Sandino's Daughters
Revisited

For Carol —
These women,
— their stories —
in struggle,
Margaret Randall

Sandino's Daughters Revisited

Feminism in Nicaragua

MARGARET RANDALL

RUTGERS UNIVERSITY PRESS
NEW BRUNSWICK, NEW JERSEY

Library of Congress Cataloging-in-Publication Data

Randall, Margaret, 1936–
    Sandino's daughters revisited : feminism in Nicaragua / Margaret
Randall.
      p.   cm.
    Includes bibliographical references.
    ISBN 0-8135-2024-X (cloth) — ISBN 0-8135-2025-8 (pbk.)
    1. Women and socialism—Nicaragua. 2. Women—Nicaragua—
Interviews. 3. Feminism—Nicaragua. 4. Nicaragua—History—1979–
5. Frente Sandinista de Liberación Nacional. I. Title.
HX546.R35   1994
324.27285'075'082—dc20   93-10819
                                               CIP

Photo on the title page:
Writing on a Managua wall: La Historia No los Absolverá. Machistas *(History Will Not Absolve Them.*
Sexists). This is a takeoff on Fidel Castro's 1953 defense, "History Will Absolve Me." *In clear reference to*
the FSLN's failure to take feminism into account, this street writer proclaims that Nicaragua's revolutionary
leadership will not *be absolved by history. The female symbol can be seen as a sort of signature.*

This book and these dreams
are for Elizabeth Lapovsky Kennedy
and Bobbi Prebis

Contents

Preface

I first went to Nicaragua in October 1979. Only a few months had elapsed since the Sandinista victory in July.[1] Invited by the new government's Ministry of Culture, I would spend three months listening to women who had taken part in the recent war tell stories of determination, courage, invention, loss, and joy. *Sandino's Daughters* was the result of that fieldwork; it was eventually published in a half dozen languages, and its English version became a resource for women and men alike who, defying increased misinformation by mainstream U.S. news media and mounting pressure by the U.S. government, were beginning to travel to Central America.[2]

In December 1980 I returned to live in Managua. My youngest daughter, then ten, came with me. Later we were joined by her older sister, just graduated from high school. Through the next four years they would go to Nicaraguan schools, participate in public health campaigns, teach arithmetic and reading in the literacy crusade's adult education follow-up program, and join the voluntary militia when defending the country became an urgent necessity.

I worked—at first for the Ministry of Culture and later in mass media—and wrote other books about the Nicaraguan struggle. *Christians in the Nicaraguan Revolution* examines the phenomenon of people of faith and those who are not religious fighting and winning a war together.[3] *Risking a Somersault in the Air*

1. The Frente Sandinista de Liberación Nacional (Sandinista National Liberation Front), or FSLN as it is commonly called, was founded in July 1961 by Carlos Fonseca, Tomás Borge, and Silvio Mayorga. Several other young revolutionaries—for the most part students fed up with Nicaragua's more traditional Left—became part of the organization in the following weeks and months. Stories are varied as to who was involved and when. Fonseca is generally regarded as the maximum leader; he was killed in action in November 1976. Mayorga died during one of the earliest guerrilla actions: the battle of Pancasán in 1967. Borge is the only living member of the original trio. The FSLN is the organization (now political party) that was able to organize the Nicaraguan people to defeat Somoza. It held power for ten years. Even today it is considered overwhelmingly the strongest and most organized political movement in the country. Many sympathizers call themselves Sandinistas, although they may not have formal ties to the organization.

2. Margaret Randall, *Sandino's Daughters: Testimonies of Nicaraguan Women in Struggle* (Vancouver, B.C.: New Star Books, 1981).

3. Margaret Randall, *Christians in the Nicaraguan Revolution* (Vancouver, B.C.: New Star Books, 1983).

is a collection of interviews with Nicaraguan writers.[4] My interest in women's lives and how we struggle to become agents of social change remained a constant.

Then, early in 1984, I returned to the United States. After twenty-three years in Latin America, my personal time to come home had arrived. It wasn't easy to leave Nicaragua, where I'd lived for the past four years, in the midst of an intensifying war. The move imbued me with deep grief and a sense of loss as well as with the relief and joy that come from reconnecting with one's roots. A series of personal and political events kept me from returning to Nicaragua for eight years, until October of 1991.

By this time the period of Sandinista government had come and gone. Forced elections had brought a pro-U.S. coalition of conservative political parties to power.[5] Few of the coalition's campaign promises had materialized, and for the vast majority of Nicaraguans life was more miserable than ever. Revolutionary social programs were being whittled away, old forms of free-market exploitation reinstated.

The purpose of my brief October visit was to attend a solidarity conference called by the FSLN and attended by people from many countries. The central question was how those of us who believed in the Sandinista vision might continue to participate in the struggle for a free Nicaragua? How could solidarity be revived in this changed political situation? What links might there be between our own issues at home and those important to people there? I have written about the conference and how it consolidated in me a renewed look at women and social change. The following is a very condensed description of what I experienced:[6]

> [It was different] for each of us, depending perhaps most of all on our age
> and the length of time we had been involved with the Nicaraguan revolu-

4. Margaret Randall, *Risking a Somersault in the Air: Conversations with Nicaraguan Writers* (San Francisco: Solidarity Publications, 1984).

5. UNO or Unión Nacional Opositora (National Opposition Union), was a coalition that came together in 1989 in order to wrest political power from the FSLN. It was composed of eleven registered political parties plus three unregistered "party tendencies," or factions. The legitimately established parties were the Social Democratic Party (PSD), the Nicaraguan Democratic Movement (MDN), the Christian Socialist faction of the National Action Party (PAN), the Democratic Party of National Confidence (PDCN), the Christian Socialist faction of the Independent Liberal Party (PLI), the Liberal Constitutionalist Party (PLC), the Neo-Liberal Party (PALI), the Nicaraguan Socialist Party (PSN), the Nicaraguan Communist Party (PCN), the Conservative People's Alliance (APC), and the Conservative faction of the National Conservative Party (PNC). The unregistered entities were the Integrationist Party of Central America (PIAC), the Conservative National Action Party (ANC), and a faction of the People's Christian Socialist Party (PPSC). It was generally believed that this coalition would disintegrate immediately following the 1990 elections. Indeed, it has shifted and changed considerably, although its adherents continue to be called UNO. See Oscar-René Vargas, *Partidos políticos y la búsqueda de un nuevo modelo* (Managua: Ecotextura, 1990).

6. Taken from Margaret Randall, *Gathering Rage: The Failure of Twentieth Century Revolutions to Develop a Feminist Agenda* (New York: Monthly Review Press, 1992), 27–33.

tionary movement. Filling out my registration form and coming to the question, "In what year did you begin your support work for the FSLN?" I realized as I wrote "1971" that it had been twenty years.

At this conference a cheerful young woman held my attention. Wearing a red and black neckerchief, she looked in her early twenties. Michele Costa, of the Nicaragua Network, told me that she is from Idaho, a farm worker whose parents are Republicans and who calls the Network at least once or twice a week to offer help with one task or another. When Sandinista dignitaries come to the United States on speaking tours, this young woman sends them little gifts, handmade by her and her friends in the country's heartland. I felt a mixture of gratitude and anxiety for this woman's eagerness and trust. Despite a few obvious differences, she might have been me two decades before. At the conference this young woman sat rapt, intent upon every word.

Some of us, although attentive and often deeply moved, were not so rapt. We had more questions than answers. We expected at least some of the answers to come from the members of the FSLN's national directorate, lined up facing us at the first plenary session and at most of those that followed.

I went on to describe the several men present and noted that there were no women. But I also did something I would not have done years or even months before: make reference to the lack of feminist understanding, the fear of feminist ideas, that characterizes most of these men. Like my Nicaraguan sisters, I now felt able to publicly express concerned criticism of these leaders. Now that they had become ordinary individuals, rather than the revered representatives of a revolution in power, it was easier to say these things. There was less pressure about revolutionaries not washing our dirty laundry in public, dividing the ranks, or providing grist for the enemy's propaganda mill.

The electoral defeat had come and gone. The FSLN's First Party Congress had come and gone. A movement to elect a woman to the organization's national directorate had failed. Many of us felt that in spite of its powerful contributions, the FSLN's inability to confront feminism (as well as racism and a generalized abuse of power) had contributed to its defeat. The mostly male Sandinista leadership continued to mouth a commitment to women's equality, but where were the actions to back up the words? Michele Costa and I took this solidarity conference as an opportunity to challenge the rhetoric:[7]

> The second morning, during a session programmed for the discussion of a variety of issues, [we] decided to accept the conference invitation for people to come to the mike with questions. Our long working relationships with the FSLN, and with Nicaraguan women, had made us attentive to concerns for both. . . . Michele spoke first, addressing women's role in the FSLN and asking what plans the Party had for implementing the impressive feminist project that was outlined . . . in the final document of its

---

7. Michele Costa was the outgoing national director of the Washington-based Nicaragua Network at this time. She has long been involved with Central American solidarity work.

recent congress. . . . She noted that much of the solidarity constituency in the United States is female, that much of it is feminist in outlook, and that there is concern about deepening the process of incorporating women into positions of political power which the Sandinista revolution so clearly initiated throughout the 1970s and early 1980s. And she had a concrete proposal, reflecting a joint collaboration with women in the FSLN.

I followed Michele's words with a few of my own, about what we mean when we speak of a feminist agenda. I wanted to make it clear that we weren't talking about some limited and misleading something called "the woman question" [but] a way of looking at the world, with half the population resituated in our rightful cultural and political space, a humanization of power and power relations, full participation, true revolutionary democracy. . . .

I could feel a shudder of discomfort running along that row of men who looked down upon the assembly, and perhaps some discomfort among the conferees as well. [One of the directorate members responded that] work with women will continue. And that if we wanted to be involved with that work, all we had to do was contact the various women's organizations: AMNLAE, the women's commissions of the peasant and union movements, among others.[8] I fought to dispel a "woman's auxiliary" image from my mind. The old "we" and "they" seemed very much alive.

Once again there were too many questions, too few answers, and too general a reticence about putting this issue out front where it might make the men uncomfortable. I spent the remainder of my week in Nicaragua outside the conference sessions, meeting and speaking with women. I looked up old friends and was introduced to women I didn't know. All told stories of having prioritized a defense of the revolutionary process at the cost of perennially putting off or ignoring gender-specific issues. All spoke of feeling betrayed by a process to which they had given their all but which, in the last analysis, rendered their needs secondary—or dispensable. It was while speaking with one of these women that the idea for the present book was born. What might be gained by coming back to Nicaragua, tracking down the women I'd interviewed for *Sandino's Daughters*, and interviewing them again—after ten years of Sandinism and two of conservative government? Women with whom I spoke were unanimously enthusiastic about the possibility.

Upon my return to the United States, I continued to think about the project, spoke to others, interested my agent and a publisher, and began the task of raising the necessary funding. By July 1992 I was back in the field. As the interviews unfolded, I became more and more aware of the explosion of femi-

---

8. The Asociación de Mujeres Nicaragüenses Luisa Amanda Espinosa (Luisa Amanda Espinosa Nicaraguan Women's Association), known by its intitials as AMNLAE, was the postvictory continuation of AMPRONAC (Association of Women Facing the Nation's Problems). Both organizations were founded and controlled by the FSLN. AMNLAE, established in 1979, was named for a young working-class woman who is believed to have been the first female to die in the revolutionary war. Throughout the ten years of Sandinista government, and since, AMNLAE has undergone reevaluations and changes. It has not, however, achieved autonomy from the male-dominated party.

nist analysis, consciousness-raising, and agency to which I've already referred. The story that cried out to be told was more than a simple "Sandino's Daughters Revisited." Some women interviewed in the first book must of necessity be included in its successor, but other dynamic feminist voices needed to be heard as well. As happens with all authentic projects, the material uncovered dictated the book to be written.

I have never been an impartial observer. I make no claim to neutrality. I am with these women in their efforts to make the liberation of their gender an integral part of the Nicaraguan people's struggle for dignity and freedom. I share with most of them, as well, the absolute conviction that the latter will not be possible without the former. The past two decades of revolution in Nicaragua have been intense with rage, determination, courage, extraordinary achievements, painful mistakes, and discovery.

In 1979 the Sandinistas showed the world that a small but heroic group of men and women were capable of deposing a dictator fully backed by the United States. During the ten years of FSLN administration, despite overwhelming and continuous pressures against the young revolution, the Sandinistas increased the standard of living in a miserably poor country, improved public health, raised educational standards, and gave an important measure of dignity back to human beings. Since the 1990 electoral defeat, Sandinista women—while still suffering the effects of a profound identity crisis—have shown themselves capable of impressive analysis and action. This book weaves their voices into a dialogue that both opens a window on Nicaraguan feminism and contributes to the ongoing international feminist discussion.

A few words about methodology. Developed through a quarter century of oral history experience, mine currently looks like this: I do a great deal of reading and thinking about a project before the actual fieldwork begins. Each recording session is preceded by a conversation that allows the informant to understand where and how her story will be used. I feel it is important for the women themselves to be in control, to own their voices.

The interviews, which took place in Spanish, were recorded electronically. I did the English translations; and that process was particularly intense, as my goal has been to present each of the women in a language and style as close as possible to her authentic voice. All the photographs were taken by me, most of them during the interviews themselves—in a further attempt to convey the women's appearance, gestures, attitudes.

Upon my return to the United States, I began to write. In deciding which of the more than thirty full-length interviews I would use, I took many things into account: class and ethnic difference, my desire to allow readers to examine important issues from a variety of perspectives, and my interest in presenting as complete a picture of Nicaraguan feminism as possible. I always alternate translating and editing with work in the darkroom. The images often influence my treatment of text, and vice versa. The women's words have not been changed; occasionally they have been reordered to make for a more coherent story.

Acknowledgments

I want to thank the many friends and colleagues who helped make this book possible. Ed Beier, Sallie Bingham, Mollie Fowler, Jack Levine, the Sandy Pollack Foundation for the Study of the Americas, the Nicaragua Network Education Fund, John and Elinor Randall, the Thanks Be to Grandmother Winifred Foundation, Kit Tremaine, the Society of the Sacred Heart, and Farley and Virginia Wheelwright all made financial contributions that enabled me to carry out the fieldwork in Nicaragua and sustain myself through its writing (and simultaneous recovery from a serious bicycle accident).

Before my arrival in Nicaragua, Daisy Zamora made contact with all the women in my earlier book as well as with more recent feminist leaders. She scheduled the interviews, found housing, and generally made it possible for six months of fieldwork to be accomplished in one. Victoria González transcribed the tapes; she also asked questions of her own and participated in an ongoing examination of issues and events. Her involvement in the project was important. Víctor Rodríguez Núñez offered invaluable computer expertise, made emergency printouts, and renewed a long-standing friendship. Doña Tere always made sure we'd find good food on the stove when we broke midday; her hospitality was comforting. And Juan Picado was invaluable as a skilled driver who knew how to circumvent sudden streetfights and never complained about "starting out early to make sure we'll find the house."

Back in New Mexico, friends and family continued to be extraordinarily supportive. My partner, Barbara Byers, contrived an ingenious way to sustain my laptop during the two and a half months I was forced to write from bed. As always, she was a consistent and invaluable sounding board for every aspect of the work—from helping me find each woman's voice in translation to discussing the ideas that give foundation to the whole. She also accompanied me for part of my stay in Nicaragua, an important experience for us to share. My mother, Elinor Randall, read every word of text, offering valuable suggestions throughout. During the time this book was in process, I also was fortunate to be able to discuss feminism and revolution with my daughter Ana, for whose experience and insights I am grateful.

I also want to mention Elizabeth Lapovsky Kennedy and Bobbi Prebis, to whom this book is dedicated. Over the years I have counted on them for the best sort of feminist discussion. I owe a great deal to my agent, Susan Herner, to my editor Marlie Wasserman and the many other good people at Rutgers

University Press who helped in different ways to turn a manuscript into a finished book.

But my greatest debt is to my Nicaraguan sisters: those whose stories I chose to present in full, those who gave of their lives and insights but whose interviews I ended up using "only" as background, and many others who shared conversation, hospitality, and help of all kinds. They were forthright and generous. Among the women whose full interviews I didn't use, I want particularly to mention Gladys Báez, Mónica Baltodano, Zulema de Baltodano, Hazel Fonseca, Mary González, Leticia Herrera, Mildred Largaespada, Angela Saballos, Dorothea Wilson, and Gladys Zalaquette. If this book could have been twice the length, their stories would certainly have been a part of it. To all, my heartfelt thanks; and my commitment to a feminist future.

Sandino's Daughters
Revisited

I believe that in the case of Latin America, and particularly in our own case, the women's movement must combine the struggle for gender emancipation with that of national liberation. Neither can be subordinated; rather, each must be included within the other. There is no contradiction between anti-imperialism and equality.

—*Sofía Montenegro*, NICARAGUA

1

Introduction

Mother and daughter, Revolution Square, Managua, during the celebration for the thirteenth anniversary of the Sandinista revolution, July 19, 1992. Sixty thousand people filled the square to commemorate a revolution no longer in power.

In the late 1960s and early 1970s a renewed feminist consciousness began to smolder among activists and academicians alike. Quickly it exploded—first in such industrialized cultural meccas as New York, London, and Paris; then in some of the urban centers of Latin America: places like Mexico City, Caracas, Buenos Aires, and Santiago de Chile. These were—and remain—the capitals of deeply troubled nations, where highly exploitative governments were showing themselves to be more and more corrupt, and where radicals were questioning traditional models of opposition and long-held assumptions about how best to struggle for social justice. Such questioning was only obliquely informed by feminist consciousness.

Ernesto "Che" Guevara had become a symbol of the era.[1] Some two and a half years before his murder in Bolivia, Guevara had written his famous "Socialism and Man in Cuba," a powerful treatise which addressed the need to

1. Che Guevara was an Argentine doctor who joined Fidel Castro's July 26th Movement and fought in Cuba's war of liberation (1956–1959). He held several cabinet posts in the Cuban revolutionary government and then left that country clandestinely to continue the struggle elsewhere. On October 7, 1967, he was ambushed in the Bolivian jungle and, on direct orders from the CIA, was murdered the following day. His attitude, actions, and writings strongly influenced generations of New Left rebels.

change human beings, not simply the society in which they lived.[2] In it he spoke of a New Man (*sic*): without greed, open, generous of spirit, filled with solidarity toward those less fortunate than himself, and capable of generating and living by more humane values. It was a breakthrough document for those of us who longed for social justice but were too young to have experienced the Communist mystique of the early years of Bolshevism; who opposed the status quo but did not feel represented by the narrow Marxism of the orthodox parties on the Left.

I was born in 1936. My generation's young adulthood straddled the stifling fifties and explosive sixties. We were ready for a different model, whose mentors nurtured a more holistic vision. Finally someone was speaking a language we understood, one that linked issues of human consciousness with a more equitable economic strategy. "At the risk of sounding ridiculous, let me say that true revolutionaries are motivated by great feelings of love"—I remember this was one of Che's statements that moved us profoundly. It has not ceased to move me. Guevara talked about painting the universities black, brown, and yellow, an early reference to multicultural education. He advocated the use of moral rather than material incentives. And we appropriated this clarity. We felt represented by ideas that addressed the spiritual and aesthetic within the workers' state—even when, as women, we were barely mentioned as protagonists.

Could we have been mentioned? Is it fair to fault the visionary men of those times, when we women had not yet begun to rise up again in search of and recognition of our full identities?[3] Perhaps, given the historical context, it is not fair. But it is very important to be clear about the fact that our arena of political struggle—as well as society as a whole—was absolutely controlled by men. Women were active in the continent's revolutionary upheaval, but neither in leadership roles nor in very large numbers. As in earlier times, they had to break with tradition in order to participate in the revolutionary movements of the fifties, sixties, and seventies; and those who did, even when they did not specifically question male leadership, opened doors for important discussions about women's role—in struggle and in the larger society.

Back then, if very few of us challenged the term "New Man," and wondered how or even if women were included in the concept, we received the stock reply of the times: Of course women were included. Didn't we understand that "man" was a generic term meaning human being? And besides, couldn't we

2. "El socialismo y el hombre en Cuba" [Socialism and Man in Cuba] was one of Guevara's most important texts and became a key reference for the Latin American New Left in the sixties and seventies. It was originally written as a letter to the Uruguayan journalist Carlos Quijano, who published it in his weekly *Marcha* on March 12, 1965.

3. Throughout history, women have risen up periodically. In the United States this happened in the 1860s, in connection with the abolitionist movement—and again in the first two decades of the twentieth century, centering on the fight for suffrage. That movement of the early 1900s is commonly referred to as the "first wave" of feminism; that which began in the late 1960s and early 1970s as the "second wave." Young women today speak of being part of a third wave. Each country has had its own feminist movement with its particular historical time frame.

see that such distinctions were a product of bourgeois feminism, popular in the industrially advanced countries but having little to do with Third World problems? Such concerns, we were told, served only to shove a wedge between men and women who should be fighting together against the real enemy.

Were we really fighting together?

As was true in the United States at that time, the Moscow-oriented Communist parties of Latin America espoused a line which clearly implied that economic equality between the sexes—equal educational opportunities, equal pay for equal work, protective legislation, and services such as child care that would make it possible for women to enter the labor force—would put an end to gender discrimination. First we needed to unite the working class; only then would we be able to rout the dictators. Later there would be time to attend to the "finer points" of social equality, including residual sexism, racism and, much later, heterosexism. That word "residual" was such a frequently used adjective; it trivialized our concerns as it shamed us for bringing them up.

LATIN AMERICA'S NEW LEFT

A number of newer political configurations active in Latin America at the time were beginning to challenge the rigidity of this view. Cuba's own 26th of July Movement, the Chilean MIR, Nicaragua's Sandinistas, and other movements of national liberation struggled with new and innovative ways of waging revolutionary war, taking power, and designing a more just society.[4] There was now more emphasis on issues of race, ethnicity, and gender (sexual identity was still taboo as a subject for discussion, at least in Latin America).

Increasing numbers of Latin American women were involved in these movements. Many were influenced by having studied abroad or by having read material translated from books published in the United States and Europe. They struggled with their male comrades for greater participation and decision-making during the years leading up to victory, in the hope of forging attitudes and actions based on a more feminist conception of power and in order to

4. After several years of unproductive legal struggle, Fidel Castro and his comrades attacked the Moncada barracks in the eastern city of Santiago de Cuba on July 26, 1953. The action was a military defeat, but it politically consolidated a vanguard in the revolutionary movement against the dictator Fulgencio Batista. From that date Castro's organization was known as the Movimiento 26 de Julio, or M-26, the July 26th Movement.

The Movimiento de la Izquierda Revolucionaria (Movement of the Revolutionary Left), or MIR as it is commonly called, was founded in Chile in 1960. Its founders were young revolutionaries tired of the ineffectiveness of Chile's more traditional Left and influenced by the recent victory of the Cuban Revolution. During Salvador Allende's three years in office (1970–1973), MIR was not a member of the Popular Unity coalition but supported the socialist government in various ways. At the time of the 1973 coup, MIR advocated armed resistance but was insufficiently armed and vastly outnumbered. Like the rest of the Chilean Left, the organization suffered factionalism and splits. It no longer exists as it once did, but a number of its surviving members continue to play an important role in their country's struggle for justice.

ensure that women's role in the society they dreamed of would in fact be different.

I say "during the years leading up to victory" because the Cuban Revolution came to power in 1959, the Chilean Left managed to hold onto a scant three years in government from 1970 to 1973, and Nicaragua's Sandinistas were victorious in 1979. Yet Chile's Popular Unity government was overthrown by one of the bloodiest coups ever to be perpetrated upon a people—by the CIA in concert with a brutal local military clique. In 1990 the Sandinistas, too, were forced out of power, their enemies having received important help from the United States. Today, only the Cuban Revolution remains, though facing serious problems from within and without.

While there is no question that these experiments in popular democracy were defeated or are being undermined primarily by international capital, it has been important for feminists and others to look at how these revolutions' failures to address certain so-called secondary issues may also have helped to weaken political structures. In retrospect we can see how the inability of almost all twentieth-century revolutionary movements to develop a feminist agenda contributed to their failure to evolve new and equitable forms of power sharing that might have helped keep them alive.

In contrast to what took place in the United States, few of us in Latin America in the sixties or seventies dared to speak about politics as they were reflected in interpersonal relations. We did not press for a feminization of power; nor did we make the connections we make today between a feminist vision and such issues as ecology, abuse, holistic health, and spirituality. Some women who worked for peace did so within the context of a burgeoning feminist understanding, but we could not yet see that gender inequality had skewed our entire sense of history—and of ourselves. In Latin America (my home at the time), our demands were generally focused on equality in defense, access to education and jobs, more sexual and intellectual freedom, a more equitable division of labor in the home, and control over our reproductive choices. Insofar as the last-mentioned struggle was concerned, because we knew what U.S. reproductive policy was doing in Latin America we were more likely to be fighting against enforced sterilization than for the right to choose abortion.[5]

Without the leisure in which to stop and consider the theoretical implications of their situation, revolutionary women taking on whole dynasties of oppression had to deal with the most obvious problems of their daily lives. It was clear that men drew up the programs, made the decisions, meted out the tasks. For women, these tasks were almost exclusively those which were also traditional to their gender: they kept the safehouses, washed and cooked for the

5. Beginning in the 1950s, much U.S. aid in Third World countries was linked to policies limiting the reproduction of the working class and the poor, including programs that ranged from laboratory-like experimentation with birth control pills and intrauterine devices to forced sterilization. In Puerto Rico by the 1960s, one-third of all women of childbearing age were sterilized. Whole villages of women in the Bolivian Andes, Brazil, Peru, Colombia, and elsewhere were sterilized without their knowledge or consent. President Dwight Eisenhower remarked that the best way to avert the threat of popular movements was to prevent revolutionaries from being born.

combatants, ran messages, nursed the wounded, made use of their "feminine wiles" in the transport of comrades and weaponry, and in all the customary ways nurtured their brothers-in-arms. A few of the revolutionary organizations in Chile, Uruguay, and Brazil were developing a discourse that addressed this gendered division of labor. Still, with few exceptions, even their female members continued to do "what women do best."

This was certainly the case with the Sandinista National Liberation Front in Nicaragua, the largest of the Central American nations, where the Somoza family had held ruthless power for almost half a century. The first women joined the FSLN in 1963; one of them, Doris Tijerino, speaks in the pages of the present book.[6] Testimony by others has also been well documented.

At first these young women—often sisters or girlfriends of the men—didn't question male authority. Their task was immense: they were among a handful of radicals with nothing but faith and fury on their side. And they intended to topple a dictatorship that not only owned close to 90 percent of the country's land, industry, and production, but was also supported and protected by the richest country on earth, the much-too-close United States of America.

No wonder there was little inclination on the part of the women, or patience on the part of the men, to challenge women's role in the struggle. Women faced a severe break with family, social, and religious norms simply by engaging in revolutionary activism. But sexism, deeply embedded in the social fabric, was also responsible for the status quo, and as women's determination and courage led to a more central involvement, stereotypes were being questioned. During those early years it was the exceptional woman who withstood the rigors of guerrilla warfare or who became an instrument of precision in an urban bank expropriation. Still, men—and other women—noticed.

Many of the women I interviewed for my earlier books on Nicaragua described the processes they went through as they acquired a consciousness of their own oppression. They battled with the men over such issues as a gendered division of labor, giving birth underground, deciding whether or not to abort when raped and made pregnant by prison guards, taking part in commando actions, and assuming positions of political leadership. Women eventually made up 30 percent of the Sandinista army, and more than a few outstanding female combatants rose to positions of leadership within the FSLN. It has been suggested that these women soldiers were generally better educated than the men, thus better qualified for professional jobs in the new government.[7] Several of them speak in the pages that follow, and they have been extraordinarily forthcoming about their personal struggles for dignity and respect.[8]

6. A more complete story of Doris's life can be found in Margaret Randall, *Doris Tijerino: Inside the Nicaraguan Revolution*, trans. Elinor Randall (Vancouver, B.C.: New Star Books, 1978).

7. Sylvia Saakes, "Particularidades del movimiento de mujeres en Nicaragua," in *La mujer nicaragüense en los años 80* (Managua: Ediciones Nicarao, 1991), 174.

8. During the Sandinista administration, many of these same women were reticent about internal political disagreements, including those having to do with their struggles as women. They were subject to Party discipline and believed that such a public airing of grievances would only be used against the revolution. Since the FSLN's electoral defeat, in February 1990, there

In its final chaotic years, the Somoza dictatorship routinely banned books it considered too political or otherwise inappropriate for national readership. There are stories filled with irony, like the time Marx's *The Holy Family* made it past the censors because they assumed it was a religious tract. Sandinista women speak of being influenced by books and photocopies of books smuggled into the country and passed from hand to hand: works such as Engels's *The Origin of the Family, Private Property, and the State*, Simone de Beauvoir's *The Second Sex*, and (much to my delight) my own *Cuban Women Now*.[9]

But it would be a mistake to say that such materials planted the seeds of women's consciousness in Nicaragua or to imply that Nicaraguan women learned their feminism from abroad. These ideas took root in fertile soil. They built upon and nurtured experiences that had been alive for centuries in collective memory, since the time when indigenous women defied the Spanish Conquest in particularly innovative ways.

INDIGENOUS NICARAGUA

Chroniclers at the time of the Conquest described Nicaraguan women as the most beautiful among the New World native peoples. The Franco-Mexican anthropologist Laurette Sèjournè believes it was "their fierce sense of independence that made them seem more beautiful." That independence shows itself primarily in socioeconomic ways. Sèjournè tells us that in pre-Columbian Nicaragua "men attended to agriculture, they fished, and took care of the home; women remained in charge of commerce."[10] Only in one other part of Latin America, on the Isthmus of Tehuantepec (southern Mexico), did women control the economy in this way. Sèjournè goes on to say that men were not allowed in the great markets—the economic centers of society—unless they were foreigners (and therefore different).

She assesses, as well, some of the indigenous social customs as these relate to gender. Virginity, for example, seemed to have been regarded quite differently than it has been since Catholicism took hold. Sèjournè explains that men frequently preferred women with sexual experience. When after the wedding night men rejected those found not to be virgins it was because a lie had been told: lack of moral rectitude, not the condition of previous use, defined the problem. Rape was punished by reducing the rapist to slavery in the service of the victim's parents. Prostitution was considered a job like any other, and it

---

has been a much broader and deeper discussion of what went wrong, including a strong feminist criticism of women's role.

9. Margaret Randall, *La mujer cubana ahora* (Havana: Editorial de Ciencias Sociales, 1972); Dora María Téllez in Randall, *Sandino's Daughters: Testimonies of Nicaraguan Women in Struggle* (Vancouver, B.C.: New Star Books, 1981), 52.

10. Laurette Sèjournè, *América Latina I. Antiguas culturas precolombinas* (Mexico City: Siglo XXI, 1979), 148, 131.

was common for young women to work as prostitutes before they married, earning their dowries in that way.[11]

Still, from these brief historical notes it would be a mistake to assume that the original inhabitants of Central America respected women's power or place in society any more than today's patriarchy does. There are contrary opinions regarding exactly how women did live in ancient Mesoamerica, but it is clear that—then as now—they existed largely for the benefit of men. Reliable research indicates that the earliest societies were the most egalitarian, and that by the time of the Conquest both dominant cultures—the Nahuas (popularly known as "Aztecs") and the Mayas—had developed thoroughly male-dominated systems.[12] In this respect, then, the invaders found gender relations in the lands they colonized to be not so different from their own.

This European exploration, which initiated five hundred years of genocide—via invasion, occupation, exploitation, violence, profound racial stratification, and impoverishment—was carried out by men: the heralded explorers who, in the name of the Spanish Crown (or the Portuguese, English, or French), are still honored in the "authoritative" texts. They claimed the land, looted precious metals and other resources, disrupted or destroyed whole social systems, and reviled spiritual traditions. And because Spanish women didn't join them in the crossing (nor did they come in any numbers until approximately a hundred years later) these men established relations of use and domination over the indigenous women that continue to define gender and race relations today.

GENDER AND RACE

I link gender and race because the two are tightly interwoven on a continent where the vast majority of people are of mixed race. Since the Conquest, identity or a strong sense of self has been a major problem in Latin America. The European "discovery" was not a meeting of two worlds, as Spain would still have us believe (in its publicity around the 1992 Quincentennial). Rather it was the domination and destruction of one world by another, the desecration of a

11. Ibid., 127–129.

12. Although the Nahuas as a people were wiped out in Nicaragua, it is generally believed that the earliest Nicaraguans belonged to the Nahua culture; that is, to the group of people who spoke Nahuatl (meaning "that which sounds beautiful"). Nicaraguan's *mestizos* (persons of mixed European and Indian ancestry), especially on the country's Pacific Coast, think, speak, and derive their culture from "Nahuañol"—a mixture of Nahuatl and Spanish. The other great Mesoamerican culture at the time of the Spanish Conquest, the Mayas, occupied territory slightly to the north of the Nahuas. Today many distinct indigenous cultures are still very much alive in Mexico and throughout Central America, among them the Zapotecas, Totonacas, Cunas, Miskitos, Sumus, and Ramas (these last three are on Nicaragua's Atlantic Coast). Although their languages and customs are quite different, culturally most can be traced to one of the two major groups.

way of life, the rape and plunder of systems, societies, cultures, and human beings—with a very special abuse reserved for women.

In contemporary Latin America the most oppressed and blasphemed are the Indians; they are lowest on the social ladder. *Te salió el indio* (you showed your Indian side) is a common jibe, indicating that a person has been brutish or unduly angry. It is interesting, after five hundred years of occupation, that such anger is not recognized for what it is: resistance. Indian women are doubly oppressed. They are the sterilized without consent, the mothers who beg food for their children in marketplaces and on the street, the slave maids, the hungry, those who never learn to read or write, those who die by the tens of thousands before they reach age thirty.

There is a story that illustrates, perhaps better than any other, the connection between race and gender oppression in the history of Mesoamerica. It is the story of La Malinche, or Malintzin as she was named at birth.[13] The year was 1519, and the young girl was fifteen when she was given as a slave to Cortés, Spanish conqueror of ancient Mexico. She became his translator, first from Nahuatl into Mayan and later into Spanish as well. Thus in Mexican mestizo culture—and throughout Spanish America—the term *malinchismo* means betrayal, a fascination with what is foreign and a disgust for or dismissal of one's own origins. In numerous cultures throughout the world, in fact, woman's "nature" has come to be linked to this idea of the deceitful or traitorous.

If we examine the story of La Malinche from a feminist point of view, it is immediately apparent that this fifteen-year-old girl was not the betrayer but the one betrayed. From birth she was used and abused. A native of Coatzacoalcos, her father died when she was still quite young. Her mother then remarried and had a son. In order for the family's considerable holdings to be passed on to this male heir, Malintzin's mother sold her to some Indians from Xicalango; the mother and her new husband also spread the story that their daughter had passed away. The men from Xicalango then sold the young woman to some men from Tabasco, who in turn gave her to Cortés.

By the time she was fifteen, La Malinche had been betrayed and disavowed by her parents, displaced from her family inheritance by her half-brother, sold several times as a slave, and then given to the white male invader. And not a single man from her family, her group, or her culture protested.[14]

This brilliant young woman, who spoke three languages before she was twenty, became an object of bounty in a hideous war. She was passed from man to man, forced into sexual relations with Cortés, then with one of his lieutenants, and finally with the conqueror's son, Martín Cortés, whose exaggerated sexual appetite has been well documented in the chronicles. This pass-

13. La Malinche is the name most commonly used when referring to this historic figure. Doña Marina is the Spanish equivalent used by Hernán Cortés.

14. Much of my material about La Malinche is drawn from Sofía Montenegro, "Nuestra madre: La Malinche" [Our Mother: La Malinche], *Gente* (Managua) 3. no. 138 (October 2, 1992), 11; and Sofía Montenegro, "Identidad y colonialismo. El retorno de La Malinche" (unpublished essay).

ing of young Indian women from one officer to another was a common practice of the times.

Nevertheless, as Sofía Montenegro explains, La Malinche "has become a malignant goddess, the creator of a new race—the mestizo—which projects her as mother/whore, bearer of illegitimate children, destroyer of a free and glorious past."[15] Montenegro goes on to show how this distortion of La Malinche lies at the root of the mother-blame or woman-blame so common throughout Latin America's mestizo society. Historically, women are made to bear the guilt for their own victimization, and therein the male is exonerated.

It is a familiar story, not unlike the more recent mythology conceived and perpetuated by such as Robert Bly in his book *Iron John*.[16] Men in control continue to portray themselves as victims of the mother, and therefore absolve themselves of any responsibility for social injustice—both against women generally and against men and women of other races or more vulnerable conditions. The raped woman, especially, has become a "thing of scorn."

In Latin America *hijo de la chingada* (child of the raped one) is a terrible and common epithet. In the language itself, then, women continue to be made responsible for the crimes of patriarchy and conquest, crimes perpetrated against our own integrity and upon our flesh. Montenegro urges us to retrieve La Malinche as the historical mother of colonialism's mixed race, thereby recognizing the defiled link that joins us to our Indian forebears. In my conversations with the women in this book La Malinche's name sounded often: a new invocation of roots reclaimed.

Indigenous women in Nicaragua resisted with tenacity and creativity the Spanish invasion of their lands, their bodies, and their minds. At one point in the terrible history of conquest, as in the story of Lysistrata, Nicaraguan women refused to have sex with their husbands. They did not want to continue giving birth to children they knew would be enslaved.

Sandinista leader Humberto Ortega touched on this when he praised contemporary Nicaraguan women who, "as our victory approached, wanted to produce more children so there would be more combatants for the cause."[17] Unfortunately, this skewed interpretation is all too common among revolutionaries. Rather than focusing on an early example of women organizing against slavery, Ortega applauded their putting their reproductive powers at the service of a cause that largely ignores their reality. He failed to grasp how social change must address women's condition if it is to mean real justice for all people.

15. Montenegro, "Identidad y colonialismo."

16. Robert Bly, *Iron John* (New York: Addison-Wesley, 1990). For a feminist critique of Bly's thesis, see *Women Respond to the Men's Movement*, ed. Kay Leigh Hagan (San Francisco: Harper Collins, 1992).

17. Humberto Ortega, brother of Daniel, was one of the nine members of the FSLN national directorate and was minister of defense during the Sandinista administration. He is still minister of defense but is no longer a member of his party's leadership body. The words quoted here come from a speech at the closing session of the Federation of Cuban Women's Third Congress, Havana, March 8, 1980.

A HISTORY OF DOMINATION

As was true for most of the region, freedom from Spanish domination was eventually won, only to be quickly replaced by a long period of dependence upon and subservience to the United States. Nicaragua offers one of the longest continuous examples of U.S. intervention in the Western Hemisphere. Armed invasions of Nicaragua took place in 1853, 1854, 1857, 1894, 1898, 1899, 1912–1925, and 1926–1933.[18] The United States, following the doctrine of Manifest Destiny, considered it within its right to invade, occupy, and control. The people were brown-skinned and primitive, after all, not to mention being in the United States' sphere of political influence and residents of its "backyard."

Indeed, for a few years in the past century, the North American filibusterer William Walker was even appointed president. And Franklin Roosevelt's comment about the first Somoza is well known: "He may be a son of a bitch, but he's our son of a bitch." It is not surprising, then, that Nicaraguans are virtually born with the sentiment—the collective memory—of anti-imperialism. The word *yanqui* became the equivalent of "thug," even in the discourse of those living in remote mountainous regions. Women from the United States were called *yankas*, their children *yanquitos*.

SANDINO'S FIRST DAUGHTERS

This unusual declension of the word "yanqui" reflects a culture of righteous rage and proud resistance, culminating in the military campaign waged by Augusto César Sandino, a nationalist leader who fought against the U.S. Marines from 1927 to 1934. He and his "crazy little army"[19] succeeded in routing the invaders from their homeland, but Sandino himself was betrayed and murdered by Somoza. His burial place remains a mystery.

A number of aging men and women still remember Sandino's war; they took part in it or knew people who did. For more than four decades after the liberator's murder, it was dangerous to keep his photograph or speak his name; you could be imprisoned or murdered for either. Nicaraguan school texts omitted these pages of national heroism, but the people kept them alive in popular anecdotes and stories. A few of Sandino's generals also kept the faith, remaining at combat readiness in remote mountain outposts, waiting a lifetime for the orders they were sure would come. Finally, in 1961, they did come—in the form of the FSLN, the next step in a long struggle for independence.

In my 1979–1980 fieldwork for *Sandino's Daughters*, I came across a num-

18. Randall, *Doris Tijerino*, 165.
19. The phrase was coined by the Argentine historian Gregorio Selser, who wrote the definitive texts on Sandino and his struggle. See Selser's, *Sandino, general de hombres libres* (Buenos Aires: Editorial Triángulo, 1959) and *El pequeño ejército loco* (Managua: Editorial Nueva Nicaragua, 1980).

ber of women who testified to the deep connections they felt between Sandino's war and the more recent Sandinista victory, connections alive in their
personal experience. A veteran of both wars, and a link between them, was
María Lidia, a peasant woman from Chinandega. She was sixty-eight when we
spoke, and relived her memories in pure poetry:

> I'll tell you, my Segovia, those pine trees, those mountains were our
> friends, do you know? That's the way it was for us with Sandino. We
> simply said light and shadow, and then we said beautiful Nicaragua: your
> lakes speak for you, and your children call you, always. You will always
> always be free. And we must keep your flag flying high. Here there were
> no chiefs, no generals; here we were all Nicaraguan soldiers, together
> against the Machos.
>
> I was a messenger. At night we would go out, it was the safest time. We
> rode a burro or an ox, and we lit our way with ocote torches. The mountain
> was tough, not like it is today. Now it's almost barren compared with what
> it was then; why, at midday it seemed like four in the afternoon. The
> Machos came with their proper jackets: fine navy blue cloth with that beau-
> tiful M and that beautiful P—standing for *polisman*, so we would respect
> them. We respected their guns but not them.[20]

María's use of the term Macho to describe the invading soldiers is linguistically
and culturally interesting. A macho, of course, is a man engorged with an
overblown sense of his own importance; we might call him bombastic, or a
sexist. María and her generation resisted a foreign army embodying both political intervention and male domination.

Women also occupied more central positions in Sandino's campaign. Blanca
Araúz, who would become the general's wife, was a telegraph operator when
they married; she continued to work in communications throughout the war.
Sandino is also believed to have had a mistress, a Salvadoran named Teresa
Villatoro who led one of the guerrilla columns—an early internationalist as
well as a woman apparently engaged in front-line combat. María Altamirano,
married to General Pedro Altamirano, was in charge of one of the camps.
There is no evidence that any of these women held a formal rank in the "crazy
little army," but their participation was nevertheless outstanding for the era.
General Sandino himself devoted much of a 1933 interview to the involvement
and heroism of these women who, he noted, came from every social class.[21]

THE SOMOZA DYNASTY

Sandino's murder ushered in an increasingly repressive period in Nicaraguan
history: the dynasty of the Somozas. Theirs was a succession of regimes—for

20. Margaret Randall, *Todas estamos despiertas: Testimonios de la mujer nicaragüense hoy*
(Mexico City: Siglo XXI, 1980), 22—30.
21. José N. Román, *Maldito país* (Río Coco, Nicaragua: Las Segovias, 1933), 136–137.

almost half a century—that required increasingly terrorist tactics simply to stay in power. The country's economic model, based in capitalist agro-export, meant entrenched underdevelopment and dependence upon the United States. Peasants were robbed of greater and greater amounts of land; the rural and urban poor were superexploited. Much of the population existed at bare subsistence levels.

The violence that accompanies this type of economy increased the destitution faced by Nicaraguan women and children by the 1950s and 1960s. And as the decade of the seventies came to a close, women made up 51 percent of the population but constituted two-thirds of those living below the poverty line. Thus women were kept subordinate in every area. While the national illiteracy rate was 50.35 percent (1979), 93 percent or in some places 100 percent of rural women could neither read nor write.[22]

Nicaragua is a largely agricultural country, and in the countryside especially living conditions are often inhuman. In the 1970s, 47 percent of the country's homes were without electricity; 90 percent lacked potable water. Malnutrition, which assaulted two-thirds of the population, affected women in special ways, as their lives were an almost permanent cycle of pregnancy, birthing, and nursing their young. Statistics for 1975 showed rural women bearing an average of 7.8 children, while in the urban centers it was 6.2.[23] Impoverished living conditions often meant a mortality rate as high as 50 percent among the offspring of the poor.

In a country like Nicaragua (and, indeed, throughout the dependent world), the idea that equality will follow women's incorporation into the labor force breaks down. Female workers generally remain exploited and oppressed in the most degrading and worst-paid jobs.

Statistics continue to reveal the trend: in 1950, 27 percent of the country's economically active population was female; that figure had risen to 35 percent by 1971 and to 40 percent in 1977–two years before the Sandinistas took power. These figures are for mostly urban manufacturing and services; but even in the countryside, toward the end of the seventies Nicaraguan women made up 29 percent of all field workers, a much higher percentage than in Latin America overall.[24]

22. See Maxine Molyneux, "¿Mobilización sin emancipación? Intereses de la mujer, el estado y la revolución: El caso de Nicaragua," in *La transición difícil: La autodeterminación de los pequeños países periféricos* (Mexico City: Siglo XXI, 1986), 358; Clara Murguialday, *Nicaragua, revolución y feminismo (1977–89)* (Madrid: Editorial Revolución, 1990); and Jaime Wheelock, *Diciembre victorioso* (Managua: Secretaría Nacional de Propaganda y Educación Política del FSLN, 1979), 27.

23. Niurka Pérez, "Subdesarrollo y población feminina en Nicaragua," Seminar on Population and the New International Economic Order, University of Havana, 1984; Secretaría de Planificación y Presupuesto, *Informe del Seminario Nacional sobre Población y Desarrollo: Hacia una política de población* (Managua: SPP, 1989).

24. Paola Pérez and Ivonne Siú, "La mujer en la economía nicaragüense: Cambios y desafíos," paper presented at the Fifth Congress of ANICS, OGM, Managua, 1986.

FAMILY

Spanish feminist Clara Murguialday emphasizes how the "[Nicaraguan] family was constructed from the cultural clash between the indigenous model—with its strong tribal and matrilineal characteristics—and those patriarchal values imposed by colonialism during more than three centuries of Spanish domination." She then explains how the family structure developed "within the history of Nicaraguan agriculture, aided by an agro-exporting capitalism's inability to create a model that included the stable presence of a man in the home."[25]

This type of agro-capitalist development, imposed by the United States, brought with it the exploitative social structures needed to keep it in place. These regulate the family and affect women in particularly debilitating ways. Feminist writer Elizabeth Maier explains that this uneven development thwarted

> the conditions that make for [more equitable] forms of family organization, such as the nuclear family of the industrialized societies. In the countryside [this type of development] basically tore the traditional family unit apart, making ever more common those sociosexual practices which resulted in families without fathers and a high degree of paternal irresponsibility, in emotional as well as economic terms.[26]

Paternal irresponsibility remains a fundamental problem. It is one that the Sandinista administration attempted to deal with throughout its decade in office. Exploitative economies have traditionally made it difficult for men to earn a decent wage, and their resulting depression, along with patriarchal attitudes situating women as objects of use and abuse, conspire in leading many men to abandon their legal or free-union wives and young children.

Mothers, so often abandoned by their men and usually having several children to feed, have migrated in ever larger numbers to urban areas where they might earn a better living. If they couldn't leave their young ones with family back home, they were forced to take them along, greatly reducing their own employability. Low educational levels and almost nonexistent experience also stood in the way of finding decent work, and so these female migrants were most often relegated to the least desirable and poorest paid jobs: domestic service, the sale of foodstuffs or trinkets on the streets, prostitution.

By the late 1970s, even the formal urban-female labor force (which does not include either domestic service or prostitution) broke down as follows: 75 percent of all employed women worked in commerce or the service sector and only 19 percent in manufacturing, which in Nicaragua is generally distributed among a variety of small or cottage industries rather than in the large plants common to the more industrially advanced countries.[27]

25. Murguialday, *Nicaragua, revolución y feminismo (1977–89)*, 14.
26. Elizabeth Maier, *Las sandinistas* (Mexico City: Ediciones de Cultura Popular, 1985), 20.
27. Elizabeth Maier, "Mujeres, contradicciones y revolución," *Estudios Sociales Centroamericanos* (San José, Costa Rica), no. 27 (1980), 131.

The first serious urban employment census in Nicaragua was carried out by the Sandinistas in 1980. It showed almost half of all women of working age laboring outside the home. Eighty-five percent of all female heads of household were salaried, as opposed to only 40 percent of those who were married or in free-union relationships.[28]

WORKING FOR IMPERIALISM

Although the history of U.S.-Nicaraguan relations had long been one of domination, beginning in the 1960s more sophisticated controls were put in place. The Alliance for Progress and similar programs began taking over where outright intervention was seen by many as too dangerous. The policy was designed to consolidate dependent economies, offer the illusion of aid, and help prevent "another Cuba" in Latin America. What this meant—and continues to mean for so many of the smaller, dependent nations—is that Nicaraguans were caught in a vicious cycle, unable to solve their most pressing problems and unable to work for their own future.

In 1963, fraudulent elections brought a pseudo–civil government to Nicaragua.[29] During this administration the country joined the Central American Common Market, compelled by the needs of multinational capital and an imperialist vision of Nicaragua's hemispheric role. An agrarian reform was instituted, favoring large landowners and further oppressing the campesino population. This land reform was especially important in that it also tended to separate and scatter great numbers of peasants who were beginning to come together under the auspices of the fledgling FSLN.

Despite all efforts to undermine FSLN growth and cohesion, however, the new generation of Nicaraguan revolutionaries succeeded in organizing throughout the country. The next "Cuba" in Latin America would not be, as the U.S. government wanted the world to believe, a Castro-exported revolution. Instead, revolution would come about as it always has in the modern world: through local resistance to years of domination by a homegrown dictator and to whatever superpower controls the local economy.

CATHOLICISM

The Christian tradition was rife with mixed messages for Nicaraguan women coming of age in the 1960s and 1970s. Strong Marist traditions promoted Mary, Mother of God, as an example—one that was gradually adopted also by

28. Instituto Nicaragüense de Estadística y Censo, *La inserción de la mujer en la producción social: El caso del área urbana de Nicaragua* (Managua: INEC, 1981), 4.

29. This was the only period from 1934 to 1979 in which a Somoza did not (outwardly) rule the country. René Schick, the Liberal Party candidate, won a scandal-ridden election and remained in office until 1967.

Christian revolutionaries who claimed Mary as a figure of liberation rather than of submission. Still, there were limits on the usefulness of a figure whose own sexuality was denied, who was "used by God as a vessel to bring forth His Son." Young girls had grown up with all the strictures Catholicism traditionally imposed upon them; they were taught to be chaste, submissive, pliant, and forgiving and to lead lives of service to others, most prominently their men. They were often chaperoned, sometimes until they passed from father to husband. Those from the working and peasant classes were taught devotion; those from the upper classes were taught to do good works.

On the other hand, profound changes were taking place on all fronts. The class struggle within the Catholic Church produced "liberation theology." The Second Vatican Council led to meetings of Latin American bishops, first in Colombia and then in Mexico, ushering in important changes for people of faith.[30] A revolution was taking place within the continent's major belief system; and Latin America—essentially, culturally Catholic—was feeling its reverberations. Liberation theology meant a new reading of the Bible, from the perspective of a "preferential option for the poor." This encouraged people to link their own disenfranchisement, poverty, and oppression to the Bible's inspiring stories of struggle.

The social justice component of the new theology, along with a weave of other influences and possibilities, eventually led many Nicaraguan women to solid revolutionary positions. An experience examined in some depth by the women in this book was that of La Asunción girl's school. The Sisters of La Asunción ran one of several schools for the daughters of the Nicaraguan bourgeoisie. Five of the twelve women interviewed in the following pages attended

30. Vatican II was convoked by Pope John XXIII in 1962. In session for years, it prescribed a Gospel-oriented content for Catholicism and a more socially conscious message than had been heard previously in papal encyclicals. A general ecumenical *aggiornamento*, or "bringing up to date," allowed for dialogue with other Christian denominations and with non-Christians. Also, laypeople were given greater responsibility for the Church's pastoral work. Liturgical reforms included the introduction of language, songs, and instruments native to each country and an end to the celebration of Mass in Latin by priests who turned their backs on the congregation. In 1968 the guidelines of the postcouncil encyclical *Populorum Progressio* were adopted by Catholic bishops meeting in Medellín, Colombia. Two years later the bishops met again, this time in Puebla, Mexico. At these two meetings, Vatican II documents were interpreted in the light of the continent's economic, social, and political context. The bishops declared that great masses of people were oppressed by the "institutionalized violence" of internal and external colonial structures which, "seeking unbounded profits, ferment an economic dictatorship and the international imperialism of money." They acknowledged that the Church exists in history, not outside its laws, and spoke of "a preferential option for the poor." Liberation theology, so important in the decades since, had taken root in Latin America. Hundreds and then thousands of "Christian base communities" would spring up throughout the continent. In them, people began to analyze the situations of exploitation and oppression in which they lived. In places like Brazil, Guatemala, El Salvador, and Nicaragua especially, that analysis yielded an authentic experience of social and political commitment born of faith, in many cases similar to the commitment of their socialist or communist sisters and brothers who were launching their own projects in an effort to change society. See particularly my interviews with Vidaluz Meneses and Aminta Granera.

La Asunción. Four of the five were deeply influenced by Vatican II's impact upon those nuns who were their favorite teachers. Something extraordinary was happening in the Church; it changed the lives of these sisters, who in turn influenced their charges.

Michele Najlis, Vidaluz Meneses, Gioconda Belli, and Aminta Granera remember how the nuns organized charitable activities through which students distributed food to the poor or built latrines in destitute neighborhoods. But they also began to ask why such miserable conditions existed and what their responsibility really was. Concern for social justice began to replace the sense of satisfaction earlier generations had derived from giving alms. The country's political contradictions were also becoming more obvious. And, with the appearance of the FSLN's student and women's fronts, alternative options became available. Each of these interviewees, in her own way and at her own pace, broke away from the humiliation of giving charity and sought an activism that attacked the structures which produce and perpetuate injustice. Meneses and Granera, especially, speak from the Catholic tradition.

ORGANIZING WOMEN

The Sandinista National Liberation Front, founded in 1961, suffered early and debilitating military defeats in 1963. All but annihilated in the mountains, it turned its attention to political education among the various social sectors: peasants, workers, students. Other, more traditional parties of the Left were engaged in similar efforts at the time. Concurrently, the new wave of feminism began to make itself felt. It was essential to the way the FSLN would develop that feminist ideas became important to a number of its female members.

It was during this period that the first attempts to organize women were made. The Organización de Mujeres Democráticas de Nicaragua (Nicaraguan Democratic Women's Organization, or OMDN) was actually founded by the Socialist Party (what Nicaragua's Moscow-oriented Communist Party was then called). Several of its members—Benigna Mendiola, Gladys Báez, and Doris Tijerino, among others—were Socialists before they tired of that party's rigidity and its inability to address society's most critical problems. They all eventually quit and joined the Sandinista National Liberation Front.[31]

The OMDN was associated with the International Federation of Democratic Women, whose many national chapters appeared together with the strengthening of the international communist movement after the Second World War. Its Nicaraguan contingent remained in formal operation for years, but stagnated as

---

31. All three of these longtime women militants are alive today, in itself a rare phenomenon in Nicaragua's revolutionary history. Benigna Mendiola continues to work with peasants. Gladys Báez is the general secretary of AMNLAE. Doris Tijerino, interviewed in this book, was the nation's first woman national chief of police before she was transferred to AMNLAE (preceding Báez). She is now an FSLN deputy to the National Assembly and works with delinquent children.

one of the many casualties of communism's general lack of political vision and its inability to speak to women's needs.

By 1966 Gladys Báez had joined the FSLN. That same year, on direct orders from its national directorate, she made another attempt to bring women together: in the Alianza Patriótica de Mujeres Nicaragüenses (Patriotic Alliance of Nicaraguan Women, or APMN). Its purpose was to organize women from the popular sectors—peasants, laborers, and students—to agitate for better working conditions, equal pay for equal work, unionization for the female labor force, day-care facilities, and like demands. Michele Najlis describes the APMN's first "national meeting" in 1969:

> Our gatherings in those days were clandestine and didn't happen all that often because women had to arrange to leave their children with family members, brave their terror of the dictator's repressive methods, and brave their husbands' threats as well. The first great national meeting took place in Juigalpa, in 1969. Present were Gladys Báez and two women who had come from Managua. Three of us, that's all; no one else showed up! Gladys insisted on going ahead with the proceedings, because she said if we didn't we'd get demoralized. I remember we entered this large hall, and Gladys walked to the podium and proceeded to give one of the most beautiful political speeches I've ever heard: filled with an unshakable faith in the future. She took her time. And slowly, very clearly, she told us that this was a memorable day in the history of the Nicaraguan women's movement, because it was the first time we women had assembled to talk about our problems, our limitations, the discrimination we suffered, and our future liberation.[32]

When Najlis speaks of the women assembling for the first time, that is a relative truth. Of course these women did meet, strategize, and make on-the-spot decisions, and their coming together under such adverse conditions was noteworthy. But the Alliance, like AMPRONAC and AMNLAE in years to come, was still part of an overall plan of struggle and ultimately responded to the FSLN's top-level, all-male leadership. In retrospect, it is easy to see that this lack of autonomy in a succession of women's organizations stifled or submerged the possibilities for developing a truly feminist movement.

The OMDN had mostly been ineffective in its attempts to bring women together, except insofar as it may have helped move some of them further along their individual political journeys. The APMN, too, proved itself incapable of changing women's image of themselves in society or of promoting substantially increased political agency. During the early 1970s, however, groups of women began mobilizing around specific issues, demonstrating once again the power of their presence. They denounced the dictator's human rights violations, supported the university students in their various political campaigns, protested price hikes of milk, gasoline, and other necessities. These women

---

32. Michele Najlis, interview in *Somos* (Managua), no. 15 (1983), 16.

were mobilizing outside a women-only structure because their children were in prison, because as heads of households they were hard-hit by the economic and political crises, because as citizens they wanted nothing more passionately than to force Somoza from power.

MOTHERS AND DAUGHTERS: A REVERSAL OF ROLES

Older women maintained a particularly moving presence. As has been seen before and since in other parts of the world, the mothers and grandmothers of mostly very young and totally involved sons and daughters often followed their children's example and became courageous and trustworthy political activists.[33] In *Sandino's Daughters* I became particularly interested in this phenomenon in which children so deeply influenced their parents, rather than the more conventional other way round. And, to a significant degree, it wasn't "parents" but mothers who became involved. The older women vastly outnumbered their husbands in this sort of participation. In fact, separation or divorce was not uncommon when a mother gave herself to her children's struggle, often against her spouse's will. The "adult men," as their offspring referred to them, tended toward conservatism and personal fear; the "adult women" were more courageous, more able to assume a radical political position.[34]

These older women formed a Committee of Mothers that was increasingly active throughout the decade. Its members visited Somoza's prisons, became an important link between the prisoners and those on the outside, protested unfair treatment, went on hunger strikes, and occupied the national cathedral and the local office of the United Nations. This group eventually evolved into the Mothers of Heroes and Martyrs, which was active throughout the Sandinista administration and remains so today. Significantly, since the 1990 electoral defeat, these women—working with the mothers of the Contras—have been pioneers in a new movement of national reconciliation.[35]

33. Argentina's "Mothers of the Plaza de Mayo" are an internationally recognized example. They have marched for years to demand that their country's former dictatorship take responsibility for its thousands of disappeared persons, many of them their own sons and daughters. A movement of grandmothers has been active as well, using sophisticated methods of matching DNA in order to find children taken from tortured and murdered mothers and then reunite them with family members who have survived.

34. Nicaraguans use the term "adult" to describe someone thirty or older.

35. The "Contras"—organized by local right-wing forces and funded, trained, and sustained by the United States—were counterrevolutionaries, most of whom left Nicaragua to join the anti-Sandinista armies mobilizing in Honduras to the north or Costa Rica to the south. Large numbers of Miskitos, confused and angered by the Sandinistas' early inability to deal appropriately with ethnic issues, also joined the counterrevolutionary movement. In spite of the enormous support from outside, the Contras were never able to defeat the Sandinista army. Just before the 1990 elections the FSLN declared a general amnesty; since the electoral defeat, thousands of ex-Contras have returned to their homeland. In the past several years Sandinistas and counterrevolutionaries have come together in many instances, claiming land and other rights

THE FSLN TAKES COMMAND

By 1977 the revolutionary struggle had become irreversible. The Somoza dictatorship, in its desperate attempt to control a population that was everywhere becoming involved, declared a state of siege. It was then that the FSLN, in the Asociación de Mujeres ante la Problemática Nacional (Association of Women Facing the Nation's Problems), finally succeeded in organizing women across lines of class, age, and activity. Again, AMPRONAC was an organization conceived of by a mostly male leadership, and responsible to it. At the time of AMPRONAC's conception, the front was still working to reunite the three tendencies into which it had split in 1976.[36]

Why did AMPRONAC take off while earlier attempts had failed? In the first place, the liberation movement itself had accumulated greater experience in its mobilization of different sectors and in channeling them toward an overall plan of action. The general level of misery and corruption was so high, and the repression against those who rebelled so intense, that many felt they had little left to lose except the dictatorship—and their misery. Women and others actively searched out structures in which to participate.

Murguialday notes that sixty women, most of them from the middle class, participated in AMPRONAC's first national assembly on September 29, 1977. Just nine days earlier, Anastasio Somoza had lifted the state of siege, and the women took advantage of this momentary lessening of repression to speak out: it was the first time that women, organized as such, had taken a position on the country's political situation. AMPRONAC considered it the opportune moment for its debut and, along with the Christian base communities, brought together more than a thousand people to listen to peasants denounce the repression in the countryside. This assembly was reported nationally and internationally.[37]

denied by conservative government policies. These groups have called themselves Recontras and Recompas (*compas* being short for *compañeros*, or comrades). Mothers on both sides have been exemplary in helping to forge this new unity.

36. The FSLN split into two tendencies at the end of 1975: the Prolonged People's War (Guerra Popular Prolongada, or GPP) and the Proletarians (Proletarios). In broad terms, the GPP was concentrated in the rural areas and advocated the development of a guerrilla nucleus in the mountains that would eventually be capable of extending itself throughout the country. This resembles the line put forth by the Cubans during the sixties and seventies. The Proletarians wanted to concentrate more among the urban working class and build a Marxist party. They were also strongest in organizing certain sectors, among them students and women. Later, a third tendency developed, calling itself the Insurrectionists (Insurreccionales or Terceristas). Some say this tendency evolved among those members of the FSLN leadership who had been attempting to bring the other two together. When the three tendencies reunited in March 1979, a nine-member national directorate was established with three men from each tendency. The GPP was represented by Tomás Borge, Henry Ruíz, and Bayardo Arce; the Proletarians by Luis Carrión, Carlos Núñez, and Jaime Wheelock; and the Insurrectionists by Daniel and Humberto Ortega and Víctor Tirado. These men became the nine "Commanders of the Revolution."

37. Murguialday, *Nicaragua, revolución y feminismo (1977–89)*, 41.

History had placed Nicaraguan women rather naturally in the forefront of the struggle. As we've seen, paternal irresponsibility had long been epidemic. Mothers were often left alone to care for their children; as single heads of household they were forced to devise ways in which to keep their offspring from starvation. Many mothers bore the special anguish of mothers whose children were at war. They had sons or daughters who were underground, in the mountains, or in prison, and they came out massively in defense of their children's rights.

By the late 1970s feminism had also made its mark in Nicaragua. In an atmosphere at least somewhat influenced by feminist movements elsewhere in the world, the time was right for Nicaraguan women to come together in an organization they could call their own. Gloria Carrión, an AMPRONAC founder who later became AMNLAE's first national director, spoke in a 1979 interview about women's participation during Somoza's last years:

> It's only been [very recently] that you could really talk about a massive incorporation of women in the struggle against the dictatorship. And it's important to point out that women's integration into the revolutionary process didn't happen in a vacuum. It took place within the context of an entire people readying themselves for combat. At the same time, Nicaraguan women developed *a consciousness of themselves as women* and of the important role they could play in the fight against Somoza.
>
> Women are pillars of their families. This is the most fundamental and objective condition of Nicaraguan women's lives, and perhaps of Latin American women in general. We don't see ourselves simply as housewives, caring for our children, attending to the duties of the home and subordinating ourselves to our husbands. Women are the centers of our families—emotionally, ideologically and economically. This is particularly true of working class and peasant women.
>
> Of course it's important to note that women's participation . . . crossed class lines. It wasn't only terrible economic conditions that prompted women to become involved. Many women from privileged backgrounds also entered the struggle. Widespread repression and, in particular, the way this repression affected our children outraged women from all classes. The situation was so bad that it was a crime to be young. Age alone was reason for persecution. We had outright political assassinations of youngsters eight, nine, ten years old.
>
> Women's political involvement had its effect on relationships between women and men. Women began to develop their own points of view and express their ideas. In homes where . . . husband and wife lived together, new relationships developed. Women started making their feelings and opinions known. They would disagree with their husbands on issues where they never had before. . . . And our women's movement became stronger through this process.[38]

38. Randall, *Sandino's Daughters*, 10–14; emphasis added.

As the Sandinistas took power, in July 1979, revolutionary feminists throughout Latin America were talking about one of the questions central to their politics: Can women be organized *as women* through general struggle, or must they be mobilized around specifically feminist issues? One of the things Carrión and other women involved in AMPRONAC often said was that in Nicaragua getting rid of the dictatorship had become a feminist issue—at the time, the most urgent of them all.

WOMEN WARRIORS

The last months and even years of war in Nicaragua saw a number of extraordinary women taking on leadership roles and successfully carrying out tasks unheard of to that point in the history of women's revolutionary participation. I will speak of some of them here, without attempting to create "stars," without ignoring the fact that each of these individual examples represents legions of ordinary women, many of whom went on to make important peacetime contributions.

I've already touched on the role of mothers; they are but one aspect of the story. In Nicaragua, market women hid weapons under fruits and vegetables and transported them in the great baskets balanced on their heads. Catholic nuns smuggled radio equipment into the country inside the hollowed-out bodies of plaster saints and virgins. One mother discovered that her daughter was involved and the daughter realized the same of her mother only when they came upon one another, blindfolded and handcuffed, in the dictator's own personal dungeon—beneath a dining room where statesmen and their cronies nightly sipped expensive wines. (Those who survived those years of brutality in Nicaragua have testified that, as an after-dinner pastime, Somoza and his buddies often came down to rape the women prisoners.)[39]

In Nicaragua, criminality and cruelty reached levels that recall ancient Rome, Nazi Germany or, more recently Bosnia—such as a blindfolded prisoner being tossed around a cell as if she were a volleyball; or another prisoner being tortured to death and his body thrown into the mouth of an active volcano; or a nine-year-old activist hunted down like an animal, shot to death, and repeatedly run over by a truck. From 1961—when it was founded by three young revolutionaries with little more than rage and faith—to 1979 when it had become an experienced political-military organization capable of defeating Somoza, the FSLN channeled that rage and faith into an accomplishment reminiscent of David's felling of Goliath. It is against such a backdrop that these stories of women's unusual brilliance and courage must be understood.

Nora Astorga was a daughter of the bourgeoisie, a lawyer who worked for an important construction company during the last years of the dictatorship. Like so many of her sisters, she at first became involved in support work: exacting

39. See Randall, *Doris Tijerino* and Sandino's Daughters.

information from her conservative business contacts and making it available to her comrades in the FSLN. Then a set of fortuitous circumstances and her own personal commitment led to her protagonist's role in one of the organization's most publicized actions—and one with particular significance for women.

It was International Women's Day, March 8, 1978. The notorious torturer General Reynaldo Pérez Vega had been a client of Astorga's for more than a year. During that time, and in line with his assumption that he could quite simply take to bed any woman he wanted, he had beseiged the beautiful lawyer with sexual suggestions and demands. She continued to refuse him, but reported his advances to her comrades while skillfully keeping him interested. By March the necessary conditions had been created. Astorga called the general, known to his victims and their families as "The Dog," told him she had decided to give him what he wanted, and arranged for them to meet that evening at her home.

The revolutionaries planned on taking Pérez Vega hostage and exchanging him for important political prisoners. Astorga quickly led him to her bedroom. She undressed him and then, at a prearranged signal, two comrades sprang from a closet. They tried to overpower the man, but he was immensely strong and offered unexpected resistance. This forced them to shoot him instead, thereby writing a different ending to the operation. The civilian population, however, could not have been more pleased: one of Nicaragua's most infamous torturers would torture no more.

Nora Astorga, of course, had to leave her two children and go underground where she would continue to participate safe from the possibility of reprisal. She spent the rest of the war on the southern front. After the Sandinista victory she worked for a time as special attorney general in charge of prosecuting the more than 7,500 former members of Somoza's National Guard who hadn't managed to get away. Later she was named ambassador to the United States, but President Reagan refused to accept her credentials because of her involvement in the Pérez Vega affair. It seemed that the general had been on the payroll of the CIA.

Astorga eventually became Nicaragua's ambassador to the United Nations, where she played a significant role during the first difficult years of covert U.S. military intervention. She was an outstanding diplomat, making a lasting impression on Nicaragua's powerful enemies as well as on its friends. Even as she was dying of breast cancer, she continued as the Sandinistas' compassionately human and politically brilliant voice through one last general assembly. She died in February 1988 at age forty-two. Almost ten years had gone by since the action that had vindicated abused and humiliated people the world over.[40]

After years of participation, Mónica Baltodano rose to the highest Sandinista military rank during the final months of the war. She and two male comrades organized the final offensive in the capital city. They were forced to devise a mass exodus, removing thousands of young fighters and civilian population under cover of darkness one night in the famous retreat to Masaya, after which

40. Some of this information is drawn from *Sandino's Daughters*, 116–128.

Somoza and his troops discovered Managua virtually emptied of combatants. This maneuver allowed the revolutionaries to circle around, occupying smaller towns and villages en route, and then take the capital by surprise, provoking the dictator's flight. Baltodano remembers the details of one surrender in particular:

> We reached Masaya and then Carazo, where we stayed about a week. Later we went on to Granada . . . knowing that Somoza was going to resign. . . . We went through at dawn and fought the whole day. By nightfall we had surrounded an area called La Pólvora. . . . [A]fter that battle I remember I even had a bath. The next step was negotiating with the [National] Guard. After cleaning up, we headed out. I remember a woman asking me where I was going. "To the surrender," I replied. We approached the hospital, keeping a good distance from the guard post, moving up house by house. When we got closer to their headquarters and had ourselves positioned around the building, we got word that they were ready to surrender. One of the Guard came out draped in a flag, and I went over to talk to him. That dialogue is taped and filmed. At first he refused to speak to me because I was a woman![41]

Baltodano went on to hold important peacetime posts. And there are other women, dozens of them, whose participation during the insurrectional period went far beyond what the world had come to expect from women at war, perhaps particularly in regions where gender roles are so conventionally defined as they are in Latin America. Dora María Téllez may be the most outstanding among Nicaragua's extraordinary female fighters. Her story is told in this book. Gladys Báez, Leticia Herrera, and others are not included simply because of space limitations; there isn't a book big enough for the full history and heroism of Nicaraguan women.

All these women worked in their country's reconstruction, in positions of greater or lesser importance. But a decade later, one thing had become painfully clear: the proverbial glass ceiling was still in place. The FSLN, despite its progressive position on women's rights, failed to promote its extraordinary female cadre the full distance. During the Sandinista administration there were few women cabinet members (although those who served did noteworthy jobs). Never more than a quarter of the legislative body was female. Men held the vast majority of top-level posts—in government, the Party, and the armed forces. Indeed, during and since the decade of Sandinista government, no woman has been admitted to the FSLN's national directorate, for years the Front's governing body. (A detailed story of the Party's failure to promote Dora María Téllez to the directorate can be found, from different points of view, in several of the interviews in this book.)

The problem is not simply that women were not admitted to the highest levels of authority, or that a male-dominated organization kept its women's association under tight scrutiny and control. These were not the causes but the

41. Ibid., 74–75.

symptoms of the revolutionary movement's general failure to allow a feminist discourse—or to develop a feminist agenda.

When we look at recent Nicaraguan revolutionary history in the light of gender—and the women who speak in the following pages confirm this—we can see that those female combatants who were able to most completely assume a style of analysis and conduct considered to be "male" rose to the highest levels of power permitted them within a structure controlled by the men. Doris Tijerino and Dora María Téllez are examples of this phenomenon. The former does not consider herself a feminist, and so expresses her discomfort in terms of attitude rather than ideology; the latter seems to have made a series of conscious choices for a historical moment in which, in her judgment, more radical change is not possible.

These interviews, as well as those with Michele Najlis, Milú Vargas, Daisy Zamora, Gioconda Belli, Rita Arauz, and Sofía Montenegro, offer insights into how the FSLN as a movement missed the opportunity of making more complex (and therefore less vulnerable) political choices—had it been willing or able to draw upon the female strength within its ranks. I am convinced that struggles for social change, in spite of the great justice of their purpose and the generosity of their human sacrifice, will continue to fail until this fundamental flaw is remedied.

AMNLAE

Despite affirmations by women and others that the level of female incorporation within the Sandinista process was irreversible, despite early protests that women would never return to subservient positions in the home, traditional gender relations did remain and resurface during those ten extraordinary years. They had never really been challenged, at least not radically enough to have permitted qualitative change.

One important reason for this failure was the inability, on the part of Nicaraguan women as well as their vanguard party, to develop a truly autonomous feminist movement. The history of the Asociación de Mujeres Nicaragüenses Luisa Amanda Espinosa (Luisa Amanda Espinosa Nicaraguan Women's Association, or AMNLAE) offers important lessons in this respect.

Women as a group had high expectations with respect to how the new people's government would change their lives. Some articulated those expectations in immediate demands; others probably just felt something had shifted, that new relationships were possible. Few who had been involved at any level of the struggle believed that women would return to their conventional roles. By the end of 1979 and the beginning of 1980 one frequently heard some version of the following pronouncement: Once women take up arms and fight alongside their men, they receive a different sort of respect.

What may not have been understood was that the men weren't "theirs," but they did belong to the men—in every spoken and unspoken aspect of the patriarchal model. Thus, male leaders of the FSLN, the most enlightened of whom had only vaguely questioned gender roles, set about to reorganize society.

One of the new National Reconstruction Government's first decrees, one month after victory, prohibited the objectivization of women in commercial advertising. Women were ecstatic (the decree would remain in effect throughout the decade and beyond, although it would become less and less enforceable). Other decrees addressed issues of equality or protection. But when the various social sectors were organized for peacetime support of the revolutionary project—when workers, neighbors, farm workers, youth, children, artists, professional people, women, and others created the unions and associations through which they would channel their contribution to revolutionary change and better their own lives—it was essentially a male-dominated vision that turned AMPRONAC into AMNLAE.

In September 1979 a new women's organization was born, taking its name from Luisa Amanda Espinosa, believed to have been the first woman to die in the revolutionary struggle.[42] At first AMNLAE had only two small groups of women, in Managua and Matagalpa. But they were enthusiastic activists and, because the history of AMPRONAC was so well known, the association grew rapidly. Its line was clear: *Construyendo la Patria Nueva Forjamos la Mujer Nueva* (Building the New Nation We Give Birth to a New Woman). The theory of women's social insertion popular in Latin America at the time was alive and well in the concept AMNLAE had of its priority task: integrating women into the overall revolutionary process as a way of bringing about the desired changes in their social condition.

During its first two years, AMNLAE put all its energies into mobilizing women for the most urgent tasks of reconstruction—and then, increasingly, for defense. Women were encouraged to take part in the literacy crusade and to join the voluntary militia. They gravitated toward such areas as education, preventive medicine, and the equitable distribution of basic necessities. A number of women's agricultural projects sprang up. As a response to the obvious phasing out of women in the armed forces, in some parts of the country disappointed and rebellious soldiers organized all-female battalions. Market women began struggling for their rights. In a very few pilot projects, prostitutes were learning other trades. And the mostly female domestic service sector organized around such demands as the ten-hour day. AMNLAE supported all these efforts.

Women were conscious of the need to educate themselves. Of the 406,441 Nicaraguans who learned to read and write as a result of the 1980 literacy crusade, almost half—195,688—were women. Young women made up fully half of those who left their families, school, or work to spend five months in

42. Luisa Amanda Espinosa, born Luisa Antonia in 1948, was one of twenty-one sisters and brothers. Testimonies by those who knew her indicate that she was almost certainly abused by an uncle for whom her mother sent her to work at age seven. Luisa Amanda completed only three years of primary school, but she is remembered as unusually inquisitive and bright. She joined the FSLN probably in late 1969 or early 1970 and carried out the tasks common among women militants at the time: she kept safehouses, cooked for the combatants, ran messages. She was twenty-one when she and a male comrade were murdered by the National Guard in León, on April 30, 1970. See Randall, *Sandino's Daughters*, 24–33.

the mountains teaching reading and writing. One out of every ten members of AMNLAE took part in this cultural revolution. In conjunction with the Sandinista defense committees (CDS), this women's association organized the 30,000 brigadists teaching people in the cities.[43]

AMNLAE women also provided the traditional female support for the crusade: they sewed knapsacks, raised money, dropped in on the brigadists' parents while their children were away, and set up small libraries, creating the infrastructure without which the crusade would not have run as smoothly as it did. This, after all, was "what women do." And when the illiteracy rate had been successfully reduced, adult education was the logical next step. Here, too, women gave generously of their time and talent. They constituted 44 percent of the students and 55 percent of the volunteer teachers.[44]

Volunteer work: what we women are supposed to do so well. Our time is "more flexible," because we can juggle our own eighteen- to twenty-hour workdays. Most of our labor is unpaid, so we are less likely to be subject to the rigors of a formal schedule. When we are excited about participating in a project we believe will better our lives and the lives of our children, we will ask relatives or friends to pick up a child from school or stay with young ones in the evenings. AMNLAE capitalized on this penchant for volunteer work so many women share, and its massive mobilizations counted on the traditional female response—in the name of a revolution that had promised to change women's lives as it made life better for everyone.

Meanwhile, the United States was not about to let this new revolution survive. The Contra war was heating up, the countryside especially was beginning to suffer increased incidents of sabotage and armed incursions, and more and more troops were needed for defense. Women, who during the war had made up one-third of the Sandinista army, were gradually relieved of duty—or relegated to noncombat positions. By 1982 there were only two mixed battalions, but women never accounted for more than 10 percent of their members. Nevertheless, women flocked to the voluntary militia in great numbers. In March 1983, the FSLN proposed an obligatory draft law to the Council of State (precursor to the National Assembly). It would affect participation in the regular armed forces.

AMNLAE was governed by the FSLN. On this occasion, however, the association's representatives voted differently, perhaps for the only time. Some members of AMNLAE felt that discriminating against women's incorporation into the military could lead to other sorts of discrimination, that it would set a negative precedent for the liberation they sought. The Party argued that, objectively speaking, women were still responsible for home and children: the government hadn't been able to create the day-care centers and other services needed to alleviate this burden. Although there was some talk of the need for men to help with domestic tasks, there wasn't much movement in that direc-

43. Murguialday, *Nicaragua, revolución y feminismo (1977–89)*, 106–107.

44. Rosa María Torres, "Los CEP: Educación popular y democracia participativa en Nicaragua," *Cuadernos de Pensamiento Propio* (Managua) (1985), 24.

tion. The war complicated everything. The FSLN, of course, had its way, and only men were subject to the obligatory draft.

AMNLAE's development defined its constituency. The kinds of issues it began to address and the types of activities it sponsored largely attracted housewives, market women and, to a lesser degree, teachers and nurses. The mothers and wives of Sandinista soldiers gravitated toward the organization because of the support it offered them with their sons and husbands away at the front. Peasant women became members in significant numbers after a December 1979 assembly attended by more than seven hundred women from remote mountain areas.[45]

A Ministry of Labor study, carried out at the beginning of 1981, polled 4,892 working women; it revealed that AMNLAE had made no headway at all among women laboring in the banana fields or during tobacco or coffee harvests. Neither had the organization touched women in manufacturing: in the textile mills, match factories, or shoe manufacture. These women workers were more likely to try to get their demands met through union participation.[46]

Professional women, more open to feminist ideas and generally more sophisticated, wanted to begin to deal with the sexism that is so much a part of the Nicaraguan (and Latin American) social fabric. AMNLAE wasn't feminist enough for these women. Some, in fact, did try to bring a more woman-centered vision to the association but were marginalized as early as May 1980, accused of being what they were: feminists.

Throughout its history it has been difficult, if not impossible, for AMNLAE to understand or accept feminism as a necessary component to change for women's lives. The word has frequently been used as an epithet, with implications that run from "elitist" and "petit bourgeois" to "foreign" and "out of touch with local reality." The strong independent feminist movement that surfaced just before the 1990 elections, however, finally forced AMNLAE to take feminism into account.

A major problem for the association has been the fact that women's issues, at least in the beginning, were somehow considered secondary, outranked by the struggles surrounding the economy and defense. A feminist analysis might have explained how women and women's rights fit into an overall strategy for change. As it was, such analysis was not accepted—in fact was vilified—during the Sandinista administration. As a result, many of the strongest women—those who were models of feminist leadership, whether or not they choose to speak in such terms—put their energies elsewhere. They may have urged participation in AMNLAE, on the organization's anniversary or from one or another podium, but personally they gave little sign of genuine involvement.

AMNLAE's early inquiries showed that many women didn't really understand why a separate association was necessary. Why should we join an all-women's organization, they asked, when we already belong to our neighborhood defense committee, a union, or the Party itself? The ideological framework for

45. Murguialday, *Nicaragua, revolución y feminismo (1977–89)*, 116.
46. Ibid.

such an understanding just wasn't there; not on the part of the general female population, and not among the Sandinista leadership—at least not with anything like unanimity.

After a couple of years in which an increasing consciousness of the above-mentioned failings developed, AMNLAE engaged in some serious questioning of its direction and methodology. Its leaders had originally conceived of the association as a women's mass organization, a vehicle for channeling women's efforts in support of the revolutionary project as well as for meeting their most pressing sectorial needs. The Federation of Cuban Women was certainly an important model. Gender-specific issues—such as battery, rape, and abortion rights—were overlooked or disdained.[47] Education, public health projects, job training, voluntary work, protective legislation, and attention to the families of combatants took precedence. Anything that resembled the demands being made by women in the developed countries was automatically dismissed as "feminist."

In September 1981, during her tenure as AMNLAE's general secretary, Glenda Monterrey expressed in an interview that

> some women may think about abortion, but not the majority! And even if they did, now is not the time to dwell upon such issues; women and men alike must make fighting the enemy our main concern. . . . In AMNLAE we believe that problems such as male-female relations, pregnancy, and divorce are complex and must be analyzed in line with our revolution's development. It's not that we aren't interested in finding solutions to these problems, no. It's just that we have other priorities.[48]

Women's issues and the needs of the revolution were too often placed in opposition to one another. Feminism remained "something foreign," an "im-

47. The Federation of Cuban Women (FMC) was founded in August 1960, more than a year and a half after the revolution took power. From the beginning it was a mass organization for women, soon counting among its members some 80 percent of all females fourteen years of age or older. A mass (rather than selective) organization offers full leeway; members can be as active or inactive as they wish and still retain their membership. The FMC mobilizes great numbers of women to participate in tasks that support the revolutionary project. It also makes grass-roots women's demands known to the government and the Party and, in recent years, has moved to include a limited concern for feminist issues; it has been less successful in these latter two areas, however.

Abortion was illegal in Nicaragua before the Sandinista administration. It has remained so during its ten years in power and since. As it became apparent that illegal abortions were the primary cause of death among women of childbearing age, some in the FSLN and AMNLAE leadership attempted to bring the issue up for public discussion. At different times during the decade of Sandinista leadership it was discussed in the press and elsewhere. But the Sandinistas never succeeded in legalizing abortion: they feared repercussions from the conservative Catholic hierarchy during the extended emergency created by the Contra war; moreover, AMNLAE itself did not have the foresight or the courage to make the issue a priority. Today, achieving the legalization of abortion is one of AMNLAE's priority tasks.

48. *Ventana* (Managua), September 1981.

ported fad" that would divide women from men, instead of being seen as an analysis necessary to the revolution's overall health and, in fact, its survival. At the same time, as a mass organization AMNLAE was clearly unable to fulfill its promise. Only certain sectors were attracted to its program. The strongest and most activist women preferred to put their energies elsewhere. In December 1981, after almost a year of reevaluation, the association decided to cease operating as a mass organization and to articulate itself as a movement.

What this meant was that AMNLAE would no longer concentrate on recruitment. Instead, it would generate small working committees of women within the different areas and organizational frameworks. For example, women in a factory or school might get together as AMNLAE. Likewise, women in a labor union or military unit might meet, if they were concerned, to deal with gender-specific problems in their particular sector. The idea was that AMNLAE could be everywhere. *Somos AMNLAE* (We Are AMNLAE) was the slogan. For a while it looked like this change might save the organization, but the conceptual problems remained. It wasn't AMNLAE itself that was at fault so much as the political vision that had engendered it. Women became frustrated that their organization had proved unable to address their problems as women. And real autonomy wasn't considered.

The 1980s would be marked by an intensification of the United States' many-pronged attempt to undermine and destroy the Sandinista revolution. Funding and training for the Contras continued; when the U.S. Congress voted against more aid, the Bush administration's shadow government took over and the Iran-Contra connection ensured covert support. For Nicaraguan women— as for all Nicaraguans—peace and economic stability were priorities. For many, in this context, juggling political interests included refraining from angering the Catholic hierarchy (Miguel Obando y Bravo—then archbishop, now cardinal—and his axis of power), even when that meant relinquishing the struggle for freedom of choice, or the struggle against domestic violence, or abandoning other so-called women's issues.

Throughout the Sandinista administration, AMNLAE led a number of vigorous campaigns for legislation beneficial to women and children. In August 1979 the FSLN had established a "fundamental statute" providing the framework for full equality between the sexes. In subsequent years, a number of reforms to the Civil Code were proposed; some passed, others failed. When they threatened "traditional family values," there was certain to be a backlash of protest from the Church hierarchy.

Some of these new laws were more successful than others. By successful I mean that they proved practicable besides looking good on paper. Responsible paternity was established, at least by law, and an Office of Family Protection was set up where abandoned mothers could go to get financial help from the fathers of their offspring. If the father held a job, and had a salary that could be attached, this was often productive.

Free union was recognized for a series of women's rights. The Adoption Law eliminated the easy buying and selling of children that had existed in the past; men as well as women could adopt, without the prerequisite of a legally constituted marriage. This law also made it much harder for foreigners to adopt Nicaraguan children and remove them from their land and culture. A new Family Code eliminated the concept of illegitimacy; and it recognized women's unpaid labor by requiring that men give financial support to their wives and children in cases of separation.

These laws and others like them generated tremendous, at times virulent, discussion. Where male dominance was most threatened, charges such as "destroying the family" or "endangering the unity of the people" were most loudly heard. The very real rigors of war, as well as increased economic crisis, made the arguments ever more complex. AMNLAE, as an organization, began to lose meaning for many revolutionary women who felt their most urgent needs reflected in more immediate and practical ways by the Association of Small Farmers, the Confederation of Professional People, their respective unions, or the Party itself.[49] Since the women's organization proved incapable of doing the one thing uniquely within its province—that is, going to battle for women around gender-specific issues—it became less and less important in women's lives. Murguialday writes that

> the fact that AMNLAE couldn't take up women's demands, or set them aside when faced with other priorities, didn't mean that these demands ceased to exist. And the idea of women spontaneously relegating [to others] their most urgent needs so that they could concentrate on defending their country was hardly proven in practice. AMNLAE lost its social base because by eternally ignoring women's demands it failed to mobilize them around their most pressing needs. This distanced many women from the association when they found themselves unable to identify with its political practice.[50]

Into this vacuum created by AMNLAE's failure (and thus the FSLN's failure) to develop a feminist agenda, stepped the organized Right with its propaganda—always rooted in traditions that are more familiar and so, when unquestioned, seem more comfortable for the great majority of women. It is often easier to retreat into a known space than to risk the social pressures and marginalization of uncharted terrain. Statistics on women's voting patterns in both the 1984 and the 1990 election show that the Sandinistas were ultimately incapable of successfully organizing women to a position that did, in fact, offer them freer lives.[51]

49. Statistics for 1989 show that women made up 40 percent of the Farm Workers' Association (ATC), 37 percent of the Sandinista Workers' Central (CST), 70 percent of the Association of Nicaraguan Educators (ANDEN), 40 percent of the Nicaraguan Confederation of Professional People (CONAPRO), and even 12 percent of the traditionally all-male National Union of Farmers and Cattle Growers (UNAG). These are all Sandinista organizations. See Paola Pérez-Alemán, "Diagnóstico de la situación de la mujer en Nicaragua: 1990," paper presented to the Canadian Agency for International Development, Managua, November 1990.

50. Murguialday, *Nicaragua, feminismo y revolución (1977–89)*, 138.

51. A study by Cezontle, a Managua-based think tank and resource center on women, reveals that great numbers of women voted in both elections (94 percent of all eligible women were

As we will see, however, Nicaraguan feminists did not allow the Right to take over. A strong and progressive independent women's movement was about to make itself felt.

COLLECTIVE TRAUMA AND THE ROAD TO RECOVERY

With the advent of the feminist movement and the new theoretical and psychological breakthroughs it has engendered, we have begun to define new parameters for talking about women's lives. Patriarchy, with its powerful checks and balances, long stifled or distorted such discussion. To be fair to previous generations of women, there were moments when such analysis did push itself to the surface of our consciousness, only to be quickly discredited. To preserve the balance of power, the male "experts" called us witches, demons, hysterics, troublemakers, Malinches, ball-breakers, brassy, strident . . . readers will surely be able to add to the list.

In her groundbreaking contribution to our understanding of how patriarchy harms women and men in similar ways, and how society's interest in why and how this happens follows cyclical patterns of inquiry and retreat from inquiry, Judith Lewis Herman makes essential connections between the private (women's) and the public (political) spheres.[52] She shows how society has periodically pulled back from examining and attempting to deal with the reality of violence against women, precisely because doing so would mean challenging its own patriarchal model. Similarly, so-called experts have resisted examining what we once termed "shell shock," because that meant questioning male virtues of virility, manliness, and honor.

Like scholars before her, Herman examines Freud's discovery of incest and other childhood abuse or domestic violence against women. She reviews his great contribution and subsequent renunciation of his findings, pointing out that "the late nineteenth-century studies of hysteria foundered on the question of sexual trauma. At the time of these investigations there was no awareness that violence is a routine part of women's sexual and domestic lives. Freud glimpsed this truth and retreated in horror."[53]

Then she makes the connection that proves so important when looking at Nicaragua: "For most of the twentieth century," she notes, "it was the study of combat veterans that led to the development of a body of knowledge about traumatic disorders. Not until the women's liberation movement of the 1970s

registered in 1990, an increase of 15 percent from 1984). Before the 1990 election, this study found that 59 percent of those women who had voted for the FSLN in 1984 intended to do so again. Four percent said they would vote for the opposition coalition, and as many as 38 percent were undecided. See *Nicaragua: El poder de las mujeres*, (Managua: Cezontle, 1992), 142. Many analysts believe this undecided group was of key importance, and that at the last moment many more women—and men—actually gave their vote to the opposition.

52. Judith Lewis Herman, *Trauma and Recovery: The Aftermath of Violence—From Domestic Abuse to Political Terror* (New York: Harper Collins, 1992).

53. Ibid., 27–28.

was it recognized that the most common post-traumatic disorders are those not of men in war but of women in civilian life." Speaking now of the United States in the seventies, Herman shows how

> [only] the moral legitimacy of the antiwar movement and the national experience of defeat in a discredited war . . . made it possible to recognize psychological trauma as a lasting and inevitable legacy of war. In 1980, for the first time, the characteristic syndrome of psychological trauma became a "real" diagnosis. In that year the American Psychiatric Association included in its official manual of mental disorders a new category, called "post-traumatic stress disorder." The clinical features of this disorder were congruent with [those which Freud, Janet, Kardiner and others] had outlined [so many years before]. . . . Thus the syndrome of psychological trauma, periodically forgotten and periodically rediscovered through the past century, finally attained formal recognition within the diagnostic canon.[54]

Nicaraguan women have, in fact, been severely victimized by the phenomena of woman abuse and wartime traumas. On the one hand, like women everywhere, they have long been weighted down by a legacy of domestic violence. Herman and others before her offer statistics showing that this is common to approximately three out of four women, and that it can and does cause lifelong symptoms of post-traumatic stress. In this respect, Nicaraguan women may not be so different from their sisters elsewhere. Early political systems had legitimized and protected the abusive power relations that became "acceptable" in their lives; and the Sandinista administration proved unable to address those relations or change them in any meaningful way.

Nicaraguan women, as we have seen, also suffer from the equally stress-producing symptoms usually reserved for men who have been forced to endure prolonged combat situations. Like women in Vietnam, southern Africa, El Salvador, Guatemala, and so many other places where war has for too long been a fact of everyday life, women in Nicaragua share the plight of a battle-worn population at large plus the special suffering reserved for women.

But Nicaraguan feminists do not only share the trauma; their feminism has made them partners in their own recovery. They are no longer simply victims, but "survivors" in the most profound meaning of the term. It takes women coming together to develop a language and a therapeutic practice *outside the patriarchal profession and its canon* for there to be a real understanding of what has been perpetrated and how best to deal with it. Paradoxically, the challenge to their identity suffered in the wake of the 1990 electoral loss shook the consciousness of many Sandinista women, and some men. They had undergone the experience of collective defeat described by Judith Lewis Herman and were free to begin building upon a movement that had already burst through the strictures of official disapproval. Feminists in Nicaragua are currently engaged in a powerful coming together—outside the traditional parameters of patri-

54. Ibid.

archal society, and outside the parameters of a male-dominated revolutionary practice as well.

I find it useful to examine the Nicaraguan situation in the light of Herman's paradigm. Traditionally, domestic violence in Nicaragua has been both acute and unremarked. Women became the strong pillars of family and also, in certain periods, of commerce. As guilt-ridden mestizas, as victims of Christianity's traditional double message to women, as housewives at war, as abandoned mothers, and as females lured onto the front lines of struggle and politics only to find themselves restrained by conventional expectations every time real equality threatened, they suffer from a collective version of the aforementioned post-traumatic stress syndrome. I would like to quote at length from Herman's description of psychological domination:

> The methods that enable one human being to enslave another are remarkably consistent. The accounts of hostages, political prisoners, and survivors of concentration camps from every corner of the globe have an uncanny sameness. . . . These same techniques are used to subjugate women, in prostitution, in pornography, and in the home. . . . Even in domestic situations, where the batterer is not part of any larger organization and has had no formal instruction in these techniques, he seems time and again to reinvent them. . . .
>
> The methods of establishing control over another person are based upon the systematic, repetitive infliction of psychological trauma. They are the organized techniques of disempowerment and disconnection.[55]

Our incipient ability to see through the web of this skewed socialization is, in and of itself, heroic. In Nicaragua, women's domestic situation is compounded by years of political repression. During the Somoza dictatorship, as we've seen, this repression achieved an intensity that saturated the population—with a special brutality aimed at women. During the war of liberation, untold horror was the order of the day.

The initial years of the Sandinista administration freed people's psyches, but certainly not for long; nor radically enough to reduce significantly the level of collective stress. Almost immediately, economic pressure from the United States and the Contra war combined to renew tensions. The 1990 electoral loss brought with it—for the Sandinistas especially—an identity crisis still very much to be contended with. Several of the women in this book speak eloquently of this crisis.

But Nicaraguan women, despite these pressures and perhaps in some strange way because of their unrelenting intensity, have reacted in ways not seen before. And because the vast majority of Nicaraguan feminists have come to their feminism through years of political struggle, the other side of this reality may be that when they tell their stories and listen to each other, they are together able to move through an amazing spectrum of consciousness, healing, and vision—with impressive speed and extraordinary potential for clarity.

55. Ibid., 76–77.

Herman insists that "the first principle of recovery is the empowerment of the survivor."[56] A community in which collective empowerment is the goal not only nurtures recovery but encourages a philosophical breakthrough as well. Many of us, from our own lives, know this to be true. What greater empowerment than that experienced by these Nicaraguan sisters of ours—who have so far survived dictatorship, war, victory, defeat, and the continued capacity to re-vision their reality?

THE NEW FEMINIST MOVEMENT

The Sandinista revolution brought young women, with their Spanish Catholic heritage of chastity and submission, out into an arena of public struggle. A decade of revolutionary government promoted women's rights in health, education, labor, leadership, and more egalitarian legislation—some of it successful, some not. Admittedly, unrelenting pressures from the United States made much more difficult many of the revolution's social programs.

The political model, heavily influenced by a male-dominated Left unable or unwilling to deal with feminist analysis, continued to keep its official women's organization under control; throughout the Sandinista administration the FSLN retained control over AMNLAE, and the women of AMNLAE proved incapable of cutting the cord that prevented autonomy. Still, it would be incorrect to underestimate the liberating effect that Sandinism has had on generations of women.

Paradoxically, since the electoral loss, revolutionary women have been able to break the binds of allegiance to male-oriented party politics. In an economy in shambles, with a conservative government in office, and amid a generalized depression that has seriously threatened everyone's sense of self, Nicaraguan women are getting together, questioning absolutely everything, developing new ways of looking at their reality, and organizing to change what is wrong.

The struggle for women's autonomy has taken place, as well, in the spiritual arena: women have been agents of change and also pawns in what amounts to a modern-day schism between the hierarchic power structure and the revolutionary Catholic Church. There has also been a retrieval of pre-Columbian spirituality. Touching upon, influencing, and being influenced in turn by other important struggles—such as the movements for ethnic autonomy, against racial discrimination, and for gay rights—feminism in Nicaragua offers a particularly exciting panorama. The women in this book share histories that span a tremendous range of struggles.

In Nicaragua, the outcome of the 1990 elections changed everything. Everyone, including the opposition, expected the Sandinistas to win. In their interviews, Gioconda Belli and Dora María Téllez provide detailed insights into the FSLN's preelection expectations, and into the type of propaganda the Party directed at the female sector. A number of the women interviewed analyze the

56. Ibid., 133.

Party's misogynist campaign slogans, its failure to address issues important to women, and the dramatic results which that failure brought—both for the outcome of the elections and with respect to the disenchantment that certain groups of women began to experience.

Many of the strongest and most feminist Sandinista women had for years faced problems when they challenged the male power structure. As members of a revolutionary party, however, they were bound by a discipline that permitted little if any revelation of grievances. As described by both Michele Najlis and Milú Vargas, some of these women struggled within the organization—to little avail. Once their party was voted out of power, however, there was less reason for such unexamined loyalty. In the subsequent collective attempt to understand what went wrong, in the private and public discussions that raged, women were able to speak more freely about the abuses they had suffered in silence.

It would be unfair not to recognize that a number of women also tried to make their voices heard before the electoral defeat. Daisy Zamora joins Najlis and Vargas in speaking of her ongoing search for personal dignity—indeed, political survival—within a highly sexist system. Gioconda Belli, charged along with others with designing the FSLN's electoral campaign, tells how she came to believe it was ill-conceived. But when she presented an alternative— feminist—approach, she was quickly marginalized. Mirna Cunningham gives us a picture of women on the Atlantic Coast.[57] Sofía Montenegro and Milú Vargas describe a radical feminist movement that got off the ground before the elections and that has grown significantly since. Rita Arauz draws parallels and makes connections between the lesbian and gay movement and feminism in general.

Nicaraguan feminists, tired of trying to get AMNLAE to understand and respect their positions, have created an independent, broad-based, cross-class, and internationally connected movement that currently boasts a number of research and education foundations, several excellent publications, and a guerrilla-like networking system. Most of the women involved consider themselves Sandinistas; they either continue to be members of the FSLN or are sympathizers. Many speak emotionally about their development within the Party and say they would not be where they are today without it. But they also feel it is time to discard the male leadership that has so overwhelmingly refused to address their concerns.

Organizationally, the new feminists remain intentionally amorphous. Some hoped that a new organization might have gotten off the ground by now. Others, still wary of traditional organizational forms, resist such a move. In the context of an International Women's Day festival held in March 1991, several

---

57. Women on the Atlantic (Caribbean) Coast of Nicaragua took an initiative unique among that country's women. As the Contra war intensified, they began to act as intermediaries between the Nicaraguan resistance and the Sandinista government. This paved the way for the peace process and also strengthened the women's movement on the Coast. See Saakes, "Particularides," 172.

hundred younger women began referring to themselves as "The 52 Percent Majority"; this, however, is a nonstructured movement rather than an organized group. PIE (Partido de la Izquierda Erótica, or Party of the Erotic Left) began during the electoral campaign as a small circle of friends interested in doing feminist analysis and attempting to influence the centers of male power. Sofía Montenegro, Milú Vargas, and Gioconda Belli describe its unique history and achievements.

The lesbian movement in Nicaragua is both feminist and revolutionary, and this combination sets it apart from similar movements in the industrialized countries. It also functions in close coordination with the gay male movement and with sisters and brothers who identify as bisexuals. Lesbians run foundations promoting women's health work, the publication of nonsexist educational materials, AIDS outreach and advocacy, and consciousness-raising within their community. The interview with Rita Arauz gives an overview of this activism.

In January 1992, after more than a year of preparation, Nicaragua's independent feminists hosted a gathering of women in Managua. The theme was "United in Diversity." The organizers expected an attendance of three hundred, but more than eight hundred showed up to fill the capital city's largest convention center. There was no fee, and every effort was made to host women from outlying regions in other women's homes.

The women attending the event were indeed diverse: working women, professionals, feminists and those who had never heard the term, Miskitos and other indigenous women from the Atlantic Coast, peasants, students, religious sisters, teenagers, grandmothers, Sandinistas, and representatives from the nation's extreme Right (Azucena Ferrey, the only woman to have belonged to the Contra directorate, made a brief appearance). The organizers invited AMNLAE to be a part of the conference's planning phase, but the organization refused. When it became apparent that the meeting was going to be such a success, however, some fifty AMNLAE women decided to attend as individuals.

Open discussion and effective democracy characterized the event. Organizers urged consensus rather than resorting to coercion disguised as expediency. Previously written position papers, to be rubber-stamped by those in attendance, were not a part of this experience. According to one participant:

> Among the proposed objectives were those of promoting an exchange of ideas about women's problems among the different groups, analyzing the impact that the current government's economic policies have on women's lives, and looking for answers through collective action. Themes discussed were the economy and environment, education and culture, relationships and sexuality, violence, and organizational participation.[58]

The meeting produced a great number of initiatives, chief among them a series of networks in which women may work together around issues of health,

---

58. Scarlet Cuadra, Guillermo Fernández, and Francis Lurys Ubeda, "Buscando unidad en la diversidad" [Looking for Unity in Diversity], *Barricada Internacional*, March 1992.

education, sexuality, violence against women, and the economy. Decisions were also taken to create a women's bank that would finance feminist projects, support the celebration of Gay Pride Day in Nicaragua, revive the deposed government's program of preventive medicine (especially as it can serve women's needs), promote nonsexist sex education at all levels, and initiate a campaign to bring back free, secular and (for the different ethnic groups) bilingual education.

The January gathering showed the FSLN, the general public, and women especially that Nicaraguan feminism is to be reckoned with; that it is not an import or a fad, but an indigenous movement reflecting the urgent needs of diverse women. Two months later, the independent women's movement hosted a meeting of Central American feminists at a beach resort outside Managua. Ties are strong with feminist groups in Latin America and other parts of the world, and there is ample evidence that Nicaraguan feminists are engaged in their own profound analysis of their history, their recent past, and the ways in which patriarchy continues to distort their perceptions of the world.

THE WOMEN IN THIS BOOK

Although I reinterviewed many of the women in the original *Sandino's Daughters*, I ended up using only two of their stories this time round: Daisy Zamora and Dora María Téllez pick up where they left off in 1979–1980 and address the ways in which a decade of Sandinista government fulfilled or failed to fulfill the FSLN's promises to women. Zamora, a poet, was program director for the clandestine Radio Sandino during the revolutionary war and served as vice-minister of culture when the FSLN took power. Téllez is one of the country's outstanding military and political leaders; she occupied the city of León at the end of war, thus securing a liberated territory in which the coalition government could be installed. During the Sandinista decade she was minister of health, and she remains a member of parliament for the FSLN.

Doris Tijerino is the first Nicaraguan woman about whom I wrote, back in 1974; she is one of the few who remains from Sandinism's early period, and her life became a book several years before the 1979 victory.[59] Among the twelve women in the present collection, she is the only one who does not define herself as a feminist. Her story is included because it is such an extraordinary one, and because I believe it is important to offer the vision of a strong revolutionary woman who is avowedly antifeminist. During the last five years of the Sandinista administration, Tijerino was the only woman national police chief in the world.

Michele Najlis, Vidaluz Meneses, and Gioconda Belli appeared in *Risking a Somersault in the Air*. All three are writers whose work is popular in their country and abroad. All are feminists. All have a great deal to say about the ways in which Sandinism helped them define themselves as social protagonists but ultimately could not deal with them as women. Meneses also gives us a

59. Randall, *Doris Tijerino*.

picture of the devout Catholic who came to the revolution through her understanding of the requirements of faith. She is currently dean of humanities at the
Jesuit-run Central American University. Najlis heads the Cultural Office at that
institution, and Belli is a full-time writer.

Mirna Cunningham didn't appear in any of my previous books. A Miskito
woman, physician, and revolutionary leader, she brings to the present volume
the voice of women on the Atlantic Coast. Cunningham made international
headlines in the early 1980s when she and a nurse coworker were kidnapped,
raped, and tortured by the Contras. Her analysis of that attack sheds light on
the fundamentalist Right's political practice of violence against women. At the
time of our interview she was working with the Five Hundred Years' Campaign, an alternative movement (set up in opposition to the official 1992 Quincentennial celebration) representing the continent's indigenous groups, blacks,
and poor.

The conversation with Milú Vargas centers on women and the law. During
the Sandinista administration, when she was chief counsel for her country's
parliament, I interviewed her about the pro-woman legislation then being introduced by the FSLN.[60] Now she was able to speak as well about her role in
writing the 1987 Constitution, her marriage to one of the few members of the
FSLN's national directorate sensitive to feminist issues, and her own problems
as an outspoken feminist within the Party.

As has been true in the United States, and for similar reasons, in Nicaragua
most of those who speak or write about feminism are from the middle and
upper classes. Thousands of working-class and peasant women lead lives of
protest and agency. Their experiences are what fuel the best analyses made by
those of their sisters who have more time and freedom to explore the issues. I
didn't want working-class women to be absent from this book: the interview
with Diana Espinoza reveals the insights, tenacity, and strength of women in
the factories and the unions, touching on the labor struggles which have become so frequent recently. At twenty-six, she is also the youngest woman
interviewed, thus broadening the age range (which, because of the type of
experience I was interested in exploring, tends to center on women in their
thirties and forties).

Aminta Granera is from a wealthy family, closely related to the Somozas.
Her personal journey led her from a protected childhood in León and attendance at a private university in Washington, D.C. to becoming a nun in rural
Guatemala, eventually joining the FSLN, and fighting for her country's liberation. During the Sandinista administration she was in charge of intelligence for
the Ministry of the Interior; now she holds a similar high-level post in the
national police force.

The lesbian and gay movement has an eloquent spokesperson in Rita Arauz,
a Nicaraguan who attended college in San Francisco, "came out" as a lesbian
and organized against Somoza within that city's gay movement during the

60. Margaret Randall, *We Have the Capacity, the Imagination, and the Will: Milú Vargas
Speaks about Nicaraguan Women* (Toronto: Participatory Research Group, 1983).

early seventies, and was recruited into the FSLN as an openly lesbian activist. Back in her country since 1984, she helped organize the lesbian and gay movement there. She currently heads Nimehuatzín, a nongovernmental organization doing AIDS outreach, education, and advocacy.

Sofía Montenegro speaks last. Like so many Nicaraguans, her family and personal histories are spliced with the painful drama of opposing political loyalties. She expresses terror, grief, loss, and an evolving discovery of self-identity. Like Arauz, she came to the revolution through a feminist consciousness—not the other way round. Daughter of a member of Somoza's National Guard and sister of one of the dictator's torturers, Montenegro had to overcome the innate lack of trust that her surname elicited in other revolutionaries. During the Sandinista administration and in spite of her iconoclastic character, she headed the editorial page of *Barricada*, the FSLN's official paper. Now she edits its popular (and feminist) weekly magazine, *Gente*. Her analysis of feminism and Sandinism seemed a fitting way to end this book.

"Women's Solidarity Has Given Our Lives a New Dimension: Laughter"

Michele Najlis

Going to interview Michele Najlis felt a bit like participating in one of those TV specials where it's been prearranged that you'll meet a long-lost sister. Behind the scenes, the connections have been made. You haven't seen one another in twenty years. Will she like me? Will I like her? Will we recognize one another . . . ? This morning you dressed with a certain amount of trepidation. Yet you know your lives have moved in similar directions, identical histories have touched you deeply, you have even chosen tools of the same trade with which to express feelings that criss-cross along coinciding routes. Both surprise and familiarity belong to this picture.

I allowed myself the imagined scenario: you are women, feminists, poets, I thought. The experience of the middle years breathes a particular excitement into your lives. Both from secular West European Jewish families, you bring the presence of those cultural roots to an energetic New World commitment. One of you is Nicaraguan and grew up on this magical land that has repeatedly overcome such a punishing history of invasion and earthquake, exploitation and war. The other comes from the country that once installed a North American president here.[1]

1. In 1854, the United States staged the first of a long series of military interventions in Nicaragua. William Walker declared himself president in 1855. Recognized and supported by

Nicaragua and I were to cross paths from the early sixties on, until it became my home in 1980. But my history with Michele begins much earlier. The first thing I wanted to tell her, when we settled into our conversation at her small office at "la UCA [Central American University]," is that she was the very first Nicaraguan woman with a personal presence in my life.[2] Although the long-lost sister image is more feeling than fact—we've come together over the years, and I've interviewed her before[3]—I first became aware of Michele Najlis, the young Nicaraguan poet, almost thirty years ago. It was Mexico City, early in the sixties.

I coedited El Corno Emplumado / The Plumed Horn *then, a bilingual journal devoted to publishing the most exciting new literary production of those years. We were stalwarts of the creative renaissance exploding throughout the Americas.*

One day a modest envelope arrived at the magazine's post office box. It was from Fernando Gordillo: Nicaraguan poet, revolutionary student leader, and wheelchair-bound critic of his country's tyranny, who only a few years later would succumb to the illness already sapping his considerable energies.

Fernando sent us poems. And he included as well a few by his girlfriend, Michele. We loved both poets' work and published it in the journal's next issue. And I remember we asked for photos; a wall in our Mexican study had become a collage of poets' faces. I can still see the Michele of those years: a serious young woman with penetrating eyes, wearing glasses, whose straight shoulder-length hair framed a face that looked directly out of a faded I.D. shot. Perhaps she had taken the picture especially for us, in some photo arcade on the streets of old pre-earthquake Managua.

Over the years we kept in touch: a letter here, a new poem or two there. When we would speak of Nicaraguan poetry, still dominated by the great men—Rubén Darío, Salomón de la Selva, Carlos Martínez Rivas, Ernesto Cardenal—someone would invariably say: "Do you know that young woman, Michele Najlis? Her work has a particular strength and charm."

El Corno Emplumado *ceased publishing in 1969, when a political repression forced me underground and eventually out of Mexico. So I missed* El viento armado *[Armed Wind], Michele's first book which came out that year in Guatemala. After the Sandinista victory of 1979, it would reappear from Editorial Nueva Nicaragua, the revolutionary publishing house that began to make available to a hungry readership the literature that had been banned or ignored under the dictatorship.*

Michele and I met face-to-face in 1981. I had returned to live in Nicaragua

U.S. President Franklin Pierce, he reintroduced slavery into the country and attempted to conquer more of Central America before he was overthrown and Nicaragua reestablished constitutional rule in 1857.

2. Central American University, the Jesuit university in Managua, has long been a center of intellectual and progressive activity.

3. Margaret Randall, *Risking a Somersault in the Air: Conversations with Nicaraguan Writers* (San Francisco: Solidarity Publications, 1984), 109–117. When Solidarity Publications folded, the book was turned over to Curbstone Press (Willimantic, Conn.).

after three months of fieldwork for Sandino's Daughters *the year before. The slim young student was a decade older now; a bit heavier, still a poet, still serious and with the same penetrating eyes. Her generation had prodded and dragged and fought its country's way to the overthrow of Latin America's longest and most corrupt dictatorship. The FSLN, of which Michele was a member, had just won a devastating war and embarked on a marvelous and transforming dream. Many, like Fernando Gordillo, had been sacrificed. Michele was one of the survivors.*

During the years I would live in Nicaragua, Michele and I would cross paths now and then. We frequented the same cultural events. We both wrote journalism as well as poetry. And we both had daughters named Ximena (although hers spelled her name with a J). In 1983 the United States launched the Big Pine naval maneuvers along the Honduran coast. Intimidation was always part of the low-intensity warfare game. A group of North Americans protested by coming down to form a human shield near the coastal battlefield of Bismuna. Michele and I found ourselves recording that experience of shared solidarity.

The headquarters of the Sandinista Cultural Workers' Association in Managua now bore Fernando Gordillo's name: Casa de la Cultura Fernando Gordillo. The names of many such heroes and martyrs graced the new people's institutions opening everywhere. During my years in Managua, Michele was chief of the new government's Department of Immigration. Then she headed an office set up to control the press; the war-provoked state of siege had become a constant and the difficult problem of press censorship a sad necessity. Eventually, before I left the country in 1984, Michele went back to writing full-time.

Although we never discussed it back then, Michele and I also shared an experience more complex than either poetry or social change. We were two strong women who reveled in the extraordinary space opened up by the Sandinista revolution. We knew from our own lives how women's roles were changing, yet suffered the indignities of a movement that was never able to deal with its sexism in any really thoroughgoing way. "About Sexism" is a prose poem from a collection of Michele's published in 1988.[4] It is short and to the point: "Sexists (which is not to say all men) are beings with short hair and ditto ideas."

These were some of the things on both our minds as we prepared for this new conversation, July 1992. We had agreed to meet at Michele's office. She is now director of cultural affairs at the Jesuit university, where she also teaches literature. Her office door was locked when we arrived—too early—but Michele appeared several minutes later. In light of the hardships of these past several years, culminating in the FSLN's electoral defeat two Februarys ago, maybe I expected a more haggard version of the woman I remembered. If anything, Michele looked younger, trimmer, stronger, with a centeredness I hadn't seen before.

Wearing freshly pressed jeans, a plum-colored T-shirt, and sandals, the poet and teacher who also works as an administrator quickly rearranged a couple of straight-backed chairs and heated water for instant coffee. A well-

---

4. Michele Najlis, *Ars combinatoria* (Managua: Editorial Nueva Nicaragua, 1988).

used bicycle was propped against a file cabinet in one corner. Posters and books brought the small room to life; a colorful and very beautiful hand-woven canonical stole from the liberated zone of El Salvador caught my attention as I set up the tape recorder and placed my camera on a corner of the crowded desk.

The camera clearly brought Michele up short. "I hate *having my picture taken," she confided. "I tense up the minute a lens points my way." And she took a copy of* Ars combinatoria *from a nearby bookshelf, turned the pages to another of its two-liners and read aloud: "The camera is like a boa constrictor; it paralyzes its victim before devouring her." The poem made its point. But I heard myself telling its author that she'd have to pretend my camera wasn't a threat. "I want to be able to see you, physically as well as through your words," I said. "And I want my readers to be able to see you, too."*

Michele agreed and, coffee finally in hand, tilted back in her chair. I knew she's given more thought than many to the experiences of these past few years, from a feminist as well as a partisan perspective. Ours was a conversation I particularly looked forward to, because I knew it would touch upon the issues most pertinent to our lives. Michele, too, seemed eager to talk, exploring her thoughts and feelings even as she offered them up:

Well, you know I'm the daughter of Europeans; both my parents are French. My father's family is Jewish. I was born in Nicaragua in 1946, into petit-bourgeois society with all its advantages and disadvantages. Of course, there are a great many advantages. But they, too, engender complexities and complications. Take my dual culture. At home we lived a European life-style, a European culture. Outside the home I lived as a Nicaraguan.

It can make for a real identity problem. There's even a name for this particular predicament; it's been called the "immigrant's child syndrome." I recently read an article about it, in a psychology book. And I remember asking myself, "How can this writer, who's not even the son of an immigrant himself, understand my history like that? How is it that he knows what I've suffered, my joys, my traumas . . . ?" It actually made me a little angry!

On the one hand, I had access to two very different cultures, a variety of different points of view. My upbringing and education had a richness my friends' lives didn't have. On the other hand, who are you? What culture do you belong to? With whom do you really identify? You're always an outsider, no matter where you are. The daughter of immigrants, if she identifies with her family's culture, is a permanent stranger in the country of her birth. If she identifies with the culture of the country in which she was born—which was what I did—then she never really feels at home within her family. This contradiction has been complex, as well as a source of richness in my life.

From the time I was a child, I always felt like a Nicaraguan. Why? I don't really know. Probably for emotional rather than rational reasons. My earliest memories of feeling different from my parents, are connected to how much I love *tiste*.[5] They considered it a disgusting drink. And, you know, it's a very

5. *Tiste* is a traditional Nicaraguan refreshment made from cornmeal and served in gourds.

strange thing for a little girl, at the age of five, to suddenly realize she's different from her mother. I grew up loving mangoes. My mother couldn't stand the smell of mangoes. I loved baseball. My parents thought it was a ridiculous sport.

Later, of course, I found a great many points of identification with my parents. I love the classics of European culture; it's something I've always valued. And I owe that to them. I don't even consider European culture to be foreign in my experience; it's a part of me. So this dichotomy is certainly something that marked my childhood. The other important contradiction has to do with growing up a woman in a petit-bourgeois family and assuming a leftist position.

How and when did you become a leftist, Michele? What was the process?

This may be true of all my major life commitments, but I believe that in my case progressive ideas came through emotion rather than reason. That is to say, the rational part came later. My first memories of this process are also linked to what I was just telling you, about beginning to realize that I was Nicaraguan. For example, as a child I'd spend a lot of time in the kitchen, with my mother's domestic help, drinking tiste and talking. I began to identify with those women, with their likes and dislikes; and I'd listen to the stories they'd tell: about their rural villages, their families, how they lived. I was learning about Nicaragua through the sensibilities of the poor.

At the same time, our cook's godson also lived at the house. His mother wasn't able to support him, so he lived with his godmother, who worked for us. He was a poor kid, and he was my playmate throughout my early childhood. At first, of course, I had no idea about class differences; Carlos and I seemed the same to me. We played together all day long; we were best friends. My blood brother was seven years older than I, which is a lot when you're five. So, naturally, Carlos was my closest playmate. He was four.

You know, I don't think Carlos or I understood there was a difference between us until it was time to start school. When that happened, I immediately knew something was wrong. Because I was sent to a Catholic school, where the rich kids went, and Carlos was sent to a neighborhood school; we didn't even know its name. My school was called *colegio*; his was called *escuela*. For the first time in our lives, I began to feel something had come between us; there was a sadness, an unnamed something that hadn't existed before. Maybe resentment is the word.

One day we were playing at home like we always did. And we fought over something. Fighting wasn't unusual for us; we'd fight like kids do and make up and everything would be fine again. But this time it was different. Carlos told me, "Okay, you win. We'll play what you want to play, because you're rich and I'm poor." I don't think I'd ever felt quite as bad as I did at that moment. I remember that I threw the ball down and ran off to my room, to cry. That whole afternoon, I cried and cried and cried. When I finally came back downstairs, I went to seek refuge with my nanny, who was Carlos's godmother.

Of course, she asked me why I was crying, and I told her what Carlos had said. "Isn't that dumb?" I asked her. And she took me in her arms and told me, "No. No, it's not dumb. It's the truth. You are rich, and he's poor." So I ran back to my room and cried some more. I couldn't understand how something that cruel could come between my playmate and myself. That's what I mean when I say that my first notion of class difference didn't come from the larger world, but from something I'd experienced right there at home.

You went to La Asunción, didn't you Michele?

Yes, I'm another of your La Asunción women.

Someone should write a book about the several generations of Nicaraguan women, revolutionary women, who studied at La Asunción. The sisters obviously had a profound effect on all of you. . .

You know, that's a great idea. And the congregation's one hundred and fiftieth anniversary is next year. In fact, I've been trying to write something for the sisters, something to give them for their celebration. And I haven't been able to. Maybe I'll interview my contemporaries, the other women who have come out of that experience. You've just given me a great idea! Because whenever we get together—Vidaluz, Milú,[6] myself—we end up talking about the sisters. They combined several seemingly contradictory qualities. The congregation was founded for the purpose of educating upper-class girls. Yet some of the sisters possessed a social consciousness that was amazing for the times.

Some of those nuns were anything but typical. There was a French sister, Mother Mireille, who was extraordinary. She's still alive, in her nineties. Mother Mireille was from pure French nobility, absolutely rancid. When she took her vows she asked to be sent as a missionary to Latin America or to Africa. She wanted to work in the Third World. She ended up at our school, but spent a great deal more time in the most miserable neighborhoods of Managua than she did with her upper-class students. And when she taught us religion, she'd talk about the poor, about the responsibility that went along with privilege. This was two or three times a week.

In general, the sisters told us how privileged we were to be studying at a school like that. And they insisted we get a good education, one that would prepare us to assume our social responsibilities. Twenty or thirty years ago you didn't hear that sort of thing very often, I mean women telling other women that they should prepare themselves for something beyond marriage and having children.

There was another sister who taught literature, Sister Amanda Escoto from León. To this day I can say that the most important things I ever learned about literature I learned from her. Who knows where she picked up the things she taught us. She always said that "women's work" bored her, that when her mother sat her down to do embroidery or something like that, she'd memorize

6. Vidaluz Meneses and Milú Vargas.

poems and recite them to herself in order to keep from being bored. She became a Sister of La Asunción, and she was the one who taught us literature. She had a very special way of exciting us with what we read! Imagine, we were fifteen, sixteen years old, and she made St. John of the Cross, *El cantar del mío Cid*—all those classics of the Middle Ages and the twelfth century—come alive for us.

Then there was the religious vision we got from those sisters. You've got to remember that this was long before Vatican II, before the renewal in the Church. So, yes, it really was a privilege to have been able to go to that school. I studied grade school through high school there, twelve years. I graduated in 1964.

Margaret, something I want to emphasize about my background is how a poetic sensibility fed my social consciousness. It really did. You know the Nicaraguan landscape, how lush and beautiful it is. And its tropical nature: you absorb it through your pores—the heat, the wind, everything. My identity as a Nicaraguan had to do with those women who worked in my childhood home, with my friend Carlos, and with this landscape. I think the landscape is something common to most of us women poets here: Gioconda, Daisy, Vidaluz.[7] Our identification as women coincides with our identification with the landscape and with the revolution.

As a child, I was a dreamer. And when winter came and everything turned luscious, you couldn't keep me inside. The school was near the lake. All you had to do was turn left instead of right; and every once in a while I'd take off. Back then you couldn't walk very far in Managua without running into the most abject poverty, especially down by the lake. That's still true. Acahualinca is down there, one of the poorest neighborhoods. And you'll find gambling houses, prostitution, utter hopelessness. What I'm saying is that in my life there was a multilayered awakening: nature, poetry, and class consciousness—which in my case meant discovering that I didn't like the class I was born into and that there was another class plagued by a great deal of pain.

Another thing I think influenced me a lot was when I started going to parties, when I started going out with boys. The boys from my social class seemed totally boring to me, right from the start. We had nothing to talk about. We'd started a literary club at school, and we'd invite different intellectuals to come and talk to us. Pablo Antonio Cuadra, Ernesto Cardenal . . . yeah, we were thirteen, fourteen, fifteen years old and we invited the country's best-known intellectuals to our little club. What's more, they came! But through that literary club we also got to know a few boys from some of the other schools.

That's how I met Luis Rocha, who went to the Ramírez Goyena. That was a public school. I met Luis before I knew Fernando Gordillo. And meeting Luis was like discovering a whole new world. Because the nuns, progressive as they were, were terrified of communism. Communism was the Devil incarnate: it was hideous; every day they made us pray for the poor little Russian children who suffered under the Communist boot. So of course I thought Communists

7. Gioconda Belli, Daisy Zamora, Vidaluz Meneses.

must be really bad. Then I met Luis Rocha, and I thought he was the best, the nicest person I'd ever known.

The sisters taught us charity as a daily practice. And I remember one day I asked Luis why he never gave alms. He said it was because it wasn't enough. "I'm willing to give my life for this revolution," he told me. I had never come across that much generosity, certainly not among the boys of my own class, who called themselves Christians. Luis called himself an atheist, and one day he confessed to me that he was also a Communist. I said to myself, "If this is a Communist, I want to meet more of them." I told Luis, "I want to know if there are others like you or if you're the only one."

My vision of the world was changing. The Communists I met seemed to exemplify the ideas the sisters taught us so much more than my classmates, who said they were Christians, did. And I liked these new friends who lived a life I didn't even see in my own home. That's how this world opened up to me. Fernando was already studying at the university in León. He was six or seven years older than me. He and Sergio Ramírez had already founded *Ventana*, where they published my first, really bad, poems.[8] I always tell Sergio it was his fault those terrible poems were published. Anyway, I knew Fernando and he was a member of the FSLN. My first connection with the organization was through him and Luis.

Tell me something about those first contacts with the Front. Organizationally, how did you become involved?

It's all a little blurry now. I can't remember making a specific contact, I mean organizationally speaking. In fact, I can't remember if I actually knew Fernando and Luis first, or if I already knew Jorge Guerrero, Francisco Moreno, Selim Shible, and the Ortega brothers by then.[9] Maybe that's the way it was. I really can't remember. What I do remember is that we just started getting together, and that each of us thought the others knew why we were meeting. It was pretty surreal! Much later, when we were adults, Jorge Guerrero admitted to me that no one had the slightest idea; each of us was waiting for one of the others to explain what was going on.

There was some military training. That must have been around 1960. The FSLN as such hadn't even been founded. Or it was about to be founded. Most of us were adolescents, fourteen, fifteen years old; and since we were willing

8. Sergio Ramírez, a novelist, was the founder of the Ventana literary movement and its magazine. Much later he became a member of the group of Nicaraguan intellectuals known as the Group of Twelve, who came out in support of the FSLN toward the end of the war against Somoza. Ramírez was a member of the first Government of National Reconstruction, then became vice-president of Nicaragua, and today is one of the nine members of the FSLN's national directorate.

9. Jorge Guerrero was an early member of the FSLN. Francisco Moreno and Selim Shible, also early members, were killed in combat. The Ortega brothers are Camilo, who was killed in 1978 at the battle of Monimbó; Humberto, now commander-in-chief of the army; and Daniel, ex-president of Nicaragua and today general secretary of the Sandinist National Liberation Front.

and eager, I guess we thought we should be preparing for something. I don't know if anyone really knew what. The clearest explanation I ever heard was when Francisco Moreno told us we needed to be prepared for when Carlos Fonseca returned to Nicaragua.[10] "We need to form a cell that can support him" was what he said.

But I remember one day we were all going off to train in Guatemala. Including me. And I felt tremendously humiliated when the guy who was our contact turned to me and asked, "Just where do you think you're going, little girl?" He stuck me in a cab and paid the driver to take me home. I must have been thirteen or fourteen; I know I was in junior high. And I didn't have the vaguest idea of where I was going or what I was supposed to do. But I knew we had to do something.

Then the Ortegas were arrested, Selim Shible too. Now it seems to me that this all happened before I met Fernando. Luis's political life was clandestine; he never told me he was a member of the FSLN, not until much later. In any case, it was a while before the Front became organized in any really structural sense. But you've read Omar Cabezas's book.[11] "The bulk of our troops are in the mountains," we used to say. And in the mountains they used to say, "The bulk is in León." In León it was, "In Managua . . ." The truth was, we were maybe fifteen people in all.

So when you graduated from La Asunción, what did you do? Where did you go?

I ended up in France, of all places, for six months. Yes, I went to France. I tried studying sociology. I thought—and it still seems to me to be a reasonable idea—that sociology could be useful for someone who wants to change society. The only problem was, I wasn't a sociologist. They fed me all those formulas and I didn't understand a word. Then, too, I was seventeen. To leave Managua, which was such a small town, much smaller than it is today, and find yourself in Paris in 1965; you can imagine. The crisis was in full swing,

10. Carlos Fonseca, Silvio Mayorga, and Tomás Borge—along with several other young men whose names have varied with the telling—founded the FSLN in July 1961. Fonseca was born on June 23, 1936. His Mother, Justina Fonseca, was a cook; his father, Fausto F. Amador, worked as an accountant at one of the U.S.-owned mines. It is believed that he chose to use his mother's rather than his father's surname because of a special closeness to his mother. He was the undisputed leader of the FSLN until he was killed in battle in the mountains of Zinica on November 7, 1976.

11. Omar Cabezas was born in 1950 in León, Nicaragua. This longtime member of the FSLN attained the rank of guerrilla commander and was political secretary of the Interior Ministry during the Sandinista administration. His novel, *La montaña es algo más que una inmensa estepa verde* (Managua: Editorial Nueva Nicaragua, 1983) won the 1982 Casa de las Américas literary award. It was a best-seller in Nicaragua, has been translated into dozens of languages, and was published in English as *Fire from the Mountain* (New York: Crown, 1985). Cabezas is also the author of *Canción de amor para los hombres* [Love Song for the Men] (Managua: Editorial Nueva Nicaragua, 1988).

students couldn't find housing, it was awful: the build-up to what finally exploded in 1968. I was totally lost. Lost in such a different world, and lost academically because sociology wasn't really for me. It's a wonderful discipline, but it's not mine.

In any case, I got a lot out of those six months in Paris. And then I came home and enrolled at the National Autonomous University [UNAN], where I studied literature. I wrote poetry. And finally I did become a real member of the FSLN. I began to work as a student leader, with the Revolutionary Student Front [FER].[12] That's how I spent my college years.

What about Fernando? What happened to your relationship with him?

Well, my relationship with Fernando began before I left the country. I was still in high school. And Fernando died in 1966, just after I returned. Meanwhile, I kept on going to school and graduated in letters with a specialty in education. But by that time I'd been much too public in my political work; I would have had to go underground—and I don't have the physical constitution for that. I would have come apart at the knees, the elbows, everywhere. Impossible even to think of someone like me going underground.

So politically speaking I was paralyzed. Right after my graduation from the university I married a man named Amaru Barahona. And I had my oldest son, Tupac. He was two months old when the 1972 earthquake hit. That's when I took him to Costa Rica. I intended to stay for fifteen days, and we ended up living in Costa Rica for seven years, from 1972 to 1979.

As soon as I arrived I became a member of the People's Vanguard Party.[13] As far as I knew, the FSLN didn't have an organizational structure in Costa Rica at the time. And that was also the beginning of the terrible crisis in the Front, when it split into three different tendencies. Many of us felt like we'd been left stranded. It was a pretty paralyzing moment. In Costa Rica I started out doing ordinary Party work, but later they assigned me to tasks in solidarity with Nicaragua. And I didn't come back here until we'd won the war.

What did you expect you'd be doing when you came back? I remember you held some pretty amazing jobs during those first years, but I've never been clear about exactly how you came to work where you did . . .

Well, my first job was in Immigration. And it was pretty hilarious how I ended up there. That was our period of total euphoria. Imagine, I'd just arrived. And, naturally, in Costa Rica I'd spoken with Ernesto [Cardenal], and he'd said to be sure to be in touch when I got back.[14] So I arrived, and you

12. UNAN, the Universidad Nacional Autónoma de Nicaragua, is the state university; and FER, the Frente Estudiantil Revolucionario, is the FSLN's organization for university students.

13. The Partido Vanguardia Popular is the Costa Rican Communist Party.

14. Ernesto Cardenal is Nicaragua's best-known living poet. Born in Granada in 1926, he participated in the unsuccessful 1954 movement to oust Somoza García, the father of Somoza

remember how things were back then: it was all so crazy. I couldn't even find Ernesto until someone told me he was at the Camino Real Hotel. I went out there to see him, and again it was chaos. He didn't have any more of an idea where I should go or what I should do than I did. "For the moment," he said, "go on over to Radio Sandino. You have some experience with radio; go on over and see if they can put you to work."

So I went to Radio Sandino. At that point families here had this tremendous need to find out what had happened with their loved ones, if they were dead or alive. No one knew where anyone was. At the radio station, there were these huge mountains of papers: lists of names, people looking for one another. We had no way of answering all the letters we were getting. So we decided that one of us would remain at the station and the rest would go to all the different army barracks and make lists of the combatants who were there. Then, we figured, we could read those lists over the air: "In such and such a camp, the following soldiers are quartered . . ."

Of course, we got to the camps and what we found there was the same general disorder as everywhere else. Who knew people's names? But the idea seemed like a good one. So I went to El Chipote; and I was sitting outside on a rock, waiting for an official to come out who was supposed to talk to me, when Tomás Borge just happened to pass by.[15] He said, "What are you doing here, Michele?" "Making a fool of myself, Comandante," I said.

Debayle. Cardenal later spent a year with Thomas Merton and the Trappists at Gethsemany, Kentucky, but poor health forced him to leave the order. Still later he studied for the Catholic priesthood at a seminary in Antioquia, Colombia, and was ordained in Mexico. In 1966 he founded a contemplative and artists' community on a small island in the archipelago of Solentiname, in Lake Nicaragua. He, like many of the community's young people, eventually joined the FSLN (Cardenal is generally regarded as the first Catholic priest to join the organization). A thwarted military action brought repression to the Solentiname community in 1977, and it was destroyed. Cardenal was forced into exile, where he continued to play an important role in the struggle until the end of the war. Immediately upon the July 1979 victory, he became minister of culture in the Government of National Reconstruction. In that position, for as long as the ministry lasted, he promoted programs that opened up a world of creativity to all Nicaraguans. It was Cardenal's idea that I come to Nicaragua to interview women for what would become *Sandino's Daughters*, and his ministry supported the project. Cardenal's own bibliography is extensive, including *Zero Hour*, *Gethsemany, Ky.*, *Psalms*, *Prayer for Marilyn Monroe*, *The Gospel at Solentiname*, and *Cántico Cósmico*. Since the Sandinistas' electoral defeat, Cardenal has run a small art gallery in Managua, continues to write and speak, and creates innovative wood and metal sculptures.

15. El Chipote is Managua's main military camp, on a hill in the center of the city; formerly it was Somoza's stronghold. Tomás Borge, born in Matagalpa in 1930, is the only surviving founder of the FSLN. He is a Commander of the Revolution and one of the nine members of the national directorate. During the Sandinista administration, he was minister of the interior. Borge is also an accomplished writer, with many books to his credit. English-language editions include *Christianity and Revolution, Carlos: The Dawn Is No Longer Beyond Our Reach, The Patient Impatience*, and *Have You Seen a Red Curtain in My Weary Chamber?*

"I want to see you tomorrow morning, at the Ministry of the Interior," he told me. I tried to explain the commitment I had with Ernesto and that I was already working for Radio Sandino, but it was useless. "It's an order from the national directorate" was his response. And you know what that meant: in those days, we were all very disciplined. So, of course, I picked right up and obeyed what I supposed was that order from the national directorate. But I can tell you, I spent that whole night in tears. I was an artist—or I wanted to be an artist—and I knew it was crazy for me to be going to work at the Ministry of the Interior. But I had to obey orders. And I will say that once I got there I had a great time.

When Tomás told me he was putting me in charge of Immigration, I said I didn't have the slightest idea what a passport was even for! All he said was, "Me neither. No one here knows anything about anything. So go and figure it out." And then that phrase you heard everywhere back then: "And if you can't find out how it's done, invent something."

To make a long story short, two Costa Ricans showed up. One was the head of their Immigration Service, a man named Alvarez. He'd done an incredible amount of solidarity work with Nicaragua, supported us in every way he could. And when we won the war, he just up-and-came to Managua, to see what he could do to help. I don't remember the other man's name. But both of them were nothing short of incredible. It was because of their help that we were able to organize our first systems of control.

I don't know if you can imagine the chaos that reigned here at the beginning. No one knew who was who. And we decided we wouldn't recognize a single document issued during the dictatorship, which of course was absurd. If the Somoza government had issued passports attesting to the fact that people were who they said they were, most likely they were. After all, they were as interested as anyone in keeping track of everyone. But we decided we had to nullify everything that came from the dictatorship. Passports were worthless, birth certificates were worthless, everything was worthless.

But how were we going to figure out who was who? With the help of those Costa Ricans, we invented a way. It was much too complicated, but the idea behind it was beautiful: put all our trust in the people. So we decided it was going to be the Sandinista defense committees [CDS] that would tell us whether Margaret Randall is really Margaret Randall, and whether she lives where she says she lives.[16] We designed a form that had to be filled out and signed by the head of your neighborhood CDS, who was supposed to know who you were and where you lived. Well, they really did know about as much as anyone. After those Costa Ricans, we got help from the Cubans, too, and the Panamanians. I remained in Immigration until 1981.

Then I went to work at the Media Office. God, those were rough times! *La*

16. The *comités de defensa sandinista* were neighborhood committees, originally designed on the Cuban model, through which people could come together to organize popular defense, carry out preventive medicine campaigns, keep the neighorhoods clean, and in other ways defend the freedom won.

Prensa launched its daily provocations against the revolutionary process.[17] Do you remember the constant barrage of lies they put out? An absolute lack of the most elemental ethics: they'd print one provocation after another. Anywhere else in the world, in absolutely any civilized country, you'd have gone to jail for less. I mean the journalist, the editor of the paper, everyone responsible would have gone to jail. You just can't publish a story that's not true, about a public servant making off with 10 million dollars, and expect to stay out of jail.

That barrage of provocations, on the one hand; and on the other, a completely inadequate system of controls. We didn't have the laws: there was nothing we could do when they'd print those lies except close down the paper. We were in a terrible legal bind. And the leadership of the FSLN didn't have the slightest idea about what it meant to shut down a paper. The consciousness just wasn't there. I had what amounted to twelve different people giving me orders: the nine members of the national directorate plus Sergio Ramírez, Córdoba Rivas, and René Vivas—who was my only legal boss.[18] And every one of them was constantly ordering me to close *La Prensa*, including Córdoba Rivas! It was a mess. No one ever agreed with anyone else. And besides, even if none of the rest of them did, I certainly had an idea of what it meant to close a major newspaper. I'm telling you, that was a difficult period for me. And on top of it all, the war kept getting worse.

Among the FSLN leadership, historically I think there's been a tendency to underestimate ideological struggle. You lived here, Margaret; I'm sure you saw this: "We're in power, we're in control, if we want to do this or that, we'll go ahead and do it. We don't have to discuss it, we don't have to give our

---

17. *La Prensa* was founded by Pedro Joaquín Chamorro, a Conservative politician with a long history of opposition to Somoza. During the dictatorship, his newspaper could be counted on for news about the resistance that did not appear anywhere else. Chamorro was assassinated by Somoza in January 1978. Though anti-Somoza, *La Prensa* never went so far as to adopt the FSLN position. Following the 1979 victory, it moved further and further to the right. After about a year, all the progressive people on the paper (70 percent of its administrative, editorial, and printing staff) quit to found *El Nuevo Diario*, an independent daily headed by Chamorro's brother, Xavier. *El Nuevo Diario* has continued the tradition of honest journalism once typical of *La Prensa*, while the latter now represents right-wing, antipopular interests. It is no secret that the U.S. embassy underwrites much of what is printed there. *Novedades*, which had been Somoza's paper, was nationalized by the FSLN and became *Barricada* with the victory of 1979. After the electoral defeat of 1990, *Barricada* was no longer the official publication of the FSLN and became a paper of the independent Left. In a situation not uncommon in Nicaragua, all three papers are run by members of the Chamorro family. Pedro Joaquín's oldest son, Pedro Joaquín, Jr., heads *La Prensa*; his brother, Xavier, heads *El Nuevo Diario*; and his youngest son, Carlos Fernando, heads *Barricada*. *El Nuevo Diario* currently has the largest daily print run, with *Barricada* steadily gaining readers.

18. Rafael Córdoba Rivas, a Conservative businessman, was one of the representatives of big business who, along with Arturo Cruz, became a member of the revolution's early Government Junta of National Reconstruction after Violeta Chamorro and Alfonso Robelo stepped down in 1980. In recent years, he has dropped out of public politics. René Vivas is an FSLN leader who held a series of positions during the Sandinista administration.

reasons, we're the ones in charge." That was the attitude, and I believe that attitude led to a great many errors.

Most of us can see that now, although it was harder for some of us to see it at the time. On the other hand, there were some structures that were more rigid than others. And the intensification of hostilities from the United States, from the Contras, the difficulties inherent in changing society: all that obscured a lot of what was going wrong. But I'd like you to backtrack for a moment, Michele. I want to know what it was like for you as a woman, specifically as a woman, to hold the jobs you did during those first few years . . .

Well, I can't remember ever having problems with the men who worked under me; they didn't seem to mind a woman giving them orders. But I certainly did have problems with my superiors—from the beginning. I remember, for example, when we were planning the first anniversary celebration. We were talking about how we were going to arrange things at the airport, for the foreign dignitaries who were scheduled to arrive. I remember one of the male leaders saying we should do things in such and such a way because that's how they're done in Cuba. I turned to him and said, "Well, we're in Nicaragua, and I don't think that will work here." And I gave my reasons. He got absolutely furious; he wouldn't even talk to me. He didn't shout or scream or anything, but it was obvious from his expression that he didn't take me seriously. Later, because I stuck to my position, he said, "I'm just sure: that *is* how a woman would do things!"

I've had this type of problem at the very top. Once I had to go to see the minister about something, a criticism I had, and his immediate response was, "Women never understand this sort of thing!" I said, "You're right, Comandante. We don't understand this sort of thing. What's more, we don't justify it, and we have no intention of understanding it. And you know something, we're proud that we don't."

There was another incident when the whole country was going through the process of decentralization. Each of the state institutions had to reorganize to fit the new guidelines, including the Ministry of the Interior where I was working at the time. I remember we'd almost finished restructuring by region; we had only one unit left to go. And the supervisors picked for almost all the units in all the different regions were men. That didn't even seem to bother anyone. I don't remember which unit it was, but there was one where all the supervisors turned out to be women. The vice-minister suddenly said, "This isn't right. We have to revise this. We can't have a unit with only women in charge."

I raised my hand then and I said, "Comandante, you're absolutely right. We should go back and revise everything we've been doing for the past six hours. Because in all the other units all the supervisors are men; and that's not right, something's obviously wrong . . ." What a scene that provoked, Margaret! I no longer remember exactly what he said, but it was something to the effect that I should remember my place, that I shouldn't show such a lack of respect for my superiors; and in general he implied that it wasn't the same for there to be all men in a unit as it was for there to be all women.

Michele, were you still married to Barahona then? What kind of a personal situation did you have? I mean, were you getting this sort of sexism on the job and also at home, or was your relationship more supportive of your personal integrity?

No, I wasn't with Barahona anymore. That marriage had ended back in Costa Rica, where we got a divorce. And it was a very bad relationship. After the divorce, and still in Costa Rica, I married a really beautiful man, Walter. He's a different story altogether, very understanding of who I am. More than understanding, I'd say. He's very special, absolutely unusual for a Central American man. Then, too, I have an excellent rear guard: a support system of wonderful women that's helped a lot.

I remember in 1981 I decided to go off with the Omar Torrijos Brigade.[19] Camilo, our youngest child, was five months old at the time. I decided I was going, I got permission at the ministry, and I came home that night and told Walter. I actually wondered what his reaction would be; I knew it was a big decision, and a sudden one. Well, Walter looked at me for a moment, and then he said: "Of course. I think it's going to be an important experience for you; and you'll be able to give a lot, too. The only suggestion I have is that you get yourself a good pair of boots, ones that really fit."

When he said, "The only suggestion I have . . ." I thought, "Here it comes." I figured he was going to say something about the kids, ask who I thought would take care of them, that sort of thing. But no. Walter is unusual in this respect. But he also works like a beast, so my rear guard was important: my mother and a woman named Mariita. She was my nanny when I was a child, and she's stayed on with me and the kids, with my older brother's kids; she's just kept on working for the family. I know that I've been able to work as I have, especially when my children were small, because there were two other women there to take up the slack. I have three children in all, two sons and a daughter.

Michele, I'd like to know how you eventually moved from the ministry and from that job as head of the Media Office—two defense positions—back into the world of writing. How were you able to make the decision to leave that type of work and go back to writing full-time? Was it difficult? Did you have some heavy-duty convincing to do? Was it something you'd been thinking about for a while?

19. The Omar Torrijos Brigade, named after the murdered president of Panama who had shown a great deal of solidarity with the Sandinista cause, was for men and women in civilian leadership positions who during the Contra war nonetheless chose to spend a month or more on the front lines. The idea was that the rank and file shouldn't be the only ones to risk their lives. Enrique Schmidt, then minister of communications, did in fact lose his life while with the brigade.

Well, of course, after those first moments of revolutionary euphoria, I came to my senses and asked myself, "What in hell am I doing here?" And it wasn't only me. In general I think there was a great deal of misplaced talent, mistreatment of individuals, during the revolution. Maybe it was because of the violence we'd all lived through—or that vertical concept of the state, the Party, power itself. A great many people were treated very badly. You know, it's difficult to find a Sandinista today who would say no if you asked whether they'd suffered that sort of thing.

I was no different from many others. Between my dissatisfaction at not being able to work in a field I was really suited for and the constant mistreatment, the humiliation, I was ready to leave, I can tell you. I don't know if you are aware that they removed me from the ministry without an explanation. I never really found out why. And when a comrade took it upon himself to ask the minister why they'd treated me like that, he said I had "an identity problem"! In other words: the woman's crazy.

To make matters worse, they'd removed me from my job but the minister wouldn't free me entirely. He wouldn't let me go. It's really a pretty ugly story. First they removed me from Immigration, without giving me a reason. Then they had me at the Government House command post for six weeks, keeping track of so and so who went home at such and such an hour, so and so who's reported that he's at the office, that sort of thing. I thought I would go crazy. After six weeks, I went to see Tomás one day. I told him, "No matter what you say, I'm not going back to the command post. It's driving me crazy." That was when I realized they didn't know what to do with me.

I don't know if you remember a magazine the ministry published; it was called *Patria Libre*, and Freddy Balzán was the editor.[20] One day Tomás took me to see Freddy. Well, I'd always admired Freddy: a great comrade and a great journalist. We talked, and we were both delighted because we thought we'd be working together. When we left the office, Tomás told me, "On the masthead you'll be the editor. But Freddy's going to be in charge."

"Why is that?" I asked. I had nothing against Freddy being in charge. I knew he had a great deal more journalistic experience than I did. I'd have been content to sign on as assistant editor, as a member of the editorial staff, whatever. But Tomás said, "No. Freddy's a foreigner, and he's got a lot of enemies here." Well, I was furious. I told Tomás, "I think it's a tremendous lack of respect toward Freddy that you recognize his capabilities, you know he's the best person for the position but, giving in to xenophobia, gossip, intrigue, you virtually take his job away. And I also think it's a lack of respect for you to ask me to participate in tearing the comrade down, instead of supporting him. Furthermore," I said, "I'm not about to let my name appear in a position over which I have no control."

After that, they really didn't know where to put me. They sent me to the Political Department, where I answered the phone for three weeks. I read and answered the phone. That's when I decided, this is just too much. I'm not

20. Freddy Balzán, is a Venezuelan journalist and longtime supporter of the FSLN.

doing anything here. So I went to see Omar Cabezas, who was my immediate superior at the time. And I told him, "Omar, I can't stand any more of this. I'm giving you two choices: you can either arrest me as a deserter, or you can release me." At that point my discharge didn't depend upon Tomás anymore; it could be signed by Omar. And Omar took a chance. "Go on," he said, "leave the old man to me." That's when I started writing my column for *El Nuevo Diario*.[21]

Michele, I'd like you to talk about the last few years of the Sandinista administration, with an emphasis on what it was like then to be a feminist woman here. It seems to me there was a period when things began to change . . .

That's true. The Nicaragua in which we lived beginning around 1985 had changed considerably from the Nicaragua of 1979. You heard the same rhetoric, but the reality was very different.

What or who do you think was responsible for this change? How did it come about?

I think a lot of it had to do with the fact that the FSLN took power through armed struggle, with the almost military structure that implies. And those very vertical chains of command remained in place. The intensification of the Contra war also favored maintaining those structures; it favored, but in my opinion, didn't justify them. Of course, we had to have a vertical line of command to topple the dictator—and afterward to fight against the counterrevolution. At least in the war zones. But that top–down discipline in Managua, in our political life, what was the justification for that?

And you know, a great many of us questioned it; but we had no possibility of being heard. Not really. Besides, a level of corruption was developing within the leadership. I won't say all the leaders became corrupt, but too many did. And this, too, tended to support the verticality of the state and the Party— because if you have someone who's corrupt at the top, he's naturally not going to permit criticism from the bottom. If he does, the first thing he's going to hear is that the bottom doesn't want him there. From 1985 on, we began to see this sort of problem.

We were fighters. And we weren't content to keep our criticisms to ourselves. I was expelled from the Party three times. The first time I cried like a baby; the second time I got mad. We were in a meeting and I told them, "Go to hell! The FSLN isn't your personal property, it belongs to all of us. And I'm not getting up from this chair unless you bring in the police to drag me out."

---

21. From 1982 to 1985, Michele wrote a column in *El Nuevo Diario*. It never had a name, but it appeared almost daily in the advertising section and with a dark gray border. In these columns Michele talked about all sorts of events, people, and ideas. A selection appeared in book form: Michele Najlis, *Caminos de la estrella polar* [Pathways from the North Star] (Managua: Editorial Vanguardia, 1990).

The third time I just laughed. I said, "You guys must have totally lost your sense of the absurd to be expelling me from the FSLN!"

Those of us who had the courage to speak up in our base committees—I was the political secretary of my base committee—or at the meetings of political secretaries here in Managua, we never got anywhere. Once I brought up the problem of corruption. It wasn't the first time, and I remember a regional official had the nerve to tell me that corruption wasn't a problem in the Party. He said it was a problem in the police force, but not in the Party. The whole thing was tremendously painful.

You asked about the women, what was going on with us. Well, AMNLAE was simply an appendage of the FSLN, run by male members of the national directorate who frequently made terrible comments about women and women's issues. Bayardo was one of the worst.[22] And Daniel [Ortega]. I can't even remember some of the things they said; there must be people with better memories than mine. Milú may remember, because we talked about it; we were together on more than one occasion when that sort of thing happened.

I remember the day Daniel said something about abortion being "one of those exotic ideas imported from Europe and the United States." He said it was something only intellectuals were concerned about, that it didn't have any relevance in the lives of ordinary people. Doctors at the Berta Calderón Hospital told him, "Comandante, two hundred fifty women a year die of botched abortions in this hospital alone. And that's not counting those who never make it to the hospital." But he kept insisting it was "intellectual claptrap." The same for family planning; he didn't want to hear about it. And this was on television, on a "Meet the People" broadcast.[23] There were some two thousand women in the audience, not to mention those who saw it on TV. All Daniel could say was that we needed to reproduce because the war was killing so many of our combatants!

So, as I say, AMNLAE was nothing more than an appendage of the Party. And, unfortunately, I think it still is. To answer your question, in the latter half of the eighties if you were a woman here in Nicaragua—or, worse, a woman artist or writer—you really didn't have much of a chance to be who you really were. And if on top of all that you were critical, if you insisted upon voicing your criticisms, you just didn't have a chance.

Take the Sandinista Cultural Workers' Association [ASTC].[24] They didn't

22. Bayardo Arce, a longtime member of the FSLN, was a Commander of the Revolution, a member of the national directorate, and political commissar of the Party during most of the Sandinista administration; he attended to the areas of culture and news media. He is also known as an alcoholic and a womanizer.

23. Cara al Pueblo, or Meet the People, was for a time a weekly event in which government officials would conduct long meetings with the people at a factory, in a neighborhood, at a farming cooperative, or a school. The generally frank discussions kept the lines of communication open and often produced innovative solutions to collective problems.

24. ASTC, the Asociación Sandinista de Trabajadores de la Cultura was an umbrella institution encompassing unions for writers, musicians, painters and sculptors, dancers, theater people, and photographers. The unions functioned as professional organizations as well as defenders of

even ask the artists what we thought, and suddenly they became the Institute of Culture. Ipso facto, everything that had been given to the different unions— regardless of whether it had been given by the state, that's another question entirely—was simply taken away. It was given to this Institute of Culture. They'd already closed the Ministry of Culture a couple of years before.

We artists decided to protest. It was a very peaceful protest, a well-reasoned letter published in the papers. But since Rosario Murillo was in there kicking, well, they called in the six members of the Party who had signed the protest. They summoned us to a meeting with Tomás, Sergio, and Daniel. And they were extremely hostile. Right off they said, "First of all, we want to know if we're talking to members of the FSLN or to progressive intellectuals who sympathize with the revolution. If we're talking to the latter, then we're ready to hear your criticisms. But if we're talking to Party members, there are some other things we have to talk about first."

I shot back with an answer I don't think anyone expected. "Comandante," I said, "I don't understand your question. I was called by the Party secretary, summoning me to a meeting. As I understand it, an organization can only summon its members; other people, it invites. So I think your question is completely out of line." Ernesto was furious; he said things that day he'd been holding back for eight years. The others all said yes, they were Party members but they didn't think that meant that they couldn't be critical. Daisy Zamora was there, and Erik Blandón, Luis Rocha, Gioconda Belli, and myself.

Those men said terrible things to us that day: that we were fence sitters, that the first to desert the revolution would be its artists and writers, things like that. You know the story. The hostility was systematic. As artists, we had become undesirables. As women, well, we were appendages. And the saddest part of all is . . . if only we could have said, "Well, that's Rosario. Rosario is a little crazy." But it went so much deeper than that. Those attitudes were part of a whole leadership style, and you began to find that style everywhere you looked.

In retrospect, it's easy to see how this verticality, this separation on the part of the leadership from what was really going on among the people, this arrogance if you will, affected the Party's ability to stay in power. In retrospect, it's all much easier to see. I'm wondering if someone like yourself, who maintained a critical stance, was surprised when the FSLN lost the elections?

The whole electoral campaign was a nightmare for me. It was truly horrible. I got more and more depressed as the months went by. We were waging a

---

artists' rights and concerns. The president of ASTC was Daniel Ortega's wife, Rosario Murillo, a poet who managed to alienate most of the country's writers and artists throughout the decade of Sandinista government. She was particularly competitive with the Ministry of Culture. Toward the end of the administration and after the electoral defeat, Murillo seemed to lose touch with reality. Her husband, however, continued to defend her conduct and attitudes, even when these were indefensible.

campaign that didn't really say anything. When someone asked him why, Sergio Ramírez even went so far as to say that it wasn't an ideological campaign, but a political one. That is, we didn't discuss what was on people's minds, we didn't reason with anyone; we just spewed slogans. We bought people, and everyone had a price—from a T-shirt to dollars and television sets. I'm telling you, it was a nightmare.

But no, I didn't think we were going to lose. It saddened me, but I thought we'd win. And then, when we did lose, my world fell apart. Because I was always hoping I was wrong. And I think this is how we all felt, all of us who were critical. We always kept that faint hope that maybe we were wrong. We hoped things weren't what they appeared to be. I was constantly depressed. Day after day you'd be talking to people and you'd hear new stories about the abuses, the graft, the womanizing, the high-handedness, that persistent inability to accept criticism . . . and the sanctions against comrades who dared to be critical.

Eventually it became impossible to write a critical article and expect it to be published. This in Nicaragua, where during the first years of the Sandinista government "Criticism" was our middle name! Women intellectuals especially felt trapped. Our own media wouldn't publish the things we knew needed saying, and we weren't about to go to *La Prensa* with our articles. Self-censorship began to be a problem then: all the things we didn't say because we didn't want to fuel the enemy's arsenal. It was pretty traumatic. Then, when we lost the election, we all felt like history had absolved us. Unfortunately, history *had* proved us right: it was like we'd lost our historic opportunity to make a revolution in this country.

Were you still writing for El Nuevo Diario *then? Where were you working at the time of the election? What concrete changes did the defeat bring into your life?*

I was at the Ministry of Education by then. That was a kind of world apart, probably because of Fernando.[25] His honesty, his work-style, his enthusiasm and ability to get us all enthused: it really set the place apart. We used to refer to it as the Sister Republic of the Ministry of Education! Of course, when we lost the election, all of us there felt terrible. And the Ministry of Education was unbelievably poor. So it probably wasn't only a sense of responsibility on the part of those of us who worked there that kept corruption away: there was nothing whatsoever to steal.

I can remember taking three pencils and two notebooks one day, because my kids were starting school and I literally didn't have the money to go out and

25. Fernando Cardenal, a Jesuit priest, longtime member of the FSLN, and brother of Ernesto, is one of the undisputed extraordinary figures of the Sandinista revolution. Selfless, brilliant, innovative, kind, and a tireless worker, he was the primary architect of Nicaragua's 1980 literacy crusade. Later he headed the Sandinista Youth Movement, and toward the end of the decade he was minister of education.

buy them what they needed. I was ashamed and I took them. The day I got paid I ran right out and replaced what I'd taken; I put those three pencils and two notebooks back. Because everything at the ministry was on inventory, and we all respected that. Fernando's enthusiasm and love of life was contagious, it affected everyone who worked with him. The sense of comradeship made it a world apart.

Still, at the ministry we felt bad because we could see the country growing needier by the day, and our ability to meet its needs was diminishing. And we'd say, "If things are this bad here, where we know we're doing absolutely the best we can, what must they be like in other places?" There's no question but that the war and the U.S. blockade must bear the major responsibility for how our programs were slipping away from us. I want to make that clear. I'm not going to go to the extreme of claiming that verticality and corruption on the part of the Sandinista leadership were our biggest problems, but I think it's important that we understand how these things played upon one another.

The war certainly made it easier to justify that top-down style. It pushed us to censor ourselves, as I've said, and that's a terrible thing. If it hadn't been for the war, I for one would have been willing to make much more noise than I did. It's very important that this be understood: many of us censored our own criticisms, not out of opportunism with regard to the Sandinista leadership but because we were afraid the enemy could, and would, take out of context anything we said and use it against the revolution. We have to remember that a war was going on here, and that people on both sides of these debates were dying.

After the elections I remained at the Ministry of Education. A group of us there, a broad range of Sandinistas, talked for a while about what we should do. Should we stay or should we leave? At first I thought it would be better to leave, because it seemed to me that the position I occupied was going to have to be turned over to the incoming administration in any case. There were others who argued that we shouldn't abandon the ministry, and I could understand the logic in that, too. It might have seemed like revenge for us to say, "Okay, we've lost, we're getting out of here." Because clearly we had a great deal of experience, we had an enormous amount of information, we'd set up a whole range of resources. More than leaving the new government in the lurch, we'd be leaving our educational system in the lurch, our kids.

I was an adviser to one of the ministry's main departments; and I finally decided to stay, to talk straight with the incoming department director, who seemed like a flexible person, someone I thought I could work with. And it might have been okay; we might have been able to work together. But what eventually happened? Five months went by, and not one of us who'd stayed on was given any work to do. None at all. As far as I was personally concerned, that was fine; I made use of the time and wrote half a book of poems I'd been wanting to write for years. On the other hand, I could see that sooner or later they were going to have to let me go. If they weren't giving me any work, they weren't going to be able to keep me on.

And I wasn't happy there either. Having an intellectual on the payroll without making use of her abilities: it's a basic lack of respect. The only thing they gave me to do that whole time was to read and give them my opinion of a book on religion. I've always liked reading theology, but I'm also convinced that our educational system should be secular. So after five months I resigned and came here to UCA to work.

My immediate reaction to the electoral loss was to feel overwhelmed, as if I were inside some sort of historic nightmare. But my second reaction was, "Okay, maybe it's not so bad after all. Because now the FSLN may be able to take a real look at itself, the Party may be able to learn from its mistakes and become stronger." And, in fact, that's exactly what began to happen. Over a period of several months, and with a great deal of determination and effort on the part of many people, an important dialogue developed. There was tremendous energy behind this, especially among the rank and file.

This culminated with the Assembly at El Crucero. And that's when I began to realize that the leadership still had an extraordinary amount of power to manipulate what people thought, to bring people into line, so to speak. And that's exactly what happened. Criticisms were aired and then put aside; unity became the watchword. By the time the First [Party] Congress came along, I didn't bother to take part.[26] It seemed to me that the Congress was a lost cause even before it happened. A great many courageous comrades did take part in the Congress. They were very honest, they made their criticisms known, and they did manage to open a space for discussion. They were even able to renovate a percentage of the Sandinista Assembly, but I think the leadership is still pretty solidly in control. And, as one comrade recently said, "It's time they pass that baton on."

You know, these guys were real heroes in their time. We must credit them with that. And they shook this country free of the most horrible dictatorship. They went as far as they were able to go. Now they need to relinquish the reins. First of all, because their project can't be pushed any further than it's already gone; and, secondly, because their leadership became corrupt along the way. Someone put it this way: "You guys are owners now. How can you lead a revolutionary party if you belong to the owner class? You're not guerrillas anymore." And that's true: the FSLN continues to operate in that extreme top-down way, and the national directorate remains virtually untouchable.

I don't think it's the FSLN alone. We're having to question the methods of most of the revolutionary parties, and of whole societies that once called themselves socialist . . .

Yes, the past decade holds a great many lessons. With what's happened in what used to be the socialist bloc, we're having to look not only at work-styles, methods, the corruption that's been exposed, but also at the Leninist party model itself. We have to look at the kind of party we need, in order to figure out what sort of alternative project we want. Because we no longer really have a clear picture of an alternative project.

26. The FSLN's First Party Congress was held in Managua in July 1991.

We're all at the stage of "What now?" We know what's wrong, but we haven't been able to figure out how to fix it. And I'm not even sure our generation is capable of producing the alternative. The sense of powerlessness is overwhelming; we're not used to feeling incapable. Women I know, and myself, we've had a political presence since adolescence. We've made a commitment and we want to continue to make it. I'm forty-five, and since I was thirteen or fourteen years old I've been accustomed to thinking of myself as a subject of history, not an object.

Actually I used to think of myself as *un sujeto*. Now I think of myself as *una sujeta*.[27] That's progress, but at this point I feel like a rather useless subject. I don't know what to do. I want to do something, but I don't know what. The other day a friend of mine said, "You know, I think the most honest thing we can do is to recognize that we have no alternatives, that the *gringos* have us by the throat and there's nothing to be done.[28] Maybe if we really accept defeat we can internalize what's happened, grieve for all the pain, and get on with our lives. Maybe then we can begin to conceptualize a new project."

It sounds hard, maybe even cruel; but I'm afraid he may be right. At some point we've got to be able to say, "We couldn't make it work." A part of me is still overwhelmed by this sense of loss. A part of me feels terrible about what's happened. But then I tell myself, "We're a whole lot better off than we were ten years ago." Because ten years ago we were still living the myth of the socialist world. And if in ten years we were able to get so messed up, with the concept of power we had, the top-down structure, the corruption, what must it have been like in the socialist countries after fifty or sixty years? It must have been a real nightmare. In some ways, I suppose, we can be thankful that the nightmare vanished sooner here.

Of course the [worst of the] nightmare has vanished, but we're left with a monolithic imperialism. In *Ars combinatoria* I have a short prose poem called "The Worst of Two Evils." It says: "Incredibly, the last decade of the twentieth century has shown us that one evil can be worse than two. Now there is only one imperialism." And that's terrible, because the U.S. government has free rein to do whatever it pleases, to commit all the atrocities it wants, anywhere in the world. And I'm not just talking about the atrocities of war. I mean their whole neoliberal project, in which a third of humanity is simply considered expendable. That's the real atrocity, the real violence, the state of permanent warfare.

You can see what a dramatic situation this is, the impotence we feel, the anguish. And there's always this ambivalence. I think about it, and I tell myself it is really a good thing that what had to happen took place sooner rather than later. But then I think some more and I say, "What horrible times we're living through." The paralysis of not knowing what to do, the ecological disas-

27. The Spanish language has masculine and feminine nouns. *El sujeto* is masculine, *la sujeta* feminine. Michele refers here to a new usage, similar to what has developed in English, owing to a feminist rethinking of the language.

28. The term "gringos"—blond, blue-eyed, fair-skinned foreigners, usually from the United States—is generally used derogatorily.

ter we face—at the rate we're going, the ecological situation is getting so bad we're not going to be able to turn it around.

I don't think humanity has ever been in such a dramatic situation as the one we're in right now. Oh, I know, every generation says the same thing. But unfortunately it seems every generation is right. I mean, they were right in the eighteenth century, and we're right now. Things get worse. But I don't think our planet has ever been in danger of extinction before.

Michele, in the midst of this very bleak panorama, is there anything at all that seems positive to you, anything that encourages and excites you?

Oh yes. What's happening with women. That really excites me, tremendously. I look at the difference between my daughter's life and my own. And I tell myself, "My daughter's 100 percent better off than I was at her age." When I was a child, I didn't want to be female. I always wished I'd been born a boy. I'd look at my mother and father, and I saw that what my mother did was absolutely boring; what my father did was much more interesting, much more fun. So I rejected my own femaleness; I wished I'd been born a boy.

My daughter's name is Jimena. When she was about five, I overheard her fighting with her older brother. He was furious at her for something, I don't remember what, and he came out with this totally Freudian accusation: "Well, you're a girl and you don't have a penis!" At age five, I would have burst into tears if my brother had said that to me. But my daughter just came right back at him: "So? You're a boy and you don't have a vagina or a uterus!" And my son was the one who started to cry.

When I hear this sort of thing, I realize how far we've come. My daughter is happy to have been born female; she feels good about herself. She's got a lesbian sister she loves and is proud of—Walter's daughter is a lesbian—and she'll tell me, "I'm going to visit my sister and my sister-in-law." My daughter participates every year in the Gay Pride march here. Some of her school friends treat her like someone from outer space, but there's a new consciousness taking root in this generation.

And I look at this daughter of Walter's, her name is Silvia; it cost her a great deal to accept her lesbian identity. But I look at her now and I see a well-adjusted, happy, dynamic young woman, living with her partner in a healthy relationship. And I tell myself, "We women have come a long way." I remember when I was growing up, how women were taught to hate each other, to see each other as rivals, enemies. We were forced to compete because we all lived the male model. A woman who was "complete" was a woman who had a man: boyfriend, lover, husband, boss, whatever. So, naturally, other women were your rivals.

My experience is totally different now. In fact, I feel a delicious complicity with other women. Right here at the UCA something happened recently that couldn't have happened a few years back. Did you hear what Vidaluz Meneses did when the president of the school offered her the dean's position? It was absolutely marvelous! Since this is a Jesuit university, people are appointed to the major posts [rather than elected]. The president came to see Vidaluz one day and asked her if she wanted to be dean of humanities. Her response was, "I'll have to think it over. I'll let you know in a week."

A week later, the president called her back to find out whether she'd made her decision. And she told him, "There's this seminar that's just about to begin. Let me get back to you after it's over, because I'll be seeing a lot of people there who work at UCA and whom I don't know. I might find someone capable of doing the job as well if not better than myself." Needless to say, the president was shocked. Most women would have jumped at the chance to be dean.

After the seminar, Vidaluz finally did sit down with the president of the school. From the beginning of the conversation, she knew what she wanted. And she was very clear: "I've thought about it," she said, "and I'm willing to take the position. But I've found two other women who are equally qualified. We've talked among ourselves, and we're all comfortable with any one of us being given the job. Any one of us would accept it. We've also decided that whomever you decide to name, the other two must immediately be made advisers to that position."

I don't think there was a person at the university who didn't sit up and take notice. That just wasn't the way this sort of thing had ever been done. Here was a woman who, when offered a prestigious position, didn't simply jump at the opportunity. She thought about it, she thought about other women who deserved it as much as she did, they consulted among themselves and then presented a collective response that couldn't be refused! People understood that women were developing a different dynamic, a whole other conception of power. A man would never have done what Vidaluz did.

Here at UCA we have our own little matriarchy. Vidaluz is dean of humanities, all four faculties have women chairs, and I'm head of Culture. And we help each other out; we're always inventing things together. If one of us has important information, she shares it with the others. This is not what any of us learned growing up; we weren't taught this kind of solidarity. We were taught to be jealous of each other, to try to get ahead at the other's expense. So this is a new experience, and it's very beautiful. Women's solidarity has given our lives a new dimension: laughter. It has enabled us to move from silence to lamentation, and then from lamentation to laughter.

You know how it's always been. Women never really told each other anything important—because we were ashamed, or because we were rivals. We didn't want others to see our weaknesses. And then one day, because of feminism, we discovered the similarities in our histories and we began to talk. The first stage was one of lamentation—and anger. We've come a long way; as I say, we've moved from anguish and anger to laughter. We tell so many of the same difficult stories: "Can you imagine what happened to me?" But laughing about it, because the wounds have begun to heal.

Being able to laugh about one's tragedies presupposes the formation of a pretty solid identity. It's like Marx said: "Humanity goes from tragedy to comedy." It's not that we've become blind to our suffering; we see it for what it is—a tragedy—but also as a kind of comedy.

Michele, the process that women are going through here is so akin to ours in the United States, or to what women are experiencing in other parts of the world. The sociocultural and political contexts are different, of course, but the process of coming to a feminist consciousness is so recognizable.

Speaking with other women here, with the lesbian women in particular, your name comes up repeatedly when there's talk of a Gay Pride event or a protest of some kind. You're one of a group of heterosexual women, and also men, who have systematically supported the gay movement here. I used to think this was simply because of your innate sense of justice. Now I realize that you've gone through your own process of coming to an awareness about homosexuality, perhaps in part because of your relationship with Walter's daughter Silvia. I wonder if you'd be willing to talk some about what that process was like for her? You mentioned that it was difficult . . .

Well, I can tell you as much as I know. Yes, it was very difficult for her. She went from psychologist to psychologist, from trauma to trauma, from one depression to another—until one day she got lucky. She found a psychologist who told her, "Silvia, there's nothing wrong with you. You're a lesbian, that's all." That woman helped her enormously to extricate herself from the swamp society had dragged her through.

Then, at a certain point, she was brave enough to tell her mother about her lesbianism. Her mother didn't take it well at all; it was a terrible problem in the house. Then she came and told her father. Walter told me, "Silvia's a lesbian." And, you know, the same thing happened to me that had happened so many years before when I found out Luis Rocha was a Communist. Until then, I thought I was terribly liberated. I used to say, "Lesbians aren't delinquents; they're sick." But when Walter came and said "Silvia's a lesbian," I immediately realized: "Silvia's not sick; she's a lesbian!"

The whole thing became clear to me. I understood that this young woman had never really had a problem, had not been "messed up." She was a lesbian, and it was society that was messed up because it didn't accept her as she is. She couldn't accept herself because society didn't make her feel acceptable. A few days after Walter told me, Silvia came over to the house and she herself told me about her lesbianism. She talked about her partner and introduced me to her. I was able to see their relationship as the most natural thing in the world. And I realized how stupid I'd been.

Silvia is twenty-eight years old. Her first few lesbian relationships weren't that good. And I don't wonder: it's hard to establish a decent relationship when all of society is against you. But now she's in a wonderful relationship with a terrific woman. And her mother has also opened up a bit. It hasn't been easy, but she's been able to welcome them into her home. It seems to me that one of the few areas in which humanity has made some progress is this area of women's struggle.

Being a woman today feels entirely different from what it felt to me when I was young. And I can see how different it is for my kids—not just for Jimena and Silvia, but for my sons as well. Because it's not just Jimena who calls

Silvia's partner her sister-in-law. Camilo also says, "I'm going over to see my sister and my sister-in-law."

You were at the forum the other night. When I heard myself say to that audience, "If the president doesn't veto Article 204, I'm going to sign on to the protest because it's my right to be a lesbian the day I so decide,"[29] when I heard myself say that, I thought: "We've come a long way in this country!" When I heard myself say those words, it was as if my whole life as a woman passed before my eyes. From my early inability to accept my femaleness, because it seemed so boring, right on up to the present.

You know, if you can't accept yourself as a woman, it makes for problems in a heterosexual relationship, too. If you don't love yourself, it's hard to have a good relationship with anyone, man or woman. So I thought about when I was finally able to accept myself, and then I remembered a time when I believed that homosexuals were sick: "Poor things, we shouldn't be so hard on them; they need treatment, they need our help." And then there I was, standing before an audience of hundreds, defending my right to be a lesbian. And I thought to myself, "How wonderful! This is an area of my life in which I can truly say I've grown!".

My daughter Jimena said something interesting the other day. She said, "You know, mother, I think we're all bisexual. Why close off either the homosexual or heterosexual possibility? Why narrow your options? I have a boyfriend now, and I've always been attracted to boys. But maybe one day I'll be attracted to a woman." I told her I thought that was the healthiest attitude.

That same night we went to the movies with a friend, a guy who's somewhat limited in the brains department. In the lobby of the theater, there was a sheet for people to sign to protest Article 204. I asked this friend if he'd already signed; I guess I thought he was more open-minded than he is. And he said no, he hadn't signed and he wasn't going to. Sexist that he is, he came out with one of those typically obnoxious expressions: "I must confess that when I see two women together, I feel like saying: 'Hey, honey, here I am!'"

Jimena turned around and looked him straight in the eye. "That's precisely one of the reasons many of us are lesbians," she said. "If I had to choose between a man like you and a woman with minimal consciousness, I'd take the woman any day." That guy turned red as a beet. Jimena is fifteen.

29. In May 1992, Nicaragua's National Assembly narrowly passed Article 204 of the Criminal Code. This article states that "a person commits the crime of sodomy by talking about, encouraging, propagandizing, or practicing in a scandalous way the sexual act with someone of the same sex," and it makes that crime punishable by one to three years imprisonment. Thirty-nine Sandinista and two Liberal senators voted against the article; forty-three government coalition senators voted in favor. There was widespread protest from many different quarters, but President Chamorro refused to veto the bill and it became law in July. Protest continues.

"I Was a Woman, a Miskito Woman, a Woman from the Coco River"

Mirna Cunningham

When we think about Nicaragua, most of us imagine an equatorial sun, smoking volcanoes, long years of a vicious dictatorship, and the Sandinista National Liberation Front, that group of guerrilla revolutionaries which led the people to freedom from a dynasty of terror in July 1979. We may conjure up the unique flavors of tiste and nacatamales.[1] *And the Spanish language is sure to come to mind. Now if we're talking about the country's Pacific landmass, all these references are applicable. More than half of Nicaragua's national territory, however, is known as the Atlantic or Caribbean Coast.[2] It's a different culture entirely.*

On that vast and underpopulated Atlantic Coast, the culture is not Latin but

1. Large, flat cornmeal tamales, generally stuffed with pieces of pork, sometimes with the addition of potato and chili. The whole is wrapped in a banana leaf and steamed. Commonly sold on Sundays or other holidays, they are considered a specialty by the poor.

2. The Atlantic Coast has roughly 300,000 inhabitants, including 180,000 Spanish-speaking mestizos, 26,000 English-speaking Afro-Americans or creoles, and three Indian groups: Miskitos (67,000), Sumus (5,000), and Ramas (fewer than 600). There is also a small Afro-Indian group called the Garífuna, which numbers around 1,500. The original indigenous population was augmented by the African slave trade and colonized by the Moravian Church as well as by

Afro-Caribbean and indigenous (mostly Miskito Indians). The language is not Spanish but an English patois or one of several Indian tongues. A large influx of mestizos (who constitute more than half the national population) has brought a strong Catholic influence to the region. But the Moravian Church is still the religion of the poor, providing much of the social infrastructure in health and education.

U.S. mining, timber, and banana interests have long exploited the descendants of African slaves and the native population in and around Puerto Cabezas, Siuna, Bonanza, and Rosita in the north. Bluefields, to the south, resembles many colonized towns throughout the Caribbean, with its scattered wooden houses built upon high stilts. Great rivers and much in the way of untapped natural riches grace this vast expanse of often impenetrable jungle. A lack of roads and communications has traditionally kept the people on the Atlantic separate from their sisters and brothers on the more populated Pacific Coast. Radio and TV from Managua first reached the Caribbean during the 1980s.

The problems of this multiethnic area proved a challenge to the Sandinistas. The FSLN had really had a viable presence there only among the miners. Indigenous music, dance, and other artistic manifestations received support from the new Ministry of Culture, but there was little real understanding of the different ways of life. Poverty, isolation, and ignorance on the part of those in office eventually pushed large numbers of Miskitos and others into a counter-revolutionary army, already being funded and trained across the Honduran border in the early eighties.

MISURASATA was an indigenous organization formed just after the Sandinista victory of 1979. The initials stood for "Miskitos, Sumus, Ramas, and Sandinistas Working Together." Some erroneous policies on the part of the FSLN, combined with the individual rivalries of certain indigenous leaders, however, led to clashes between the Front and the local authorities. War and natural disasters took their toll. Then, in September 1987, after important

---

U.S. mining, timber, and banana interests. The Atlantic Coast has long been Nicaragua's ultimate isolated region, abandoned by a succession of political forces until the Sandinistas took power in 1979. Although the mestizo majority has brought a Catholic and Spanish-language presence, the Coast's identity is still profoundly Indian, black Caribbean, and English-speaking. The conservative and ostensibly apolitical Moravian Church continues to provide much of the social infrastructure. During the Sandinista administration, the Coast was the scene of much turmoil. After a series of problematic government policies and several years of debilitating war, in September 1987 the Sandinista National Assembly voted in the Autonomy Statute. This called for two forty-five-member coastal governments, one in the North Atlantic Autonomous Region (RAAN), the other in the south (RAAS). Autonomy meant that the regional governments could control their own resources, trade with the Caribbean, distribute their own basic goods, health, education and culture, and control their own finances. It is an innovative model that is still in the process of being tested. The 1990 Sandinista electoral loss, which installed a conservative central power, has greatly challenged the autonomy process. But new alliances are being formed, and the experiment in multiethnic self-government continues.

work on both sides, the central government's National Assembly voted in the Autonomy Statute.

Tellingly, even today, the Caribbean population commonly refers to those on the Pacific as the "Nicaraguans." And autonomy now faces implementation by a conservative government that would not have promoted it in the first place. Nevertheless, the statute provides the context for a new experiment in multiethnic autonomy never before attempted anywhere in the world.

Nicaragua's Atlantic Coast: a land that is culturally more Caribbean than Spanish, traditionally isolated and superexploited, remote but very much a part of this war-ravaged nation; a land where the story I will tell shocked but did not surprise those whose lives it touched.

In December 1981 a young doctor, her nurse, and their driver were kidnapped outside the small hospital in the village of Bilwaskarma. The doctor was Mirna Cunningham, well-known medical authority, part-Miskito–part-creole native of the area. The kidnappers were also indigenous to the locality; they had joined the counterrevolutionary forces organizing by then in Honduran camps. They forced their hostages across the river, where a drama would unfold that eventually would make news far beyond that border.

The driver was released almost immediately, but the doctor and nurse were subjected to twelve hours of almost constant torture. As they raped the two women, the terrorists intoned fundamentalist hymns and chants. The events were clearly engineered by Moravian pastors, whose anticommunist crusade had already begun to target other revolutionary and community leaders. That fateful night, a sort of trial was staged in Bilwaskarma. Some agreement was evidently reached, for the women were spared execution and released. All the inhabitants of the village packed up and left their homes, though. As a result of this incident, the community where Mirna was born virtually ceased to exist.

In 1982 the Center for Constitutional Rights, in New York City, represented Cunningham and others in the first of two court cases.[3] The cases were designed to bring public attention to the Reagan administration's complicity with Nicaraguan counterrevolutionary forces in violation of international law. As the Contra war heated up, increased numbers of Nicaraguans on both coasts were falling victim to its violence: a small boy lost a leg, a teenage girl lost part of one arm. Most of these losses were sustained in the poorly armed popular defense of peasant cooperatives and fishing villages. In its efforts to unseat the Sandinistas, the United States was once again funding and training brother against brother, sister against sister.

Because she was a principal plaintiff in both Dellums *and* Cunningham v.

---

3. The Center for Constitutional Rights is an institution with several dozen staff attorneys and hundreds of collaborating attorneys who take on a broad range of human rights and civil rights cases—everything from violence against women, gay and lesbian rights, voter rights, affirmative action, and First Amendment cases to helping those in other countries who have been victims of U.S. foreign policy or U.S. refusal to comply with international law. In its more than twenty years, the Center has handled many hundreds of cases and won important victories. Emphasis has been not only on the litigation itself but on educating the public on political issues.

Smith *and* Sánchez Espinoza v. Reagan, *Mirna Cunningham came to be known outside her own country.*[4] *In Nicaragua she had long been known for other reasons. When the FSLN was forced to remove some ten thousand Miskito people from their homes along the Coco River in order to deliver them to safer ground at Tasba Pri, Cunningham was the doctor charged with making sure they reached their destination safely and in good health. Later, she was the FSLN delegate to the area and, still later, the medical authority for the entire coastal region. During the Sandinista administration, she held a variety of Party and government posts.*

Today this short, solidly built woman with an open face, smiling hazel eyes, and closely cropped Afro holds a seat in the National Assembly. She also heads the Nicaraguan office of the Indigenous, Black, and People's Quincentennial Campaign. When I interviewed her, she was in the middle of organizing its next continental meeting, to be held in Managua during October 1992. She gladly took time away from these preparations and received us at the lovely old building now called Popul-na, where the campaign has its offices.

We made our way back to her office. There was an enormous map of the coast covering one wall. If I reached out to touch its jungles and rivers, this map seemed to say, the authentic vegetative nature of the region would exude its aromas, moisten my skin. Almost as if we were "there" instead of "here," we set up the tape recorder, ordered the indispensable coffee, and began to talk. Before getting into the story of Mirna's life, I was curious to know what the outcome of her legal cases had been. "Did anything ever come of them?" I asked:

You know, those cases never really succeeded in the courts. Still, I feel they were worth the effort, because we waged a tremendous educational campaign. We were able to make what was happening in Nicaragua known to women, to workers, to many people in the U.S. who might not otherwise have known what their government was doing. That was back in 1982; the war was beginning in earnest. Those cases contributed to the important solidarity movement that was getting off the ground at the time.

4. *Dellums and Cunningham v. Smith* was filed in California in the summer of 1983. On behalf of a U.S. representative and a Nicaraguan victim of Contra terror, it asked then Attorney General William French Smith to appoint a special prosecutor to investigate Reagan administration violations of U.S. criminal law, especially of the Neutrality Act, in its support of the Contras. The plaintiffs won in District Court, where the judge ordered the attorney general to appoint the special investigator. Three years later they lost at the court of appeals level, where the judge reversed the earlier decision, arguing that the plaintiffs were not the proper persons to have brought the case.

In 1983, *Sánchez Espinoza v. Reagan* was filed. A dozen other victims of Contra atrocities joined Cunningham in this case. Its two main arguments were as follows: 1) the Reagan administration was jointly responsible with the Contras for human rights violations in Nicaragua, thereby enjoining U.S. support for those violations; 2) the Reagan administration was violating the U.S. Constitution by funding an undeclared war. This case, too, was eventually dismissed, on the grounds that it raised political issues the court did not feel it could address.

I always wondered how they turned out. And I remember that they played an
important part in the solidarity movement. But I don't want us to start that far
along in your life. Let's go back to the beginning: where you were born, your
childhood . . .

I was born in that same village of Bilwaskarma, on the banks of the Coco
River near the Honduran border. The U.S. banana companies were still ex-
ploiting the region then. My father worked as a mechanic on one of the ships
that transported bananas down the Coco. I grew up in Waspam, which was a
slightly larger community, and I went to grade school there.

I studied with the Catholic sisters—at least I was accepted at the convent
school after an initial period in which the sisters wouldn't take us because we
weren't Catholic and didn't speak Spanish. Faced with that rejection of their
kids, a group of our parents had to get together and open a public school. Later
I transferred to study with the sisters, when they finally agreed to admit us.

For junior high, I had to travel to Bluefields, because in those days you
could only go as far as grade school in Waspam. In fact, back then there wasn't
a junior high school in the entire North Atlantic Autonomous Region. The
sisters helped me get a scholarship, and I went on to study to become a teacher.
And after I got out of school, I worked as a teacher for a year in order to earn
the money I needed to study medicine. Then I headed for León, where I eventually graduated as a doctor.

It was there in León that I made my first contacts with the Sandinista National Liberation Front. The FSLN was just starting to gain strength in the
universities at that time, after the terrible defeat at Pancasán and the massacre
in Managua in which Julio Buitrago was killed.[5] From the beginning, my work
with the Front was clandestine. Oh, I participated in the usual student demonstrations, some of the public protests and that sort of thing; but mostly I was
doing underground work.

After graduating as a doctor, I went back and got a job with the Moravian
Church in Bilwaskarma. They had a hospital there, so that's where I did my
internship. Later I was part of the extension program they had going in the
Coco River area. But the Moravians eventually fired me. At that period in my
life I was married to Carlos Alemán, and he'd been taken prisoner, so the
Moravians accused me of having connections with the Communists. Still, during my time with Carlos I had four wonderful children.

After the Sandinistas won the war, I came to Managua to take a job with the
Ministry of Public Health. And I didn't get back to the Coast until 1981 when I

5. The battle of Pancasán, in August 1967, marked one of the earliest military encounters
between the newly founded FSLN and Somoza's National Guard. It was a defeat for the revolutionaries, one in which Silvio Mayorga and other valuable men were lost, but it brought public
attention to the fact that a guerrilla movement was consolidating itself in the mountains of
Nicaragua and had not been eliminated, as Somoza repeatedly claimed. Two years later, on July
15, 1969, Julio Buitrago, another important member of the FSLN leadership, was ambushed and
killed in an urban battle in Managua.

was appointed FSLN delegate there. That's when the kidnapping episode took place . . .

The incident in which you were kidnapped has been out of the news for almost a decade. Could you go into some detail about exactly what happened?

I was kidnapped in December of 1981. That was the year the political and military situation here began to change radically. Reagan took office, and immediately young Miskitos were being trained in Honduras. It was mostly preparation until December, and then the program really got off the ground. Of course, at the time I had no idea what was going on. I had come to the region to work as a doctor, and one day I was visiting the hospital at Bilwaskarma. The incident occurred when a nurse, the chauffeur who was driving the Jeep we were in, and myself had just left the hospital and were headed to our next call. A group of armed men stopped the vehicle—they had been shooting at us— and then they forced us across the river.

These guys were members of MISURASATA, the indigenous organization that had recently been formed. They took us at gunpoint, as I say, and they held us in several different camps throughout that night and in the early hours of the following morning. They let the driver go, but the nurse and I were repeatedly roughed up, hit, and raped. Something that made a particular impact on me was the fact that they sang religious songs and prayed while they beat and raped us. It was ritualistic. They kept telling us that they were soldiers for Christ, warriors in the fight against communism. They said we were Communists and so they had to wage war against us.

Those were Moravian hymns—I recognized them—and those guys prayed all night long. From time to time they'd converse with us, explaining why they had taken us prisoner. Their whole attitude was fanatical. And except for that generalized anticommunism, they couldn't really give a reason for having taken us like that. I mean, they weren't accusing us of specific crimes or acts of war, even from their point of view. That helped later on when they agreed to let us go.

Early the next day they brought us back across the Coco, back to Bilwaskarma. It was clear there was a connection between the Miskitos who captured us and some mestizo police. We think it was the police who gave the order for them to take us, but they hadn't authorized our execution. When they brought us back to the community, it seemed like they were still waiting for that order to be given.

But, as I told you before, I was born in Bilwaskarma. And by the time of this incident, I'd worked as a doctor there for eight years. The ordinary people in the village were very upset over what had happened: the women, the old people. They were anguished about the kidnapping. So around 4:00 or 5:00 in the morning, the whole community began to pack up their things; they were terrified. But they also put enormous pressure on MISURASATA for a public trial; they wanted them to set us free. And at 5:00 in the morning, with the entire community assembled, they made the decision to let us go.

We'd been prisoners for twelve hours. And there's no doubt in my mind that the pressure from the community was what kept it from being longer, or from ending differently. They brought us back across the river because of that community pressure, and they let us go because of it as well. And, you know, it's strange . . . but the whole thing seems to have been an operation against women; because, in our case, they let our driver go. And that same night they also kidnapped two male doctors from the same hospital, but they didn't take them to the camps: they kept them prisoner on the Nicaraguan side of the river, and they beat them up but didn't rape them.

The aftermath of all that torture and rape must have been terribly painful for you. What did you do, where did you go immediately following the incident?

I returned to the community. But of course the community no longer existed; everyone had gone. A thousand people crossed the river, and they didn't return to Nicaragua until 1985 or the beginning of '86. The incident with us provoked the destabilization of an entire village. And it's important to keep in mind the religious aspect of this whole thing, because that contributed to the confusion people felt. The political chief in the camps at that time, the guy who was responsible for the political formation of MISURASATA, was the Moravian pastor.

This is something that hasn't been talked about as much as it should: throughout all those years of Contra war, here in the Pacific but also on the Atlantic Coast, there was always an intimate relationship between the fundamentalist pastors and the counterrevolutionary movement. I remember another time—this wasn't something that involved me directly, but as a doctor working at the hospital I witnessed what was going on—when the battle at Pantasma took place.

That was also on the Atlantic Coast. We lost fourteen or more members of the armed forces in combat that day. And I remember when the wounded were brought into the hospital; it was horrible. The hospital staff, the nurses and all, were accustomed to singing a hymn together at 7:00 each morning. And it turned out that the hymn they chose to sing that day was the same one the Contras had been singing when they ambushed those soldiers the night before. The wounded had been brought in at around 11:00 at night, and at 7:00 in the morning they suddenly heard the same hymn their attackers had been singing when they'd surrounded them. You can imagine the trauma that caused!

If you go back and look at the hymnals, the little songbooks the Moravians were distributing in the early eighties, you'll see that the words changed radically between 1980 and 1981. The music stayed the same, but the words changed. And in all the religion classes, in all the seminars that people were attending, they began singing hymns that urged them to participate in a veritable anticommunist crusade, a kind of holy war.

But you asked what happened to me. I remained in the region working. Of course, it wasn't the same. My kidnapping marked the beginning of a whole series of evacuations: some, like the one at Bilwaskarma, forced by the circumstances of the war; others decided upon by the Sandinista government, which began evacuating people for their own safety. The Coco River area, as such, disappeared. My own family, living in Waspam at the time, was evacuated to Puerto Cabezas.

We still live in Puerto Cabezas, although we've rebuilt our home in Waspam and we're in the process of moving back. Now I divide my time between here and there. Two of my children are on the Coast, and two are in Managua. Carlos José is nineteen now; he's studying sociology at the university here. The girls are younger; they're still in high school.

Mirna, how have these experiences affected you as a woman? I mean growing up in a small community on the Coast, in a working-class family, suffering racial and language discrimination as well? And then studying medicine, also as a mixed-blood woman from the Coast? Coming back to practice medicine, and then being attacked as you were, so violently . . . ?

That's just it. I think the problem for a woman from the Coast isn't simply that she's a woman. Gender profoundly marks social difference, but you also have to face the difference of ethnicity. As an Indian, as a black woman, you're different from other women who are mestizas. I told you what happened to my sister and me on our first day of school. They wouldn't accept us. We arrived freshly bathed, dressed in our finest clothes, and we were ready to start school like the rest of the children. And the sisters refused to accept us, because we weren't Catholic, because we didn't speak Spanish. Right there we suffered a particular kind of discrimination.

It wasn't only my sister and I. A whole group of Miskito children were rejected by that school. Our parents had to get together and found the first public school in Waspam, so we could study. But, you know, throughout my years of primary school I always suffered discrimination; we Miskito children always knew we were different. The other kids taunted us. They said our blood was a different color. They'd beat up on us for no reason except their racism. And then we were also Moravian instead of Catholic, so we suffered religious discrimination as well. On Sundays we'd be at church, and everyone from the local Catholic priest on down would stand outside throwing stones; they'd attack us like that the whole hour the service lasted.

So I always felt different. Later, when I went to junior high, the attacks continued. The Atlantic Coast was rampant with racism. There was a regular scale of acceptability, depending upon how light or dark you were. First came the white people from the United States: those who were connected with the multinationals, the managers of the big companies. Then came those who spoke Spanish, the mestizos or mixed-bloods; then the blacks; and the Indians were at the bottom of the pile. I suffered from that hierarchy all through junior high school.

This kind of oppression made it necessary to work much harder for everything you needed or wanted. For example, in order to win a scholarship: for me to be able to go on to junior high, I had to be number one in my class; number two wasn't good enough. It was something that we were always conscious of. We just knew that we had to study harder, do better, be the best. And this didn't let up once you got out of grade school. I had to take two programs—regular high school and teacher's training—at the same time, plus be the best in my class, just to be able to keep my scholarship. And this was because I was a woman, a Miskito woman, a woman from the Coco River. It was almost unheard of that someone like myself would go to school, much less graduate.

Nor did my experience with prejudice end when I left the Coast. León is a very conservative city. And back when I was in medical school, the people there looked at women from the Atlantic Coast as if we were prostitutes. Actually, that was true for the Pacific in general: I mean, if you were black, you were a prostitute; that's the idea people had. But in León, in that conservative León society, it was even more extreme. To make matters worse, I think we were all of two women from the Coast studying in León at that time: Marlene Chow and I. And on top of being black we were poor. The discrimination we suffered certainly pushed us toward the FSLN, and our sense of what the FSLN was about was much more emotional than political back then.

Would you say that within the organization you also suffered some discrimination?

Yes. And I think I continue to suffer discrimination in the Party. The Sandinista National Liberation Front, besides being sexist, is an ethnocentric organization. At a certain level, politically, I believe that the comrades have tried to understand and deal with the problems of the Atlantic Coast. But in more subtle ways there's still a lot of sexism, a lot of ethnocentricity, and this puts Sandinista women at a disadvantage.

I'll give you a concrete example of how this can play itself out. During the Sandinista administration, in the last three years or so before the electoral defeat, the majority of government representatives to the North Atlantic Autonomous Region were women. I was the delegate from the presidency, Dorothea Wilson was a deputy, Hazel Lau was a deputy as well; the regional committee had nine members, and five of us were women. So we were in the majority. And with all of that, we were never permitted to develop as we might have.

There was this unspoken rule that a man had to be in charge—and not even a man from the Coast, but a man from the Pacific! As we say, "a white man from the pacific," supervising the people from the Coast and supervising the women. We suffered continually from those men lording it over us. I don't mean sexual harassment or anything like that. No. It was *political* harassment. They just never completely trusted us. And I believe they didn't trust us because we were women and because we were from the Coast. If we asked questions, if we expressed doubts about a particular issue, they immediately assumed we were confused because we were women. They couldn't see that we wanted a more profound political discussion of the problems specific to the Atlantic.

And I think that this failure on the part of the FSLN at the national level, this failure to deal with us as they would have were we men from the Pacific, really had a negative effect on the Party's work on the Coast. We're talking about a region where the vast majority of the men had either gone over to the counter-revolution or were in the army. In the indigenous communities, women were doing most of the work. Women in general needed support, we needed a vote of confidence: women in the communities and, of course, we women who were in leadership positions. And the FSLN was never really able to give us that.

Right now we continue to see this problem, and not only in the FSLN. It's also true in Yatama—Yatama is an organization of indigenous peoples that comes out of the earlier MISURASATA—and there's not a single woman at the top level of Yatama leadership. That's saying a lot when we take into consideration the tremendous role women in general have played on the Coast.

During the Sandinista government, we managed to achieve a 50 percent female participation among the institutional delegates to the regional committee. That was during my administration. Under the current administration, there's not a single woman. Not one! So I wouldn't say this real lack of confidence in women is something peculiar to the FSLN. We can see it in all the country's political parties, and in many of them much more markedly than in the Front. In fact, with all its sexism, the Front was considerably better than those in power now.

Mirna, how do you think the FSLN might confront and deal with its sexism and racism?

That's a very difficult question. And it's a complex problem all over the world, not just here on the American continent. Problems of gender and ethnicity, the problem of nationalities: around these questions the whole socialist bloc began to fall apart. And those of us who have been working on this campaign to commemorate five hundred years of indigenous, black, and people's resistance, we believe it's impossible to talk about a viable alternative for the continent—be it a political party, a government, or a grass-roots movement—that doesn't take both these issues very seriously: gender and ethnicity.

Those of us who have been working all these years in the popular sectors, we're convinced that all the models up to now have lacked this vision: a genuine understanding of women and race. We haven't been able to develop authentic movements that retain sufficient autonomy while at the same time articulating the larger, overall struggle. We don't have the formula yet, and I don't think there's anyone who does, but we're certainly aware of the problem.

If we're going to talk about democracy, if we're going to talk about true "people's participation," we've got to start discussing this. A real honoring of women and a real honoring of race must be included in our demands, and not merely in a formal way. Because we've known how to talk the talk; we've got the discourse down pat. What we haven't been able to do is raise people's consciousness in a more profound and far-reaching way. You know how few men and even women are aware of the importance this has. We have a few feminist women who are aware of the gender issue, and we have a few men and women who are aware of the ethnic issue. But on both counts it's a fragmented consciousness—very limited.

We need to put some effort into these two areas. Because if we don't manage to reach people with this message, I don't think we're going to be able to change anything. Not really. Here in Nicaragua, for example, you're not going to find anyone who will tell you we'll have democracy without women's participation. From Doña Violeta on down, everyone has the right line. But the question is, How must women participate? How do we achieve full participation?

Sometimes you hear people talking about polling women, consulting with them, or about the need for a national women's program. Or, when we talk about the Coast, we hear people saying, "Oh, yes, we respect the different ethnicities." I say, we don't want to be "respected"; we want full economic participation. When the resources are distributed, we want to know exactly how the peoples of the Coast are going to benefit. In the discussion of each important issue, we want to be making the decisions, not looking on while someone else makes them for us. And I don't think the consciousness yet exists that this is what we mean when we talk about "participation."

The Autonomy Statute was approved in September 1987, but it wasn't until 1990 that we were able to elect our first autonomous authorities. And this new conservative government, which neither approved nor understands the statute, has inherited a complex transitional process. The UNO [government] has practically refused to recognize our indigenous authorities; it consistently ignores our leaders and the laws we pass. So the question now is, Is it even possible to continue to develop a project of regional autonomy under a neoliberal political model? For example, we're demanding collective ownership rights for inhabitants of the Atlantic Coast while the central government is giving away concessions left and right.

As people from the Coast, this is our great challenge. Political and economic independence is ours on paper. We fought for it long and hard, and we won. But what we need now is for this independence to be respected, for them to allow us to exercise it, to administer our own natural resources, to run our own factories, to decide for ourselves how we want to redistribute their profits. If this isn't understood, we're never going to be able to participate fully in the construction of a new Nicaragua. And the struggle for autonomy continues.

In the National Assembly we have five seats: two held by deputies from the South Atlantic and three by deputies from the North. There are four men, and I'm the only woman. And that's not the only division: two of us are Sandinistas, two belong to UNO, and one is a Christian Socialist from Yatama. The political divisions as well as the gender division create significant problems.

Furthermore, since we of the Coast must also involve ourselves in the political struggles of the Pacific—I'm talking about the problems between the different political parties—those parties frequently influence the deputies' decisions. More often than not, these problems have nothing at all to do with the reality of the Atlantic. So this makes for a situation in which we representatives from the Coast not only have our problems of ethnic polarization, but we must deal with these political problems as well. And all of this pushes the real situation of the Atlantic Coast into fifth or sixth place.

I wonder if you would explain the Quincentennial campaign? In the United States, Indian peoples and others are also organizing around this anniversary that marks five hundred years of invasion and repression; and I know there are working contacts between some of the indigenous peoples north and south. But it's mostly in Latin America that I've heard blacks and the poor included in the name of the campaign. Can you talk about your work with the campaign, about what you're hoping to achieve?

The campaign got off the ground three years ago in South America. It began as a kind of countercelebration to what the different gove   ments were planning for the quincentennial of the European conquest of th. Americas. But as we've gone along, we've broadened its goals. One of our objectives is certainly to provide an alternative to the official celebrations. Those of us who are working on the campaign are in complete agreement that there's nothing to celebrate; these five hundred years have been a time of exploitation, of oppression. On the other hand, we're not satisfied with simply denouncing what happened five hundred years ago—because we're still suffering the consequences of that conquest today, and we're suffering new forms of colonization as well.

Bush's initiatives in all our countries, the stance taken by the international banking institutions, the incredible unemployment, the misery in which the indigenous, black, and poor mestizos of our continent live: it's all a product of that model of colonization which began five hundred years ago and which remains in place today. So, for us, the campaign is a broad space in which the struggles of indigenous, black, and poor people can come together and articulate shared ways of rising above our oppression. It's not just a campaign of denunciation but one in which we can look for alternatives to continue our struggle. We've experimented with alternatives that take poverty into account; what we haven't been able to develop over these five hundred years is an alternative that includes attention to the ethnic question. Peasants and indigenous peoples started the campaign. In the course of getting together, however, we've seen that there are other sectors, people whose situations and demands may be slightly different but who are just as trampled upon as the rest of us. So now there are women, young people, artists, field workers, the urban poor, blacks, indigenous peoples; in other words, all those who have traditionally been marginalized.

We've been able to set up organizations in thirty countries from Alaska to Chile. You probably know that we have a central event scheduled here in Nicaragua on October 12, 1992. But the campaign goes far beyond this one event. After October 12, we want to be able to keep discussing a strategy for making this movement a viable alternative of struggle. For us, October 12, 1992, is a date we can use to help us build our movement. But none of this is easy.

It hasn't been easy in the first place because of all the various interests involved. The various governments are the ones staging the celebrations and, of course, they have all the resources, all the money. The poor are the ones who are interested in the campaign, and we don't have any money—not even for the kind of promotion we should be doing. Another problem is unity. We represent a diversity of groups in the campaign, many of which have been pitted against each other over this five-hundred-year period. These divisions have naturally bred distrust. There is an enormous amount of distrust, for example, between the Indian and the black, the black and the mestizo poor. And those who are trying to keep the campaign from succeeding are taking advantage of that distrust, encouraging it.

There are those who say that the Quincentennial campaign should be waged only by the indigenous peoples who were here when the Europeans came. What do blacks have to do with it, they argue, what do the popular sectors have to do with it? There are those who accuse the popular sectors of trying to upstage the Indians, of taking the emphasis away from our demands. As I say, there's a great deal of mistrust on all sides. Still, I believe that one of the things we've achieved in these three years is the shared conviction that we cannot launch a viable alternative at the continental level if the Indians continue to struggle by themselves, if the blacks go it alone, if the poor think only of their own situation—as they have up to now. We've seen where that's gotten us.

We're clear about one thing: unless all the marginalized sectors join forces, we'll never be able to influence the struggle for an economic model that will work for us. That's our long-range goal in this campaign. And that's what we've been working toward in each of the countries. It's meant real grass-roots organizing, planting seeds we know won't produce results by October 12, 1992. We may not even see any significant results by 1993, but we're in this for the long haul. And, you know, already there have been some interesting byproducts, at least here in Nicaragua.

Here all the different popular sectors are represented in the campaign. The National Workers' Front [FNT] is involved, which means [we will see] the initiatives of groups of workers facing the reprivatization that's going on.[6] Because, for example, the workers are saying, "We're not necessarily against

6. FNT stands for Frente Nacional de Trabajadores. The CST (Sandinista Workers' Central) and the ATC (Association of Field Workers) were the most powerful FSLN unions during the Sandinista administration. They argued that the strongest defense of workers' rights was a defense of the revolution itself, even when that sometimes meant compromising immediate demands. During the height of the Contra war, most workers accepted such a stance; but as the war wound down, this argument held less weight with rank-and-file members, who were particularly hard-hit by the government's austerity measures of 1988. With the FSLN's electoral loss, its unions were in a position to defend workers' rights against UNO's obviously antilabor policies. It was then that the FNT was born, giving new energy to labor struggles in the context of President Violeta Chamorro's harsh economic plan. Besides the CST and the ATC, the FNT includes UNE (National Employees' Union), the UPN (Nicaraguan Journalists' Union), CONAPRO (National Confederation of Professionals), FETSALUD (Federation of Health Workers), and ANDEN (National Educators' Association).

privatization, but we want to own a percentage of the industry. We've been workers all our lives, now it's time we get to be owners. So we want our own industries, or a part of them." This type of thing can happen in other countries as well. Or, take our autonomy project for the Atlantic Coast: that might be viable elsewhere.

This is the first time I've heard someone talk about the Quincentennial campaign not simply as a commemoration but as a new form of political organization . . .

Yes, and we're breaking with previous models. Because when we talk about autonomy, for example, we're talking about a multiethnic autonomy. We're moving away from previous models, in which a particular ethnic group wanted its own territory. On the Atlantic Coast of Nicaragua we're articulating an autonomy project in which several different ethnic groups are working together for an integrated set of rights: political, economic, legal, religious, cultural. We're dealing with all these elements within a single model. And we can certainly share this experience with the Talamanqueños in Costa Rica, with the Cunas in Panama, with the different ethnic groups throughout the continent.

In every one of our countries, in each of our ethnic groups, there are experiences worth sharing. I'm talking about people's experiences at the grass-roots level, about new ways people have attempted to resolve their problems, to meet their own needs. If we find that some of these projects are viable, that they work, we may be able to offer a real alternative of regional integration, something designed by us rather than by our oppressors.

One of the big problems I see is that the governments are co-opting our discourse. Under the guise of supporting our ideas, they twist them around to meet their own conceptions. Right now, all the governments are talking about integration, democracy: the ideas we've been putting out there for the past twenty years. In other words, our discourse is no longer new. What we've been saying about the environment, what we've said about everything, it's all been co-opted by official rhetoric. And they use a diluted or changed version of our demands for their own purposes, not ours.

The political parties are in crisis. What political party at this point in time offers a real alternative at the continental level? Even our leftist political parties: what alternative have they been able to offer when faced with the neoliberal economic model? Oh, the discussions continue to rage, all right. But what real alternatives have they been able to come up with? I'm not suggesting that political parties have no role. Obviously they've played a role by channeling the demands of the different social sectors toward the governments and toward society as a whole. But the truth is, people want greater participation. They want to be protagonists, not topics or objects. Society needs a mode of expression the political parties haven't been capable of offering.

When we talk about developing a more democratic process, that's where the basic problem remains: real people's participation. Each social sector must work out its own alternative. Of course, this isn't going to be easy—not at all.

We're talking about something that's very complex and very ambitious. But if we don't keep looking for new models of viable people's participation, we're going to become utterly frustrated. We've got to keep on looking, and struggling. I think we're on the right track, because we can see that what we want to do is possible, at least on a small scale.

Mirna, did the electoral defeat strike you, coming from the Coast, differently than it might have had that not been the case? I mean, was it less surprising? How did people on the Coast experience the electoral campaign, and how did they vote?

On the Coast we expected to lose. I mean, we expected to lose locally but win nationally. You have to understand that in the North Atlantic Autonomous Region the FSLN had serious problems with the Miskito population. Even with the creole population there were very serious problems. In some of the coastal areas, we believed we would win—for example, around the mines where the FSLN has a twenty-year history: Siuna, Rosita, Bonanza. But in Puerto Cabezas, in the Coco River area, it was a different story. You have to remember that between 1982 and '84, almost the entire population in those places had taken up arms against the FSLN.

Starting in 1984, when we began to talk about autonomy, we slowly began to win people back from the counterrevolution. Autonomy became the important issue, and it began to create a bridge of trust between the population of the Coast and the Sandinista government here at the national level. In 1982, it's safe to say, almost no one on the Coast supported the Front. That means that between 1982 and 1990, when the election took place, we were able to win over 46 percent of the people. Because that's who voted for the FSLN on the Coast, 46 percent of the population.

Nevertheless, preelection polls we took in the area of Puerto Cabezas were telling us we only had 20 percent of the population with us. So we knew for sure we were going to lose there, in the region. But nationally, well, we were as confident as the rest of our membership; we were convinced we were going to win nationally. Although we figured we weren't going to be able to pull off a Sandinista autonomous government in the region, we did think we'd win a percentage of council members; and we believed we'd have a central government that supported autonomy. But that's not what we got.

I don't know if I would say that we Sandinistas on the Coast suffered the electoral loss with less anguish than those in the rest of the country. On the other hand, maybe we did. The Sandinista movement on the Coast is a good deal younger than it is in other places. The FSLN didn't really take root there until after 1979, when progressive forces became convinced that of all the political parties it was Sandinism that supported us most fully. Still, it wasn't easy for us to win this support. We had to fight against, as well as with, the FSLN in order to get the Party to take our demands seriously, to take our demand for autonomy seriously, to take us into account.

So in some important ways we've always played a kind of oppositional role.

Because—to be seen as protagonists, to be taken seriously—we've had to struggle so much harder than people in other parts of the country. On the other hand, like the rest of the FSLN, we've had to deal with this whole matter of suddenly becoming a political opposition force. For Sandinistas on the Coast this has presented some special problems. For example, we knew we stood in opposition to Violeta Chamorro's government. But we also stood in opposition to Yatama, the indigenous organization that backed autonomy. And how could that be? Because we're committed to strengthening autonomy! How could we be the opposition and in favor of strengthening autonomy, both at the same time?

You can see how complicated it's been. We spent quite a while discussing all this. How to support the autonomy project without becoming a part of Yatama? And the truth is, we've come to the conclusion that we must work closely with the local Yatama government because our goals are long-term, not for this moment alone. We're working for the future of the Coast. And we have a ways to go in terms of being able to articulate a Sandinism that is truly multiethnic. Sandinism on the Atlantic Coast has to be mestizo, black, Miskito, and Sumu.

It can be complicated achieving unity between the different regional ethnic groups, which are at one and the same time members of a Pacific-based political party. Too often the Pacific party's interests dominate the ethnic interests of the region. And, of course, many of the decisions made at the national level affect us on the Coast. The FSLN, the central government, just about everyone tends to prioritize their interests above ours. Still, we Sandinistas of the Atlantic continue to work so that Sandinism won't disappear from our area.

I think the future of the Atlantic Coast depends upon our ability to articulate the people's needs and put Party interests in second place. For us, those interests may be less relevant than in the rest of the country; it's time we prioritize the specific interests of the region.

What can you tell me about women on the Coast during the past several years? What problems are important there that might have less relevance here in the Pacific? And are women organizing in any way?

Women on the Coast live with an inordinate degree of violence. And the degree of violence against women there is intimately linked to what I've already mentioned: our triple oppression as women, as ethnically different, and as poor. I'd say the indigenous woman is subjected to an almost institutional violence. Take death in childbirth: there's been a tremendous increase in that among indigenous women. The majority of coastal women start having children when they're thirteen, fourteen years old—while they're still children themselves—and these children having children face a very real possibility of dying.

We don't have the programs we should have to deal with this. Men on the Coast have traditionally worked for the multinational companies. So it's the women who stay in the communities, grow the food, and take complete charge of the upbringing and education of their children. And they're the ones most affected by fluctuations in the economy, by the policies and measures that come down. A recent example was the closing of the seafood processing plants. Three hundred heads of household, most of whom were women, lost their jobs. On the Atlantic Coast, of the four thousand or so who have been put out of work, the great majority have been women.

Social decomposition of all kinds is on the increase. Drug traffic and drug consumption has risen dramatically, and this in turn has increased the number of muggings, of rapes. Again, women and children are the most directly affected. When you consider the fact that our women have always suffered an extreme level of violence, we're talking about a very serious situation. Battery is "normal" on the Coast; in the communities, men consider women literally to be their property. And it's the classic situation of the man who beats his wife, his children, and so on down the line.

But women have been organizing against this state of affairs. Women's organizations have existed for a while, but traditionally they've been connected with the Church. So it wasn't a matter of teaching women to struggle against their [unjust] situation but, rather, to do needlework, to make crafts—or simply to accept their lot because that's what the Bible teaches. But new organizations have emerged. We now have an association of women on the Coast called Women's Movement for Peace and Autonomy; there's a chapter in each of the municipalities.

You've got to remember that we're talking about a region where there's 90 percent unemployment. The economic situation is so critical, there's so much misery, that the women try to address their problems as women—battery, rape, and so forth—but survival is still their number one concern. There are women who try to address gender issues, but the economic struggle still takes precedence.

Still, we're beginning to see some change. There have been mobilizations to try to free women who are imprisoned for killing men who've raped them, and women on the Coast are demanding a law that would punish batterers. So there's some movement in this direction. And indigenous women are organizing, black women are organizing. There's also a movement, in which women are very active, to retrieve and preserve our culture.

Mirna, what's your life like at the moment? Are you still practicing medicine? How do you divide your time?

No, I don't practice medicine. I try, but there isn't enough time. It's still a dream, but next year I want to begin a traditional medicine project I have in mind. I want to plant the herbs and have my own little hospital where I can heal in the traditional ways. I don't know, I may have to wait until I retire!

The thing is, I'm a senator in the National Assembly. I'm also a member of the Regional Autonomous Council, and I'm secretary of the Natural Resources Commission, which is the body that's negotiating with the central government over mineral rights, forestry, fishing, and so forth. In the National Assembly,

I'm on the Women's Commission as well as the Commission for Ethnic Affairs. And as if all this weren't enough, I've got the [Quincentennial] Campaign; we're responsible for the next continental meeting. So my agenda is pretty full at the moment.

What I'm hoping is that once we turn the campaign over to the country that wins it in October, I'll have a bit more time to dedicate myself to beginning this traditional medicine project. It'll be on the Coast, not here in Managua. One of the things the Autonomy Statute establishes is the importance of retrieving and developing traditional medicine, and that's really where I want to put my energies.

On the Atlantic Coast, do women traditionally practice herbal medicine, or are the doctors mostly men?

Both. Among indigenous people and blacks in the coastal communities, traditional medicine has been kept alive all these years. When we speak of "indigenous resistance," I think one of the things that most exemplifies this resistance is the practice of traditional medicine. In fact, we want to begin our continental meeting October 7 through 12 with a gathering of indigenous doctors, doctors from all over who practice traditional medicine. And we want to make it clear that this medicine is a form of resistance, in as sensitive an area as that of people's health. In the Miskito communities, for example, everyone practices traditional medicine.

Each community has its *sukia*, its *curandero* [shaman]. Sukias are higher than curanderos, because the sukias don't cure with herbs alone; they also use prayers, songs, vaporizations, and other rituals. And we have curanderos who specialize in treating snakebites, for example, or who work only with a particular disease. Aside from the sukias and the curanderos, we also have "prophets." A prophet is someone who got struck by lightning and didn't die. That person then becomes a prophet and can do special types of rites. So, to answer your question, I'd say about half the sukias, curanderos, and prophets are women. It's about half and half. The first two inherit a family tradition; the third requires being hit by lightning, and that can happen to a man or a woman.

"The Only Way for Women to Fight for Their Rights Is If They Get Together and Do It"

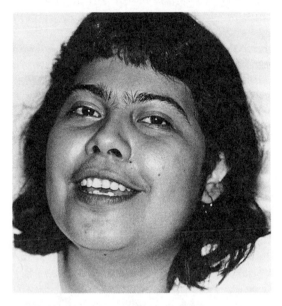

Diana Espinoza

I'm twenty-six and I was born right here in Managua. I have four brothers and sisters; I'm the second of the girls. And, well, my life has been a normal one, more or less comfortable. At fifteen I got married, and at sixteen my first child was born. I had my second at seventeen, my third at eighteen, and my fourth when I was twenty-five . . .

Diana Espinoza began telling us her story, her seemingly disinterested manner covering shyness or uncertainty, or both, about what we might want to know. I was particularly struck by the fact that this young working-class woman, whose childhood and current situation was so obviously filled with hardship, would use the word "comfortable" when describing her life. The daughter of a cab driver and a seamstress, with four children of her own by the time she was in her mid-twenties, her choice of phrase startled me. Middle- or upper-class Nicaraguan women we'd spoken with usually emphasized the difficulties.

When we asked the receptionist at the factory's front desk if she would call Diana, she had motioned us over to a yellow couch, its tired stuffing bleeding through ragged splits in the upholstery. It was clear she was accustomed to people coming to visit this particular employee. While we waited, she located our interviewee by calling around on an ancient black rotary telephone.

El Caracol is a small factory in one of Managua's old central neighborhoods, not far from the city's fouled lakefront. A caracol *is a snail or snail-like shell. By the plant's main entrance a small stone replica of such a shell lends a touch of interest to an otherwise plain façade. Its spiral might be a symbol of these workers and their tenacious struggle for autonomy in a country where manufacturing has been made all but impossible and goods cost 10 percent more than in Miami.*

The building has seen better days; its "technology"—if the term is even applicable—is outmoded. Some one hundred fifteen workers, slightly more than half of them women, handle different phases in a process that washes kernels of corn and pulverizes them into the fine flour known as pinolillo, *from which tiste and other traditional foods are made. We learned that El Caracol also has a line of powdered cacao for making delicious Nicaraguan chocolate.*

Victoria González suggested this interview and accompanied me to the factory.[1] She had met Diana during Diana's recent tour of the United States, where she'd gone to speak about the Nicaraguan labor movement during this new and complicated postelectoral period. Victoria had shared her impressions of this young labor leader, who didn't speak a word of English yet bravely made her way alone from city to city.

A couple of times she'd arrived at unfamiliar airports and no one had been there to meet her. On the flight between Chicago and Washington, D.C., she began to bleed uncontrollably. She hadn't known she was pregnant, she later confided, but discovered it when she miscarried that night. Confronting loneliness, a language she did not understand, strange landscapes and stranger customs, she continued the tour to its very successful conclusion. Diana Espinoza isn't one to let circumstances get the better of her.

I was thinking about how much more I knew about Diana than she knew about me when a heavyset young woman descended the circular girder staircase and glanced from one of us to the other. She gave Victoria a hug of recognition and held out her hand to me. As I grasped it in both of mine she smiled; and it was that smile, frank and inviting, that gave me my first inkling of how much quiet strength this young woman possesses.

Diana wore an oversized Disneyland T-shirt and a pleated, mustard-colored skirt that hung to the middle of her sturdy calves. Delicate gold loop-earrings were just visible beneath her shoulder-length brown hair. Gradually, as she

---

1. Victoria González, whose father is Nicaraguan and whose mother is North American, grew up in Matagalpa until her mother, siblings, and she moved to Detroit when she was fourteen. She is a poet and a graduate student in history at the University of New Mexico, Albuquerque, who frequently spends her summers in Nicaragua. Victoria was involved in this book in several ways: giving me the benefit of her views as a Nicaraguan woman of the younger generation, she transcribed the interviews, participated in some of them, and offered invaluable insights to the project as a whole.

unlocked her history, she became more animated, her broad mouth opening more easily in laughter that revealed a row of strong white teeth. Her brown eyes were intelligent and kind. I had the immediate impression that she was someone who takes on extraordinary tasks in a forthright but almost mechanical way.

"Follow me," she said simply, turning to lead us up the narrow steps and into a dim hall lined with offices. We went through several of them, where men and women worked with antiquated typewriters or poured over figures in large ledgers. "These women are going to interview me," she announced matter-of-factly to a young man who rose and came with us into the small conference room in the rear. And to us: "This is the head of our union."

The young man nodded and shook our hands. He offered us coffee and served it. Then he coughed and said he was sure Diana herself would be able to give us all the information we might need: if we'd excuse him, he needed to get back to work. We sat on opposite sides of the modest table, tape recorder and camera in place, ready to begin. I started out with the usual questions. Diana's responses were brief at first, almost awkward. I searched for a way to put this woman at ease, to help her share a life I knew was, like so many others here, extraordinary.

But I needn't have worried. Diana relaxed and became more eager to talk as she moved into her story. Although having married at fifteen and becoming a mother of four by the time she was twenty-five didn't seem to be something she thought of as unusual—or even interesting—as she began to speak of her experience at the plant, a clear passion gripped her words:

I came to work here at El Caracol on March 1, 1984; it's been eight years now. This was my first job. I started out cleaning offices but, well, I'd finished high school so, little by little, they trained me for other things. That's an advantage we have here: the women and men who want to get ahead have the opportunity. In two years' time I had the job I have now. I'm the plant's bookkeeper.

The union was already active when I came, and women have participated in our union movement from the beginning; they've been outstanding. In fact, the secretary general was a woman when I started . . . Yes, our union belonged to the Sandinista Workers' Central [CST].[2] And since I've worked here, I can say there's always been respect for the workers, the women workers especially.

Do a lot of women work here?

2. CST stands for Central Sandinista de Trabajadores. When the revolution took power in 1979, there were only 183 workplace unions in the country. By the end of the eighties, there were more than 2,000, with 55 percent of the workers unionized. Nearly two-thirds were affiliated either with the Rural Workers' Association (farm workers and others in the countryside) or with the CST. Other, smaller workers' confederations existed to the right and left of the Sandinista labor movement.

In the packing department it's all women. In administration, well, I've already told you that the general accountant is a woman. Women work in every part of this factory, although it's never been easy for us, especially if we have children. For example, when I first came to work I didn't have anyone to take care of my kids; I had to take them to a child-care center. I had to drop them off at 6:00 in the morning, and when I left work at four I'd go and pick them up: 4:30, 5:00. Sometimes their teachers waited; sometimes they'd have to take them home with them.

What about your husband? Did he help at all?

My husband worked, too. We needed the two salaries. In Nicaragua salaries are very low; it's impossible to live on one. There's a lot of single mothers here, and I don't know how they manage. They're mother and father to their kids, and I'm telling you, I don't know how they do it. They have to make more sacrifices than the rest of us. And still, we have lots of women like that who have played important roles in our struggle.

Tell me about the struggle here at the factory. How did it begin?

When the revolution came to power here, this factory kept on producing under its original owners. But they cut back on personnel. Maybe sales went down or something; they told us that they couldn't keep as many people on. They applied for a loan from a bank that used to be here in Managua, the Calley-Dagnell, and they got it. We thought that was a good sign. They said they needed the money to invest in the business, to build it up; but what they really did was transfer it to a bank account in Miami. And then, right after that, one by one they left the country. They abandoned the factory without raw materials, with no money and with lots of debts.

We workers were left out in the cold. We asked the revolutionary government if it could take over the factory, if the People's Industrial Corporation [COIP] would administer it.[3] And in 1981 they took it on.

Did that make an immediate difference in people being able to keep their jobs or in the working conditions? Did the workers' lives improve?

Yes, because . . . well, no. Not at first. The first few months were hard. The factory was in the red, so the workers had to make an extra effort. We gave up

---

3. COIP is the Corporación Industrial del Pueblo, established by the Sandinista state in 1979 to organize its takeover of 168 factories previously owned by Somoza or his close associates. The total original value of what was confiscated came to 197.3 million dollars, representing one quarter of the country's industry and employing 13,000 of the 65,578–strong labor force. Six months after the Sandinistas took power, 81 of these factories were up and running; the rest were still idle. The eight major industrial groups were plastics, textiles, timber, foodstuffs, pharmaceuticals, building materials, paper, and metal and machinery.

our salaries; we were working for food alone. For three months we worked like that, but everyone pitched in. People volunteered extra hours—"red and black time," we called it—and we managed to get our sales up.[4] We paid our debts, and the factory became solvent again.

When we got things going, that's when the union was able to negotiate a new collective contract. We got benefits, like a monthly basket of subsidized minimal necessities: twenty pounds of rice, twenty of sugar, ten of beans, a gallon of cooking oil, six cakes of wash soap, and bath soap, too . . . we got all those things after COIP took over. And we were also able to hire a doctor who would treat the workers' children free. The factory provided the medicines. I mean, if the health center didn't have a medicine the doctor prescribed, then the factory gave you the money to buy it on the outside.

By 1990 things had gotten a lot better here. We'd been able to contract a gynecologist to attend to all the women workers. We all had our yearly Pap smears. And if we were pregnant, we got the attention we needed. This was a big step. Things were going well until the FSLN lost the elections. Then everything changed.

What were the first changes?

Well, in September of 1990, Magelda Campos and Oscar Campos [the former owners] came around with their lawyer. They showed up with the guy who was the administrator at the time, and they called me and another worker in— there were just two of us working with the books back then—and they said we had to turn them over.

There was no warning, you didn't have any idea this was going to happen?

No. We didn't know they were trying to get the factory back. But when they came and demanded we turn over the books, I told them no. I said I didn't think the workers would agree to something like that. Saving the factory had cost us a lot. Then these people started talking about the capital they'd invested, how they built the place up, what they paid their workers, all of that. And they said they'd only left because it had been confiscated.

I told them that if they were willing to face the workers, fine. I didn't have a problem with that. But I didn't think it was such a good idea because I could tell them we were united in not allowing a takeover. We weren't going to accept their proposition. But they insisted. They went down to talk to all the employees, and that's where they got the surprise of their lives. The workers told them that, as of right then, they were occupying the factory.

Those of us on the union board had to support the workers in their decision. They were the majority. And it turned out I was the one who had to protect the lady, to see that she got out of the plant that day without getting hurt. I knew that if anything happened to her it would go badly for us; the police would

---

4. Red and black are the colors of the Sandinista flag.

come and they'd make us leave. Women and men together occupied the factory from that moment on. Fifteen to twenty of us stayed here every night just to make sure the owners weren't going to force their way back in. To this day, a group of us come around on weekends, just to check that everything's all right.

You mean the Camposes gave up their claim to the factory, just like that?

No, they kept on fighting us. They froze our bank accounts, they cut the telephone wires, they even cut our electricity off at one point. But we were able to get the electricity turned back on by going to talk with Emilio Rappaciolli, who was the minister of energy. He sympathized with us. We even had to get legal documents protecting our right to keep on working. Because if they'd caught us in the street with a plant vehicle, they could have taken it away from us. Or they could have burned it. We knew the risks . . .

How did you know your rights?

We hired a lawyer. He was a movement lawyer who took on our struggle out of conviction more than anything else. He's a revolutionary, too, and he's been with us right along. We pay him a monthly salary; it's as if he were just one more factory worker . . . it's cheaper that way. And this lawyer isn't only helping us. He has a number of cases like this one: workers who are fighting to keep their factories.

That's an amazing story of cooperation. Diana, is El Caracol the only factory here where the workers have been successful in not letting the former owners come back and take over, or are there others?

El Caracol was the first, and our factory has been an example for others across the country. The workers here have been an example: we sacrificed so much to get it up and running again, we weren't going to let them take it back just like that. When other workers saw what we were able to do, they started their own struggles. There's the Prego soap factory; they joined us when we went out. In a matter of days, the old owners of Prego gave up and they're working now, just like we are. The workers at Bimbo Bread and Luna Beds also tried, but they gave up.

It took us two years here at El Caracol. Finally, on June 8 of this year [1992], we signed the papers that say the factory belongs to us. We'd already incorporated as a legally constituted entity, a workers' cooperative; and that's who's buying the plant. The only thing is, they're asking 400,000 dollars. We don't have that in a lump sum, so we're still working out the details about how many years they'll give us to pay it off. We asked for ten years and they only want to give us six, so we're still working on that. But the agreement should be ready soon.

We have the advantage that the person we hired as our director has already been legally empowered to administer the plant. He can make legal decisions.

And the company—Caracol Industries—isn't just this factory. There's a discothèque called Lobo Jack; it's very popular, maybe you've heard of it. And there's some land, farms, a number of different properties. We just negotiated with the government for this factory; we said they could keep the rest.

Then we entered into negotiations with the workers at Lobo Jack. We asked them to give up their 25 percent of the discothèque in exchange for 30 percent of this factory. Their 25 percent is worth twice what this whole plant is worth, but they said yes—because it looked like they were going to lose anyway. Our goal was for the workers to own the industry. We weren't thinking just of ourselves, but of all the workers. So we signed that agreement with the workers at Lobo Jack, the discothèque has been returned to its original owners, and we've got the factory.

So the original owners have virtually given up?

No, not yet. They still bother us because there are fifteen workers who sided with them. We didn't kick them out; they left of their own accord. They said they were fighting so the factory would go back to the old owners, but now that we've won they've decided to claim their rights as workers. We don't think that's fair. We say they've lost what rights they had. Are they kidding? No one's going to accept them back after they deserted us like that. The workers who held fast wouldn't stand for it.

Diana, when and how did you first become involved with the FSLN?

It was before the insurrection, and I was still in school. I belonged to an organization called CAP, People's Action Committee; it was mostly young people. CAP raised political consciousness among the students back then. I was thirteen at the time, and I got involved. Then later, during the National Literacy Crusade, I participated in that too: I taught reading and writing. And then when I came to work at the factory, I joined the Sandinista Youth. I've been a member of the union board four years now, and I was just reelected. I'm grateful that my fellow workers have that kind of confidence in me.

Does your husband share your politics, Diana?

No. He belongs to the Council of Trade Union Unification [CUS].[5] That's a workers' confederation that takes the side of the bosses, the capitalists, the

5. CUS, the Consejo de Unificación Sindical, was founded in Nicaragua in the mid-1960s with the assistance of the U.S. government–funded American Institute for Free Labor Development (AIFLD). CUS represents a very small number of Nicaraguan workers (2,000 according to Sandinista sources, 35,000 according to the Council itself). It has been virulently anti-Sandinista, staging opposition demonstrations in 1988 and 1989. Although it denies political affiliation, it is closely linked to the Social Democrats and was a strong backer of UNO in the 1990 elections.

guys who have all the money. I don't know if they're just ignorant or getting paid off by someone. At the beginning, I know, the CUS union leaders had dollars; my husband had dollars in his pocket all the time. So he and I have our differences. It's ugly to say this, but he's even told me: "You people are thieves. Give the factory back to its owner. She worked hard for it. She deserves it. You never worked for it. All you Sandinistas are nothing but thieves!"

I was thinking about leaving when he said that. But I told him, "Look, I don't mess with your politics. If they've pulled the wool over your eyes, it's nobody's fault but your own. The real blind man is the one who chooses not to see. So if I don't mess with your politics, you have no business messing with mine. If I respect your ideas, you have to respect mine too. If you don't, I'm sorry but I'm leaving. I'm not going to subject my children to this lack of respect . . ." So he said he'd stop saying those things. And our home life calmed down for a while, although things flare up every now and then.

Where does your husband work?

Over at Pepsi-Cola. He's a union leader there, too.

It's interesting, a couple that stays together in spite of those kinds of political differences . . .

It's not easy. As long as he watches himself, what he says around me . . . Maybe another kind of woman would be arguing with him all the time, tit for tat. But I think of my kids. I stay because of the kids . . .

Do you love him, in spite of the political differences?

Not really. Like I say, it's mostly for the kids that I stay. The little one more than anything. When a couple gets divorced, it's always the children that suffer. They don't see their father or their mother. To avoid a fight I don't even talk with my kids about what I think. He does, though. But, you know, it seems like they're more attracted to my ideas than to his. I don't know why, maybe it's their friends, but they've even taken to arguing with their papa. When he says "our president" or whatever, the oldest are nine and ten years old and they'll tell him, "Come on, Papa: whose president? You're not even working now! When the Sandinistas were in power, when Daniel was in power, Mama bought more things than she does now." That kind of thing. Kid's talk, but it's the truth.

I'm interested in how you came to your political ideas. Were your parents politically involved?

No, my parents weren't political. My grandfather was in the National Guard, in Somoza's time. But none of them talked to me about politics. I got interested on my own, when I was in school. I began to understand the injustice there was, and I got involved in the student strikes . . .

Victoria was telling me about your U.S. tour. Can you talk about that?

Can you imagine? I'd never been out of the country before. It's the first time I ever had an experience like that: traveling around, visiting the different solidarity committees, telling people about the struggle here at El Caracol. I was nervous, I can tell you. Sometimes my hands would shake. My whole body would tremble. I could feel myself blushing!

But it was a good experience, too, one I don't think I'll ever have again. You know how it is: you wonder how people are going to accept you, how they're going to treat you, what they're going to say. But they treated me very well. At first it was hard for me to talk to so many people I'd never seen before. And I was on my own; once I even got lost in an airport.

What happened?

That was when I got to Kansas. The person who was supposed to meet me wasn't there. And I didn't know what to do, because I don't speak English. That was the time I was most scared. A black man came up to me and asked if I was lost. I tried to tell him I had to call this telephone number I had. He called a policeman, and then he started to dial the number I gave him. But the policeman came and asked me what I needed.

I told him I didn't speak English, and he called on his radio for a bilingual person to come and help. The bilingual person came right away. He asked me where I was from and I told him: Nicaragua. What was I doing there, [in Kansas], he asked, was I working or visiting or what? I told him I was a tourist, that I was visiting some friends. Then the cop began asking what I was doing there. I had some of our flyers in my hand, so I told him I was on an exchange, talking to some union people.

I was scared to say too much. But the policeman, when he saw the flyer, shook my hand. And he began to talk. I couldn't understand too much, but the translator told me he was saying that he was proud a Nicaraguan would come visit his country to talk about the democracy we now have, with Doña Violeta's presidency! "We're proud to receive a representative of Doña Violeta" was what he said!

It caught me off guard. I was just about to put both feet in my mouth when this other guy appeared and said he was the one who was supposed to have met my plane. He said he was sorry he was late but he'd had to take his child to school. The policeman repeated all that stuff about Doña Violeta and democracy, and everybody shook hands and we left. Once we were in his car, the comrade started laughing out loud. "What are you laughing about?" I asked him. "That cop thought you were a representative of Nicaraguan democracy!" "You should laugh," I told him. "I could have gone to prison and no one would have known where I was . . ."

How long was the tour?

Twenty-five days.

What did you husband say when you told him you were going to be away for that long?

Well, I left my baby with my mother, but the older kids stayed with my husband because of their school. When I told my husband that there was this idea of sending someone to the States, that the union elected me to go and the workers agreed, he said, "No problem." But the day I was getting ready to leave he told me, "You know why I'm letting you go? So you'll know how well people live up there, how much money they make and how they live." "Fine," I told him, "I'll keep my eyes open."

Of course, I saw lots of pretty things. Some people have a lot but there are lots of poor people, too. And, you know, I always thought that *no one* was poor in the States. That's the way they show it on TV. That trip taught me there's suffering everywhere, the same economic crisis hurting poor people wherever you go.

Diana, what did your family say when you got involved with the FSLN?

My mother didn't find out right away—not until the day we occupied the neighborhood, which was June 16, 1979. One of the neighbors knew I was involved, because she was with the Prolonged People's War tendency, which was another part of the movement. So she went and told my mother she should get out, that she should pick up and go to my grandfather's house because they were going to occupy the neighborhood. I didn't even know at that point, no one had come to tell me. But this neighbor, she told my mother: "Get out while you can, and take little Diana with you." "Why?" my mother asked. "Because she's involved and she's going to get hurt. She's too young. I don't want anything to happen to her," she said.

So my mother left and she made me go with her. And she read me the riot act; she said I had no business getting involved in politics, that I was too young. She said when I was older I'd know what was good and what was bad, that she didn't want me getting mixed up in all that at my age. She really bawled me out, like mothers do. Now that I'm a mother myself, I understand.

And my father said I was crazy, that I couldn't possibly know what was going on. He said that until a girl is eighteen years old she doesn't have a head on her shoulders, she can't reason or know what she wants, and that someone was taking advantage of my innocence. But I always knew what I wanted, even though I was young. And I always felt responsible. Because, you know, if I hadn't been so sure, I would have given up right then and there. And I didn't. Of my sisters and brothers, only one thinks like I do. He's older than me, and he's the only one.

What kind of work did your father do? Did you mother work, too?

My father drove a cab and my mother was a seamstress; she still sews.

As a woman, as a young woman, did you have any special problems when you started working as a union leader?

Not really. My biggest problems were from my own lack of experience. It's not the same being a member of an organization as it is being a leader, where you have to look out for the workers' best interests, fight for justice for them all. Sometimes there are workers who think they know what's best, and they don't. It can be hard negotiating between one position and another, but the more you do it the more you learn. It was hard at the beginning, but then I learned how to get my message across, how to explain things so people will understand. That's what being a leader is all about.

At home I had another kind of problem, though. My husband liked to say union work isn't for women, that only men can do it. He says women don't have what it takes to be leaders. And he's wrong, because here in Nicaragua it's been proven that women have the same ability as men.

Here in the factory, weren't there men who also thought the same as your husband?

Maybe. Maybe there were some who thought like that. But you can see that they're in the minority. Because, even when we women stayed here all night long—you know how lots of us stayed when we took over the plant—and people around here began saying we were staying for other reasons, that we had something going with the men . . . Some of the women whose husbands worked here thought that, too, and you know there were men whose wives ran them out of the house because of that. In the end, though, the men respected the women, and they saw that they couldn't push us aside anymore. Because we showed during that takeover that we can do whatever the men can do, just as well as the men. And we're still showing them.

Do you think maybe it's been easier because so many of the workers here are women?

It could be. But, you know, men with those backward ideas: I don't think it's easy to change them. They're always going to say things like, "That lazy bitch; she should go home and take care of her kids. That's where she belongs." I've heard a lot of men say things like that. But here at the plant the men have come to respect the women—for the most part. Here at El Caracol you don't hear that kind of thing anymore. Over at the Pepsi plant there are two different unions. The one my husband belongs to has only men in it, so things are different there. The other union has women but not that many, I don't think.

Diana, how do you think the revolution affected your life, as a woman I mean?

I was fourteen when the revolution came to power. But I could see that a lot of men beat up on women; they liked mistreating women. There are still a lot of men who do that, but before it seemed like there were more. And women didn't have anywhere to go where they could complain about it. No one listened to women. The revolution built women's centers: for example, the Luisa Amanda Espinosa women's organization. Now they even have a legal office, a special place for women to go and file their claims if they're being beaten or mistreated. And they listen; they call the man in, and they can even take him to court. That's been a change with this revolution: women aren't shoved aside so much, as if we don't matter. The idea that women should stay at home and only men should go out and work, that's changed.

Did you ever work with a women's organization?

Well, when the woman who had the women's secretariat here at the plant was on leave, I had to take over her job. Since I was the only other woman, they said I should do it. There were workshops, and I went to some of them, where they trained us in how to organize women so that there should always be a representative of the women. But I haven't specialized in that.

Exactly how many women do you have working here? And are there any other special services for women, aside from medical attention?

There are 115 workers here; and I think that, at the moment, 60 of us are women. What we've been able to get is the doctor I told you about. And when a woman is going to have a baby she gets a month's pay, equal to the salary of a grade-eight worker. She gets diapers, too. And if she has special problems of some kind—the baby's sick or she needs extra medical attention—then she can put in for 50 percent of whatever expenses she has. Compared to a lot of places, I think we've done pretty well.

All this is part of our collective contract that comes up for renewal every year. And it depends on how well the factory is doing, because right now we're going through pretty tough times. Right now we're managing with what we get from the solidarity committees. We're lucky there are people who want to help us. For example, they're going to send us a shipment of cellophane, because we haven't been able to get the cellophane we need and that's slowed down production something terrible. Many of our personnel are on vacation now because of this. And we're looking at ways to solve the problem: giving new powers to the administrator, working with the banks—because we've never really worked with the banks here.

Have you been able to get day care for the workers' children?

We don't have a child-care center here at the plant. Most of our workers' children are older; they're already in school. And the women who have babies, well, they leave them with relatives or the older kid takes care of her little brother or sister. We want to have a child-care center on site, but that's going to have to wait a while; we just don't have the money right now.

Diana, what do you think is going to happen with the factory? How do you think things are going to work out?

I think we're going to be able to buy the owners out. Because we have this plan for paying the money out of what the factory makes: 6 percent of our profits. The workers are also going to donate a part of their salaries. We've had the problem of changing from one type of society to another, such that the paperwork and registration cost 6 percent of the sales for a single month. If we continue that in July, it will be 6 percent of July's sales: about 30,000 córdobas.[6] And we think we're going to be able to swing that—with the help of the solidarity committees, of course.

Is there anything we haven't covered that you'd like to talk about? Anything else you'd like to say?

I'd like to tell women everywhere that they should learn to fight for their rights, for their place as women, and not allow men to treat them like objects, not be satisfied with being paid less just because they're women, even though they do the same work as men. But the only way for women to fight for their rights is if they get together and do it. The unity of all women is the answer.

Diana asked us if we wanted to see the plant. As we walked through the half-empty buildings, the machines mostly quiet, we could feel an underlying tension. Clearly the great majority of El Caracol's work force has been laid off, owing to the lack of materials and the negotiations aimed at ensuring ongoing work. It's the old story of workers bearing the brunt of the sacrifice as they struggle courageously for survival.

Along one wall a mountain of kernels in a large cement trough waited to be washed. Old funnel-shaped metal vats were arrayed like columns of armored knights. Everything was very clean, and very old. Here and there a small cluster of workers, most of them young women, packaged and weighed measures of pinolillo they scooped off a slow-moving conveyer belt.

They chatted with each other and willingly posed for our pictures. But the concern in their eyes was as uniform as their bright yellow cotton shirts, tie-back kerchiefs, and red aprons. It needed no verbal expression. Every one of them greeted Diana with the bottom-line question: "Hey . . . How're things going today?"

6. A córdoba is the Nicaraguan monetary unit. In late 1992 the exchange was approximately 3,000 córdobas to the U.S. dollar.

5 DAISY ZAMORA

"I Am Looking for the Women of My House"

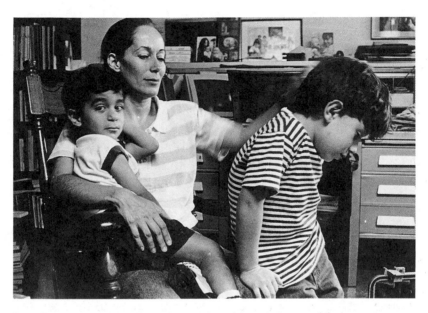

Daisy Zamora and her sons René Alberto, left, *and Joaquín Ernesto,* right.

I interviewed Daisy Zamora for the first time in 1979.[1] The revolution was not even six months old, and she was vice-minister of culture, aiding Ernesto Cardenal in the magical and sometimes overwhelming task of channeling people's natural creativity into everyday accomplishments. For these two poets and their enthusiastic staff everything was possible: converting abandoned houses into centers where people could paint and make music and do theater in the country's most remote mountain villages; encouraging poetry workshops in army units and factories; supporting the cultural life of the Atlantic Coast; or flooding Managua's elegant National Theater with street kids who listened, energized, to Theodorakis or Joan Baez.[2] When the United States unexpectedly cut its wheat sales to Nicaragua, the Ministry of Culture promoted a Festival of Corn—getting people excited about the history and tradition of corn and the variety of ways that the plentiful local substitute could be prepared.

1. See Randall, *Sandino's Daughters,* 94–115.
2. The National Theater, an imposing edifice down by Managua's lakefront, was the only building in that part of the city to have survived the 1972 earthquake. During the Somoza era it

The site of all this activity was a mansion called El Retiro. *It had belonged to Hope Portocarrero, Somoza's wife who'd been cast aside when the dictator began living with his longtime mistress Dinorah Simpson. The house was sprawling and decorated with unusually subtle taste; most of Nicaragua's ruling class preferred the birthday-cake models of the nouveaux riches. And the Ministry of Culture opened this house—including its swimming pool, tennis courts, and lavish grounds—to anyone who wanted to have a look or explore its mysteries. What had long been off limits to anyone but its owners and their servants, in 1979 welcomed—indeed embraced—the old men who came to record their stories of having fought with Sandino, the primitive painters from the tiny islands of the archipelago of Solentiname, the local and visiting artists, and the neighborhood children.[3] Two great Indian laurel trees served as landmarks, and a flamboyant parrot lived in a cage that hung from one of them.*

Ernesto and his vision were at the heart of the ministry; Daisy kept it going. Our first interview took place in her office, which I described at the time as "piled high with papers, projects, plans, problems and solutions. I can't help thinking," I wrote, "that this woman with her tender but penetrating gaze must wish . . . to remove herself from the pressures of the revolution and hide in the seclusion of her poetry."[4] Everything was new, everything possible. As forthcoming as Daisy was, I couldn't have known back then just how intense those pressures were—and how much more so they would become.

Several years later I interviewed Daisy again. I was then compiling a collection of conversations with Nicaraguan writers, and my interest was the poet's literary production rather than her political history or vice-ministerial duties.[5] But I continued to describe the loner, a woman whose façade hides as much as it reveals. "As a small child," I wrote, "Daisy Zamora was shy and sometimes remote, and as a woman she continues to be seen by many as reserved. She is a person who listens more than she speaks. Someone with strong revolutionary convictions—and matching history—she nevertheless retains the image of a middle-class woman concerned with appearances and manners. One doesn't expect to see Daisy without the appropriate dress or outside the context of a certain subtle elegance."

featured elitist programs, frequented by the country's small bourgeoisie. When the Sandinistas came to power, they changed the name of the theater to the Teatro Popular Rubén Darío (Rubén Darío People's Theater), priced events so they would be accessible to a much broader audience, and brought in the best international talent as well as staging local groups. Since the FSLN's 1990 electoral defeat, the theater has changed its name back again and once more caters to an elite.

3. Solentiname is an archipelago of thirty-eight islands in the southeast corner of Lake Nicaragua. From 1966 to 1977, Ernesto Cardenal had a contemplative community on one of the larger islands (see Chapter 2, note 14, above). During Solentiname's heyday, indigent peasants were inspired to write poetry and to paint. Under the Sandinista administration, the Ministry of Culture promoted both the Solentiname community and the peasant poets and artists nationally.

4. Randall, *Sandino's Daughters*, 96.

5. Randall, *Risking a Somersault in the Air*, 155–163.

But, I continued, "those who know this enigmatic woman see beneath all that. She comes from a well-to-do family . . . in which bourgeois politics became the nightly dinner conversation. Her father participated in the 1954 movement against the elder Somoza, and he was discovered and imprisoned because of it. Daisy was four then; she was told that he was away on a business trip but she recognized his picture on the front page of the daily paper. Faced by her family's refusal to admit she was right—that it was really his face she saw—she suffered with nightmares for years." [6]

Physically, Daisy has changed little. Tall and slender, her flawless oval face is framed by an abundance of honey-colored hair. Sometimes it fans out in a fountain of shoulder-length curls. At other times, she pulls it back into a bun at the nape of her neck. Her forehead is high and smooth, her cheekbones prominent. But her extraordinary eyes are what people comment upon most often: they are very blue and very steady. When Daisy listens, which she does well, she listens most conspicuously with her eyes.

Others besides myself have written about Daisy's origins, which are similar to those of so many upper-middle-class Nicaraguan women of her generation. Daisy herself has explored her early life in poems that aptly evoke the culture and the times. One of the most poignant, in retrospect, is "Death's Makeup," written for her childhood friend and sister revolutionary Nora Astorga. In it she remembers "the childhood we shared / our diligent grandmothers, ceremonious grandfathers / in linen and Panama hats, / benevolent and tender." In the same poem, she traces as well the intensity of almost unimaginable changes: their "Adolescence plagued by ambiguous fantasies," becomes an "age of conspiracy, of contacts, carnage for the operative, / absence and exile the price we paid for action." And, not one to remain at the surface of experience, she digs deeper to speak of ". . . our beloved men, our children, sister grief." [7]

It's all there. And yet, there is so much more. Daisy Zamora grew up profoundly influenced by her grandfather and a great-aunt. She didn't study at La Asunción, *but at another convent school for daughters of the bourgeoisie, the* Colegio Teresiano. *Later, at the university, Daisy majored in psychology and became involved in student politics. But instead of going to work in her profession, she married her first husband, Dionisio Marenco, before finishing college.* [8] *His engineering career took them to a sugar mill near Chinandega. In 1974, together with other young people in the vicinity, the couple organized a formal FSLN cell. Those years saw their participation in the purchase and*

6. Ibid., 155.

7. Daisy Zamora, "Death's Makeup," in *Clean Slate: New and Selected Poems*, trans. Margaret Randall and Elinor Randall (Willimantic, Conn. Curbstone Press 1993).

8. Dionisio Marenco is a civil engineer with a master's in business administration. During the revolutionary government he was at first minister of construction and transportation, then minister of domestic commerce, and finally minister of planning. He continues to be a member of the Sandinista Assembly.

transport of arms, the hiding of comrades, the raising of funds, and other support tasks.[9]

As Nicaragua's political climate intensified, so did Daisy's and her husband's involvement with the revolutionary forces organizing to defeat Somoza. In August 1978 their home was the safehouse from which members of the FSLN commando *left to occupy the National Palace.* A month later, during the September insurrection, they themselves took part in a frustrated military action. And then, during the last months of the war, Daisy's became the woman's voice on Radio Sandino, the Party's clandestine station broadcasting from "somewhere in Nicaragua."[10] Throughout the country, and beyond its borders, her words were listened to by millions—for whom they became a unique source of dependable information about the war.

When Daisy speaks of her revolutionary history, she often reminisces about what she used to describe as her petit-bourgeois upbringing and the contradictions she had to overcome. Of her early college years she once said, "I held back . . . I was very insecure about my . . . background. And that made me even more shy. Others of my age were more radicalized. Most of them didn't have much patience with those of us who hadn't reached their level." Now she realizes that she was responding to an innate insecurity as much as to the sectarianism of those who might have helped her to grow politically. Later, in Chinandega, she opted for teaching workers' children. She speaks of the dramatic inequalities between laborers and bosses at the mill, and she remembers that her response "was to deal with it in an individual way, as a teacher."[11]

In 1972 Managua suffered a devastating earthquake, and Daisy had to cope with severe personal loss as well; her beloved grandfather became ill with cancer, and she returned to the capital to nurse him for the last five months of his life. Over the next several years, Dionisio's decision to join the FSLN's insurrectional tendency and Daisy's own increased involvement in armed struggle pushed the young, delicate, almost aristocratic-looking woman beyond the point where class origin was any longer an impediment. Experience tore through hesitancy or shame, bringing courage in its wake.

And courage was something Daisy would be called upon to nurture in a variety of arenas as her country's struggle unfolded. More than a few revolutionaries have pointed out that actual warfare is often the easiest stage in the complex process of social change. As vice-minister of culture, Daisy Zamora would be forced to confront manipulation and power plays that decimated her innocence as well as many of her expectations. As a woman within the male-dominated Sandinista power structure, she would suffer the indignities common to her gender. As a poet, she was sometimes dismissed as a dreamer.

9. This and subsequent history can be found in *Sandino's Daughters.*

10. One of Zamora's major poems is the long and powerful "Radio Sandino," a re-creation of bits and pieces of those historic broadcasts interspersed with her memories of those months (included in *Clean Slate: New and Selected Poems*).

11. Randall, *Sandino's Daughters*, 100.

But there was still more. Daisy's personal life was also destined to bring her pain and to help her grow. With her first husband, Dionisio, she faced the difficult but rewarding adoption of an undernourished and somewhat fragile baby girl. Together they nursed her to health. Then, in a very traditional Spanish-Catholic milieu, she divorced Dionisio and began living with another man: Oscar-René Vargas.[12] Individualists who rejected the Party line when they believed it to be wrong, considered iconoclasts by some, Daisy and Oscar-René suffered a certain amount of political as well as social stigma. But they trusted in honesty, dignity, and time to help them through.

Still, Daisy's trials continued. She and Oscar-René had another child, a little girl, who died at birth; a better doctor might have avoided the tragedy. Their second, a boy, is now a healthy five-year-old. But their third child was born with a cleft palate, necessitating a series of operations for which mother and child have had to travel to the United States once every year of the young boy's life. He is a lively and loving three-year-old, with regular features now, but there are still more operations in his future. At forty, Daisy's luminous blue eyes hold a serenity but also a centeredness, the kind that comes from consistently having to struggle in order to make it through.

Since the FSLN's electoral defeat Daisy, like so many other Sandinistas who once held important government positions, has had to forage for work. She has managed to pick up a class or two at the Jesuit university; her students say she teaches Sor Juana Inés de la Cruz better than anyone they know.[13] A major project was her recently published anthology of Nicaraguan women's poetry, an important contribution which greatly enriches her own bibliography.[14] And she has teamed up with the popular Nicaraguan singer Norma Elena Gadea in programs of poetry and song. Over the past several years, Daisy has also been active in her country's independent feminist movement.

When I decided to revisit "Sandino's Daughters," and do fieldwork for this

12. Oscar-René Vargas is an economist and sociologist; he joined the FSLN in 1967. Exiled because of his political activities, he lived in Brazil, Cuba, Chile, Switzerland, and Mexico, where he continued to do solidarity work. With the revolutionary victory of 1979, he returned home. His many books include *La intervención norteamericana y sus consecuencias: Nicaragua 1910–1925* (Managua: Ecotextura, 1989), *La revolución que inició el progreso: Nicaragua 1893–1909* (Managua: Ecotextura, 1990), and *Nicaragua: Desafíos y opciones* (Managua: UNICEF, 1992).

13. Sor Juana Inés de la Cruz (1648–1695) became a sister of the Convent of San Jerónimo in Mexico City at age twenty. Her religious confinement, perhaps the only way for a woman of her time and culture to avoid marriage and domesticity, placed unfortunate limitations on one of the most extraordinary minds of the seventeenth century. An innovative and passionate poet, essayist, and playwright, she was forced to renounce her literary vocation during the last years of her life. Sor Juana's brilliance has long been admired, but her lesbian longings have only recently been recognized and researched.

14. *La mujer nicaragüense en la poesía / Nicaraguan Women's Poetry*, ed. Daisy Zamora (Managua, Editorial Nueva Nicaragua, 1992). See also her *La violenta espuma / The Violent Foam* (Managua: Ministry of Culture, 1981), *En limpio se escribe la vida / Clean Slate* (Managua: Editorial Nueva Nicaragua, 1988); and *Clean Slate: New and Selected Poems*.

*new book, Daisy immediately offered to help me locate the women I'd spoken
with a dozen years before. She made contacts, scheduled interviews, found me
a place to stay—and, when it came to her personal contribution, put it off as
long as possible. This continued to be a difficult period in Nicaragua. For
Daisy, juggling her life as poet, worker, mother, wife, Sandinista, and feminist, the issues remain complex, the pain and anger beginning to articulate
themselves in necessary, sometimes accusatory ways.*

*Finally, several days before I would leave Managua, Daisy and I got to-
gether in the library of their museumlike home. A wealth of contemporary
Nicaraguan painting covers the walls of the entryway, living room, and dining
room and then threatens to invade the tree-lined courtyard off which the library is a recently built addition. In the library, though, it's all books . . .
books and family photographs, poems pinned above a desk, one computer that
stores economic treatises beside another that houses literature.*

*There was an added dimension to this particular afternoon. Exactly one
month earlier, Daisy had lost the woman who had raised and loved her more
than any other: her great-aunt Anita Gámez. Anita had been another of my
interviewees for* Sandino's Daughters. *Now, at age ninety, the tragedy of Sandinista loss had undermined her will to live. She had come down with a sudden
case of pneumonia and died within days. For her great-niece this new grief
was very fresh.*

*Daisy consented to locking the library door against the conspiracy of con-
stant interruption from her young children and their friends. As a mother she is
always ready to stop everything and listen to a child's question, need, or demand. Indeed, with her children I have yet to hear her raise her voice beyond a
tone of steady and deeply felt interest. Today, though, she had committed herself to responding to my desire to bridge the years since our previous interviews. And, as with all else she does, she took the commitment seriously.*

*We were seated in those wonderful rockers traditional to Nicaraguan houses
large and small. Daisy leaned back in hers, growing thoughtful. Through a
corner window, opening onto the courtyard, I could see two little boys trying
hard to get their mother's attention. For a while, she pretended not to hear
them; occasionally she'd relent and briefly address their demands. She was
wearing jeans and a simple striped polo shirt of pale blue and white; her hair
was pulled away from her face and pinned up. It had been an overwhelming
morning, buying food at one of the city's markets, she said. But she was ready
to talk about her life:*

About my class background, I don't think there's that much about it I can
add to what you already know. I was raised largely by my great-aunt, in a
home with Liberal politics—"Liberal" as in the political party, though my
father opposed Somoza. And my grandfather was an important influence in my
early life. Since our interviews a decade back, though, today I would talk more
about the women in my family. My grandfather was important, but I realize I
never even mentioned my grandmother.

My grandmother was a very cultured woman for her time. She spoke perfect

English, perfect French. She completed high school and was a voracious reader—voracious and indiscriminate. When my grandmother died it fell to my great-aunt, another sister of hers who was living at the time, and myself to go through her things. Her library was amazing! I remember she had everything from romance novels—whole collections of M. Deli and Rafael Pérez y Pérez, who were the Corín Tellados of her day—to Jack London and Alexandre Dumas.[15] She was an utterly eclectic reader.

In my childhood my grandmother evokes imagination. She told me endless stories (derived from all the reading she did, I realize now). Looking back from where I stand today, I continue to think of my grandfather as the person who most developed my sensibility, but my grandmother developed my imagination. She gave me a sense of the fantastic. She inhabited a world that was magically unreal.

My great-aunt, who died a month ago today, was the one who gave me self-confidence. She made it possible for me to believe in myself, and that's such an important thing for a young girl growing up. It's really what allows you to make it through. Self-confidence and what little practical sense I have, I owe them both to my great-aunt.

So those are some of the particulars I'd add to the story of my class background. And I'd reiterate that I was extraordinarily protected as a child. In fact, even when you and I first met, Margaret, at the beginning of the revolution, I don't think I'd been able to break all that much with the protection of my childhood and young adulthood. I was still pretty innocent.

I've always wanted to ask you, Daisy: although you'd participated in combat and done things that many people couldn't even imagine, it's true that in some ways you were still quite protected . And in a certain sense clandestine activity and armed struggle involve life-styles that are set apart somehow, isolated from the mainstream. So how was it for you, when the war ended in 1979, suddenly to find yourself in the position of vice-minister of culture?

The whole time I was vice-minister, I don't think I ever thought of exercising power for power's sake. I don't know if I can really explain this, and of course I'm speaking in retrospect so many years later, but what's clear to me now is that Ernesto imbued the ministry with a work-style that was profoundly revolutionary. We were truly there to serve people, all the people; to promote a type of creativity in which the people themselves would become the protagonists of their own cultural pageant.

I remember those years at the ministry as years of incredibly intense work—so intense that it cost me my marriage, my relationship with the man I was with at the time. Being a man, he had a clearer vision of power, I think: power in its patriarchal dimension, the way it's exercised pretty much throughout the

15. Corín Tellado is the pen name of the author of hundreds if not thousands of Spanish-language romances, published in book form or included in popular women's magazines such as *Vanidades*.

world, the way power has been used for thousands of years and the way it continues to be used. I didn't understand that use, or misuse, of power; and I don't think Ernesto understood it either. Maybe because of his dual standing as priest and poet: the priest who dedicates his life to serving others; the artist, the poet, who is rooted in sensibility and who nurtures himself through the sensibility of others.

So, in a sense, I never really *understood* that I was vice-minister of culture, certainly not in the way my colleagues must have seen me. What I remember is just working like crazy, day and night, wanting so badly to solve every problem that came up and being absolutely convinced that we were laying the groundwork for a truly revolutionary project; that is, that we were making a real difference in people's lives. The literacy campaign was only a beginning in our minds. We wanted higher levels of culture and cultural expression for everyone.

I'm interested in what you say about power. Because I remember that your husband was also involved in the revolutionary project in a different area, but one just as important. So I'm wondering what kinds of problems arose . . .

Basically it was an ethical problem. It had to do with being faithful to the principles in which I believed. I guess in a certain sense I'm not political enough. Well, we're all political, of course, but I never understood the art of political maneuvering. At the ministry we'd see a problem or launch a project we thought important, and we'd just plunge ahead with it without worrying about who stood in the way or what political ambitions they might have. I'd simply follow the principles in which I believed; and I wasn't careful enough of other positions, or I overlooked them entirely. And those positions existed, they were real.

I was naive enough to believe that the revolution had put an end to all that jockeying for position. That's why I say it was an innocent point of view. I'd been overprotected; I hadn't lived enough. It didn't matter that I'd been involved in political struggle for a while by then, that I'd marched at the university, even seen combat in Managua, gone into exile, been underground . . . Those experiences were important, of course, but through them all I somehow retained a kind of candor, an innocence, that prevented me from understanding political life as it existed. And, you know, I still don't understand it. Not really. Or maybe I don't want to. I simply won't go against my principles.

And my husband would give me advice. He was always telling me that there are limits, times when you have to make concessions, give in. And it wasn't that I was closed to what he was saying; I don't think I'm a closed or rigid person. It's just that I believed that the revolution had a cultural project; and when that project came up against certain individuals' personal ambition, the problems became insoluble.

I never understood this. I really didn't. And it's what provoked my leaving the ministry. Bayardo Arce, who was the member of the national directorate who dealt with the area of culture at that time, made it very clear. He was really very sympathetic. He said there was nothing wrong with me personally but that I'd become the target of all these opposing forces. Ernesto remained above the fray but I was the one who had to make things work, and I got blamed. I always said what I meant, I always played clean. And since my counterpart in the artists' organization was a master at maneuvering, we were playing two entirely different games. So they had to remove me and replace me with someone more docile, someone who was willing to play their game.

What they really did was eliminate the position. After I left there was one ephemeral vice-minister of culture; he lasted only nine months because he couldn't take the pressure. And then there was Vidaluz [Meneses], who was never officially named. Now I can see that this was the policy: not to give any real power to another vice-minister. I don't think it's an accident that I was the only formally appointed vice-minister of culture in almost eleven years of revolution.

If we look at the history of the Ministry of Culture and of the revolution's cultural policy in general, we can see that things began to disintegrate from the moment you vacated the position. A couple of years later, the ministry itself was closed. What happened to you, Daisy? Where did you go to work after that?

By that time I was known as a troublemaker. I could be counted upon to defend the principles in which I believed, to argue, to be confrontational when necessary. So after the vice-ministry they sent me over to the national directorate's secretariat, an internal Party structure. Later, I went to work at the FSLN's International Relations Department. A rigid discipline went along with both those jobs; there was little room for discussion.

But, of course, I didn't last long in either place because I continued to open my mouth when I had something to say. It wasn't that I always thought I was right; I just couldn't stand this "correct line," where there was a single vision, a single right way of doing things, without any recognition at all of the possibility for error. Maintaining a democratic process seemed important to me. From the time I was in Culture I never could accept imposed ideas, no matter where they came from. I preferred to discuss the various opinions, and everywhere I went I faced the same problem.

I know you want me to be more concrete. In the ministry, for example, I was never willing to cancel a cultural program that had been advertised for weeks, simply because there was a call from Comandante Daniel Ortega's office advising me that the president had decided to cart the artist off to some sort of last-minute function. They'd call, and I'd say I was sorry but the tickets had already been sold—whatever. And whoever it was, a secretary usually, would be astonished. "But it's for the comandante," she'd say; and I'd tell her it didn't matter, that if the comandante wanted to come to the phone, I'd be glad to explain the situation. Of course, he never came to the phone. But this sort of problem was a constant. You can multiply it by hundreds.

The most important conflict was probably around the poetry workshops. It would be hard to find another country where the teaching of poetry became a national issue, worthy of the front pages of the daily papers. Here *Ventana* waged a virtual war against the poetry workshops.[16] There are entire issues of the supplement devoted to the claim that we were turning out hundreds of little Ernesto Cardenals, that the workshop teaching methodology produced Cardenals in series. *Ventana* accused us of making only one kind of poetry available to the participants.

All you have to do is read the back issues of *Poesía Libre*.[17] You'll find poems by Lord Byron, William Carlos Williams, Nicolás Guillén, Vicente Huidobro; you can hardly imagine a more varied list. And those were the poets the workshop participants read. It's true that Cardenal published a brief set of initial instructions, things to do and not to do when beginning to write poetry. But as he himself said, that it was cautionary rather than regulatory. Basics, like being clear about what you wanted to say, or being specific—for example, talking about a willow or a palm tree, instead of just a tree. I don't really think those suggestions were so harmful to the people of Nicaragua.

The poetry workshops weren't conceived of only so people who wanted to write poetry would have a place to do so. They were an attempt to get people to *read* poetry, too, and to understand that creativity belongs to us all; we have only to tap it. But the experiment, which I believe was a profoundly revolutionary one—one that retrieved the most important cultural tradition we have here, which is poetry—became an object of continual attack, until the workshops ceased to exist.

These personal vendettas shouldn't have been allowed to flourish within the revolution. No one person, just because he or she liked you or didn't like you or wanted your job or had some personal motive for attack, should ever have been able to destroy a revolutionary project like that. But they were able to do so. And in my particular case, from the time they removed me from the Ministry of Culture to the moment we lost the elections, I never again held a job in which I was able to make decisions that would affect large numbers of people. They kept an eye on me.

I have another story, and it will probably sound unbelievable to you. When I was working at the DRI [FSLN's Department of International Relations], Julio López Campos, who was the office chief, once called me in to let me know it had come to his attention that I sometimes failed to have lunch with the rest of the staff in the dining room, where we all had half an hour to eat. He said he had been told that I sometimes stayed in my office by myself, reading poetry instead of going over my work for the North American desk. At the time, I was

16. *Ventana* [Window] was the weekly cultural supplement that appeared every Saturday, folded into *Barricada*, the FSLN newspaper. The original Ventana, after which it was named, was an important literary magazine, published in the 1960s at the national university in León by Sergio Ramírez, Fernando Gordillo, and others. During the last year of the Sandinista administration, the more recent version became a personal showcase for Rosario Murillo and her vendetta against Ernesto Cardenal.

17. *Poesía Libre* [Free Poetry] was the Ministry of Culture's poetry journal.

in charge of Party relations with the United States. It was hard to know how to respond to such an accusation!

Even more painful was the issue they made of my personal decision to leave a relationship that had worn itself out. And it was complicated by the fact that I went off to live with someone else. They actually punished me for that, politically! My first husband was important in the revolutionary government; he was a minister of state. And it's not that they took my Party membership away, nothing like that. It was more a campaign of silence: they stopped inviting me to important functions; people stopped talking to me; or if an invitation for me to participate in an international poetry festival arrived, it just never came to my attention. Occasionally I'd even find out someone had written suggesting they invite someone else instead.

This was how they punished me for deciding to leave a marriage that wasn't working and start a relationship with another man, who is also profoundly revolutionary but has his own opinions, speaks his own mind, a person like myself who challenged what wasn't right. Now that we've lost the elections and everything's changed here, plenty of people have been willing to tell me what was going on; but at the time no one wanted to risk his position.

It took a while for those of us who put the revolution first to understand what was happening. You know, at the Ministry of Culture when one of us was invited to an international event or had to travel for some reason, we'd go with two hundred dollars in our pocket! And if our hosts paid our expenses and there was anything left over, we'd bring it back and turn it in! When I talk about this today, well, I don't know whether people believe me or not. There are hundreds of anecdotes. I remember once I was invited to an event in Paris. I went off with two or three hundred dollars, and Ernesto told me if I had anything left over to buy materials for the ministry. I came back with a ton of paints and brushes, things for our artists, and materials for a new jazz group we were starting besides . . .

I'd like to stop for a moment and ask you to consider another aspect of all this. I worked at the Ministry of Culture in 1981, and I know what you're saying is true. But I wonder about gender as well. Do you think your status as a woman affected the way you were treated, or that you experienced the attacks any differently because you're a woman?

So much in life is paradoxical—and dialectical. I'm sure I was treated differently, but I wasn't the only one. I don't know how many other truly revolutionary women paid a tremendous political and even economic price, as I did, because they held onto their personal dignity and spoke their mind when it was necessary. But, ironically, all the things I've been telling you somehow reaffirmed in me my sense of what it is to be a woman. It gave me an inner strength, a moral authority, and although I don't talk about this much I think it was something that allowed me to grow. Because you know, Margaret, it's interesting—and sometimes disappointing—to see what power can do to women as well as men. It was painful for me to see women I knew, women who were my friends and whom I valued and admired, make all sorts of trade-offs in exchange for what might turn out to be only the illusion of power.

It would have been a different story if some of those women had made their concessions and then, from the positions they acquired, concerned themselves with helping to change things for women in general. But that didn't happen often. Unfortunately, most of these women played the male game; they ceded important territory as women, and their "leadership" didn't do a thing to better the situation for the rest of us in the revolutionary process.

This has been particularly painful for me because we women did everything during the period of armed struggle. We risked as much as the men, we carried the same sort of responsibilities: there was no way we hadn't earned the right to leadership positions in the revolutionary government. But there were women who, once in those positions, forgot they were revolutionaries and forgot they were women. I'm speaking from my own experience.

I don't know if you want to put this in your book, but I can tell you there were plenty of sexual pressures. In the eyes of a number of our male leaders, women continued to be seen as "meat" or "cattle," as our macho slang would have it. The quickest and easiest way for political women to acquire a "protector" and gain direct access to power was by sleeping with someone in power. And who knows what my life would have been like if I'd had that sort of safety net.

In fact, when I left the Ministry of Culture, one of the comandantes wanted to send me to Foreign Relations, also in the capacity of vice-minister. I was never privy to the behind-the-scenes discussions, so I don't really know what was on his mind. But I can tell you that some time later this same man started literally stalking me: it was invitation after invitation, insinuation after insinuation. One day I called him up and invited him to lunch. I had to tell him, "Look, I admire you tremendously. I respect you. You're one of the leaders of this revolution. But I need you to understand that I'm a free person, with all the rights that implies, and I'm absolutely capable of deciding with whom I want to have a relationship. Believe it or not, I'm not attracted to you just because you're a comandante. So I'm asking you to respect my decision, and I hope we can remain friends." I remember he hardly touched his food. He left the table and for quite some time he wouldn't even say hello.

And it gets worse. When I made the decision to leave Dionisio and live with Oscar-René—a person considered controversial at the time—I suffered truly sordid consequences. And I use the word "sordid" intentionally. I was working at INIES then, and unfortunately the Comandante with whom I'd had lunch was the Party liaison with that institution.[18] He called me in one day and told me they had plans to appoint Oscar-René director of INIES. But, he said, it wouldn't look good for both of us to be working at the same place (I was the executive director). So if I would resign, they'd relocate me somewhere else and he could have the job. He said the Party had its reasons. So I resigned and

18. INIES, or the Instituto Nicaragüense de Investigación y Estudios Sandinistas is the Nicara-guan Institute of Sandinista Research Studies.

they accepted my resignation. Then they didn't name Oscar-René after all, and I was left without a job.

When people found out what had happened, one of my friends —Antonina Vivas—told me I might be able to get a job at the United Nations. Jaime Balcázar was the U.N. representative in Nicaragua at the time and he was a progressive person, very supportive of the revolution. I applied for a job, I filled out the forms, and I heard that Balcázar wanted me. But the U.N. office had to run its applicants by the government. I later found out that this same comandante, with a single telephone call, kept me from being hired.

What I'm saying is that not being willing to go to bed with that kind of power broker not only cost me my own power niche, it prevented me from finding work. Around the same time, Oscar-René had a program on Radio Sandino; his boss, César Estrada, was honest at least. He said, "Listen, Oscar-René, I've just had a call from so-and-so"—the comandante I'm talking about—"and he told me to cancel your program."[19] You have to understand how seriously everyone took Party discipline back then. This is why I said that in spite of all the experiences I'd had, when you interviewed me twelve years ago I was still an innocent, because that behavior is typical of traditional bourgeois society. But I had no idea these things could happen, and even be encouraged, in a revolutionary process.

All of this has led to my profound belief that we need a totally different conception of power, one that includes a truly humanist, feminist perspective. And when I talk about a feminist perspective, I'm not talking only about so-called women's issues: I mean a different conception of the world, of relations between people, of power relations at all levels.

Which is what real democracy is all about . . .

Of course. At the time these things were happening in my life, I wasn't as clear as I am today about the theory concerning inequality. I mean I had read some of the more-or-less classic feminist authors, but I hadn't internalized their ideas to the point where I acted consciously upon them. It was more a case of my life experience pushing me to look for other answers, and then in turn to search for some of the more radical texts.

Daisy, I wonder if you might be willing to reflect upon how the revolutionary women of your generation and those who are a bit younger than you experienced the decade of Sandinista power? One hears two sorts of testimony which seem to a certain extent contradictory. On the one hand, Sandinism as a political movement certainly opened an enormous space for women to become subjects as opposed to objects: women began to think, act, participate, and hold positions they had never held before. On the other hand, the type of experience you describe is all too common. Can you talk at all about a balance?

---

19. Years later, Rodolfo Tapia Molina, the director of Radio Sandino, confirmed what César Estrada told Oscar-René Vargas about the orders received to cancel his program.

Yes. It's absolutely true that the revolution opened up a new space for women here. We fought alongside our male comrades and that produced an explosion of new possibilities. By the end of the war the old order had been completely disrupted, and all the women who had taken part had the opportunity of working in our respective fields to help construct a more just society. I think the problem was that this new space wasn't accompanied by a new mentality on the part of most of the male-dominated leadership. What this meant was that there was a gap between what the revolution offered its women and what we women found in our day to day relationship with "Comandante X," a man still very much formed in the old ideas.

Personal honesty has always been very important to me, Margaret. Some of our revolutionary leaders made beautiful speeches, everything sounded good on paper, but so much of it wasn't substantiated in practice. So, yes, a space was opened up. No question about that. The revolution provided free education for all, health centers, medical attention, new hospitals, and medicines accessible to the poorest strata of society. There were massive vaccination campaigns which eradicated health problems that had been endemic here. Our infant mortality went way down, and we were able to open day-care centers in the rural areas as well as in the cities. There were dozens of extraordinary projects. And revolutionary ideas were on the agenda; people talked about them. But, as I say, many of those women who thought they were making tactical concessions in order to achieve a better situation for all women, they eventually ended up trapped in what had become a way of life. And others, who refused to make concessions, who held on to their personal dignity, well, they simply were displaced as I was.

I know this is very much a topic of discussion now, since the electoral loss. Did women talk about these things before the elections? Did you discuss them among yourselves?

Yes, very definitely. A number of us who had these concerns talked among ourselves. But the problem was that no one in power paid any attention. They didn't take us seriously—not even the women, not even AMNLAE, none of the channels that were supposed to have existed [to address] these very issues. We never managed to get answers that seemed real to us, that convinced us of anything.

There was always the war, our boys at the front, production, the economic crisis . . . and, of course it's true these things were priorities. But that doesn't justify dishonesty, it doesn't justify continuing to look the other way when gross injustices are being committed. And I have to say that I think we needed a much more belligerent attitude than we had, on the part of those women who were aware and in positions of power, who did have the prestige to call some of this discourse into question. I include Milú Vargas, Sofía Montenegro, Dora María Téllez—all those women who hadn't been demoted and pushed aside as I was. I wasn't the only one, of course; a number of us were relieved of our positions early on. Sometimes I think I had one of the most difficult battle-fields, given who my Party counterpart turned out to be . . .

But there were women who had survived, and who had prestige. And they were our hope. Now that the FSLN is no longer in power some of these women have spoken out: Dora María has taken a stronger position; so have Sofía and Milú. Milú was particularly important because she was married to Carlos Núñez; she had the ear of a member of the national directorate. And Carlos was one of the few male leaders of this revolution whose daily practice seemed to match his rhetoric, who respected his partner, supported her work, really supported women. He and a very few others.

But I keep talking about individuals, and I don't want to do that. The issues are more important than the people who did or did not understand them. To answer your question more specifically: yes, we discussed these things before the electoral defeat, but there were two levels. Even those women who understood the issues and had enough prestige to speak out: it was as if they had an official rhetoric and then their own private discourse. Milú, Sofía, Gioconda, and some of the others got together. They had a group they called PIE—Party of the Erotic Left, the name was a kind of joke—and that's where they developed their more private discourse. I remember asking several of them why they didn't invite more women to join them, but they never really responded. And when we would get together—a larger number of women in more public forums—those women always assumed a position of listening to our questions, our concerns; but we were all quite clear that we weren't going to be able to take it very far.

You can even see this reflected in the 1987 Constitution. Because in spite of the fact that a number of women had an active role in writing the Constitution, the truth is that abortion or freedom of choice isn't established as a right. The most they could do was to get abortion decriminalized. Why? Because even those women always had to be careful; in this case, they had to make concessions to the institutional Catholic Church.

You know, in a country like Nicaragua, where 71.7 percent of all women begin to be sexually active between the ages of nine and fourteen and are considered fertile until the age of fourty nine, only 26 percent use any form of birth control. For this reason, among others, there are many unwanted pregnancies. A study carried out at Managua's Berta Calderón Hospital reveals that of the 780 women who gave birth there during the month of June 1991, 31.5 percent were adolescents and 68.5 percent were of what's considered to be childbearing age. But of all of these women, 50 percent said their pregnancies were unplanned and unwanted.[20]

In Nicaragua there is a very high rate of maternal mortality, of death related to childbirth. Although official statistics list 159 mothers dead for every

20. See "Factores sociales y conductuales que influyen en el embarazo no deseado de adolescentes y mujeres en el período reproductivo ideal que dan a luz en el Hospital Berta Calderón durante el mes de junio de 1991," a thesis submitted to the UPOLI Nursing School, Managua, 1991, by Edelma Dávila Hernández, Julia Urbina Aguilera, and Maritza Rizo Centeno.

100,000 live births, in 1989 our hospitals reported the figure as 209.[21] Today, illegally induced abortions are the leading cause of maternal mortality in our country's hospitals. These are the cold hard facts, Margaret; every statistic is a woman's life. As revolutionaries, as women who identify with all women and who are in solidarity with them, it is unacceptable that we prefer to cater to the Church instead of searching for real solutions.

So, as I was saying, the women who helped write the Constitution were undoubtedly convinced that they were looking out for women when they conceived of this new basic law of the land, but in practice they could go only so far. And I know they are honest, that they are honestly convinced of their feminist positions. It must have been tragic for them to feel they had to limit themselves to such an extent.

I do believe it would have been healthier to say, "All right, this is our situation. This is as far as we can go right now. It's not far enough, but it's the best we can do, under the circumstances." I think it would have been healthier to say that than to pretend they could do more when they couldn't. But then, that's the way I've always felt. I know I can't impose my feelings on everyone else.

We get back to the problem we were talking about before: the concessions you have to be willing to make in order to keep a position where you may have some degree of influence. The women you mention are all feminists. But each one of them undoubtedly has her own particular history.

I know, which is why I'm not criticizing them. I'm simply saying that the situation was such that none of them had the courage to publicly argue for positions I know they defended in private.

Rather than criticize those women, I criticize the system that kept them down. Daisy, would you give me your view of the electoral campaign, the election itself, and the dynamic produced by the FSLN's loss?

First of all, I want to say I've always thought that the revolution, besides belonging to the Nicaraguan people, is also my personal project. That is, it's the only thing I can really believe in and from which I expect something in return, the only thing capable of helping us build a better way of life. So in spite of everything I've told you, in spite of all the ugly stories—my own unhappy experience—I've stayed right here, working for the revolution in whatever way I could. Ernesto would hire me to do translations; I'd find jobs here and there; there was always someone able to give me some kind of work, for survival if nothing else. And, of course, Oscar-René had a more stable job.

But the revolution isn't abstract. It's designed and directed by men and

21. When we speak of mothers dying from causes linked to childbirth, a figure of 19 or fewer out of every 100,000 births is considered low, from 20 to 49 is considered average, from 50 to 149 is considered high, and above 150 is considered very high.

women, human beings, and that's where the problems come in. Over a period of years I think this leadership showed us that it lacked the vision necessary to do what people expected of it. Let me be clear. I'm not forgetting the price we paid in terms of low-intensity warfare, the economic blockade, and all the rest. All that took a tremendous toll. But it doesn't explain everything. Unfortunately, I think many among the upper echelons in this revolution became addicted to power. They were corrupted by power. And corruption and the abuse of power effectively separated them from the masses of people, because they no longer shared their lives.

Many of us felt that the FSLN's electoral campaign was utterly divorced from this country's reality, as if it were a campaign imported from who knows where. It was all about dancing in the streets, being happy: "Everything Will Get Better" was the main slogan. And, yes, we are a joyous people who get together to party at a moment's notice; we'll celebrate anything and everything. But the campaign played on all that in a totally superficial way. Because that happy-go-lucky attitude is a *part* of our culture but it's not our whole culture, and we were living through a particularly difficult time just then.

You could turn on your TV and watch the campaign: people did get out in the streets and dance, people danced with Daniel. But then they had to go back home to their everyday reality. They probably had at least one son at the front, and any day they might get the word he'd been killed. The FSLN's electoral campaign seemed like a saint's day celebration to me: like people celebrating [the feast of] St. Sebastian or St. Dominic. Maybe they even went so far as to spend everything they had on a costume or a new dress for the occasion; but when the party was over, that was that. The campaign didn't leave people with anything tangible, anything they could hold onto. It didn't mean anything in terms of pointing to real solutions to people's problems.

I almost never heard a concrete idea or proposal in one of Daniel's speeches. And they're the same today: most often reiterative, with lots of mottoes and slogans but no real alternatives. I don't think people voted against the revolution, not really. They voted against the pressures of war, and probably also against certain individuals and certain life-styles they identified with the Front at that particular time. Too many people must have said, "That's what the FSLN is, and I'm not going to vote for it." Because not everyone is at the same ideological level.

If I hadn't been at the ideological level where I am, for example, I might have voted against the Party, too—with everything that's happened to me over the past several years. Or at the very least I might have refrained from voting. But I didn't vote for individuals or for what the Party did or failed to do for *me*; I voted for the FSLN because the revolution is my project, quite apart from the failures of some of its leaders. Still, I believe we need a new leadership.

Were you as surprised as everyone else when the Party lost?

During the campaign I was scared. For years now I've lived the life of an ordinary housewife in this country—in the sense that I go to the market, I stand in line to get chicken, or I struggle to make my money go further. And I hear what people are saying. This place is like a small town; it's not hard to be in touch with what people are thinking, with what's going on. People complained loud and clear about the ostentation, the waste. Criticism was on the rise and it was aimed at certain leaders, not everyone of course.

By the same token, Oscar-René also heard and saw similar sorts of things. I remember three days before the end of the campaign, we were talking and for the first time we actually began to contemplate the possibility that we might lose. We were afraid. But then on February 21st so many people crowded into the square: it felt like July 19, 1979, all over again! And I said, "We're wrong. In spite of everything, people are still hopeful." But it wasn't true.

And, of course, the defeat devastated me just as it did all Sandinistas. Despite all the errors and the problems, I wanted us to win. But early that morning, at the Olof Palme Convention Center, Daniel's words were strangely comforting. When he said, "We're not wedded to power, we're revolutionaries who made the revolution in order to effect a change, in order to achieve a more just society . . . and since we're not wedded to power, we came in poor and we'll go out the same way." When I heard Daniel saying that, I thought to myself, "This is a historic moment, because the Party is going to come out of this stronger than before."

I thought the Party might really have learned something from the defeat. Because it's true: we made mistakes, there were people who became corrupt or took advantage of their positions, there was a certain amount of administrative disorder as well— which wasn't corruption exactly but maybe just a lack of experience, or irresponsibility. But listening to Daniel saying the things he was saying cheered me, it gave me the feeling we were moving in the right direction.

But almost immediately came the *piñata*, a real disaster![22] And, of course, the Right took full advantage of the situation. If we had a list of every single leader who was involved, we probably wouldn't have a thousand names: that's not the FSLN. But the Party has been immeasurably hurt by those who *were* dishonest. And some people still pretend that it wasn't such a big deal, including people among the leadership itself, the honest leadership. I've talked to Dora María about this—she's one of the leaders I most respect—and even she says it's true. But then she doesn't come out and say anything publicly. Maybe

22. During the Sandinista administration, most government officials hadn't bothered to legalize ownership of the houses they lived in or the cars they drove, many had simply taken over property left by Somoza and his friends when they fled the country. After the electoral defeat, then, these people had to put deeds and other proof of ownership into their own names. In the process, an indeterminate number abused their positions, signing over to themselves more than one house or including relatives and friends in the spoils. This was discovered and dubbed the "piñata," after the traditional decorated clay pot which, stuffed with candies and small toys, bursts when hit successfully by a blindfolded child, at which point all the children at the party scramble for their share. It was a situation that continues to shame honest Sandinistas, and it has been used repeatedly by the Right to characterize a party that, overall, has had a record of honesty and frugality matched by few.

she doesn't believe that what she could say would make a difference. It's the same old attitude we were talking about before, on the part of so many of the women in positions of power: they don't want to be critical because maybe it's the only way they can maintain that small quota of power that allows them to keep on working for all of us.

Since the electoral defeat, Daisy, are you saying no one is really talking about these issues?

People have talked about them. But the expectations many of us had with respect to the Party Congress were never fulfilled. It seems to me that the discussions served more to allow people to vent their frustrations than to lead us to decisions or actions that might promote real change. What change have we seen, really? Maybe you couldn't say anything to the leadership before, and now you can—and they'll listen, to a certain extent—but what difference does that make if it's not accompanied by a change in behavior? I don't see that change in behavior.

How do you envision the possibility of a different political model? Because I agree that the revolutionary project itself remains pertinent and viable. It's the model that proved itself inadequate . . .

Well, I think you and I are hopeless utopians. We embrace one utopia after another. What I see as viable today is socialism with a large dose of humanity. That is to say, if we're really going to effect social change, I believe we're going to have to start with the central issues women have placed on the agenda. I think that we women see things more clearly and that we have a great responsibility when it comes to bringing forth a new type of socialism. Not only women but the ecologists, too: all those who are genuinely concerned with creating a more humane world, those who take human beings and our habitat into account, those who take our relationship with the planet seriously.

I don't know how we're going to proceed from here. I've gotten enthusiastic about some of the gatherings we women have had, but then we're the ones with the least real power. And we all know about those women in the world who do have power but who waste and abuse it as much as any man—which is why we need to be talking about a model that crosses lines of gender, class, race; a model that embraces everyone. We need to be able to take power and also to transform it.

I was talking to some friends of mine the other day, lesbian feminists, and they were saying that the most advanced relationship is the one between two women. "We have a whole different concept of the world," they said. But I said they have to consider heterosexual women, too, those of us who have the same global concept but are also trying to recruit all those men on the other side. Because it's not easy. We women understand one another. We may come from different cultures, we may have had different life experiences; but you and I, for example, understand one another almost without words. On the other hand, the amount of explaining we have to do with our men is something that constantly wears us down . . .

Daisy, I'd like you to talk about the women's movement here and now. After the electoral defeat, what happened to Sandinista women?

Even before the electoral defeat, the women's movement here had begun to move in several different directions. There was AMNLAE, the official Sandinista women's organization, which some women had already begun to challenge: principally Sofía and Milú,[23] who were the most visible, or the most vocal. And women like María Teresa Blandón; a number of women. To be honest with you, I wasn't really a part of the movement then. Not having been at the center of the movement back then, I can't really give you many details about how it developed. But at a certain point I sat up and took notice, and then I began to participate.

When they held that huge meeting of women at the Olof Palme Convention Center, I went because I read about it in the paper. I just went on over of my own accord. Afterward, they interviewed me on the front page of *Barricada* because, they said, I was the only poet who had shown up; but the thing is, they never contacted any of the poets. I remember I used to tell Milú and Gioconda [Belli]: "There's a whole movement of women poets in this country. You should take us into account. Invite us to your meetings; we've got things to say." I don't know if you've noticed, Margaret, but my poetry has changed in recent years. As far back as '88, I was writing about waitresses and seamstresses, and those poems about our female historical figures. But I think my newer work is much more profoundly feminist.

So I think for a while we poets were overlooked by the most active feminists. But I went to that event; there were nine hundred women! And then I began talking to the other women poets. I talked to Vidaluz, to Michele,[24] and others; and they've gotten interested, too. Over the past year or so, we've been a constant presence at all the feminist activities.

But, you know, during the whole revolutionary period we poets were . . . I call it the teddy bear syndrome. It's a syndrome I've invented. But it's like with a child: when a child is tired and wants to go to bed she won't let go of her teddy bear, but then when she doesn't need it anymore she tosses it aside. As a poet, that's the feeling I used to have: when some of our leaders needed us to read a couple of poems at a cultural event or something like that, they called and invited us; but then they'd go back to ignoring us.

When I talked to the women that's what I said: "We poets have things to say. Call us, invite us, take us into account. In Nicaragua poetry has a social function. Use it." But, you know, of all the many recent books that have been written about women and the women's movement, none of them mentions this

23. Sofía Montenegro and Milú Vargas.
24. Vidaluz Meneses and Michele Najlis.

country's women writers. That's one of the reasons I put together my anthology; and when it appeared, women here were really glad to see it. They felt like it belonged to them.

I think we women who are poets suffer a double marginalization: as women and as poets. We're even overlooked by other women, though they may not realize it. I've had feminists tell me, "The thing is, you poets live on the moon." It's an attitude that situates us somewhere between the prophet and the clown. We're the continual target of comments like, "Oh, she's a poet. She can't run a house . . . or a business . . . or a political project." Or they say we're forgetful: a quality that's considered charming in a man but makes a woman ridiculous.

I'd like to have your poet's vision of that meeting of nine hundred women . . .

For me, I guess the most important thing was that so many women showed up spontaneously. When I read about it in the paper I thought I was probably one of the few who hadn't been invited. But no. Literally hundreds of women saw the event announced in the newspaper just like I did, and they came because they wanted to find out what was going on with women.

So that was refreshing. And for me the whole experience was like a ray of hope. I got to the convention center, and the first thing I did was sign up for a commission on a subject about which I knew practically nothing: the economy. I wanted to listen and learn about something new. And I found myself in a room with women from the Atlantic Coast, from remote regions of the country, peasant women, women who work on the cooperatives, factory women, engineers, economists . . . And they were all talking about the economic crisis, what they think can be done about it, but particularly what we as women might be able to do. The consensus that we women constitute a political force was something that really made an impact on me. For the first time, I found myself participating in a congress of women who were conscious of the fact that if we wanted to, and if we worked together, we could change history.

Another very positive aspect of the conference was that it wasn't at all manipulative. Most of us were familiar with the way AMNLAE works: it's a work-style in which women have always been afraid to go beyond a certain point, for fear of doing themselves in politically. And I naturally wondered whether this conference would be the same. I was hopeful, but also a bit scared that my hopes would be frustrated. And throughout the conference it really felt different, like we were able to work with a new concept of power. Maybe I'm being too enthusiastic, but it's something I felt very deeply. The women weren't being manipulative; no one had a preconceived agenda, that such and such a plan must emerge from the meeting. Now some of the women are saying that this was a mistake, that something more concrete should have come out of it all, that networks in the areas of health, education, and so forth aren't enough. But I disagree. I think it would have been premature to establish a more formal organization.

There's a great deal that still needs to be decided, of course—whether we want to consider ourselves a movement or participate as a whole other political party, whether we want to be a part of the FSLN or provide an alternative to it—and all those considerations are important. But I think discussing them at the conference would have been premature and artificial. The important thing that time around was for all of us to recognize this elemental truth: we're here, we share similar problems, and we constitute a political force. Needless to say, this political force requires its particular expression, but the majority weren't prepared at that point to decide what that expression might be. And those who had their own ideas about it were careful not to impose their point of view.

Some of the AMNLAE women showed up, but my understanding is that they came as individuals, not as representatives of the organization. The organizers of the event told me they'd originally tried to coordinate with AMNLAE but that AMNLAE hadn't responded. But since the conference I think there's been some degree of communication between AMNLAE and the movement that calls itself "The 52 Percent Majority." On the other hand, there have been discussions that have provoked certain divisions within the independent women's movement. But none of this really concerns me. I believe these are logical moments in a movement that is beginning to develop within an atmosphere of a more internalized freedom.

Then too, I think that as the networks develop they're going to create the conditions we need for an organized movement to emerge. Women are free to work in whatever network interests them. It feels good to me; there's none of that sense of imposition, of being forced into a particular mold with particular rules. And when you're involved in socially useful work—in health or education or whatever—you're also meeting other women, getting to know them, how they think, what they feel about this issue or that. And that's all very important.

Solidarity among women is important. I don't know if you remember, Margaret, an interview Angelita Saballos did with me some years ago, in which I made an irresponsible remark—I was protesting something or other and I said that "the women's movement doesn't have to be about burning bras or coming out as a lesbian." When you read it, you wrote me that letter telling me you are a lesbian and saying that you felt my comment was gratuitous. I told you then, and I'll repeat it here: that criticism was important in my development. Because it was after your letter that I became much more interested in getting to know lesbians here in Nicaragua, in finding out what they think and feel, how the lesbian feminists especially see our movement.

What I'm saying is that your loving criticism was important to me; and that's what solidarity among women is about, or at least that's one of its aspects. I feel a need to reassess my relationships with my women friends, from a feminist perspective, in a common search for what we share. I'm not talking about those friendships we always had, with their petty conversations about clothes and men . . . the competitions, the jealousies. I'm talking about strengthening and nurturing a level of basic solidarity, real communication.

The other day you commented on my having included so many of Rosario Murillo's poems in my anthology of Nicaraguan women's poetry. I know it was a joke, something about your "admiring my fairness." And other people, who know about how Rosario tried to destroy me when I was vice-minister of culture, have also commented on that; they've been amazed that I included her at all. Oscar-René says it's my professionalism, but I want to say that for me it's more than just professionalism. Giving Rosario the space her poetry deserves is a part of my overall commitment to women, demanding its rightful place for the whole phenomenon of Nicaraguan women's poetry.

That's an important clarification. Daisy, I also wanted to ask you about your daughter. She's a preadolescent now, but she was literally born with the revolution. How do you see her growing into womanhood here? Have the recent changes in particular affected her life?

Yes, they have. The revolution's loss of the government—which means the loss of public education, of a certain mystique, a whole culture—has had a profound affect on young people here. And on young women in very special ways. María Denise is twelve. We have a very good relationship, she and I; at least we have had up to now. She's entering a complicated period, of course. But it grieves me to see how society changes daily now, and how my daughter is being subjected to many of the same social pressures I felt growing up. The same old false values are back in vogue.

María Denise goes to a prestigious school, just like I did when I was young. She's at the Centroamérica, which is mixed now—girls and boys—and is where most of the well-known families send their kids. Some of them are revolutionary families; they've been here all along, but in several cases they seem to be changing their values now. And some are those who have recently returned from their self-imposed exile in Miami, people who left because they were scared of socialism or because some of their property was confiscated. I'm not even talking about counterrevolutionaries; just people with money who didn't care about what we were trying to do here and so they left the country. Now they're back, and their children are at the Centroamérica.

And what happens? It's really sad to see how even the sons and daughters of revolutionary leaders who came from bourgeois families are now once again cultivating life-styles and values typical of those families. During the revolution they professed an entirely different set of values. And there's the added pressure of those who have come back from abroad, of the cultural distortions they've brought with them. I see all this reflected in my daughter and I relive my own youth. María Denise comes home and says, "Ay, Mamá, guess where Sonia's parents took her over spring break? They went to Disney World!" Or she talks about another friend whose mother took her clothes shopping in Miami.

Miami has become the mecca once again—the fashion mecca and also the cultural prototype—for the Nicaraguan bourgeoisie. And, of course, this makes someone like my daughter feel confused. We're very close, and I'm sensitive to the opposing forces in her life. She knows we have different values, and I can tell there are times when she doesn't want to mention something that maybe means a lot to her but she thinks will hurt me.

Then we've also had other sorts of problems. Because, for example, she'll come home from school with her book bag and she'll tell the maid to put it away for her, or to get her a drink of water. And we have to remind her: "Honey, you always used to put your own things away . . . and since when do you ask people to get you a drink of water?" It's not that she acts like this when she's alone with us, it's mostly when her friends come over. I can tell she wants to put on certain airs. I've had problems myself with Oscar-René about all this, because he expects her to be consistent, to understand that we have other values and that's that. I tell him that we have to talk to her, gently; that, no, of course she mustn't act that way—not because we tell her not to, but because she herself understands that it's wrong. She's caught in a series of conflicts that are very difficult for someone her age.

And it's complicated. Because María Denise sees that in her friends' families, even families that call themselves revolutionary, things have changed. "They're Sandinistas," she says, "they're leaders of the revolution. Why do we have to be different from them?" There are so many values that I believed we were changing, profoundly, during those ten years. And I can see they didn't change at all. For example, the matter of family: what family you belong to. Those things are beginning to make a difference again, or maybe they never stopped making a difference. It's tragic that we weren't able to effect a deeper change in people's way of thinking.

It's complicated, this problem of changing values that have been around for generations. And ten years is a pretty short time, especially when the ideological work was neither unified nor particularly thorough. I know how difficult it can be to deal with this with your children. How has all this affected your poetry, Daisy? Has it been more or less difficult for you to write during this period? And have you written about issues that didn't appear in your work before?

Well, I don't know if this is true for all writers, but in my case what I write is always a reflection of what's going on in my life. My first and second books of poetry were very different from one another, and the poems I'm writing now are very different again. Ernesto was talking about this with me recently. He said he reads a great many poets where there's an evolution, of course, but you can always tell it's the same poet, throughout his or her life. But, he said, in my case he reads my work from different periods and it's as if he's reading another poet entirely. I think my work depends to a very great extent on what's going on in my life.

And problems call forth the muse within me. Maybe an absence of problems, a life without conflict, would silence me. But what happens is that when I'm working my way through problems, at the most intense times, I tend not to write. It's when I've digested those problems, when there's some distance, that they show up in my work. For example, when my baby died . . . or the problem René Alberto had when he was born . . . those were traumatic experiences, but I was able to assimilate them later and then to write out of them.[25]

I remember with René Alberto's birth, Ernesto came to see me at the hospital. He was one of the first of my friends who showed up—he'd heard about what happened—and he told me, "I know you're going to make something worthwhile out of this; it will become a poem." And I remember thinking to myself, "What a terrible thing, telling me I'll get a poem out of this." But he knows me. Because this is the type of thing many of my poems are about. It's not something we can choose: our own particular demons as well as those things which most nourish us are what inform our creativity. If I lived one of those tranquil, boring lives, I might not write at all.

Those ten years of revolution helped me grow. That's a good thing, when adversity helps a person become stronger. And, of course, those ten years introduced us all to new forms of solidarity and hope. One of my greatest joys is that I was able to find that solidarity and hope among those closest to me, my sisters in struggle. I'm warmed by the fact that women are among those most clearly able to envision change. We may not know at this moment exactly where we need to go. But I feel I am a part of this movement that's growing and spreading.

And this movement is also important because of the hope it represents to thousands of women in this country who are hit hardest by the electoral loss. The extreme Right and the institutional Catholic Church have promoted a return to the most archaic values. And the economic crisis is also critical. More than 34 percent of all Nicaraguan families are headed by women, and 70.1 percent of those families live in poverty.[26] You know, we're only 4.1 million Nicaraguans, and it's estimated that 70 percent of the population is poor. And, of course, the tendency is that we grow ever more impoverished, especially with the massive unemployment we've had over the past two years. Obviously, it's women who are most affected.

In your own work you've talked about stages: working-class women in the United States in the early years of this century, the movement of the late sixties, early seventies. But I feel that we're making a qualitative leap right now—because we women are conscious that we're not struggling for ourselves alone; we're struggling for men as well, and for our children, for all of humanity. And we've got a holistic vision of change.

What hurts is seeing my daughter, who could be reaping the harvest of all this that's cost me so much—so much experience bringing me to where I am now—what hurts is having to watch her pick up on so many of the values I left behind. When I'm most conscious of this, it's almost as if we're back where we started from. You can't imagine how it moves me, what a terrible tenderness it evokes in me, when I see her competing with one of her friends—

25. René Alberto is Daisy's and Oscar-René's youngest son, who was born with a cleft palate.
26. Daisy cites data that are close to, but may not be exactly the same as, other figures in this book.

because she considers her prettier, or her body is more . . . whatever. That competition for attention from the boys: all those things that I experienced and hoped she would never have to go through, or at least that she would experience them differently, from a different perspective.

I frequently write letters to my daughter. And she reads them. Often she doesn't respond immediately. Sometimes she hardly comments on them. But the days pass and I can tell that she's thinking about what I've written, that she's reflecting upon it. Or maybe she'll ask me a question or two.

I think we have to fight against these conflicts wearing us down. Because sometimes I feel myself becoming utterly exasperated; I get impatient having to struggle against the same thing over and over. Sometimes I come back here to this library by myself, and I sit in this very chair, in the dark. Everything is still and then I meditate; it renews my feeling that all of this is part of life. That's why I like that line of Manuel Bandeira: "uma agitação feroz e sem finalidade."[27] I often feel like that.

We hadn't turned on a light, and outside the library window it had been raining for a while, a daily event this time of year. The tropical sky filtered dark through palms, large banana leaves, and other thick vegetation shading the adjacent patio. We were both silent for a while, thinking about the poet's words. Then I told Daisy I'd like to end our interview with one of her most recent poems. She calls it "Lineage," and it speaks powerfully of this moment on her journey. It also reflects the idea with which she began this interview, that of retrieving and exalting the important women in her life:

Lineage

I am looking for the women of my house.

I've always known my great-grandfather's story:
scientist, diplomat, Liberal politician
and father of many distinguished sons.

But Isolina Reyes, married to him
from the age of fifteen until her death,
what story could she have told?

My maternal grandfather graduated cum laude
from the University of Philadelphia.
We still preserve his dissertation written in 1900.
He oversaw the construction of miles of railway
and only a sudden death cut short his dream
of opening up the Atlantic Coast.
Nine sons and daughters mourned him.

---

27. Manuel Bandeira (1886–1968) was a Brazilian poet. The line Daisy quotes means "Life is an endless ferocious movement."

And his wife Rudecinda, who gave birth
to those children, who nursed and cared for them,
what do I know of her?

I am looking for the women of my house.

My other grandfather was the patriarch
beneath whose shadow the whole family lived
(including brothers-in-law, cousins, distant relatives,
friends, acquaintances, and even enemies).
He spent his life accumulating the fortune
they wasted when he died.

And my grandmother Ilse, widowed and impoverished,
what could she do but die?

I am looking for myself, for all of them:
the women of my house.

"Our Experience in the FSLN Is What Gives Us This Strength"

Milú Vargas

Milucita:

The earth turns, life goes on, years pass, days pass, hours are lived and minutes flow like water. When I pronounce your name I want to say so many different things! And here I am, pondering each new image with which I might open my handful of surprises to delight your eyes. It's May, love. Let me give you this hand of mine, writing your name in the sky. I adore you!

C.N.T.

This is one of dozens, perhaps hundreds, of little notes scrawled hurriedly on scraps of paper, signed with first name or initials, and passed from Comandante *Carlos Núñez Téllez to his wife and comrade Milú Vargas over the almost ten years they were together. She keeps them all. Theirs was a relationship born in conflict, and never entirely free of moralistic attack. They both fought hard to set a new standard of equality in a context that, increasingly, prioritized public policy over the revolution within. And when Carlos Núñez died unexpectedly in October 1990, Milú Vargas was left with profound personal loss as well as with a legacy that richly complements her own extraordinary life.*

When I interviewed her for this book Milú was fully back into her daily rhythm: a demanding work schedule, a dozen different projects in hand. The Carlos Núñez Téllez Center for Constitutional Rights, which she founded following the Sandinistas' electoral defeat, was up and running. At a forum held at the Jesuit university only days before, I had heard her speak with brilliance and passion against the country's recently instituted antisodomy law. The attorney, the organizer, the political militant seemed like her old self again. But Milú the woman was just beginning to emerge from overwhelming grief.

I met Milú Vargas for the first time in 1982. She was then chief legal counsel to Nicaragua's Council of State, the one-chamber legislative body inaugurated just after the Sandinistas took power. In her small office on the second floor of the Senate building, we talked about women's rights. I remember Milú launching unabashedly into a discussion of the urgent need to legalize abortion, to address violence against women as a growing social concern, and to deal with other issues that at the time were hardly considered priorities. Priorities? Mostly they weren't even mentioned. The Contra war was beginning to seriously threaten the young revolution back then; everything else was secondary.

But these issues were never secondary to Milú; not then and certainly not now. In the early 1980s, when the Sandinista dream was still new, this woman, slight and wiry, with red hair, dancing eyes and prominent freckles, leaned across her cluttered desk and spoke excitedly about the day AMNLAE's representative and the delegate from the FSLN had argued with one another on the Council floor. The question had been whether or not the recently instituted compulsory draft should be extended to women. Milú, long a champion of women's rights, agreed with the women's organization that the draft must not discriminate against them. It was a rare dispute between the Party and its female arm. The Party, of course, won.

A great deal has happened since then. The years from 1982 to 1992 bridge the change to conservative government as well as the decade of revolution in power. These dates also bracket the period in which the United States eventually managed to push the Sandinistas to positions that would lose them state power—and in which the FSLN itself became more entrenched in sexist practices, eventually alienating some of its female support. Throughout, Milú has nurtured a steadfast feminist vision, a position from which she can see what went wrong as well as understand Sandinism's extraordinary potential for change—by no means exhausted, even now.

When we first met, rumor already had it that she and Comandante Carlos Núñez Téllez *were seeing one another. He was estranged but not yet divorced from his previous wife, and in this overwhelmingly Catholic country the new relationship was tinged with scandal. Ten years later, Milú is recovering from early widowhood. She and the man who was certainly the most open, the most feminist, the most forward-looking of the FSLN's leadership remained a couple until his death.*

We sat at a simple round wooden table on the back veranda of the home they shared. A large garden, with a profusion of tropical trees and plants, spread out before us. Behind, the walls of a formal living room were crowded with paintings, mostly by Nicaraguan contemporaries: Julia Agüirre, June Beir, Roger Pérez de la Rocha, Leoncio Sáenz. An exercise bike in that same large room and a rowing machine in one corner of the dining room didn't surprise me, given Milú's lithe, muscular body: not an ounce of fat. A Pekingese darted here and there, staking out her territory.

Milú has been involved in women's struggles for most of her life. She was one of the founders of AMPRONAC, back in 1977. She remained on the national executive of AMNLAE until she and other feminists no longer felt they could work within the organization. To the important process of writing her country's Constitution she brought a consistent defense of women's rights. As a child, her father had established a family atmosphere where women's equality was respected; as an adult, she insisted that her comandante husband be responsible for half their household management.

From a bourgeois, intellectual, and political home, Milú started out with dreams of becoming a dancer; she ended up an attorney. She studied law at the Jesuit-run Central American University, in Managua, and received a graduate degree in constitutional law at the University of Pittsburgh. Recently, when asked how she felt about being called a feminist, Milú responded to a local reporter: "It's one of the best things people can say about me. In my view, being a feminist means struggling for equal rights for everyone, and that's good for men as well as women."[1]

A few days before our interview, I attended that forum at the Jesuit university where I heard Milú tell the audience that the antisodomy law, just passed in the National Assembly, offended her personal freedom "to choose a lesbian life-style in the future, if I wish." There, too, I picked up a copy of her newly published treatise on violence against women. Both because she is a public defender of women's rights and because I know her to be a woman of profoundly held feminist convictions, speaking with her for this book seemed particularly important. Now we faced one another, two cups of steaming herb tea on the table between us. Milú's enthusiasm and dynamism are contagious.

"There's so much I want to know," I began. "Your experience with the legal aspects of the Council of State, the process of writing the Constitution, your own immersion in the revolutionary movement, your views on the women's movement here, your life with Carlos . . . I guess it would make sense for you to begin by telling me something about your origins. What kind of a family do you come from? Tell me something about your early years . . .

Well, you know, I come from a Conservative family; and in Nicaragua that means the Conservative Party, longtime opposition to Somoza. But it was also a traditional family, traditional in its composition: father, mother, kids. I'm the fourth, the youngest after three older brothers; but much later, ten years later, there were two more children. At any rate, I was the youngest for quite a while.

Then, at a certain point, we were no longer a traditional family. My mother died when I was seven. My father actually became a widower twice, and each

---

1. Interview with Mildred Largaespada, *Gente* (Managua), 2, no. 54 (January 1, 1991).

time he married again. I used to hear him refer to "my kids, your kids, and our kids," meaning his own children, his wife's children, and the children born to both of them. Losing my mother at such an early age left a void in my life; it was the first of what would be a series of terrible losses. But, growing up, my father was definitely my strongest influence. I've often said that he was forced to be a sort of MaPa, mother and father in one.

Ours was a very political home. We breathed and ate and talked politics every day. Lunch always meant a political discussion. As a member of the Conservative Party, my father was solidly opposed to Somoza. And he was a lawyer, prominent professionally as well as politically. As my brothers grew, they and my father talked politics more and more; and when I was old enough I took part in these conversations, too. We were always discussing what was going on in the country.

For example, my earliest memories of Somoza's National Guard are very vivid. In 1956—I was five years old—a young man named Rigoberto López Pérez shot Somoza García. Somoza's son ordered the guard to round up all the prominent political opposition in the country; they were looking for anyone who may have had anything to do with what happened. They tortured these suspects, interrogated them, what have you. And, of course, among that political opposition was my father. My mother had urged my father to go into hiding, so he wasn't actually at home when they came looking for him. But I'll never forget the guard that day: stomping around our house, throwing things on the floor, searching through everything.

Later, my most immediate political sources were my brothers. My oldest brother, Gustavo Adolfo, was involved in the student movement Juventud Patriótica and, later on, in the FSLN during its early days. My brother Oscar-René was also a student leader and participated in the founding of the Front. I followed in their footsteps. And then, of course, there was the school I went to, because I'm another one of your La Asunción women.

Mine was pretty much the usual life of a young girl of my social class and culture: I'd go to school, come home, maybe visit a friend, attend the parties people gave. But there was this one sister at La Asunción—Mother Mireille was her name, she was a French nun—and she began taking us to teach catechism classes in one of the poor neighborhoods down by the lake. In those days it was called La Tejera. That was my initiation into the reality that something was really wrong here, because the people in that neighborhood lived in subhuman conditions. They ate garbage, none of the men had work, the children's bellies were swollen with parasites, the women were battered and downtrodden.

That experience made me think. Here I was, living in such happiness and order, and there were these other people living like that. And I began to ask myself what difference it could possibly make to them that I came down there to teach about the Trinity, about "the one true God." What difference could those catechism classes make in their lives? "Father, Son, and Holy Ghost," I'd tell them, and they'd just sit there staring back at me. As young as I was, I understood that with those kinds of problems this sort of teaching was senseless. I was sixteen then. We're talking about 1965, before Vatican II.

I was upset, and I began talking to my father about all this. I remember I whispered when I said these things, because my brothers teased me about my concerns. I'd pray for the poor, and my brothers would make fun of my prayers. I'd ask my father what we were going to do to change the way things were, and he said it wasn't enough to pray. My father said that when Jesus told us to love your neighbor as yourself, it meant wanting for others what you yourself had, in very concrete terms.

I tried to find others who felt like me. And so I explored the Christian base communities, the Christian life groups, and talked to other young people in my social set. And I participated in activities with those Christian youths until I got to college, to the Central American University, which is run by Jesuits here. I started college in 1969/70, and almost immediately a guy named Alejandro Gutiérrez, who was a member of the FSLN, asked me if I wanted to join.

I was ready. Alejandro didn't have to do a lot to convince me. I'd been looking for an alternative for a while. I studied law and I began to take part in the student movement; they elected me class representative my first year. That's how I started with the takeovers of the churches, the street demonstrations, the congresses, and all the rest. By this time, my brothers had been forced into exile. So I was on my own.

Of course, one is influenced by a number of different people in one's life. I was certainly influenced by that nun, who by the way is still alive and still fighting for the poor in her own way. She's a very old woman and she's never stopped struggling for what she knows is right. My brothers were also an influence in my life. My father, as I've said, was probably my greatest influence. In his last years he was a parliamentarian from the Conservative Party; he was very progressive. And he was always very respectful of his children's political views, even when it was hard for him to respect our differences.

You know, he often told us how hard it was for him to respect our views. Because not a single one of us made the same choices he did. Sometimes he'd ask me, "Why did all of you have to take this road?" And I'd tell him we're the products of his contradictions. On the one hand, we lived this comfortable life that he provided, but with a certain political participation. On the other, he taught us a set of principles: he always talked to us about loving others, about having a social conscience, moral values, the ability to transcend one's personal situation and think about the larger picture, about what was going on in the country. And he was also able to respect the choices we made, and to accept the consequences of those choices.

Milú, how was it for you as a female growing up in your father's home? It's clear from what you say that you enjoyed a political respect, but what about your role as a woman—particularly as your mother died so early? What was expected of you in what must have become a very male-oriented home, as opposed to what was expected of your brothers?

You know, I'm really not that conscious of the nuances of what that was like, because I didn't really acquire an awareness of sexism until around 1974.

By that time I was twenty-four. My real gender consciousness came with my first marriage. But I can tell you that as a child, and growing up in the household I did, I had the sense that my father treated us all the same. And he always spoke eloquently about women. I even remember feeling a bit superior because my brothers had to serve me: in my childhood home, women enjoyed a privileged position. My father always said that women should be treated with special attention.

That in itself was a kind of subtle sexism, a kind of discrimination if you like, though of the more positive variety. My father would talk about women as givers of life; everyone of us is born of a woman, he would say, and therefore we deserved the respect and attention of men. But he went further than that. My brother Oscar-René was my playmate, we'd swim and compete together in swimming meets; and when he'd win, my father always told me that I could be as good as my brother. All I needed to do was try harder.

I remember going into the student movement believing I was as capable as any of the guys. And the same with the university. Of course, I noticed how few we women were; but my father always said that was because women in general were being educated for marriage, and he'd stress how important he thought it was for us to be independent. He'd always tell me, "Don't get married until you can take care of yourself." He'd say that without economic independence there *is* no independence for women, and he insisted that he was the only man we'd ever depend upon economically who wasn't going to ask for anything in return. It's pretty amazing when I think about it now.

At the university I was an excellent student, better than many of the men. Right away, as a freshman, I was elected class representative. So I didn't feel discriminated against, not until I married. It was in my first marriage that I really became conscious of gender discrimination. I made the mistake of thinking that things with my husband would be like they'd been with my father.

As you might imagine, we had servants in my father's house; but they had their days off, and then my father distributed the household chores among us all, himself included. And he didn't distribute them according to sex. I have plenty of memories of my father sweeping, mopping the floors, going to the market for food; and of my brothers doing those things as well. And I guess I grew up thinking that that's the way it was in every family.

But my marriage changed all that. Carlos—that was my first husband's name, too—was in government. He was minister of transportation first, then vice-minister of finances. Later he was in the army, a lieutenant colonel and chief of the rear guard. It was during that marriage that we went to the United States for a year and I did my postgraduate work at Pittsburgh. While my husband and I were in the States, we more or less shared the household chores, depending upon who had the most time. But when we returned to Nicaragua in 1974, that was when things changed.

I began to notice that my husband had certain expectations of me. He wanted me to be your typical housewife, overseeing our homelife, taking charge of all the usual domestic tasks. By that time I also had my daughter Denise. And my husband didn't want me to work; he thought I should stay home, be a mother, take care of the house. He'd ask me where his tennis shoes were, and I wouldn't have the faintest idea; and, you know, I just never thought I had an obligation to keep track of his tennis shoes. I'd been brought up to believe that each of us is responsible for our own things.

That's where the problems began, the conflicts. And I didn't consider them my problems alone. We both had problems. We just had different visions of male and female roles, so we separated and eventually were divorced. But it was an amicable divorce because we both realized that we'd had a different set of expectations. We respected and cared for one another, but we understood that I wasn't the type of woman he needed and he wasn't the type of man I need either.

Around the same time that I began to experience this discrimination in my relationship I also started having problems in my professional life. I became a lawyer in 1975. I went to work at the law office where my father had been a partner. The two remaining partners were old friends of his, Somarriba and Medina. In fact, all the lawyers in that office were men; and they all had twelve to fifteen years of experience, much more than I. I'm pretty sure they hired me there because of my father; he'd recently died.

I was twenty-four, twenty-five years old at the time. And as I say, I was the only woman lawyer in the firm. Of course, I began to notice the sexism that was simply habitual among the men. Even on the part of the male clients: they tended to treat me as a sexual object, while they treated the other lawyers as equals. For a couple of years I was constantly upset: upset in my marriage and upset on the job. My political life had become somewhat sporadic, support work rather than full-time militancy, and I was beginning to feel more and more alienated both in my relationship and in my profession. I felt terribly alone. It was a very difficult period.

All that changed in 1977, when the FSLN founded the first successful women's organization. Personally as well as politically, AMPRONAC came along at exactly the right time for me. I remember it was Lea Guido, Nora Astorga, and a few others who got the group going. It was Lea who came looking for me to ask if I wanted to join them in launching a women's organization. For the first time, I was able to talk to other women about what I was feeling, other women who shared my politics and who were experiencing the same sort of discrimination.

I remember it as a tremendous relief, the first time my political work seemed intimately linked to what I was going through personally. And the political became personal because our area of struggle within the Front provided connections in that respect. My participation in AMPRONAC marked an important shift in the direction of my political work, and I've never stopped working with women.

I can understand that your experience with AMPRONAC must have been important, and that working with AMNLAE also provided the space for a developing feminist consciousness, even with the problems that have existed within that organization. But what about the FSLN? What's it been like for you as a feminist militant in the Party?

I'll tell you something, Margaret. And this is the first time I've spoken about this publicly. In 1980, not long after our victory against the dictatorship, Carlos Núñez and I fell in love. And our relationship didn't begin on an easy footing. You'll remember the processes back then through which those of us who had been part of the struggle officially acquired our membership in the FSLN. The first induction included the top leadership, the national directorate and a number of other men and women. There was no question about them. But then came the process leading up to the second induction. I was being considered for membership, and that coincided with the beginning of my relationship with Carlos.

The duo—two men—charged with looking into my background, and at the qualities that might make me membership material, also looked at this relationship which was with a married man. Carlos was estranged from his first wife, but they were still legally married. And, of course, I was the one being questioned, not Carlos. It was clear enough what this was about: Carlos was a man and he had power. I was a woman, and didn't.

When I told Carlos what was going on he was furious, of course, and his immediate reaction was to try to protect me. He was upset because this was happening to the woman he loved; he wanted to go right out and "fix it." But I wouldn't let him. I told him that if he spoke to anyone about this, if he used his influence in any way, our relationship was over; because I'd leave. I explained that I was determined to go through this ordeal like any other woman being considered for membership in the FSLN.

This macho mentality had hurt many women, of course. And I felt I had an advantage because I was willing to fight—for myself and for them. I wanted to take what I saw as an unfair decision and lodge a protest, carry it to its logical conclusion. And I hoped to set a precedent so that women wouldn't have to suffer indignities like this in the future. Carlos thought about what I was saying, and he realized I was right.

That whole process around my being denied Party membership lasted several years. It was very important for our relationship. It allowed us to discuss a great many aspects of gender discrimination that otherwise we might not have been able to tackle. And it consolidated our understanding of two issues that remained constants in our dialogue throughout the years we were together: discrimination and power. Carlos read a lot, of course; but it was through experiencing situations like this one, with people he loved, that he came to understand how power could be misused and what discrimination really meant. Not just with me, but with other women comrades as well. Carlos became a real ally in feminist struggles.

Understanding issues of power and discrimination isn't just important in terms of gender equality. I think it's essential to changing society as a whole . . .

You know, I think a central problem with this sort of thing is when you begin to separate the private and public spheres, to make different rules for each. We tend to look at our political leaders one way in terms of their public image and quite another in the context of their private lives. We forget it's the same person. And so there's a problem of coherence. The richness of multi-layered experience is lacking. When we think of revolution only in terms of economics, agrarian reform, literacy, state-controlled industry and the rest, when we think of revolution only in terms of external and not internal change, I think we fail to go as deeply as we must.

And the Party never adequately addressed the political aspects of so-called private conduct. We never reflected on this, not collectively in any case. Personal conduct was seen in a moralistic way, if it was seen at all, and that was a big mistake. Because change comes about only as a result of perceived necessity. If we recognize our need to have more complete relationships, a fuller and more integrated life, that's what pushes us to change.

And it's not just women who gain from this change; men gain, too. Patriarchal attitudes also deny men important possibilities in life: the expression of their feelings, the relief at not always having to be "the strong one." Men are conditioned to feel that they have to provide the answer to every problem; they're not permitted to feel weak. We're all products of the education we receive, and of the ideology which that education promotes. We need to do some serious thinking about this.

I don't believe there's any such thing as a good Party member who mistreats his wife at home. And, of course, this isn't uncommon within the FSLN: we have plenty of men who do excellent jobs in their public political life but who have very abusive relations with their wives and children. It's this kind of thing that's brought a great many of us women within the Front to the conclusion that, in this area at least, our Party isn't giving us the answers we need. These issues just haven't been on the agenda.

Are they on the agenda now?

No, they're not on the agenda yet. Not really.

Tell me more about the process through which you eventually did arrive at your militancy. You left that story in the middle . . .

It was a complicated process. One day they called me to meet with my base committee, which is the group that handles the preliminary evaluation. They told me I had all these excellent qualities, that the evaluation had been satisfactory on all counts except that, well, these two comrades considered it a problem that I was having a relationship with Carlos, a married man. They said that since Carlos was a member of the national directorate and president of the

National Assembly, they thought I was with him as a way of acquiring power. When they concluded that phase of the process, I wasn't granted my membership.

Then they called me before the Party sectional for state workers. I had a job with the state at the time, so that was the board designated to hear my case. That's when they accused me of "not protecting the image of a comandante." I remember I asked them who was protecting *my* image, and they didn't have an answer for that. It was 1982. I refused either to confirm or deny that I was having a relationship with Carlos. I told them to ask Carlos if they were so interested in knowing. I knew they wouldn't dare do that, and of course they didn't.

From there the thing went on up to the next level. I wasn't present at that hearing, but I heard that Mónica Baltodano and Sergio Ramírez both said they weren't going to stand for a woman being judged in that way. Nevertheless, my case seemed stuck at that point. There may have been other discussions— I'm giving you a synthesis—but the fact is that it took them a long long time to give me my Party membership. It was some four years later that they finally called me in and gave me my card. And don't think I took it as calmly as I'm telling it to you now. Back then, it hurt a lot. Because, you know, I'd look at the other members of my generation, with their cards and their little lapel pins, and it all seemed much more important than it does now.

Still, that experience helped me through my own process surrounding all this. I remember telling Carlos I was willing to pay the price for what I was doing, and that my feminist consciousness helped me internalize an ideological position. Comandante Bayardo Arce was also very supportive. He knew me from my days in the student movement; he respected me and tried to help. But I had to tell him also that I didn't want that kind of help. I needed to go through this on my own.

I remember Comandante Arce calling me in one day and telling me that I was a stubborn woman, that it just didn't make sense, that I deserved my Party card and why didn't I just let them give it to me and be done with all this nonsense? But I stuck to my decision to see the process through on my own. And Carlos was right there beside me. In fact, he got to the point where he said that there are militants and there are "militants." If I made concessions just to get my card, he said, that would be the day I'd stop being a true militant. We agreed that a real Party member has to stick to what she or he believes in and fight for what's right, with or without official recognition.

These discussions Carlos and I had, which were very important in our relationship, are reflected in a poem he wrote to me. It's called "To a Militant without a Card." I remember telling Carlos that the only thing I wanted him to promise me was that if I died, if I were killed or died somehow while this process was still going on, he wouldn't let them make me a Party member posthumously. Because when you die, you know, everyone suddenly thinks you were perfect. He promised, and that's when he told me that if things turned out that way he'd put an epitaph on my tombstone: "Milú Vargas: Militant without a Card."

Milú, why do you think no woman has made it to the highest echelons of Party leadership? Women have played such important roles in the struggle here, and within the FSLN. Why has it been impossible for the national directorate to accept even one woman member?

Well, in the first place, because the Sandinist National Liberation Front is a sexist party. The failure to allow a woman onto the directorate is a reflection of the Party as a whole in this respect. The FSLN is a party that's been open to women's participation, and a great many women have risen to positions of importance in its ranks; the Party has taken official note of women's participation, but it's not yet a party that recognizes the need for women's full representation at all levels. Here in Nicaragua, ours is the most advanced political party in terms of female participation: at the grass roots, tremendous numbers of women are taking part. It might even be the least sexist party in Latin America. But it's certainly not a party of real equality, not yet.

Concretely, I think the failure at last year's Congress to elect Dora María to the national directorate can be traced to two factors: discrimination against women and an undemocratic electoral process. I was secretary of the electoral commission. And, you know, in any election the rules you follow are fundamental. There were basically two positions there: the traditionalists, who wanted to vote for a previously chosen slate, and others of us who wanted to vote for individuals. If we'd voted for individuals—casting our votes for nine separate people, and the nine with the most votes would make up the new directorate—I think we might have had one or even several women members. But the preselected-slate position won out. And that decided everything; it sealed the outcome.

The Party leadership had already agreed that the seven members of the old directorate plus René Núñez and Sergio Ramírez would make up the new governing body. Once that was accepted, we didn't have a chance. I'll tell you something else, and this isn't hearsay. It's something I can vouch for because I was there and I heard the discussions: there were those who said that nominating Dora María Téllez was "a feminist plan to divide the directorate!" There was a real campaign to take prestige away from Dora María. They called her a lesbian, even on the radio.

So that's the kind of thing that was going on. Certainly gender discrimination played an important part in the outcome—with that old patriarchal fear of a feminist position. Because outside the Olof Palme Convention Center there were demonstrations, groups of women from Managua in support of Dora María's candidacy. And, of course, there were men who just couldn't take that. Maybe they thought they should have been elected, but they were afraid to put themselves forward as candidates, and the thought of a woman candidate was just something they couldn't handle.

Inside the Congress, women and young people generally supported the alternative position. But, of course, we were in the minority. On the other hand, the fact that the discussion took place at all, out in the open like it did, was a step forward in my opinion. The discussion was very important.

What do you think about the next Party Congress? Do you think there's a chance there'll be a woman elected to the national directorate then?

Well, we'll have to see if women are even interested by that time. This whole thing provoked such a public discussion that Comandante Daniel Ortega, in his closing speech, was forced to promise a place for a woman the next time around; he had to commit himself to that. But I'm not at all sure that's what we women want, at least those of us who have done some reflecting on the matter, because we have to ask ourselves whether their Party model even represents our interests at this point.

We'd have to ask a number of questions. What would it cost us to have a woman on the directorate? What benefits would accrue? What degree of representation would we find satisfactory? In recent years, at least, we've seen that the struggle for change is reflected much more honestly and fully in the mass organizations than in the Party per se. So I think we'd have to analyze whether or not we want to invest a lot of time and energy in campaigning for female candidates to the national directorate. We women ourselves haven't really discussed this, so I honestly don't know.

The important thing is the overall struggle. We know that women's participation in the mixed organizations is important, and that means it's important at absolutely every level. And, of course, the FSLN is the party we have, at least at the moment. In that sense, yes, I suppose it's important that women serve on the directorate.

Would you talk about the electoral defeat?

I think our electoral defeat can be traced to several basic problems. There's no question but that women wanted an end to the war. All the women of my generation or older had sons in the military. A vote against us seemed like a vote to bring those sons back from the front lines; because there was the generalized feeling that with the FSLN in power the United States would continue to wage its war against Nicaragua. And, of course, the economic situation took its toll. We'd already had to take austere economic measures here. In 1989 alone, thirty-five thousand state workers lost their jobs. It's true that we had occupational conversion plans, because those workers were given the option of going to work on farming cooperatives, that sort of thing. But all that affected the election.

On the other hand, I don't think our campaign prioritized the right issues. Take women and young people: prioritizing the issues important to those sectors doesn't just mean holding meetings every once in a while and asking a few perfunctory questions. It's important how you communicate. The FSLN should have been capable of understanding how women here really felt about the policies that were being imposed.

I was head of the women's secretariat of the organization of professionals,

CONAPRO, at the time.[2] We had our own campaign to empower women, and we ran a hundred workshops in which we trained ten thousand women throughout Managua and in some of the departments. One of the themes was "Women's Political Rights." We didn't tell them to vote for the FSLN; we gave them some basic information so they would know they had the right to vote for whomever they believed would best represent them. And we taught "Women and Political Parties: The Electoral Platforms." We'd analyze each party's platform and what it said to women specifically. It was clear that the platform which offered most to women was the one put forth by the FSLN. But we were the only organization that ran this kind of workshop.

Ten thousand women reflecting together in an atmosphere that encouraged them to figure out what they thought and to speak their minds: it was extraordinary. But in the national context it was a drop in the bucket; I mean, it just wasn't enough. For those women politics meant the state, the people at the top. Over and over again they'd say, "That stuff doesn't have anything to do with me." To get a working-class woman to understand that politics could be a part of her life, you had to explain things, get an honest discussion going, find out what she really wanted. What was her idea of a government that served her needs? What were her needs in the first place?

What I'm saying is that the FSLN's electoral campaign wasn't aimed at ordinary women; it didn't speak to their experience, to their way of looking at the world. Anti-imperialism is fine, but there wasn't the slightest attention to the problems women face every day: physical abuse, rape, family planning, job training, relationships, access to leadership positions, difficulties with their children. These are the important issues for women, and we didn't even touch on them. As a Party, our discourse was much too general. It wasn't aimed at any particular sector because we didn't really listen to what people were saying.

These are some of the things I think we have to consider before we launch another campaign in the future. And the women candidates themselves: who among them was given the sort of public exposure we gave the men? It wasn't until the very end of the campaign, January I think it was, that we produced a few T-shirts with images of some of the women candidates. And at the public meetings it was always the men who gave the main speeches; the women remained on the sidelines. And the male candidates never addressed those problems which are central to women's lives.

I even remember one day, in the Fourth Region I think it was, I heard one of the women candidates saying: "Here come the men. They're going right up on the truck. And we women candidates are down below, on foot." That's the kind of thing that just can't happen again, the next time around, not if we're interested in the female vote.

Another thing was the type of publicity we produced. While the opposition presented Doña Violeta as this gentle soul, with her simple language—people

2. CONAPRO is the Confederación Nacional de Profesionales, the National Confederation of Professional People.

laughed, if you please, when she'd make those grammatical mistakes: "with me or unwith me," she'd say[3]—but it got people's attention. It was sweet, accessible, very much a popular language. And she'd dress in white, all virginal, with her arms outstretched like the pope, and talking about "my children." Laugh if you like, but people who were hurting were comforted by that maternal image.

Meanwhile we used a slogan that in our culture is tremendously warlike: *El Gallo Ennavajado* [The Cock with His Fighting Blade]. The fighting cock represents a fight to the finish, in which one or the other of the opponents inevitably dies. The image evokes blood, and it's also tremendously sexist. I heard women saying things like: "What do I want another cock for? I've got as much cock as I can handle at home!" And the worst is, when the whole thing was over and we sat down to analyze what went wrong, there were still a great many in the leadership who couldn't see it. They said, "That's a feminist critique. That has nothing to do with what the people really think."

The saddest part of the whole thing is, I don't think we can say we've engaged in any really deep analysis about what happened. Not yet. The men continue to say, "Oh, you're an intellectual, a feminist intellectual. You don't know what ordinary women feel." But, of course, ordinary women aren't going to express their feelings to them. They're not going to stand up in an assembly that's rigged for a certain model of behavior and say what they feel. Their feelings come out when they're talking to us and in a particular type of setting—in a workshop that lasts for two days, for example—with some attention to group dynamics, where they feel safe enough to let their hair down.

Milú, with all your experience, did the electoral defeat surprise you?

Of course it did. Because in spite of everything I've said, in spite of all the criticisms—which we did voice during the campaign itself—we were still absolutely sure we were going to win. I was sure of it. The alternative was unthinkable. So unthinkable in fact, that the UNO people themselves didn't even imagine they would win! Here the winners as well as the losers were products of overconfident attitudes. They were overconfident that they were going to lose, and we were overconfident that we were going to win. They didn't prepare for victory any more than we prepared for defeat.

Our loss and their victory caught everyone by surprise. Understanding and assimilating what's happened has been a learning experience for both sides, and for the FSLN I think there are a lot of lessons to be learned from all this. For the next elections or the next whatever, it just can't be that small group at the top believing it knows what's best, designing the campaign, making all the decisions. We've got to process other types of information, really listen to the different sectors, take them into account. And we need a discourse that addresses people's needs, one that's not so general, so superficial.

---

3. In Spanish, "conmigo o sinmigo."

But you say there hasn't been any real analysis of all this?

No, there hasn't been. Not yet. Oh we've discussed a few of the issues, there's been some criticism. But if you understand that this kind of error didn't begin with the electoral campaign, that this situation comes out of an increasingly worse separation of leadership from ordinary people over a period of years leading up to the elections—affluent life-styles, authoritarian attitudes, that type of thing—then you know it's not a matter of criticizing a slogan or two. We still need to go through a process of understanding how things got so bad. And we need to open up the Party structures to a more democratic discussion.

Milú, could you talk about the feminist movement here, what women are doing and how the events of the past couple of years have affected women's organizing?

I see an explosion of women's energy, ideas, organizational abilities—including many women who once held leadership positions within the FSLN, who mouthed the official line—taking on certain responsibilities, trying to fit ourselves into the mold of a single organization. The process began back in 1987. I think that was when women began to see things more clearly, to realize we had important differences with the official line. And sometime in 1990 we began to see the results of that process.

Yes, the discussion began in 1987, within the different sectors. For example, I was one of the professional women and we began to talk about these issues; but women farm workers also began to talk, and women in the labor unions, health workers, teachers. We all started talking to one another about the need to change AMNLAE; none of us felt that the organization spoke to our deepest needs. We began to ask ourselves why we didn't have a movement capable of addressing those needs—within the sectors—and we also began talking about what we had in common.

The common thread included concerns about motherhood, abortion, family planning, abuse, rape, and labor laws aimed at dealing with the widespread discrimination against women. And these issues were seen differently by women in the different sectors. In other words, any one of these issues might be treated differently by a teacher than by a farm worker or a lawyer. They were issues common to all our lives, but we needed to address them according to who and where we were. We were tired of getting the same old set of guidelines as if we were all the same.

This discontent began to be articulated in 1987, and we all grew through struggle. We grew through discussion, up against the general inability to understand our needs within the FSLN and within AMNLAE. Finally, in 1990, we simply came out in defense of our differences. We insisted upon a recognition of diversity and of the existence of different currents within the women's movement. That's when we proposed autonomy. That was one of the most important points.

And autonomy for us didn't mean we no longer wanted to be part of a larger project, the project for overall social change, but we demanded the right to elect our own leadership. We wanted our leadership elected by women at the base, not appointed by the all-male national directorate. And we wanted to design our own programs, manage our own funding, decide our plans of action. This didn't mean that we weren't going to take the country's general situation into account; of course we were. But we wanted an autonomous women's movement.

And how was this demand received? What happened?

Well, there were different groups of women. Some of us were considered more radical (which to our detractors meant less militant) members of the Party. Others were considered more traditional, exponents of a more traditional line, more readily influenced by whatever the national directorate might say. Often the issues themselves fell by the wayside because there was a tendency to see the discussion in terms of personalities: "Those are Milú Vargas's ideas, or Sofía Montenegro's ideas . . ." They couldn't understand that it wasn't a matter of the ideas of one or two women but that a great many women felt as we did, a great many of us who were leaders in the feminist movement at that time.

It wasn't until after the elections that we began getting together on our own, without the men, that we really began talking about the issues. And we generated a profound discussion—sometimes a bit violent, at other times on a higher plane—with women who continued not to understand where we're coming from: it was a discussion in which important ideas were expressed. And we began to understand what we needed to do in order to find a way to remain united while still recognizing these different ideas. That's when we came up with the phrase *Unidas en la Diversidad* [United in Difference].

"United in Difference" was the theme of our January conference. And it was an extraordinary experience, really excellent. That's where we could really see the results of these three years of discussion. We put a wealth of ideas out there. But we also had to figure out who we were. Many of us said, "I became who I am, politically, in the FSLN." It was as if we'd given birth to ourselves in the Party. So, for some, there was also this sense of betrayal, the fear that maybe we were somehow betraying our political selves.

You know, I consider this a real gift. The FSLN enabled us to grow to the extent that we were able to claim autonomy, think for ourselves, create new alternatives and new possibilities for struggle. I believe we women are an important part of the Front's rich history. Because if the Front had enabled us only to mimic what we heard, if it had kept us down—incapable of creating anything new—then it wouldn't have been much of a political organization. Our experience in the FSLN is what gave us this strength, this possibility for change.

It's like what happens when you have children. If you're a parent who raises her children so all they'll know how to do is repeat your ideas, your voice, then you're a parent who hasn't given them anything. But if you're able to give your children their own ability to see, think, act—well, then you've enriched them immeasurably. They become what they've managed to get from you plus what they're able to create with what you've given them. So I see this whole process of breaking with a kind of blind obedience to the FSLN as a very positive thing. But there are other women who still see it as betrayal.

This fear of betrayal is something that's been used against us, that's been manipulated, no question about it. Another idea with which they've tried to manipulate us is the accusatory "Be careful, you'll divide the Party!" At this stage of the discussion, it's pretty clear to most of us that we're not dividing anything. We're strengthening the real Party. Because we're an alternative not only for women within the FSLN but for other women as well: women who may or may not belong to a political organization but who are interested in trying to improve their lives within the overall struggle for a society that includes a goal of justice for everyone.

As members of the FSLN I think we have a historic responsibility to develop and strengthen the feminist project. Not only for women inside the FSLN but for all women, no matter what their affiliation or whether they even have a political affiliation: women who are moved and excited by feminism. There's a tremendous richness of experience and creativity out there among the whole range of women who want to participate, whether or not they're members of the Front.

Milú, what kind of work are you involved in now? What specifically are you doing?

I'm an alternate member of the National Assembly. That means that when the delegate who holds the Senate seat isn't able to attend, I'm there participating. And, of course, I'm in close touch with what's going on all the time. I'm also president of the Carlos Núñez Téllez Center for Constitutional Rights. I named the Center after Carlos and in honor of the extraordinary work being done by that group of lawyers in the United States,[4] many of whom are long-time friends of Nicaragua, and also personal friends. We've worked closely with a number of these men and women over the past ten, eleven years.

In our Nicaraguan Center for Constitutional Rights we currently have five lines of work. There's "Women," which is our main emphasis at the moment; then there's "Local and Centralized Power." We have an area we call "Autonomy and Municipalities," which we believe will gain in importance as we achieve a greater decentralization and a higher degree of democratization, and we have a line we call "Defense of the Constitution."

When you heard me speak during that panel at the Central American University the other night, I was defending the Constitution. Because Article 204 violates our Constitution in several different places, besides violating international human rights treaties. We at the Center take cases like this to the Supreme Court if we consider a law itself to be in violation of the Constitution or if a particular citizen's constitutional rights are being violated.

Our fifth line of work is "Labor Law," everything that has to do with

4. The Center for Constitutional Rights, New York (see Chapter 3, note 3, above).

workers' rights. Naturally, we deal with the problems of women workers. We've held workshops with every one of the unions, independent of their political affiliation, in which all the women have made suggestions as to the writing of a new Labor Code from their points of view as women. The Center also has a publishing program. At the moment we're putting together a book of commentaries on the Constitution; it will be a reference book. Nothing like that exists in Nicaragua.

There are fourteen of us involved with the Center, though only five of us are full-time staff. We're the group of lawyers who worked as legal counsel at the National Assembly during the Sandinista administration. When we lost the election we said, "Well, if we don't get together and do something that makes sense collectively, each of us is going to go her or his separate way." And we didn't want that. Creating the Center seemed like a way of returning to the Nicaraguan people the [benefits of the] experience they've given us. It's the people who permitted us to work with the creation of laws aimed at meeting people's needs, and we learned so much in that work.

So we got together and made this project happen. We've got a women's program going in the poor neighborhoods, in which we train outstanding women to know and understand their legal rights; we call them "people's defenders." These women in turn train other women in the locality, and they provide a sort of legal first aid in cases of rape, battery, problems like that. Another women's project we have is the People's Law Office, and I think we're going to make it into a mobil unit. To begin with, we're selecting four neighborhoods and we'll take the service to the women there.

We're also working with women labor leaders. Our National Assembly has been contemplating a new Labor Code, and we've been working with women leaders in the unions in order to get their input about what should go into that code. We want women's rights to be included: not just equal pay for equal work but an extension to legal maternity leave, day-care centers in the factories and in other workplaces, employment security, attention to issues like sexual harassment on the job. We're demanding an eight-hour day for women who work in domestic service—as maids—and overtime when they have to work longer. Now we're entering the second phase of this work which involves designing a strategy that will ensure that our ideas are included in the law when the Assembly votes.

Milú Vargas is a woman of courageous thought and creative action. Her political involvement consistently combines "think tank" strategy sessions with coalition building and concrete projects that promote constructive change. Before I left her home she wanted to show me a sunny, window-encased sitting room, one wall of which displayed bits and pieces of her life with her late husband. "This was our favorite retreat," she said. There were poems and letters, snapshots in which their joy was so contagious that it transcended the recorded moment, and a heartfelt "diploma" awarded to Carlos by Milú for his successful handling of half their household chores.

On another occasion, Milú had told me the story of how she got the news of her husband's death. She was on a speaking tour in the United States. She had stayed with friends in Pittsburgh. One of them drove her to the airport where she would board a plane for the next city on her tour. Somehow they got to talking about love, more specifically about how one can know another human being for a while and then suddenly realize the relationship has changed. "You're in love," she said, "and you know that everything is different. I said to my friend then, 'If anything ever happened to Carlos, I don't think I could go on.'"

The two lawyers, both women, hugged good-bye. Milú boarded a plane to Chicago. And it was her host in that city, meeting her flight, who had to tell her something had happened to Carlos: he had died unexpectedly in Havana. She flew home then to begin the long process of grieving that hasn't yet ended. Milú says she spent some time in a small bare cell in Diriamba, with her longtime mentors, the Sisters of La Asunción. "At first it was too hard to be here in this house," she admitted. "Everyone kept asking me if I was all right, wanting me to be all right. How could I be all right?"

Loss like hers is never all right. But on another level Milú has always been— will always be—all right. She is a woman unafraid to follow both head and heart, indivisible as they continue to lead her toward her own political center. And she's not moving toward that center by herself. She's bringing a legion of women with her.

"As a Woman, I Think It Was Worth Living the Revolutionary Process"

Vidaluz Meneses

When I first interviewed Vidaluz Meneses in 1983, she summarized her background as only such a careful and studious person would: "After the revolution one realizes more than ever the need to define oneself, to identify . . . within a certain class. And that led me to study something of how classes are divided in Latin America. My family, my development, belong to the middle class. I remember that among my first critical poems, I wrote some which point out how 'having' came to be an integral part of 'being.' My father was a member of Somoza's National Guard. And that also had extremely important repercussions in my life."[1]

Long before Vidaluz's class consciousness or revolutionary option, though, she understood her deep identification as a Christian. In her infancy and childhood she was nurtured by three pious aunts; her family observed the rituals and practiced the values of a peculiarly Nicaraguan Christianity. Remembering the music, soft lights, incense, and sense of comfort, her hazel eyes assume

1. Randall, *Risking a Somersault in the Air*, 42.

a special softness. Her celebration of saints' days and the Purísima, and later her Catholic social service and spiritual retreats, informed the years of her growing up, conformed her ambience and culture.[2] All else was its logical extension.

But a deep passion runs just beneath the surface of this woman's serene and amiable exterior—reminiscent of Sor Juana Inés de la Cruz, or even Joan of Arc. Vidaluz, too, attended La Asunción. And when the time came for this young woman to choose a life of political struggle, her choice was conditioned by what was happening in the Church at the time: by the impact of Vatican II upon the life of Latin American Christians; by the "preferential option for the poor," as it was called by the bishops gathered at Medellín, Colombia, and Puebla, Mexico.

For many young men and women in Nicaragua's Christian youth movement, contact with the ideas and endeavors of their secular comrades eventually distanced them from their earlier religious practice. As dramatically as the Church was changing, its programs still fell considerably short of the radical warfare necessary to rout a dictator or win a war. Vidaluz's journey was different. She made a revolutionary commitment without straying from her Christian faith—or from its daily manifestations. One sparked the other, in fact, and they became fused in a passionate and principled code of personal conduct. (The story Michele Najlis tells, of how Vidaluz responded when named dean of humanities at the Jesuit university, was not an anomaly in this woman's response to opportunity.)[3]

Vidaluz Meneses—born in 1944, full-figured though youthful, curly dark-brown hair, a warm presence—is a woman in love with her faith and with the experience that nourishes it. Her intimate, tangible spirituality has provided her with the courage to consistently opt for life—through a succession of diffi-cult, often painful, choices, dilemmas, sorrows, and disappointments. Some of these have been shared by many in Nicaragua, where families have often been torn apart along political lines. Others have been uniquely hers.

Her father, Somoza's ambassador to Guatemala during the last years of the dictatorship, was executed by that country's revolutionary movement. Already involved secretly with the FSLN, she nevertheless flew in an air force plane to where he lay dying, so she could say good-bye. She married a man who shared her concern for justice, and they joined the FSLN together. Later, however, he distanced himself from the struggle and eventually joined the counterrevolu-tion. Faithful to her ideals, she left him. Three of her four children eventually followed their father into exile. Vidaluz has had to juggle respect for their

2. Purísima is the celebration of the Virgin Mary that takes place from November 30 through December 8. It is a popular tradition in Nicaragua, where families and institutions construct elaborate altars in honor of the Virgin, often outside or in the doorways of homes. People circulate, singing special songs, and the hosts offer fruit, pieces of sugarcane, and other sweets. After the Sandinistas came to power, some altars began to incorporate a revolutionary theme; the Virgin became symbolic of freedom and solidarity.

3. See Chapter 2.

choices with a mother's desire to keep her family together, and to keep it together in the country she so deeply loves.

Ten years ago, when she was just approaching forty, she wrote a short prose piece eloquent in its synthesis of where she felt herself to be at the time. It's called "About the Revolutionary and Some of Her Weaknesses"[4]

> In May I'll be forty years old. I have four children and I'm in love with a poet. I was born into the upper class, yet I go out with the brigades to pick coffee and cotton, and on the cultural sojourns as well. I passed my first Militia course.
>
> In the coffee fields I am awkward and slow; the shape and color of the berries distracts me (perhaps because I see the world through poet's eyes). Picking cotton I spend hours cleaning the pods that have fallen to the ground (because "cotton tossed is cotton lost"). In the cultural brigades I lament the fact that my poems are not epic, that my voice is neither as loud nor as clear as the heroism of our border patrols. I destroyed my Militia ID card signed by "Cain," as our people call him.[5]
>
> I read in Luke what I would later discover were also the words of Che Guevara: "Our brothers and sisters are not of our blood, but of our faith"—revolutionary faith, Che added.
>
> Commander Guevara also said that "everyone has a right to exhaustion, but not everyone can be a member of the vanguard." I admit that I frequently declare myself an efficient member of the rearguard. The important thing is that I will never stop aspiring to reach the goal along with my brother and sister workers and peasants—although I may be the very last in line.

Currently dean of humanities at the Central American University, Vidaluz is one of a very few Sandinistas—respected by friend and foe alike—who since the FSLN's electoral loss has been able to retain prestigious work in her field. During the previous administration, she headed the country's library system and was briefly vice-minister of culture before the Culture Ministry suspended operations. And through it all she is a poet.

Her poetry has faithfully chronicled her life experience. A first slim book, La llama guardada *[The Hidden Flame] was self-published in 1975. She sometimes talks about how she herself took the material to a printer, saw it through publication, and then tried to peddle hundreds of unsold books. "I finally ended up donating them to the library system where I worked," she laughs.* El aire que me llama *[The Air That Calls Me] appeared in 1982. Commercially produced and promoted, it includes some of her most important work and marks her as a poet of note. In 1990* La llama en el aire / Flame in the Wind

---

4. "Del revolucionario y algunas de sus debilidades" (1983), in the collection *Llama en el aire / Flame in the Wind*, trans. Margaret Randall (Managua: Editorial Nueva Nicaragua, 1990), 121–122.

5. Edén Pastora, FSLN commander, headed the National Militia and had therefore signed its members' I.D. cards. When he defected and went over to the counterrevolutionary forces, people showed their outrage by publicly burning their cards.

was published. It is an anthology of Vidaluz's production to date—including selections from the earlier books and her most recent work.

"Wailing Wall" is the last poem in that collection. It is clearly a response to her revolution's shocking fall from power, and—again—it conveys her unique vision. The poet promises

> This time I will not drown memory,
> I will absorb the dead and those lovers forced to separate
> which is another form of death.
> Bearing the flag of this holocaust we've lived,
> I will not wander through life schizophrenic
> nor silence the voices of those still clamoring
> for the reign we could not build.
> I will not ignore the blood on the clay,
> the scream rising from my bowels,
> this roar of multitudes accumulated in my breast . . .

The poem goes on to speak of the need for tears, and it claims a time and space for them: the wall of lamentations. But it ends with that hope and faith the true Christian does not lose, "beyond all that which has been seen and lived, beyond it all." And yet Vidaluz is not possessed by naivete or blindness to the human condition. As an epigraph to this last section of her book, she chooses the words of Bertolt Brecht: "Still we knew / that hating brutality / also disfigures us. / Anger at injustices also / uses up our voice. Unfortunately we / who should have paved the road to love, / could not be lovable."

This time around I found Vidaluz on the campus where she mentors students and faculty alike. She suggested I come out to the tiny wood-frame house in the country where she lives with Sergio Morazón, a veterinarian who makes house calls and who prepared a delicious pork roast for the occasion. Friends and I arrived to the welcoming scent of the loin in its juices, newly picked garden vegetables simmering atop the rice, and the unmistakable scent of fresh corn tortillas.

The half-finished structure—barely containing a sitting room, kitchen, bedroom, small writing space, and bath—is dwarfed by the luxuriance of the tropical vegetation that surrounds it. Vidaluz, who had come straight from work, was wearing an AMNLAE T-shirt. It's not difficult to see how her insistence upon following her ideology and her heart must continue to bring traditional society up short. The devoutly Catholic young lady, the general's daughter, the properly situated wife and mother became in time the divorcée, poet, and revolutionary. Now she is this T-shirted university dean, a woman obviously in love and at ease with her amiable partner amid building blocks and cages of small sick animals. Through the transitions, she has never stopped being the daughter or the mother, the Christian, poet, or revolutionary. Today she professes as well to being a feminist.

We took our time over drinks, conversation, and the delicious meal. Then Vidaluz dispatched her husband and the others and we settled into her modest writing space, surrounded by books, articles, papers, and mementos evoking *half a century of memories. Vidaluz's manner combines reflection with curiosity and a constant search for answers, interrupted by moments of sudden excitement. She finds it easier to speak of others than of herself; that I remembered from our earlier encounters. But she feels a deep responsibility to tell the story of these times, and she knows that includes her own:*

Well, you know about those three great-aunts of my childhood. They are common personages in the biography of most Latin Americans. All three were schoolteachers, and very religious. Catholicism predominates on the Pacific Coast of Nicaragua. Those three great-aunts were very pious, very devout.

My mother and I lived in Matagalpa, and my father would come up to see us on his days off; at that time he was in cadet school. So my earliest years were very much influenced by those three great-aunts and their world of magical religiosity. I call it magical because it was a fantasy world, almost entirely given over to religious ritual, with organ music—all the sounds and sights and smells of Nicaragua's old colonial churches. Little blond angels fluttering around the image of a wise and generous God: it was all part of our Catholic vision. The Church was absolute in its teachings about Hell and Heaven, and we all aspired to the latter.

This was the experience of my childhood: a profoundly religious one. And then my mother also sent me for a time to Bonanza, the mining region in the eastern part of the country. I went one vacation and ended up going to school there for several years. Another great-aunt of mine was married to a North American who worked for one of the companies at the mine, and they were like grandparents to me. They loved me very much and gave me a great sense of security, just as I had with the rest of my family.

So I think I've been fortunate in that respect. I had the love of my parents, a number of very loving great-aunts, and that couple who were like my grandparents. I should say that my maternal grandmother died when my mother was still an adolescent, and my father's mother lived in another city.

Getting to know something of the Atlantic Coast was also important during that period of my life. I'll never forget the landscape, so different from that of the Pacific. Those were happy years, very happy years.

When I was twelve I returned to my mother's and father's home. My father was always being transferred, though. As a military man he was stationed all over the country, in almost every city, which meant that I attended almost every school in Nicaragua! But by the time I got ready to go to high school we had settled in Managua. And, yes, like so many of the other women you've spoken with, I went to La Asunción, the school where most of the girls from wealthy families studied. I went through La Asunción with Angelita Seballos, Michele Najlis, that whole generation. Then I went on to the university.

Wait a minute, Vidaluz. I'd like to hear about your experience at La Asunción. Was the school as important in your formation as it was for so many of the other women?

Yes. The sisters were very intelligent. It was a Catholic education with a certain degree of social consciousness. We were upper-middle-class girls, and so we were given exercises in charity. It was paternalistic, of course, or maybe "maternalistic" would be a better word. The goal of that type of work is to patch society's wounds. There were organizations like Caritas, charitable institutions that donated meat to the poor, and the sisters would take us to the poorest neighborhoods to distribute the meat, that type of thing. It was all designed to motivate us to perform good works.

La Asunción was oriented more toward service than toward excellence in education. I've talked about this with Michele and Angelita, with a number of the women of my generation. Because, for example, Daisy Zamora, who went to another school for rich girls, El Colegio Teresiano, studied other things. The sisters there were more modern, it was bilingual, and they taught typing; the curriculum in general was more demanding.

But La Asunción put more emphasis on formation than on instruction. We were the rich young ladies who would be presented to society; we'd eventually get our engagement rings, get married, and be happy. And so their goal was to turn us into *generous* rich young ladies, *good* women. But the flip side of that was a certain sincerity, an openness and honesty. And, you know, when we run into one another there's instant recognition. I don't know anyone who went to La Asunción who doesn't have this certain frankness about her. It's marked us all. And it may be the most interesting quality shared by those who graduated from the school.

Wasn't Fernando Cardenal one of the priests who attended to the Sisters of La Asunción? I remember talk of spiritual retreats, after Medellín or Puebla, where Fernando and the sisters questioned the type of charity work they'd been doing . . .

That's true, but it was after I left. Generations that came after mine were influenced by those changes: the sisters went through a social and political transformation, and interesting things began to happen. Then there was the 1972 earthquake; that earthquake destroyed the building that housed the school, and the sisters had to decide what to do, how to proceed, and they made some important decisions then. They moved to a prefabricated building, and the school became much more democratic: lay teachers came on board, and many of the sisters went out to work in the ghettos. Only La Asunción in León kept the characteristics of the old Managua school. But that all happened after I left. The Conference of Bishops at Medellín caught most of my generation already at the university. Or we were married.

My own development was a bit slower than the norm, I think. That was because of my family, my father being a military man and all . . . I had a wonderful relationship with my family, but I knew that the FSLN espoused the only real possibility of changing society. On the other hand, working with the Front meant going underground, giving oneself over to something dark and unknown, where death could so easily be your destiny.

There's another interesting phenomenon I want to mention while we're talking about the sixties, and that's the profusion of literary groups. Where I studied we had what we called "literary academies"; we had one, and there was also one over at La Salle, which was the pedagogical institute. The students who wrote or painted got together to develop our talents. It was in this sort of activity that I met a poet from Diriamba named Alvaro Gutiérrez; he's a painter and a poet. Today he heads the Artists' Union at Praxis.[6]

What I'm saying is that we were young people, students, practicing Christians who were inclined toward literature and who began to have contact with some of the first-year students at the university: there was the Ventana group that included Sergio Ramírez, Fernando Gordillo, Octavio Robleto, and others. Michele Najlis, who went to La Asunción, identified with the poets of Ventana. Michele was a model for the rest of us: she went to our school and she was from a wealthy family with that educational background, that cultural level . . . but she made a political commitment which was anti-Somoza and, later, openly revolutionary.

Literature and the revolution went hand in hand for us. The Cuban Revolution was also an influence, and what was happening in Paris in 1968; everything we heard from other parts of the world naturally had its impact here. And we were involved in endless discussions in which literature and politics each played an important part. Ventana was the most important group here, and Fernando Gordillo was the student leader who impressed us most. He was a great speaker; the only thing was, people said he was a Marxist.

I admired Fernando, and of course the other members of the group were my friends; I loved them and believed in them. But I was also troubled because in those days Marxism meant atheism, and I wasn't prepared to give up my faith. So I respected those people, I read *Ventana* but I didn't formally belong to their group. There was another group, I remember, sort of modeled after the beatniks. Roberto Cuadra was the moving spirit there along with Beltrán Morales and Edwin Yllescas. They called themselves La generación Traicionada [The Betrayed Generation]. They assumed a snobbish stance, pure rebellion. In fact, I remember someone asked them once who had betrayed them, and they said no one.

In the midst of all these different currents, I received a letter from Alvaro Gutiérrez inviting me to join a group in Diriamba called Presencia [Presence]. It was very ephemeral, absolutely unimportant. The only reason I mention it is that I went and met with them once. And in the only issue of the magazine we published—it was called *Presencia*, too, the same name as the group—we said we were in favor of radical change, nothing halfway. But we identified ourselves as [Catholic] believers. There was a Christian Brother with Presencia who left his order and entered politics; he became a Christian Socialist and later

6. Praxis is an art gallery and café in the center of Managua. It is run by Nicaragua's Artists' Union and schedules regular shows of local artists as well as occasionally giving wall space to those from outside the country. As a group, Praxis has a long history of bringing artists together in support of Nicaragua's revolutionary process.

a counterrevolutionary, but at the time he was progressive. His name was José Estéban González, and he did a lot of damage later on. In some almost undefined way this was all a preview of what would later turn out to be liberation theology, since there was no such thing at the time—I'm talking about the years well before Medellín—and those concerns hadn't manifested themselves yet within the Nicaraguan Church. This literary group existed, then, although it existed for only a very short time.

So I continued with my questions and my concerns. I married a man named Carlos Icaza; he was of my same generation and he studied law. We were married, we eventually had our four children, and as a married woman I became involved with the usual Christian groups. It was the traditional route for the times: we took what we called *cursillos de cristiandad* [little courses in Christianity], which were for people of all ages. I went like everyone else, and they filled a void because they included the idea of social commitment. By this time, the Church was beginning to be more conscious of what was happening throughout Latin America.

We would meet once a week for prayer and reflection, usually with another couple older than ourselves. For a while we also sponsored a series of premarital talks, because we wanted the young people to have some sort of preparation; we knew that we hadn't been prepared for marriage or for being parents. The series included a lecture on the legal aspects, another that was theological—the priest gave that one—and one on sexuality.

I had been lucky because in matters of sexuality my parents were pretty open, at least for the times. I mean, my father had his affairs and such, but my parents were clearly in love and managed to stay that way throughout their marriage. It was an easy relationship and comfortable to watch. Of course their rules for the oldest daughter were the usual ones for those times. I wasn't allowed to date without a chaperon, and I was a virgin when I married. I obeyed all the rules and rituals of my generation.

But it wasn't an exaggerated sort of thing, and I didn't mind the restrictions. My concerns were more social in nature, and religious—mystical—because of the kind of life I had. I don't think this was an experience peculiar only to me; it was very much the Latin American experience of the times. I was looking for some coherence between what my Church taught and the social reality I saw around me.

At the university I had taken part in all the strikes; it was something we just naturally did. But it was more at the level of civic duty. I remember being very impressed by Gandhi, and by pacifism. And when I talk to others of our generation—and even to someone like Ernesto Cardenal—I realize that we were all influenced by Gandhi; we all shared similar concerns. The two big problems for us were atheism and violence: atheism as a philosophical doctrine, because we couldn't turn our backs on our deep religious faith; and armed struggle because it meant violence. It wasn't until we read the Medellín documents that we were able to deal with those fundamental discrepancies.

Pacifism was our ideology at the time. I remember I had books by Gandhi and by Martin Luther King. King's thought was also very important to me.

And, you know, even though I accepted the necessity of armed struggle and came to understand that there are moments when you have to resort to that, I continue to believe in passive resistance. It can have enormous power. Besides which, pacifism makes you stronger as an individual; it helps strengthen your willpower and makes you more coherent in your principles. The results can also be much more positive. Armed struggle is an extreme solution, unhappily necessary at times, but it should always be the last resort.

After all these influences I've mentioned, all these different possibilities for changing the world—and the society in which I lived, here in this country where I was born—the Medellín Council came along. And, of course, we members of the Christian groups were busy with our reflections, the political movement was maturing as well, and we Christians were ready for a change. At that moment the Sandinista National Liberation Front showed a great political clarity. The Sandinistas were clever in their ability to capitalize on the concerns of those of us with religious faith.

I remember at the time we had something called the "Course of Courses"; it was for the Christian leadership. We were discussing whether our goal was to change the structures so we could live our Christianity better, or to Christianize the structures that existed. That was the sort of thing we were discussing then—until we became convinced that it was impossible to Christianize Somoza's structures. Then we knew we had to destroy them.

By that time, we were talking about "social sin," giving our own name to a category that the ideologues and politicians called "exploitation" or the "profit system." For us, selfishness and injustice became social sins. And we began to reflect upon what the liberation theologians were offering to the general discussion: about violence, how they were going to justify armed struggle as an option. We began to understand that it was easy for us as Christians to respond if we saw someone bleeding in the street. So why weren't we responding to the institutionalized violence all around us: the misery and hunger that killed so many every day? As Christians, we knew we were responsible for this situation that was being perpetuated and maintained; and if we couldn't end it by civic means, then we had to legitimize armed struggle.

So this was our journey. And in our discussion groups class differences began to break down as well. Because it's true: my friends and I were middle class. But we'd go to the assemblies where all the different Christian base communities were represented, and there we had the opportunity of listening to people from the urban working class. And the peasant experience, too: people would come from the countryside and give their testimony; they began to be known as "delegates of the Word."[7]

---

7. After Vatican II and in the context of the democratization of the Catholic Church, delegates of the Word were laypeople with a certain amount of training who took on many of the tasks traditionally performed by priests. They weren't permitted to marry or to give Communion or carry out some of the other rituals limited to the priesthood; but they functioned where priests were scarce, and they gave religious authority a more human face. During the Contra war, many of these delegates of the Word were targeted and kidnapped, tortured, and murdered by the counterrevolutionary forces.

When I was a child we didn't read the Bible; in fact, there was a real bias against it. I remember my great-aunts telling me that if you read the Bible you'd get confused, almost as if you'd go crazy. Everything was a great mystery. But all that changed with Vatican II. All those courses I took as an adult were totally different from what I'd heard as a child. And we began to read the Bible; we read the Old Testament and began to feel we were living the history of the people of Israel in their struggle against Egyptian slavery. It was all very symbolic for us, and very relevant. And through all of Latin America the same thing was going on.

We had to rid our people of the tyrant, who was Somoza. All the biblical figures and events were applicable to our situation here in Nicaragua. The Psalms became instruments of struggle and of comfort, too. I remember reading the Psalms and asking the Lord to protect me. After the revolution I wrote about this, I wrote down that testimony and published it in *El Nuevo Diario*. It was when the Contras began bombing the cities. I lived with my children in Pancasán at the time, and I was afraid.[8] They hit nearby neighborhoods, although the bombs never reached our house. But, of course, no one could be sure we weren't going to be next, not when we knew they were targeting the civilian population. And there were Psalms that helped, number 91 for example, where it says, "You need not fear . . . the arrow that flies in the daytime."[9] It was interesting, as Christians, how we made use of those instruments.

We prayed when we felt fear or when we needed guidance. I remember once we had a young man hiding at our house, he was wounded and . . . Well, I should tell you how we got involved in all that first. I already mentioned that I'd participated in the demonstrations throughout the sixties, in the strikes at UCA when I was a student and then later when I was working there. It was in 1977 that I became more formally involved. Two things influenced my conscious decision. One was the Group of Twelve.[10] Sergio Ramírez was one of the twelve, and we'd been friends since we were young. When another friend of mine called to tell me Sergio was at a safehouse on the Southern Highway and that there was danger in the area, could we take him in, I told her yes right away. Because he was a friend. When he came to our house we just naturally became involved in the network; you hardly noticed it happen.

I don't even remember now if that was the first incident or if there was something else. Because Boris Vega Sánchez was a law student at the time I was working at the university; he had to move a group of combatants from Catarina, near Masaya. They'd thrown some contact bombs or something, and they'd been wounded. He had to move the comrades to Managua so they could see a doctor. Juanita Bermúdez came around, I remember, and we began to

8. Pancasán is a neighborhood in Managua, named after the battle of 1967.

9. Translation from *The Jerusalem Bible*, Reader's Edition (New York: Doubleday, 1986).

10. The Group of Twelve included prominent intellectuals, businessmen, religious leaders, and other well-known Nicaraguan citizens who came together toward the end of the war in support of the FSLN. Among them were Sergio Ramírez, Carlos Tunnerman, and Father Miguel D'Escoto. It is believed that, had he lived, Pedro Joaquín Chamorro would have joined the group.

transport this group that had been in armed confrontation with the [National] Guard. That must have been where I said yes. I accepted the fact that the FSLN was the vanguard and that I was prepared to take part.

What about your husband, Vidaluz, and your parents? Did you become involved without your family's knowledge, or did you have some support?

My husband went through the same process more or less, out of his own experience as a Christian. But we had our differences; he wasn't as convinced as I was. And, of course, I'd been wanting a clearer relationship between my life-style and the struggle for a while. For example, I agreed that we needed a house, the usual middle-class conditions for raising a family and so forth. But I hated the excesses, and I wanted to establish a more democratic system with the domestic help. I realized that any little gesture was like a Band-Aid; it didn't change anything. I guess I was becoming more radicalized and that provoked quarrels between Carlos and me.

With my father, well, it was much more difficult. I was relieved when he completed his thirty years with the guard and was ready to retire. They had promoted him to the rank of general, and he returned to civilian life to live on his farm. I was incredibly relieved because, years before, when I'd been involved in those student demonstrations, I remembered the guard showing up on the street that borders the campus. My father was a comandante with the police at the time. They launched their tear-gas bombs and it was horrible for me. I suppose I was afraid like everyone else, but my worst fear was having to confront my father. I didn't think I could do that; it was so complicated. It just hurt too much: the thought that my own father would be forced to arrest me. That day I'd run away from the demonstration.

And I lived with that all along. There were a number of us in the Front who were daughters of Somocistas. Another example was Marta Cranshaw, who'd been a member for a while by the time I came along; but her father was a politician, and mine was a military man. The sons and daughters of the National Guard were constantly faced with the possibility of having to face our fathers in battle . . . in an armed confrontation, or if they picked us up. Emotionally I knew I wasn't strong enough for that, so I was very relieved when he retired; I felt like a great weight had been lifted.

All that year I talked with my father. I urged him to accept civilian life. I told him, "It's going to be so nice for you, at last, to be able to tend to your land and so forth." But Somoza had other ideas. He asked my father to accept the appointment as ambassador to Guatemala. I argued against his going. I told him he was just going to complicate his life. At this stage of the game, everything was in crisis. But Somoza was something unbelievable for the guard. What he said was law. My father accepted the appointment and left for Guatemala.

As his daughter, I tried at least to help my father do an acceptable job as ambassador. I gave him a book; it was called *The Diplomat's ABC*. I wanted him to learn something about diplomacy. I didn't want him to be seen as ridiculous, as one of those ignorant law-and-order types. My father had the usual middle-class education, nothing out of the ordinary. I remember telling my mother that it would be a good idea if my father organized a library there at the embassy, with Nicaraguan books—that he could invite the Nicaraguan students in Guatemala to use it; that it would be a nice gesture, a contribution. My father agreed. One of my younger sisters went to help him set up that library; I bought books for it here, and she and my mother went to organize it.

By now we're talking about 1976/77. The crisis was becoming more and more acute. My father had gone off to Guatemala, representing the Somoza government, and I stayed here in Nicaragua, more and more involved in the struggle against the dictatorship. I wanted to separate my life from his, as completely as possible. But it was hard. There were a number of incidents I can remember in which the fact that he was a general in the National Guard made me extremely uncomfortable. I always thought he might find out what I was doing. And I also didn't want anyone ever to have to ask him for help, I mean in terms of getting me out if I got arrested.

When they killed Pedro Joaquín Chamorro, in January of 1978, sectors of the bourgeoisie that opposed the dictatorship began getting seriously involved. Their interests and the interests of working people began to converge. And then there was the struggle in the countryside: the disappearances, the torture and murder of peasants was becoming an everyday occurrence. Catalino Flores was a peasant leader who'd been captured, and no one knew if he was dead or alive. So a group of peasants occupied the United Nations office in Managua. And a number of us Christians gathered in front of the building; we sang, prayed, brought them food, whatever was needed.

One day we'd planned a Mass right there on the sidewalk. I went, and we were shouting slogans: "Where are our brother peasants? Let the assassins respond! Who murdered Pedro Joaquín? They say it was El Chiguín!"[11] As soon as we began to form a group, there came the guard with their tear gas: they threw a series of tear-gas bombs at us. We ran to take shelter in some houses we found open, and protected ourselves with lemon and water. Some of the women were arrested. But the whole thing was filmed by a TV cameraman. And I didn't know it, but my father was in Nicaragua on business at the time.

I felt the same kind of fear I'd felt years before as a student. I was afraid to leave that house, afraid someone would see me on television and my father would hear about it. And, in fact, he did. He happened to be in the country, as I say, and he was at my sister's house just after the demonstration. When I

11. "El Chiguín" translates as "The Kid" in Nicaragua; it was what the people came to call Somoza's notorious son, Anastasio Somoza Portocarrero. He headed an elite unit of trained killers known as the EEBI, or Escuela de Entrenamiento Básico de Infantería (Infantry Basic Training School). Founded in 1948, the outfit went through a number of changes in its concept and operation. By the time the war against the dictatorship was in full swing, this unit of young recruits, generally between the ages of eleven and eighteen, was being employed in the repression of political opponents and the torture of prisoners. After the victory of 1979, the Sandinistas called on criminologists, psychiatrists, psychologists, and others to help design a rehabilitation plan for these young people, many of whom had been recruited out of poverty and drugged to encourage their hideous work. Many were later reintegrated into society.

finally got home that day, they told me some of my cousins had shown up where my father was, with their clothes smelling of tear gas. "They're a bunch of cowards," they told him, "El Chiguín was lobbing tear-gas bombs at a group of women at Mass, and Vidaluz was there." My father took it very hard.

My father didn't talk to me much after that. He kept his thoughts to himself. A few years before, he had tried to question me about my activities. Someone had told him I was involved; and he said he was concerned, he didn't want me to get in trouble. At the time, I was working on a magazine; it was mostly analysis and a place to denounce what was going on. Some Jesuits put it out, Father Luís Medrano mostly, and a few of us laypeople were on the editorial board. I told my father, "It's true. I work with some priests on a magazine that publishes an analysis of our reality and denounces the injustices being committed. That's what I'm involved in, not armed struggle or anything like that. But yes I'm with them . . ." and I gave him a whole liberation theology sermon. My father wasn't a violent man. He was serious but, well, he listened and he didn't have an argument against what I was saying. So it wasn't the kind of thing where I was ever disrespectful to him or he shouted at me. Nothing like that. This great silence just grew between us, because he had one ideology and I another.

The daughter has told the story of her father's death many times. She has repeatedly been asked to record it in interviews, one of them with me those many years ago. And she has written about making her own particular peace as well as about the event itself. I decided to spare her yet another telling. What follows, then, is largely transcribed from what I reported after my conversation with her in 1983, with the addition of a few other sources.[12]

Vidaluz made more than that one attempt to speak with her father about their political differences. She wrote to him on two separate occasions; and although she describes the first letter as somewhat abstract—"I just felt the need to talk to him about our transformations as Christians"—the second represented a definite ideological break. "I had to be very clear in that letter," she says. "I told him that I would always love him but that, unhappily, 'I can't agree with you.' I even said that history would condemn him but that I as his daughter would forgive him."

The daughter understood that the father had joined the National Guard in order to have a career, but she knew that she had to respond to a different calling. She often reminded him that it was the very education he had provided that had brought her to a place where she now saw history and responsibility in a different light. The father never answered the daughter's letters. The silence grew, but their deep love for one another survived.

The FSLN had just carried off the spectacular and successful takeover of the National Palace. Toward the end of that month the Front was about to embark

---

12. This account is taken primarily from my *Risking a Somersault in the Air*, 41–54, and from Teófilo Cabestrero, *Revolucionarios por el Evangelio / Revolutionaries for the Gospel* (Bilbao, Spain: Editorial Desclée de Brouwer, 1983), 209–245.

*on a coordinated insurrection that would further change the balance of power
and push the war to a new level. In Guatemala a commando of the Revolutionary Army of the Poor, in solidarity with the Nicaraguan struggle, shot
Somoza's ambassador from a moving car. He was about to enter a barbershop
two blocks from his house. One of the four bullets destroyed General Meneses's lung; another pierced his spine. It was September 16, 1978.*

*Somoza immediately ordered a military plane to take the general's family to
Guatemala City. Vidaluz traveled with one of her children and her younger
sister. There they kept company with the badly wounded man until his death on
September 29. It was a time of conflicting allegiances and acute anguish for
this woman who so deeply loved her father but who was by that time fully
incorporated into the struggle against everything for which he stood.*

*"My father had a bullet in his spine," she says, "so he wouldn't have been
able to walk if he'd recovered. He would have been a quadriplegic. I prayed to
God that he would die . . . And I remember speaking with the German doctor in
charge of his case. In the middle of the conversation I realized the man was a
fascist. He was surprised when I said my father was also a victim of the
Somoza regime."*

*"My family always thought of me as the one with a higher cultural level or
something," she explained. "So my mother asked me to be the one to speak
with the press, give statements, that sort of thing. When my father's condition
deteriorated, I told one of the journalists that I hoped his sacrifice would help
bring peace to Nicaragua. I remember that a member of the embassy staff
showed up after that. He said I should be careful of what I told reporters, that
it could be used against our government. I told him as a Christian I stood
behind my words."*

*When the general died and his family returned home, Vidaluz was left with a
legacy of conflictive pain. She remembers telegrams from Somoza's people;
one of them read, "We beg you to accept our condolences." But she also
received strength from her comrades, among them Father Fernando Cardenal,
"who sent me a beautiful letter, comforting me and acknowledging my commitment to the people. And another poet, Alejandro Bravo, managed to send a slip
of paper with the words 'I'm with you.'"*

*After the war, during the first year of revolutionary reconstruction, Vidaluz
would write a poem that expresses her love for her father as well as her conscious separation from his way of life. "Last Post Card to My Father, General
Meneses" also characterizes this woman's coming to terms with so many difficult contradictions:*

> *You should have celebrated your birthday today*
> *but you are gone, and it's all to the good.*
> *I cherish your words and subsequent concern*
> *for how I would turn out,*
> *because history did not allow you*
> *to look upon this moment,*
> *much less understand it.*
> *Judgment has been given.*

I tell you I keep for myself
your generous love,
your hand on the spoon
as you feed that last breakfast to your grandson,
lightening the atmosphere
of our goodbyes.
And we remain, each on his or her side:
two noble knights of antiquity
embracing before the final, fatal, duel.[13]

I now asked Vidaluz about the next separation in her life, how she and her husband grew apart:

That was something many of us here went through, I mean we who committed ourselves to the revolution. Many of us shared a hatred of Somoza, we were anti-Somoza, but when the Sandinistas took power other divisions naturally surfaced. Those who simply wanted the dictator out weren't necessarily prepared for profound social change. And it was in this context that my separation from Carlos took place.

My husband didn't really have a strong ideological position. He was from a Liberal family—the Liberal Party here was Somoza's party. The farthest they really strayed from the dictator was as Liberal Independents. But my husband had never been political. He was always a petit-bourgeois professional, relatively successful at what he did; and I think perhaps a revolution is particularly traumatic for a lawyer, unless he's a lawyer interested in human rights or something like that. A revolution is like the wellspring of a new type of law, and the old laws are relative in many ways, especially when it comes to property rights. Revolution brings with it a whole new concept of ownership.

So Carlos came out of the Christian process, as I did, and his law clientele were made up of "the good rich," as I call them. But many of them began to become involved in a different manifestation of Catholicism: City of God, it's called, and it's profoundly reactionary. I don't think Carlos experienced any great crisis of faith, but his contact with his clients began to have an effect on him. It influenced the way he saw things.

You know, the revolution is a very complex process. And along with class struggle there's going to be some class resentment. People find it difficult to communicate with one another. And if you're a middle-class professional, people may tend not to trust you completely—until you've proven yourself. Carlos also had a difficult nature. So it was a combination of things. I'd say he just didn't have the character, the ideology, or the strength to stay with the revolution.

And that's what happened in our marriage: we just moved further apart. I

13. "Ultima postal a mi padre, General Meneses" / "Last Post Card to My Father, General Meneses," in Meneses, *Llama en el aire / Flame in the Wind*, 69. Salmon Russel is working on an anthology of four contemporary Nicaraguan women poets, including Vidaluz, and his translation of this poem is slightly different from mine.

was more and more in love with the revolution. And, of course, my area of activity was very exciting, with great projects and extraordinary change. It had always been my dream to build libraries, and that's exactly what I got to do. The whole program of cultural and educational development: I just wrote an article about women in art and culture here, and I said that of all the revolutionary projects those were among the most successful, where men and women worked together in the creation of something truly extraordinary.

I was more and more in love with the revolution. Of course, I wasn't blind; I saw the mistakes, and the abuses. The first year I had a hard time with certain things, because I wanted the revolution to be impeccable. I wanted everything to be perfect. Communism was to be God's kingdom here on earth, as Ernesto Cardenal would say. So every single error, every abuse—small as it might be—completely mortified me.

After a year and a half, or two years, I remember asking myself, "What's happening to me?" And I asked the Lord for humility. Maybe it was my family, too. My whole family was on the other side! Two of my mother's sisters had also married guard members: one was a colonel, the other a general. And then my father's death . . . I wanted the revolution to be perfect, to give me something absolutely contrary to my family's politics.

I wanted to be able to say, "My decision is the just one, the correct one." But after that I realized I had to take it as it was—with all its humanity. I knew that the human beings who make a revolution don't change from one day to the next. So I was able to grow with the revolution; Carlos wasn't.

Vidaluz, I wonder if you can talk about how you lived this experience as a woman. I have a sense of your experience as a Christian and of how you developed as a revolutionary. What about as a woman?

I don't know. I'm sure my life as a woman has been different. But I haven't given that as much thought as [I have about] how I experienced this phenomenon as a Christian. For example, when we say "Between Christianity and Marxism there is no contradiction"—that slogan you've heard so often—well, there really *isn't* that much difference. As a Marxist you're convinced of your project, and that conviction gives you strength. The same was true of me. I wanted a different kind of society, a more humane society. And I still think the communist model is valid. If we failed, that was because of our human weaknesses, not because it wasn't a society worth building.

This loss we've suffered has been something terrible. We were up against tremendous odds. I'd ask the Lord not to let me give up, and not to let me feel guilty. When you read the Bible, I think it's in Matthew where it says, "We are not brothers who are of the same flesh, but those who share a faith." A revolutionary faith, I would like to believe; but I couldn't bear the loss of my blood family either.

I've talked to Cuban comrades about this. And you know the Cuban experience; we can't compare it with our own. It's much more radical, a different phenomenon altogether. The revolution here in Nicaragua took place at another moment in time, and it was much more open in terms of respecting familial relations. But I don't think it's healthy, psychologically speaking, for families to be wrenched apart—especially in countries as poor as ours.

No, not poor. For a while now I've refused to describe our countries as poor. They're rich and they've been impoverished, are being impoverished, by those who would keep us down. It's such a difficult thing to transform society that to do the job I think we need healthy, whole people. A person who is frustrated and bitter can't really make profound changes. In one way or another he or she is going to project those frustrations onto the work being done.

That's why class struggle concerns me. Oh, I know there are conflicting interests. Your maid doesn't have the same interests as you do, or your employee if you're the boss. As a Christian, I have to recognize the truth of that. And I know that if we want real change we must change the economic relations of production, eliminate those differences which better the lives of a few at the expense of so many. But, on the other hand, class resentments trouble me because I don't think people who are resentful can really do anything worthwhile.

My position with my family was that my mother, my children, they all had to understand that my father's death was a direct result of his own historic option. I loved him deeply, I recognize everything he was in my life, and his death was tremendously painful for me. But he made his choices and lived his moment. I made mine, opting for what I consider to be just.

Maybe this is where I can address your question about my experience as a woman. My husband tried to make me feel guilty—and I've seen this happen with other women—guilty about my children. He'd tell them, "Your mother is more interested in the revolution than she is in you. For her, society comes first; before her own children." It was systematic. And, of course, this is something we women have talked about. Making a revolution is a very absorbing task; it takes a lot of time and effort. It wasn't easy for us to juggle our roles as mothers and revolutionaries.

Many of our children, particularly in the middle class where we had the privilege of having domestic help, were left alone for long periods of time. It's one of the contradictions you have to deal with. But when I've talked to my sons and daughters about this, I've told them, "Look, what you have to understand is that the revolution is for everyone, and we must all situate ourselves in that reality." Of course, my dream was to have one of those families where everyone was committed to the struggle: husband, wife, and kids. I dreamed about a family where everyone went out to do whatever task they were involved in and then came back together and were able to share that, to share their experiences with each another.

The impossibility of this in my own life has been very painful for me. All the insinuations, the pressures, my children's father trying to turn them against me: "Your mother is more interested in the revolution than she is in you," all that sort of thing. Instead of motivating the children and one another: "Let's go out and teach literacy! Let's participate in this or that!"

As a mother, I fought against that sense of guilt. And I tried to interest my sons and my daughters in the tasks of the revolution, although I wanted to respect their decisions as well. The other day I was thinking about a cassette I made early on. Much of my family had already gone to the United States, and I was sitting around with my four children and we were making this tape instead of writing a letter. My son Carlos was upset; he was upset from the time he was very little. Because it's hard for children when you break up their family for political reasons. My son's grandmother had left the country, like his cousins whom he played with every day. You can hear his pain on that tape.

I was talking to a friend of mine the other day, María Socorro Gutiérrez; she's a wonderful friend and a Christian, we've shared a great deal. We were talking in particular about our sons. You know the history of my oldest: his father involved him in counterrevolutionary activities when he was only fourteen, and the revolution handed him over to me instead of putting him in prison. I worked hard to give him something he could hold onto here, but he eventually left the country. And then my youngest: I took him with me to pick coffee and all sorts of things. But I couldn't get him interested either.

But what I told María Socorro is that I don't know what I would have done if either one of them had stayed and had to face the draft. I told her I didn't think I would have had the strength to force them to go down and sign up. It's entirely possible I might have ended up sending them out of the country myself. And then I would have felt enormously guilty. María Socorro is very honest, she's very frank, and she said: "Well, I don't think I would have been able to face that either."

I don't know. I always tried to respect my children's choices, even when it hurt me terribly that three of them didn't opt for the revolution. It hurt me because they're my children. And I believed and continue to believe in the ideal of a society with justice for all—a society different from the one I grew up in. And it's frustrating to realize that I wasn't able to pass that ideal on to all my children. It makes me very sad. If I find political apathy unpleasant in an adult, I find it all the more disagreeable in a child.

Who among your children continues to live in Nicaragua? Or have some of them returned, now that the Sandinistas have been defeated at the polls?

My daughter Vidaluz is the only one who remained.

In a way, she's repeated a version of your own history . . .

Yes, and she knows that. She gave a testimonial interview. Roxanna Lacayo made a film called *Un secreto para mí sola* [A Secret for Me Alone]; she got the title from a short story of mine.[14] It's my story, the one I'm telling you now, and my daughter appears in it. Roxanna caught up with her in militia training. She filmed her on a march, in her uniform and all, and then she went out to the camp and did the interview there. She asked Vidaluz how she felt about me.

14. Roxanna Lacayo is a Nicaraguan photographer and filmmaker.

And that was when my daughter said that maybe she identified with me more than her sister and brothers did because she and I had suffered the same sort of conflict with respect to our fathers.

But, you know, it's still not easy. Throughout our ten years of revolution I had so many discussions with friends of mine, friends who identify as Marxists. They always accused me of being too Christian, too soft. What they find hard to accept is that I'm not willing to totally condemn, forever. I know it's a part of my Christian philosophy . . .

Do they mean condemn your ex-husband . . . or your children?

Condemn my family in general. Or speak implacably about whomever . . . I mean, when we were being threatened with armed intervention, when people were being murdered and mutilated here, and the United States was sending all that money to the counterrevolution, of course I condemned them. One hundred percent. But when it comes to human relations, it's hard for me to totally write off individuals . . .

I think it's only logical to consider human beings as complex creatures. That rigid kind of mentality is typical of the more classic Marxist stance, but there's a great deal of rethinking going on today . . .

What I'm talking about clearly comes from a Christian perspective; it's a profound humanism that reflects the respect Jesus has for us all. Still, like I said, I felt a terrible frustration that all of my children didn't choose the revolution. I was envious of other families where the parents were able to inculcate revolutionary values in their children.

I remember talking to Fernando Cardenal once, and I said I was worried—actually frightened—that I might not be doing the right thing in allowing my children to continue having a relationship with their father. I said that maybe I should keep them from going to see him, or try harder to convince them. But I also said I was afraid: the revolution isn't perfect, and maybe when they reached adolescence or even later they might resent the fact that I'd prevented them from having their father in their lives. Besides, in my own life I'd given them a different example: I never cut off my personal relationship with my father. So I didn't feel that I had the right to stop them from seeing theirs. Fernando said, "No. To educate is to know how to let go." I'll never forget his words.

Getting back to women for a moment: how do you assess the changes for women during the revolutionary period? And since the electoral loss?

For me, the balance for women during the revolutionary period is a very positive one. As a woman, I think it was worth living the revolutionary process. And we had victories (although, it's true, some of them seem somewhat intangible now). The most important achievement may simply be that we began to see ourselves as women. But that's an important beginning. Unfortunately, when we look at the legal aspect, most of the changes in the laws—like the revolution itself—were hampered by enormous institutional failure. We didn't have the time we needed to do as much as we wanted. The Constitution remains as a sort of outline of what we would have liked to have been able to pass into law.

But I think the proliferation of organizations working for women in Nicaragua today is significant. I personally had the opportunity of overseeing the edition of a book called *La mujer nicaragüense en los años 80* [Nicaraguan Women in the Decade of the Eighties].[15] I think it gives a very objective picture of those ten years of revolution insofar as women are concerned. And the fact that there are so many different feminist groups now is a positive sign, I believe. Marxism has taught Christians a great deal, especially about analyzing society. It's important that we recognize that the different social classes express themselves according to their interests. Although the majority of the women interviewed for that book are middle class, intellectuals who think about the issues, I believe the different sectors of Nicaraguan women have been attracted to the various groups that exist.

I'm a woman interested in the entire phenomenon. On the one hand, I support some aspects of AMNLAE. I know there's been a negative analysis of the organization—and, of course, it's not something that's happened in this revolution alone—because it put the interests of society as a whole before the interests of women per se. And I agree, it's true. But AMNLAE has opened up in the past year. The leadership of AMNLAE has had to reevaluate a whole series of questions; above all, it's had to look seriously at women's issues and take them into account.

I support AMNLAE's magazine for example. [The Nicaraguan poet] Christian Santos is the editor, and she's done an excellent job. And I support Gladys Báez because I respect her enormously. I think she's a great woman, the same as Doris Tijerino: they're two important women in the history of this country. They may have made mistakes; who hasn't? There are those who blame Doris because, they say, she doesn't have a feminist consciousness. She's said publicly that when she became a member of the FSLN she didn't have a feminist consciousness, and that she remained without one for a very long time. I'd be willing to say that Doris began to understand women's issues when she became general secretary of AMNLAE, where she had to confront both her own contradictions and those of the [women's] sector. I think Gladys's case is different; she came to the women's organization from the more classic political jobs and not like Doris, who was the first and only woman in the world to be a national chief of police.

The kinds of criticism that have been made of both Doris's and Gladys's leadership style have been made of men as well as women. They're always positive, although they sometimes wear people down, but they have nothing

15. *La mujer nicaragüense en los años 80 / Nicaraguan Women in the Eighties*, ed. Ada Julia Brenes et al. (Managua: Ediciones Nicarao, 1991).

to do with the criticisms being made of other leaders because of corruption and ambition, which have a more negative effect. The important thing is that AMNLAE is out there, it continues to exist, to do its work; and I support that.

Then we have the group of feminists who have been influenced by what's going on in the more highly developed countries. They have a higher intellectual level, a better grasp of theory. And I think they have a role to play. I support them, too. Then there are literally dozens of nongovernmental organizations [NGOs], many among them run by and for women. That was a strategy we developed when we lost the elections, to get as many projects as possible out of government hands. Women are running NGOs that address issues of health, legal issues, education . . . and they have become tremendously important.

All in all, what we have is a great many active women. And that's a great sign. Women are doing things. I think it's important that women are so dynamic, so full of life. You've probably noticed—it may be characteristic of Latin America as a whole—that in our countries we generally pay more attention to the experience itself than to systematizing that experience. We never seem to have time to write about what we're doing, to analyze it, because there's always too much to be done.

We women have always been marginalized. The revolution signaled a great potential for us. But reality itself left us with the overburdened responsibility we've always had. You know how many homes in this country are headed by single mothers.[16] So when we talk about women we're talking about a group that's historically had to take responsibility for much more than our share of society's problems. I saw a cartoon the other day, I think it was in a Colombian magazine: a woman was saying, "I don't know why they don't just make us economists; we do wonders with twenty pesos!"

Women here do incredible things in order to make sure there's food on the table, in order to keep their families going. The age-old division of labor has placed men in the political sphere, dealing with abstractions; women are right in there where it counts, solving the concrete problems. So maybe this crisis we're in isn't anything new for women; it's just a slightly larger version of what we've always known.

Vidaluz, as a woman with a certain level of responsibility—you ran the library system during the revolution, you were vice-minister of culture for a time, and now you are dean of humanities at UCA—have you had any problems in regard to men who find it difficult to relate to women in positions of power?

16. Twenty-five percent of Nicaraguan families are headed by women according to Paola Pérez-Alemán ("Diagnóstico de la situación de la mujer en Nicaragua: 1990," unpublished paper). According to another study, 32 percent of all women with children in Nicaragua support their families without the help of a husband or any other financial contribution. See Mercedes Olivera et al., *Nicaragua: El poder de las mujeres / Nicaragua: Women's Power* (Managua: Cezontle, 1992).

I've thought about this. One of the things I've learned from Marxism—maybe one of the few things I've learned—is that women's emancipation is essentially economic. It doesn't matter what a woman's job is, whether it's a trade or a profession, if she does it well and assumes her responsibilities she's naturally going to experience less of that traditional competition with men. It's always there, but the more sure she is of herself the less she's going to feel it.

I can't honestly say I've had any problems with men, not on the job. Right now I'm one of two women deans. The structure is as follows: there's the president of the university—we call him the rector—then a rector general, then three vice-rectors, and finally six deans. Two of the vice-rectors and two of the deans are women. But I can't say I've had any gender-based problems at the school.

And as a poet, it's been more or less the same. In the art world you're always going to have your petty problems, rivalries and the like, but I don't believe it's any worse for the women than for the men. For women who take themselves seriously, who develop themselves as professionals and assume the responsibilities of their field, I think competition or other problems that have to do with gender are minimal. At least I haven't noticed any blatant sexism in my professional life. Where I see sexism taking a terrible toll is in politics, in the struggle for power.

For women, education is such an important thing—for everyone, but especially for women. Something that's made me happy, in this respect, is that both my daughters wanted to get an education: one under capitalism and the other one here, during the revolution. And now, of course, [the latter is] doing something else. My oldest daughter, the one who left the country—well, she left but she has a feminist consciousness. And I think I provided her with a model that wasn't that of your typical housewife.

Karla, my oldest daughter, went to the United States at the age of fourteen; at seventeen she got her own apartment and started working in a bank. And when she came back here the year before last, she had finished two years of college in business administration, she had paid her own tuition, her English was perfect, and she had computer skills. Now she's the assistant manager of credit at the Mercantile Bank, one of those private banks that's opened up here. She's twenty-four years old, and she earns three times what I do.

And her relationship with her husband is not at all traditional; there's a great deal of solidarity between them. They have a small child, they both work, and he does his share of the work around the house. That's not something that was easy to come by here. It's still not easy to come by. Karla plans to continue studying, too.

My younger daughter, Vidaluz, is single. She's in her third year of law right now, and she works part time in her father's law office. She's also an assistant to Gladys Ramírez, who's the director of culture. Vidaluz likes what she does, and she has a great sense of self-confidence. So I feel good that both my daughters are so self-assured, that they haven't taken the "easy way out." I love seeing them confident, strong.

My son Carlos is twenty. He never really liked to study; but he went to vocational school, he has a trade. He learned to repair air conditioners and refrigerators, and in the United States you can earn a decent living with that. But I never worried very much about him, because he's a man: even if he hadn't learned a trade, he wouldn't have been as vulnerable as the girls. Without an education they would have ended up submissive, or worse.

My youngest is Mariano. He's studying in Miami, in his last year of high school.

What do you think about Dora María not being elected to the national directorate? How do you analyze what happened there?

When the FSLN had its First [Party] Congress, after we lost the elections, I was in favor of changing some members of the national directorate or enlarging the directorate; and I wanted to see a woman included because the Party has had so many outstanding women, since its inception. Dora María was my candidate, and she was the candidate of a sizable faction within the FSLN that supported her. When I decided to write an article, in order to make public my reasons for supporting Dora María, I found there was a whole campaign already under way, a campaign endorsing her. I wasn't a delegate to the Congress, so I couldn't take part in the debates. Sergio and I were invited to the opening and closing sessions, but we weren't delegates—which was another reason why I wanted to publish my article.

What I stressed was that I felt it was important that a woman be part of the highest level of leadership, so that we women would be represented by her; but that she shouldn't be elected simply because she was a woman, but rather for her qualities as a political leader. And I added that the FSLN had a great many women who would do us proud in that respect, women who had extraordinary military histories, political histories, women who had served in the cabinet, and so forth. And then I proposed Dora María as my candidate, because she certainly had all those qualities—in abundance. She was a heroine during our period of armed struggle, she was a talented political negotiator, she was selfless as minister of state, and of course she's intelligent and sensitive to women's issues. Besides, she's an absolutely charismatic leader. I submitted my article to *Barricada*, but in the end it wasn't published. In any case, there was a very intense campaign in Dora María's favor.

But that's what I'm asking you and others here: why was there so much pressure against Dora María being elevated to the directorate, when she clearly had so much support among the rank and file?

What she said—in fact, I remember Sergio and I were coming out of the convention center, and we ran into her and asked her ourselves, and she said this to us—is that she decided to decline the nomination. Her candidacy had been discussed in the Sandinista Assembly, before the Congress, and the support just wasn't there. So she declined. It was a matter of Party discipline. Why the support wasn't there is another question. My very personal opinion is that our perennial sexism, with all its crudity, manifested itself in the power struggle. It seems than none of our current male leaders is sufficiently developed to be able to share the highest level of power with women comrades. And we women haven't yet found the way to effectively take that power.

The rhythm of our conversation had begun to slow. It was clear we were both tired. Vidaluz's husband, who had tactfully gone to attend to his sick animals during the interview, reappeared and asked if we wanted something cool to drink. The sun was lower in the sky now; all the amazing surfaces of the stalks and leaves and fruits and flowers refracted a different light: softer, inviting more informal talk. Vidaluz wanted to say something else, though, about witness:

You know what I think? I'm an extrovert by nature, but as a Christian you learn the usefulness of bearing witness. And since that's something the revolution has also cultivated, I've talked about my life a great deal. We recognize how useful it can be, how much we can learn from sharing our experiences. People listen, and they identify with the experiences they may also have had, or with the feelings, fears, hopes.

It's interesting that you bring up witness in the Christian sense because I believe it functions similarly in a book like this one. You can write about something, and people can read it, but when you let a woman tell her own story, in her own words, the reader identifies much more closely.

That reminds me of something that's provoked a great deal of discussion here of late, among the feminist groups: whether or not women bring a new style or meaning to what we do. So many women here have held positions that were traditionally reserved for men. And we've asked ourselves, "Do we handle those jobs differently? Not just in terms of our manner, or personality, but as women do we really have a different style?"

My feeling is the same as when I think about women's and men's poetry. If it's well made, effectively done, that's the important thing. It doesn't matter whether we're women or men, the important thing is effectiveness, knowing what we're doing. And I believe this is what brings equality. Still, I think women do bring a different style to our work. Historically we've developed this terrible habit of always prefacing what we do by saying "I'm sorry," asking to be forgiven for this or that. But I think we bring an authenticity to our work that's very much about being a woman. The unadorned simplicity and clarity of womanness is a beautiful thing.

"We Were the Knights of the Round Table"

Gioconda Belli

The Blood of the Others

Alive, I read the poems of the dead,
I who laugh and cry and can shout
"¡Patria Libre o Morir!"
on the back of a flatbed truck
the day we enter Managua.

I read the poems of the dead,
watch the ants in the grass,
my bare feet, your straight hair,
the curve of your back
after hours of meetings.

I read the poems of the dead
and fear this blood that fuels our love
does not belong to us.[1]

1. "La sangre de otros" / "The Blood of Others," in Gioconda Belli, *From Eve's Rib* (Willimantic, Conn.: Curbstone Press, 1989). The book's English translations are by Steven F. White, but here I offer a new translation of this poem.

This poem, perhaps as well as any of her others, evokes a sense of the place Gioconda Belli defines for herself in her country's history. It is a place she inhabits with explosive joy and profound sorrow, with a frank smile and the intimate dignity of a woman who knows that the battle lost is worth infinitely more than the battle never fought.

Gioconda is a slender woman with fair skin, dark vivacious eyes, and a great mass of curly dark-brown hair which frames her face in lush and artful disorder. Her gestures can be almost childlike at times, and then quickly serious. In a single conversation she may be playful, subdued, filled with whimsy, or almost petulant. Long a poet—whose verse has been set to music and sung by tens of thousands in the public square—in the past several years she has added two successful novels to her repertoire. When we met for this interview she was working on a third.[2]

"The first was autobiographical," she said, "as most first novels are. The second showed me I could write about characters who are completely fictional. And this one? It's an Arthurian drama, because I think we were all like Knights of the Round Table here . . ." She smiled. "It's taking its toll on me, though," she confessed. "The identity crisis we've suffered has made everything more difficult."

Like so many Nicaraguans of her generation, Gioconda is a study in contradictions. She has lived here, there, wherever the struggle demanded her participation; yet she is the mother of three generally happy and well-adjusted children. Tormented romances dot her personal history; but in recent years she has settled into what appears to be a very solid relationship. She is largely self-taught, yet was called upon to provide utmost professionalism during the decade of Sandinista government. She enjoyed a privileged childhood, yet opted for a revolutionary project aimed at bettering the lives of her country's poor. And, like so many others of her place and time, her immediate family is split by stark political difference.

Gioconda is married to Charles Castaldi, a journalist from the United States who lived and worked in Nicaragua during the last desperate years of Sandinista government. They currently divide their lives between both countries, so it was by some stroke of that magic realism one expects from Nicaragua that she happened to be in Managua when I was doing the fieldwork for this book.

I drove south from the city to their home, high in the lush hills that gradually assume an ever more dramatic view of the capital. From this distance, the lake looks placid and clean, Momotombo Volcano's perfect cone rising majestically

2. With her book of poems *Línea de fuego* (Havana: Casa de las Américas, 1978), Belli won the prestigious Casa de las Américas poetry prize. Other books of her poetry are *Sobre la grama* (Managua: Gradas, 1974), *Truenos y arcoíris* (Managua: Editorial Nueva Nicaragua, 1982), *Amor insurrecto* (Managua: Editorial Nueva Nicargua, 1985), and *De la costilla de Eva* (Managua: Editorial Nueva Nicaragua, 1987). *From Eve's Rib*, her first collection in English (bilingual, trans. Steven F. White), is not identical in content to *De la costilla de Eva*. Her novels are *La mujer habitada* (Managua: Editorial Vanguardia, 1988) and *Sofía de los presagios* (Managua: Editorial Vanguardia, 1990). Belli's poetry and fiction have been translated into Danish, German, Greek, Italian, and English.

from its surface. A reflection of tropical sun obliterates the sharp edges of misery so that the city appears beautiful, almost grandiose.

I was struck by this quality of enchantment surrounding the dreamhouse Gioconda and Charles are making their own. Floor-to-ceiling glass separates a spacious living room from the expanse of velvet green sloping toward a perfect red barn with fresh white trim. "That will be my studio," Gioconda explained, following my gaze, and she opened the sliding doors to let in the moist air of this balmy winter morning. "When we're in the States we'll have to rent the house itself, and that barn will be my hideaway, a place I can always come back to." A stand of graceful palms seemed painted on the horizon. Miles below, an unreal Managua sparkled at the edge of its shining lake.

From various corners of the sprawling house, I could hear the insistent hammering that goes with every remodeling job. People walked in and out of the sunny space we'd chosen for our conversation: her friendly husband, her teenage son—redheaded Camilo, with his wonderful shy smile, whom I remembered as a toddler from times that suddenly seemed less remote—workmen, a maid clearing breakfast dishes from the dining room table and whose lunch preparations could already be heard beyond another set of doors. Still, we managed to take possession of this corner of Gioconda's world that we had invaded with recording equipment, camera, and a rush of memories.

The poet tucked her feet beneath her at one corner of a comfortable couch. A profusion of charms on several long necklaces rattled against one another as she reached to pull a cigarette from a pack on the coffee table, lit it, and took one draw in preparation for the revelations to come. Each of the charms looked as if it possessed a tale of its own. But I was after the larger story. This wasn't the first time I'd interviewed Gioconda.[3] We'd worked together in the early eighties, sharing the anxieties, triumphs, and questions of those first years of revolution. Now it would be important not to let this familiarity prevent a complete and rigorous telling. "I know this may seem redundant," I said, "but I think it's important to start at the beginning, to talk about your whole life as you feel it now."

Gioconda's life has prepared her well for questions like mine. She isn't the least bit flustered by having a microphone thrust at her:

I was born here in Managua, into an upper-class family. My parents were Conservatives, opposed to Somoza's rule. I was the second of five brothers and sisters, and my childhood was the usual one for a young girl of my class in Nicaragua. I studied at La Asunción, like so many other daughters of the wealthy here . . .

Another student of La Asunción! Did you study with Michele Najlis?

Not exactly. I was younger than Michele. She was finishing high school when I was just beginning; I mean she was in her last couple of years and I was

---

3. See Randall, *Risking a Somersault in the Air*, 141–154.

coming up. But I remember talking to her once. She was the guru, the "real" poet at the school. And later she was its scandal. She ran off with the Communists, the story had it, with Fernando Gordillo and others "of his ilk." Her fame was legendary! But I remember the literary salon we had; Michele was one of its most enthusiastic promoters. That was my first contact with poetry, and I wrote my own earliest poems in that salon: the poems of a child, really.

But when I was fourteen years old my parents sent me off to study in Spain. That was a terrible shock; everything was so different. I was barely a teenager, and all of a sudden I was at a boarding school in Madrid. I began to feel a sort of consuming sadness, a nostalgia for home. And as if that weren't enough, from Spain they sent me to the United States, to Philadelphia, where I studied at the Charles Moore Price School of Advertising and Journalism. After a year there I was allowed to return to Nicaragua, fully programmed to marry and have children.

Wait a minute. Whose idea was it for you to study advertising?

My dream was to study medicine. But it didn't take my parents long to convince me that medicine was "inappropriate" for a girl. They said it would take too long, and I'd never get married. Or if I did my husband would leave me; because I'd get all these emergency calls in the middle of the night and I'd have to dash off to the hospital, that sort of thing. They painted a very grim picture. And I bought it—hook, line and sinker.

The real problem was that I finished school very young, so I had to make my decision before I knew enough to rebel. My father wanted me to be an optometrist! [Gioconda remembered the absurdity and let a little giggle escape.] But, of course, the idea repulsed me. I think optometrist and executive secretary must have been the two "young ladies' careers" that were in vogue here back then.

So one day my father started talking about publicity, and he explained what it entailed. He had a friend—from Philadelphia—who was a publicist. It sounded exciting to me. And well, he convinced me.

You know, I didn't even go to college. I just took this specialized course, it was a year all told, and then returned to Nicaragua. But I was "graduated in publicity in the United States." It sounded good. And besides, I spoke English. So I was eminently marketable. I came home and got a job right away, and I began to earn a fairly good salary. At age seventeen I became the first woman publicist in this country. We're talking about 1967.

I don't know why but I grew up with this notion that I wanted to be independent, and I was always very clear about the fact that if I earned my way that would give me a measure of independence. At the same time, about a month after I'd come home, I met my future husband. And we were married seven months later: the big society wedding, of course. And even though I kept working—I insisted on continuing to work—I began to feel an emptiness. It was the life every young woman of the upper classes had here: the country club, the parties. I couldn't bear the thought that this was what I was going to do for the rest of my days.

But then things took one of those unexpected turns. After my daughter Maryam was born, I went to work at an advertising agency where some of the early members of the FSLN used to come around: Francisco de Asís Fernández, Carlos Alemán Ocampo, Camilo Ortega, among others. It was through them that I began to have contact with a whole other world vision. And I began to read. Oh, I'd always been a kind of library rat; I mean, I'd read Shakespeare, the world classics, but I didn't know Latin American literature at all. I wasn't familiar with my own people's culture. I also read *The Wretched of the Earth* by Frantz Fanon, which was popular at the time. And I felt like I'd been hit over the head with a rock. These guys talked to me about the Sandinista National Liberation Front, and it seemed like a real option to me. Plus I liked them: they were different, involved; they cared about Nicaragua.

These contacts, these experiences, were totally outside your marriage?

Totally. And as I became involved—with the people, with their vision of the world, with the FSLN—I began to break with everything that had been my life up to then. It was pretty schizophrenic. I'd escape from my home, from my marriage, and go off with these guys. It was also a kind of bohemian scene. But there's something interesting: as soon as I became involved in the political work, Camilo Ortega took me aside one day and he said: "The bohemian lifestyle is one thing; this is something else. You can't tell anyone about what we're doing." So I started working seriously with Camilo. He was always very careful to keep our political activities separate from the artistic milieu.

Camilo began giving me the Front's documents to read. I hid them in a sort of false ceiling at home. I'd lock myself in the bathroom, and—you remember those ceilings the houses in Altamira have, made of squares of plaster board?— I had all the FSLN's documents hidden there. I'd read them without my husband knowing—because he wasn't about to let me get involved.

My husband actually threatened me. He wouldn't allow me to go to the university because, he said, I'd turn into a rebel. All that sort of thing. Even though I was economically independent, I earned as much as he did and contributed the same amount to our household, he always tried to maintain that male control. I'd tell him: "Quit trying to be my father!"

Little by little I pulled away from all that. Little by little I committed myself to the organization. It was a perfect depository for all my social concerns: because I was filled with ideas, filled with a sense of anguish about what was happening here in Nicaragua; because of my Christian upbringing and, of course, because of what I saw all around me.

Do you think La Asunción had as much of an influence on you in this respect as it did on some of the other women?

Not as much. But I did have [formative] experiences there. For example, the sisters took us to Acahualinca. And I saw something there, an image I'll always carry with me: it was an old woman eating wet paper because she was hungry and had nothing else. Another memory I have from *La Asunción*, something I really hated, was when Christmas came around each year. They'd line us up and we had to give gifts to the poor children, who also had to form a line . . . it was horrible. I'll never forget that. I could feel how humiliated the poor kids were. It was the worst kind of "charity."

Meanwhile, my home situation was getting pretty precarious. My husband and I had gotten on badly almost from the beginning of our marriage. But as I became more and more involved in the FSLN, and was called upon to do more important work, it was less and less possible for me to live that double life. I was twenty at the time, and I'd begun to write poetry. Actually, poetry and politics entered my life at one and the same time—poetry, politics, and an awareness of my female power.

And it's interesting, I'd really always had a sense of my womanness, from the time I was very young. If you look at my earliest poems you'll see a celebration of that, a veritable tribute to the fact that I was born a woman. Somehow I'd always understood that; and when I began to write, it just came tumbling out.

Where do you think you got that positive sense of yourself as a woman, entrenched as you were in a society that hardly values womanness?

I think my mother had a lot to do with it. Our relationship was filled with conflict, especially later on. But my mother really was a strong woman who appreciated intellect, who wanted to know things, and she hated domesticity. So she always urged me to read. And she'd talk to me about culture, about Europe. In her own way, she believed that women deserved better. Of course she'd say, "Women should be well informed . . . besides knowing how to keep house."

The other interesting thing about my mother is that she never spoke to me negatively about sex. And that was unusual among mothers in our milieu. In fact, one of my most beautiful memories of growing up with my mother was when she told me about menstruation. It was absolutely lovely, not filled with shame and secrecy like it might have been. I can still remember how she told me my body would change, that once I had my first period I'd be able to have a child of my own, the wonderful responsibility of motherhood, that sort of thing. And sex was beautiful, too, not ugly like others portrayed it. My mother said sex was so very beautiful that one shouldn't share it with just anyone. Of course, she didn't explain how it was done; she talked about "the union be- tween a man and a woman," "the most profound of all communication," am- biguous phrases like that. I wanted to know how you did it, but I had to get that information from a book.

In any case, I joined the FSLN. I had two children by then. My marriage had failed. I told my husband, "I can't live with someone incapable of taking a stand, with someone as apathetic as you are." We separated and then we got together again—briefly—because he began wanting to help, to take part in some way. He even bought me a pistol, I remember. But it was really an effort to get me back; he himself wasn't interested in the struggle. And so we ended up getting a divorce.

I had to go into exile in 1975. Even before the Chema Castillo operation, state security was on my case.[4] So the comrades had to get me out of the country. They told me to get out and stay out, not to return until it was safe. They were sure that the attack on Castillo's house would provoke a sweeping dragnet. And since I was already singled out, because security had detected my movements, they wanted to make sure I wasn't picked up.

I left, but there was a communication problem. Eduardo Contreras sent word that I shouldn't come back, that I should go somewhere else—to Mexico or wherever—but I never got the message. Somehow the instructions got waylaid, and I returned. And it was horrible, because I returned to find all my friends in prison, and I was sure they were going to arrest me as well.

Still, some time passed and they didn't pick me up. I was able to spend one more year inside the country. But I was indelibly marked. The following December there was another roundup in which my immediate contact, Jacobo Marcos, was captured. When they picked up Jacobo, Carlos Fonseca and Pedro Arauz told me, "Okay, this time you've got to get out and stay out." I ended up leaving three days before the police agents came to my office and tore the place apart.

I went to Mexico, where I stayed for five months. I started working with international solidarity, then I went on to Costa Rica. That's where I remained until the end of the war. In Costa Rica I worked for the FSLN's foreign relations commission. It was a pretty multifaceted job: logistics, accumulation of materials, running guns, just about everything. Mostly I was representing the Front at international forums, speaking on behalf of the organization, explaining our objectives and needs. I traveled a lot throughout Europe and in Central America, informing people about what was happening in Nicaragua, making

4. On December 27, 1974, in the elegant Los Robles neighborhood of Managua, an FSLN commando made a surprise attack on a holiday party that was being held at the home of one of Somoza's inner circle, José María "Chema" Castillo. Although the Front had been planning such an attack for some time, they didn't decide upon the precise target until early that same morning. Somoza himself was in Miami, but guests at the reception included a number of important diplomats and other politicians, among them Guillermo Sevilla Secasa (Nicaraguan ambassador to the United States and dean of Washington's diplomatic corps—the uncle in Aminta Granera's story), Guillermo Lang (Nicaraguan consul in New York), and Noél Palláis Debayle (Somoza's first cousin and president of INFONAC, responsible for managing 90 percent of the country's foreign credits). At 10:50 P.M. the commando—consisting of thirteen, including three women—forced its way into the house. After a sixty-hour siege, the FSLN won its demands: the release of eighteen political prisoners; 2 million dollars in cash; publication of lengthy communiqués; salary raises for many industrial and agricultural workers, domestics, and the National Guard's enlisted men; and safe conduct out of the country for the released prisoners and members of the commando. They flew to Cuba. When they arrived at the Havana airport, one member of the commando told a journalist: "We are not supermen. We are mothers of children, nurses, workers, peasants, students, the humble whose lives sum up all our peoples' exploitation."

contact with the different political parties. My main area was keeping in touch with the parties that belonged to the Socialist International.

Gioconda, I want to ask you a two-part question about the period you've just described. In those years before the victory did you ever feel discriminated against because you were a woman? And, looking at those times from the viewpoint of the feminist consciousness you have today, does it seem to you now that you suffered discrimination back then?

At the time, I didn't feel discriminated against; on the contrary, I used to say what a remarkable thing it was that there was no discrimination. I remember talking about this on a number of different occasions. I recall someone showing me a document in 1970 in which some of the women questioned the fact that they were largely being assigned "womanly" tasks, like cooking for the comrades, managing the safehouses, that sort of thing. But I can't say that I noticed any gender discrimination at the time. I felt that there was a large degree of equality, especially in the cities.

In my particular case it was the comrades who'd encouraged me to leave my husband. I remember them asking me things like, "How can you stand the fact that you have to do everything behind his back?" And when I had to go into exile, my interpretation at the time was that they really believed I'd be more useful on the outside. I wanted to stay here. I begged to be allowed to go underground, but the decision was that I should leave; and I saw that as logical back then. I didn't take it as discrimination.

Looking back, this all seems like some sort of golden age in that respect. Women participated to an extraordinary degree, and there were a number of women who had positions of real responsibility. But there is one thing: there was sexual promiscuity. Not a whole lot, but some. And you know that in our society this always affects women's lives much more than it does men's. It was accepted that a comrade would have an affair, and then another, and another. They justified it by saying that since any one of us might be killed at any time, we had to live our lives as intensely as possible. And then, too, there was the mobility; you slept one night here, another there, for reasons of safety. That life-style, with its ever-present dangers, generates its own dynamic. This is the only thing I couldn't quite reconcile myself to, as a woman.

But, you know, it's interesting. Because as soon as victory began to seem like a possibility, things began to change. It's not true that things changed after the war ended; they began to change before. For example, I remember in June of 1979, when the tendencies reunited and they began to organize different groups of comrades to carry out different tasks, all the leaders were men. I complained. I remember how I protested; I said, "I've been in charge here for a while, I've been responsible for this group. Why is a man suddenly being put in charge?" No one even bothered to give me an answer. That sort of thing began to happen. If you accepted it, fine. And if you didn't, there was nothing you could do.

I was a member of the foreign relations commission, for example, along with two men. The idea was that there would be one of us representing each of the tendencies. But I never felt like we were treated equally. I always had this sense that I was treated differently because I was a woman. Looking back, I don't think we women fought for power the way the men did. It wasn't something I was aware of then, not in those terms. Maybe I was too romantic. "Let the men have the glory," I said. And we paid for that romanticism, because where were the women all of a sudden? In the new government we had Lea Guido, the first minister of social welfare. And that was pretty much it.

What I'm saying is that we didn't analyze the discrimination at the time. We felt we had gotten what we wanted, by being allowed to fight. And you have to remember, everything was very chaotic, very intense. But in retrospect it's quite clear; the moment victory became a possibility, that's when we women who had been active participants in the struggle began to be forced out, to lose power, to be marginalized. We'd been on the front lines, and then we weren't.

Many of the women with whom I've spoken talk about this in retrospect. At the time it was happening, do you remember talking about it with any of the other women? Did the women talk about it among themselves?

No.

After the FSLN won the war, what was your first job?

I had several. I was all over the place. But I guess the very first thing they did was put me in charge of the television system. First they actually sent me over to occupy the government channel, which was full of Somocistas. I went with a group of comrades—we were all armed—and we walked into Channel 6, which was where Radio Sandino is now.

This was July 20th or 21st. Things were in chaos, but we didn't have to use our weapons. We'd won the war, and that was that. I gathered everyone together and spoke to them. Our attitude, especially with those who had the menial jobs, who weren't Somoza's trusted employees or anything like that, was that they could stay on if they wanted to. We didn't have any money, so I told them we wouldn't be able to pay them right away but that we'd provide their food.

That was an interesting moment because I was in charge. And, of course, half the country's population wanted to work in television. There were a number of comrades who had fought in the international brigades and who stayed on to help build the new society: I remember a Chilean and an Argentine in particular, and of course they acted as if they knew everything there was to know about the industry. But I was in charge, and a woman to boot, so they insisted on showing me how things should be done.

The Nicaraguan men were much more cooperative: "Of course, Giocondita," they said. They accepted my authority. So I didn't feel discriminated against. But it was because I was well known, my picture had been in the papers: "Gioconda Belli Speaks in Paris," that sort of thing. That undoubtedly brought me a certain degree of respect. They even called me "comandante!"

But then we were all "comandantes" back then. In that kind of atmosphere, in the euphoria of those first few months, who was going to feel discriminated against? But when I look back, it's very interesting. I was in love with Henry Ruíz—"Modesto"—when I went to work at the television station.[5] And he began to call me on the phone.

He was a member of the national directorate. And, of course, he was all over the place: at the central command post, in the Bunker.[6] Our relationship wasn't really defined at that point, I wasn't his fiancée or wife or anything like that. Besides, we'd begun the relationship in totally different circumstances, circumstances in which he might have been killed at any time: we met in Costa Rica and he was headed back into the country.

Anyway, right after the war Modesto started calling me and insisting I come to work for him. I'd been at the television station for a month or a month and a half by then. And he kept calling and calling. I didn't know what to do. Should I stay where I was or go with the man I loved? He was telling me he needed my help, he wanted me by his side. And I ended up sacrificing my job, which was much more interesting and certainly more in line with my talent and training, to go to work with Modesto. And what was I doing for him? I ended up as a kind of combination secretary and bodyguard . . . organizing his papers, whatever.

Bayardo Arce and René Núñez criticized me for that. The discrimination wasn't automatic or across the board. I remember both those men telling me, "You're acting like a woman. You're leaving a job that's perfect for you in order to follow the man you love. It doesn't make sense." And that mistake really cost me. It really never stopped costing me, because things were never the same after that. I never again received the same kind of respect.

So I went over to work with Modesto at the Ministry of Planning. And, like I say, I handled all sorts of odd jobs there. Then I worked at the DAP [the FSLN's Department of Analysis and Propaganda], where I was once again in charge of television; later I became executive secretary of the electoral commission. And then I headed the Council of Political Parties, for the Front. From 1984 on I played a more important role, you might say.

I'd like to hear about your work in the electoral campaign . . .

I was talking about the first campaign, in 1984. From January of 1984 I was executive secretary of the FSLN's first electoral campaign. I organized a commission that included Bayardo, Sergio, a series of comrades. But I was the operative there. I did the work, but when it came to electing the person in

5. All the revolutionaries used war names. Henry Ruíz was known as "Modesto" and the name stuck.

6. "The Bunker" was Somoza's stronghold, an underground headquarters at El Chipote military camp in the center of Managua. When the dictator fled, the Sandinistas took over offices and living quarters containing everything from expensive wines to a completely stocked hideout.

charge, of course, they elected a man. I really fought that then; I was furious. "I've been doing this work," I said, "I'm as capable as anyone, if not more so!" Their response was simply that "this is a sexist society." Clear as could be. Still, I kept on doing the work. I was in charge of all the campaign's publicity and its spokesperson as well.

In 1989 they called me again. As you know, throughout the decade I worked pretty consistently in propaganda, so they called me to participate in the new electoral campaign. They wanted me to work with the propaganda commission. I knew we had a difficult problem on our hands: the situation the country was in, the economic situation particularly. The commission was composed of Iván García, Bosco Parrales, Erik Blandón, Margarita Suzan, Carlos Alemán . . . diverse criteria, but we were all very conscious of how difficult things were. Pretty soon everyone seemed to be in denial.

Maybe it was the campaign itself, that craziness which tends to pick you up and carry you along. It all began to sound like a Coca-Cola commercial! The idea was to push that myth: the Sandinista impetus, unbridled excitement, young people dancing in the streets, that sort of thing. That was what our leaders wanted to see. You know, the country was immersed in misery, people were having a very hard time; it wasn't as if we'd just won the war . . . their perception of how to run the campaign just had nothing to do with reality.

By then, the Party had separated itself from ordinary people in this country for a while. And I began to sense this. I was more and more upset. I was living with Carlos by this time, and I think that did a great deal to bring me down to earth. Carlos is a journalist and, besides, he's not Nicaraguan. He shares our dreams, but he isn't blinded by them. I remember he used to tell me, "I was down at the market today. I talked to people. And they told me . . ."—whatever. So I had someone in my own home who was causing me to doubt our perception of reality.

Carlos and I began living together in 1984, and through him I began having contact with a number of other foreign journalists. They sympathized with the Sandinistas, but they hadn't lost their critical sense. In a way, they retained the capacity for criticism we had somehow lost along the way.

In any case, when I realized that the electoral campaign was being designed as it was—a string of slogans, very little content or serious attention to the problems people were confronting in their daily lives—I wrote a document which I presented to the commission. I said that I thought we had to prepare ourselves for the worst possible scenario. And I presented an alternative campaign, based on the only thing I believed we had to offer: class consciousness and the power that can come from that.

I said, "It's true. The economy is terrible. The war is killing our kids. But we've won a place for ourselves in this society. We have a dignity we didn't have before, and we've got to defend that dignity." I wanted to emphasize the fact that unless we could defend our dignity we'd never be able to achieve a better life, or a new kind of economy.

It sounds to me like you weren't just proposing a more realistic campaign, but a more ideological one as well . . .

That's right, much more ideological. But you should have seen the reaction to my proposal! It was just about that time that they came out with the famous phrase: *¡Todo Será Mejor!* [Everything Will Get Better!]. And since it was Daniel Ortega who thought it up, no one else dared change or criticize it. I said, "If Comandante Ortega has employed a team of professionals, if we're the ones who are supposed to know about advertising, we've got an obligation to tell him that's a terrible slogan—and that all those arrows and other symbols they're using are utterly counterproductive."

I was anguished by the fact that in Nicaragua, particularly in the situation in which we found ourselves, we were launching that kind of a campaign: just assuming we were going to win. It was completely absurd. There was such a lack of respect for what people were going through. And what did I get for my concern? They kicked me off the electoral commission. Of course, they never came out and told me to leave; they didn't want to create a scandal. They just stopped calling me for meetings. I'd realize everyone was gathered behind closed doors and I hadn't been notified. It seems Daniel Ortega said I argued too much. At least it freed me from historical responsibility. Because the campaign was really horrible, extremely sexist along with everything else.

Gioconda, do you think the sexism of the campaign influenced the fact that women voted against the FSLN?

Maybe subliminally, or unconsciously. Consciously I don't think so. Because here in Nicaragua, unfortunately, women in the popular sectors do have this image of the male as a cock; it's part of the culture. But subliminally, if you like, it's possible they identified more with Doña Violeta: the mother, the virgin, the woman dressed in white, with her crutches and all the rest.

Can you tell me about the PIE?

PIE stands for Party of the Erotic Left. A group of feminists began getting together, more than anything to talk about what was going on in the women's movement. Because it was clear that the Sandinista women's movement operated more in line with male interests, with the so-called national interests. They kept telling us that we had to put off talking about women's problems until we'd won the war, until the economy was back on its feet, until . . . whatever. After all that had been accomplished, then we could talk about feminist issues.

By that time, we women had experienced a real loss of power. We'd led troops into battle, we'd done all sorts of things, and then as soon as the Sandinistas took office we were displaced from the important posts. We'd had to content ourselves with intermediate-level positions for the most part. Besides, I remember at the beginning of the revolution, it was practically a mortal sin if you mentioned your family. If a woman said "I can't go to that meeting on Sunday because I have to be with my children," that simply wasn't acceptable.

We argued that this wasn't productive, that our own children were going to turn against the revolution because they were inevitably going to identify it with the loss of their parents. We had family obligations and they were important. I remember quoting a phrase of Jean-Paul Sartre's: "I don't believe in the revolutionary who says he loves his people but is unable to love those closest to him." But this wasn't a popular point of view. And a whole process of displacement had begun—even in our own organization, in AMNLAE, where we thought we would have a voice. But it became apparent that we didn't. Women's issues just kept on being put off, eternally.

Our most important problems always seemed to be considered secondary. We couldn't talk about abortion "because that means fighting the Catholic Church." So, as I say, a few of us began getting together to talk about these things. We didn't call ourselves PIE at first, but later—joking around—we adopted the name. It comes from Ana María Rodas, a Guatemalan poet who has a book titled *Poemas de la izquierda erótica* [Poems of the Erotic Left]. That's how we chose the initials: PIE. We even thought of designing a logo, a woman's foot with painted toenails!

We were Sofía Montenegro, Ana Criquillón, Malena de Montis, Milú Vargas, Alba Palacios—who was with the Farm Workers' Association—Olga Espinoza, Vilma Castillo, Ivonne Siu. And it varied; sometimes there were more, sometimes fewer. It never got to be a large group, because we were selective. Lourdes Bolaños was a part of the group; later she founded the Ixchen centers. What we had in common was that we were all women who were well placed here; we all exercised a certain amount of influence. And we began to figure out how we might bring our ideas to bear upon public opinion, each of us working with women in whatever sector we were influential—or wherever.

We'd get together and talk about the issues, what was possible, what wasn't possible. And then each of us, in our own particular area, made sure the issues were out there—being talked about. Sofía worked through the newspaper. I had access to the different cultural sectors and the mass media. Several of the women were connected with the Farm Workers' Association. Milú worked in the parliament. Together we did an extraordinary job, considering what a small group we were. People listened, not to an organization called PIE but to each of us individually. We counted on that and developed a common strategy.

It was in this context that we began discussing the possibility of forming a political party, with an eye to the elections. We knew that the women's vote was being co-opted by the Right. We women were the ones who suffered from the reality of this country on a daily basis, we knew how difficult things were. And, of course, those of us involved in PIE were privileged compared to most women; but even for us it was getting more and more difficult to buy a loaf of bread, to find eggs or milk. The shortages were becoming extreme. So we knew that for poor women things had to be that much harder—to say nothing of the war, the draft. And we thought of building a party capable of running candidates and everything. We even drew up a program.

So by that time it wasn't such an exclusive group?

No, we'd grown. And we had plans for men to join as well as women. If we had gone for the elections, we would have expanded, of course; but since we ended up not going for them, we remained a closed group. If we had launched ourselves as a political party, we would have opened up to anyone who wanted to join. The idea was that we would run some women candidates, but at the last minute we'd withdraw and throw our support behind the Front. We didn't want to take votes away from the FSLN, but thought that this was a more realistic approach. It would allow us to use whatever strength we might be able to bring to the electoral process, and then to negotiate our support of the Front by getting the leaders to give us our share of power—positions—once they had won.

We decided to present our idea to the FSLN's leadership. But when we went to talk with Bayardo Arce—we had our program and everything; our slogan was "Start at the Beginning . . . That's the Only Way to Grow!"—he didn't take us seriously. And then he forbade us even to joke about anything like that. It was our mistake to believe they would buy the idea, compounded by our further mistake: that of remaining disciplined and accepting his decision.

And, you know, we had some very good ideas. In our program we placed a lot of emphasis on self-sufficiency in food production. We wanted land titles for peasant women, an institute of consumer protection, and we talked about domestic violence. Women are absolutely vulnerable here when it comes to sexual abuse and battery. Our program included changes in labor legislation. And, of course, we were pro-choice: we wanted legalized abortion, control over our own bodies, and all the rest. It was a great program, infinitely more attuned to reality than the Front's.

I think we should have gone ahead. But we did what we had always done: ask permission of the boys. And we're not about to do that anymore. Of course, many women in the Party wouldn't agree with this, but there are quite a few of us who will never again ask permission. And every day we see more women here who are growing in consciousness. We had a meeting in January of eight hundred women, and in March there was the Central American Feminist Conference.

Women have told me that the January meeting was extraordinary . . .

I wasn't here for the national meeting itself, but I might as well have been. I know what happened. The event was entirely planned and carried out by women, totally at the margin of the national directorate, at the margin of the whole political apparatus of the Front. Women were identifying our problems and looking for alternatives to the conventional model. We were looking for answers that the parties weren't able to provide. But, you know, the FSLN did manage to frustrate our efforts to a certain extent.

The central goal, in my opinion, should have been the formation of an independent women's movement; that is, an autonomous women's organization. But at the conference, when women began to talk about what kind of an organization we wanted, one group [of women] who are pretty influential—because they're well-known Sandinistas, respected by the others—began to argue against the idea of an independent organization, saying that this wasn't the time, that we should organize networks, echoing anything which would guarantee the status quo permitted by the men and which those men had already decided must not change. Once again, they were following orders, being "disciplined."

That frustrated our efforts to build an alternative women's organization, something that would work for us as AMNLAE never had. I felt particularly sad about this because the moment was right. It really was. But now they say a committee is getting together to prepare for the Latin American Women's Conference. Maybe we'll be able to get the whole thing going again.

Gioconda, were you here in Nicaragua when the FSLN lost the elections?

I was right here, in this room where we're sitting now. It was horrible. I'd been in the States the November before, and I returned in December. When I left in October I remember I was very concerned, because the situation seemed dangerously uncertain to me. But when I came back the comrades managed to convince me that I was wrong. Things were fine, they said; everything was going super-okay. And once again I began to doubt my own instincts. I thought I'd been wrong. I was always somehow caught between what I was hearing at home—from Carlos and his friends—and what my comrades in the Party said. And it was contradictory. The journalists were more skeptical; they were out listening to what people were saying in the streets every day. But then my Sandinista comrades would ask, "What do these gringos really know?"

I'm not dumb. And I listened to both sides. I was uneasy, because I knew that Carlos and his friends were pretty objective. So I always had that gnawing doubt. But when February 21st came around and all those thousands of people gathered to hear Daniel, I thought: "I guess I'm wrong. I shouldn't be listening to these guys who don't really understand how things are here." That was an impressive demonstration of support for the FSLN, I can tell you. At that point I really believed we were going to win.

But then again, when the electoral campaign ended and we had a couple of days for reflection—all the propaganda stopped, and we had a chance to think—I began to feel something just wasn't right. It was strange, like something in the air; you couldn't put your finger on it exactly. And when I went to vote I could feel it, too. I noticed that a great many people were wearing blue and white, the colors of the opposition. And I felt something, deep in my heart, a kind of premonition. We had a number of journalists staying with us, and they began to tell us how they'd conducted a kind of exit poll, talking to people coming out of the polling places. And they said they couldn't find anyone who had voted for the FSLN.

That's when I really began to get scared. Still, Sandinistas who dropped by the house all acted as if we were crazy. They didn't understand why we had any doubts at all. You know, Margaret, the day before the elections I went to see "Modesto." I wanted to ask him what we were going to do in the event we lost. But everyone was so sure of winning, I ended up not even posing the question. I was ashamed to ask it. I desperately wanted to know if we had a contingency plan, and I couldn't even ask.

I remember election day as being very oppressive. I think I felt sick all day. But it was like I was fighting this internal battle between my intuition, those negative vibes I was getting, and my need to believe we were going to win. So when I realized that we were in fact losing, it was tough to accept. I had gone over to Sofía's place. And my sister called to tell me, "We've lost. They've just called Humberto over to Doña Violeta's house.[7] And [Jimmy] Carter's already called to congratulate the new president."

Sofía and I still couldn't believe it. "It's some kind of political maneuver," I remember she said, "on the part of the Right." We didn't want to believe this was happening. But I did believe it, in some part of my being. I went home then. I didn't want to go over to the Front's campaign headquarters, I just wanted to be at home in my own house.

And, you know, I experienced something similar to what I felt when we won the war. I began to think of the dead. All those faces flooded my eyes. I began to see them: Ricardo Morales and the rest. What a terrible thing, to have died for this, so the people could vote against the FSLN! It was an overwhelmingly awful sensation. And then the other thing was knowing [Ronald] Reagan had gotten his way—that they'd finally really beaten us. Even the landscape began to look different then. It was as if these hills, the volcanoes and vegetation, the lake, all began to speak to me with a different voice. Everything had changed, turned hostile in a matter of minutes. And it would never be the same again.

Gioconda, in your family how many of you are revolutionaries?

Of the five siblings, only two: my sister and I. My mother died the December before we lost. My father was never really opposed to the Sandinistas, but he wasn't a Sandinista himself. Compared to others of the bourgeoisie, he was pretty moderate. But my mother became depressed from the moment the revolution took power. It was just too much for her to see her children going in different political directions.

I'd like your analysis of the defeat. Obviously the United States did its part. But I'd like your point of view on what the Sandinistas did wrong . . .

For me, the main problem was the separation that developed between the Party and the people. The FSLN began to lose its ability to identify with what ordinary people were feeling, with what they needed. We were living the illusion of what we wanted people to feel. That was the main problem. I don't see the UNO victory as a repudiation of the FSLN, not really. I don't think those who voted for UNO ever really thought the Front was going to lose. It was a message, if you will, a way of making it a close race and sending a message

---

7. "Humberto" is Humberto Belli, Gioconda's brother and a member of City of God, a charismatic Catholic sect. One of the opposition's ideologues, he would become the new government's minister of education.

that people were against the war, against the draft. And it was a very female vote. The women's vote was important.

On the other hand, I don't know whether this women's vote came out of a feminist consciousness as such. I just don't know. It seems to me that women suffered the consequences of the war most directly: their sons were being drafted, their husbands too. And then there was the problem of the economy, how to keep putting meals on the table, that sort of thing. And this is where I think our biggest error was: we just didn't address those very serious problems in a realistic way. People can't eat abstract ideas and promises.

To be honest, there were all kinds of errors. The Party had gone off on a "development" tangent. It didn't pay enough attention to the small problems; our programs were too ambitious, and we overlooked the more realistic goals—things we could have done that would have meant real improvements in people's lives. And then there was that mistake I think a lot of revolutionaries commit: sacrificing the workers and peasants on the assumption that ideology is going to keep them going, that they'll be able to get by on ideology alone. The FSLN made concessions to the so-called patriotic industrialists and to the middle class, and always at the expense of the workers and peasants who got the short end of things. The FSLN made economic adjustments here that were as brutal as any designed by the International Monetary Fund, with the difference that the Monetary Fund wasn't even asking us to make them.

What about corruption?

I don't think corruption was that much of a problem, not really. But people thought of the Front as a reflection of themselves, and the Front had earned that: we fought together in the trenches, side by side. And people here came to expect the leadership of the FSLN to stay with them to the end. So when a few of the leaders began to partake of a different life-style, to live better, people resented that. It wasn't corruption like you'd expect to find in other countries—not that terrible level of corruption you see in Mexico or Spain. But here people had come to expect something else. They expected the Sandinista leadership to live like them, and they were disillusioned when they didn't, especially in a place as small and poor as Nicaragua.

Later on, it's true, the piñata was a terrible thing; that *was* corruption. But even that was exaggerated. The opposition tried to make it look like the entire Sandinista leadership had been involved, when in reality it was a few individuals. I think the differences in life-style affected people much more.

It's a question of how you understand power, and how you live it. Power can become manipulative . . .

It's the model itself. I now believe that all the conventional models lead to an authoritarian abuse of power. It's not a matter of gender either, because . . . you insert a woman in the conventional model and you get a Margaret Thatcher. I don't believe that women are inherently different in this respect.

It's the model that drives you to act in one way or another. What I don't have clear, as yet, is what the alternative might be.

But there is something I'm afraid of, and that's the kind of absolutism that I sometimes see reflected even in our own women's discourse. And it's that old cycle that really scares me: "The truth belongs to me alone" kind of thing. I'm terrified of that. It prevents the possibility of discussion, the ability to listen to others . . . we believe we have a patent on truth, and that anyone who doesn't agree is just plain wrong. The seed of a new kind of democracy must be the ability to accept a point of view different from your own and really look at it, not just throw it out as we've been wont to do, telling our opponent, "You're talking like a rightist, or a reformist, or a Social Democrat . . ." or whatever "because you're not talking like me."

This tendency, so typical of all of us on the Left, so much a part of our history, is also something I believe we have to fight against within the women's movement. I mean, if we really want to do something different, to transform the model. And it's hard. Because where does real democracy begin and false democracy end? Real democracy implies equality. So how do we achieve democracy among people who are at very different levels, who are subject to a variety of influences?

Take the United States: how would you define democracy there? We know how influential the U.S. media are, and how the market determines what people think. It's very complicated. We can't just talk about democracy in the abstract, as if it were the panacea for all ills. We have to understand what people's freedom is made of, what it's based upon.

Gioconda, speak to me as a poet now. What has your work meant to you throughout these many years?

During the ten years of Sandinista government the most beautiful thing for me—and it's what I feel as my greatest loss since our defeat—is having participated in a great collective project. It offered extraordinary hope, and it created a tremendous communal energy. It was like living inside a mighty river that constantly renewed you—spiritually, even physically.

At the moment, I'm trying to write a novel that uses symbols from Arthurian mythology. Because it seems to me that in a certain sense we were the Knights of the Round Table, all of us searching for the Holy Grail. We were on a quest. We were creating a better world. And that sense of collective creativity imbued life with beauty, ethics, heroism. It was all this that fueled my poetry and my novels. The experience was important to me creatively. It was multitudinous. Since the defeat, it's as if we've suffered a tremendous blow, and I'm having a great deal of trouble writing.

I thought you wrote your second novel after the electoral defeat.

No. I finished it afterward. My second novel was an attempt to write about those areas left untouched by the revolution: the depths of women's feeling, magic. The revolution didn't really touch on that fundamental experience you find in people here, especially among women: superstition, that whole mythic world women understand so well, especially rural women. I didn't want this to be a political novel. I wanted a different kind of creative challenge, to write a book that wouldn't be in any way autobiographical, something absolutely and totally fictional. And I wanted to explore Nicaraguan popular culture. I was able to write what I wanted. Some people were disappointed because the novel wasn't "political"; they expected a sequel to my first one. But I loved writing this novel. For me it was an act of magic.

What I feel now: I feel the need to learn from what we have been through. The need to talk about this experience and study the alternatives. As a writer, I know I have a powerful tool. I want to keep writing about women, the world women experience. I want to lay out the real issues in this quest for the Holy Grail, issues that for me have to do with a world where a new kind of ethic must be born. I see women playing an important role in this struggle to look inside our societies—which means looking deep down into our own humanity.

I believe in the need for utopias. If we are to survive spiritually, we must strive for better relationships with each other. We need to find a way to feel less alienated, less lonely, a way that will really bring us together. And when I say "we," I mean all of us, everyone who inhabits this planet Earth. Humanity has been able to produce great scientific ideas, great economic ideas, great material achievements; yet we find ourselves lacking when it comes to ideas that would help us solve some very basic problems: for example, the problem of drug use by young people who are dissatisfied with their lives, who want to escape their reality because it isn't giving them the spiritual fulfillment they need.

We can't give up dreaming, even if it sounds romantic and obsolete. And when you live in a country like Nicaragua, you know it's particularly important to hold onto the dream. Because people simply cannot go on living as they do. It's unacceptable that we as human beings tolerate this degree of poverty, misery, injustice. The dream shouldn't be formulated as a kind of panacea, the way it's been formulated in the past. We aren't looking for a recipe that takes two pounds of this, two teaspoons of that. What we need is not simply a formula for improving the economy; it's something much more profound, which we're not going to come to quickly or easily. But I think women and our wisdom must come into play.

Are people involved in that sort of reformulation?

There's a lot of searching going on. People are concerned, and people are concerned in the midst of the ordinary everyday struggle to survive. The political issues are all mixed up with the problem of where you're going to find work, how you're going to live, and the structural problems of the Party itself. Because in Nicaragua the interesting thing is that we're not only linked up politically to the FSLN, but emotionally as well. Our personhood, our very identity, is linked to the Party's identity.

We're not just questioning the Front as a party. We're questioning our own identity as well. That's why it's all so difficult. It's so hard to say, "Okay, maybe the FSLN isn't the answer. We have to create something new"—which is what I personally believe. But it's not easy, because breaking with the Front is like breaking with oneself. One would prefer an act of magic, a miracle: for all the members of the national directorate to realize suddenly that they've been using us in a certain sense, that they've usurped our identity. But we don't have the courage to confront them, either.

Gioconda, were you here during the Party Congress?

I was here until just a few days before; I had to leave before the Congress started. But I was involved in all the lobbying. I was at the Managua Assembly just before the Congress itself, where Dora María's candidacy was discussed and ultimately rejected.

What's your interpretation of that?

It was sexism, pure and simple. I don't have another explanation. And when I say "sexism" I'm talking about a series of prejudices—terrible prejudices. And I'm telling you: that was the beginning of the end of the national director-ate as far as I'm concerned. If we can't renew the directorate, it's going to be the end of the FSLN. The national directorate is playing a very negative role. It's become an obstacle to the healthy development of the organization, be-cause it's forcing the Party to remain stagnant; the old Front is obsolete under these conditions.

When you talk about the national directorate, are you talking about every one of its members?

Every one of them. Of course, there are some who are better than others. But during those ten years in government, I think power generated an authoritarian attitude in them all. They're all guilty of not being able to listen. The proof is the situation we're in today. So I think we need new blood. A party incapable of changing its leadership in ten years has failed in a very fundamental way.

Leadership is something you develop, you're not born with it. So it's not that I have a particular candidate in mind. There are a great many valuable people in the FSLN. There are a great many men and women with extraordin-ary experience. If they were allowed to think for themselves, to show what they can do, new leaders would evolve. And they'd be better than the nine we have now precisely because they wouldn't be burdened by the weight of his-tory. There's a conditioned reflex on the part of the rank and file with regard to the current leadership, and neither they nor we can overcome that. The only solution is to break with it and move on.

Do you feel it's important there be women on the directorate?

Of course. It's inconceivable to me that there are no women on the national directorate. Particularly here in Nicaragua, where women have played such important roles—politically, militarily, in the economic and social spheres. Besides, I think that if we're going to talk about a new model, a different model—and this is a challenge for us as women—we're in a privileged position. We don't have a formula to go by; we have to develop one of our own. And we can begin to elaborate a formula according to our own vision, a feminist worldview. It's a feminist vision that's going to be capable of producing a truly viable social model.

I don't see it coming from anywhere else. It seems to me that the current crisis is a product of sexism, of patriarchy. And it's not just the model we were trying to apply: we're going to be witnessing the failure of all models tried to date. Historically, patriarchy justified itself in the context of repeated wars. When wars end and people enter into a period without conflicts or antagonisms, patriarchy itself goes into crisis. So I think this is a very important moment for women.

A lot is going to depend upon how we present our model. Because we don't want to speak only to women; we want a society that's going to work for everyone. I don't know . . . we were talking about this just last night. It's not that we have the answers yet, but we've got to put our ideas out there and start them circulating. We can't just sit here; we've got to do something.

Is there anything else you'd like to say?

Just that, in a way, I feel we lost the revolution to a form of political machismo. Our men felt powerful, and they stood before the world like gorillas banging their breasts. The pride in what they had been able to do, the war they had won, that was what was most important to them. They felt powerful, invincible. And everyday life, the common concerns of common people—including the situation of women—they just weren't interested. Of course, they wanted to improve everyone's lot, but that wasn't what really excited them. What gave them joy, and absorbed most of their energies, was standing up to the world, the sheer pleasure they got out of telling the United States, "Here we are. We won and you can't do anything about it!"

That macho rhetoric which felt so good to them—and very often to us all—was what made them tick. They seemed not to measure the consequences of their words. They seemed not to realize that they weren't mythic *guerrilleros* any more, that they were heads of state and had to look after the well-being of four million people. In their political speeches, of course, they said they were doing all this for "the people," and maybe they thought they were. But the truth is, they lost sight of what the people felt and needed. They confused what *they* thought with what the people thought.

People's main concern here wasn't to beat the U.S. That's not what they fought for at the barricades; they fought because they wanted a better life, to feed and dress themselves and have a roof over their heads. So our leaders ended up having to eat their own words. What was all that rhetoric good for?

At the end, they were cornered; they had to give up. The rhetoric hadn't gotten them anywhere, and they had to accept the fact that they are not invincible.

And still, they tried to make defeat sound like victory. On the one hand, they negotiated; on the other, they stood there in the plaza talking as if they didn't have to concede a thing. Like raging bulls they undid in one stroke the negotiations they had just made. Daniel Ortega still does this—even now. He can't accept the fact that he's no longer president. He still thinks he can shake the world with his words. I feel sorry for all of them, because at some point they're going to have to see things as they are, and it's going to weigh on their consciences.

As for us, we're guilty of buying into this macho concept of power, of going along with it, of singing hymns to the greatness of our David and Goliath struggle. We lost sight of the real issue: the needs of the people that were not being met. I think we feel a responsibility. But I must say, in all honesty, that we did speak up, and we weren't heard. The issue, according to our leaders, was always the war, the military might we had to amass, the parades, the rallies in which we chanted the glories of our army.

Our authentic words got lost. That's why, now more than ever, I believe in the need for public debate, for bringing these issues out into the open and discussing them in democratic forums. Because, as it turns out, everything that we—the Sandinista rank and file—said during those years of revolution we said in private, at Party meetings, out of reach of those same masses whose interests we were supposed to be defending. And the leadership wouldn't have it any other way. They set the rules, and we had to play by those rules or be left in a political limbo.

Having lived through an experience like this sobers you, believe me. It makes you realize how unacceptable it is that your individuality be subordinated to some notion of "truth" that you are supposed to accept against all reason and sensitivity. Subjectivity is valid; it must nurture collective thought. After all, collective ideas are born in individual minds; and often, behind the defense of the "correct interpretation," there's a power struggle going on to see whose subjectivity will prevail.

So, the reformulation of the same project of social justice I talked about before, the same project we attempted and failed to bring off because of this political machismo, has to be based in real democracy, in an authentic struggle to achieve consensus, in people's participation not in feats of war but in the solving of everyday problems.

I think we women are particularly well suited for this task. But the problem is, the models we are forced to use are based on moral decisions reached through deductions from principles and not drawn from the real interaction that takes place in real life among real people. If you operate from a principle of care, based on real needs that must be met and not on some notion of patriotism or Party loyalty, you'll be in a much better position to start solving the problems of misery, hunger, underdevelopment.

Women have been operating from a principle of care for most of our history. We are trained to care for and nurture others. And instead of seeing this as a handicap—much like our capacity for giving birth has been turned into a handicap—we should be able to generate and socialize a new kind of ethic, new rules of the game. I think the reason we women have so much trouble with power is because the applicable rules very often go against our deeply grounded sense of ethics. The only way we can make a real difference is by changing those rules, by defending the way we behave and operate as women, not by disguising ourselves as men and competing on their terms.

"It Doesn't Matter What Kind
of Uniform You Wear"

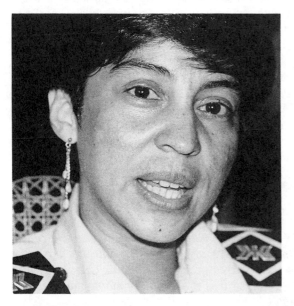

Aminta Granera

In late July 1992 the streets of Managua bore continuous evidence of protest. On any given day the smoldering remains of at least six or seven bonfires could be seen at scattered intersections. The protestors made giant piles of old tires and set them aflame in the people's traditional sign of communal rage. University students were demonstrating for their promised 6 percent of the national budget. Members of the armed forces, who had been forced into early retirement in the midst of a stagnating economy, were marching for minimal severance pay and benefits. Frequently these marches and demonstrations made it impossible to move from one part of the city to another.

The night before I was to interview Aminta Granera a group of ex-military people confronted the police near the Sandinista Trade Union Central. The demonstrators had homemade grenades and Molotov cocktails. The police had orders not to shoot. In the fray eight people were wounded, most of them policemen. They had followed explicit instructions not to fire on the protestors. Granera, a slender woman who was once a nun, now occupies a high-level position in the Nicaraguan national police. I wondered, as we approached her office, if in the aftermath of this confrontation she would be able to receive us as planned.

Getting into the compound was tinged with the surreal bureaucracy typical of such establishments in Third World countries. In spite of periodic attempts at streamlining the process, you inevitably feel you are in some dubbed comedy where language and action don't quite match. We needed to pick up a pass at one gate, but were instructed to use an entrance many blocks distant. On a low concrete wall and under scattered trees, groups of police sat eating and talking. Once inside the building, though, there was no receptionist who could tell us where to go. We wandered for a while until we turned a corner and almost ran into an elderly officer with a kindly face. He responded to our plea for directions by offering to take us to Aminta's office.

Aminta Granera in person presents a more astonishing image than her occasional newspaper photographs or the brief interview in Gente *that had caught my attention the week before.[1] Forty, her face and body might be those of a twenty-year-old. She is almost too thin, her obviously high energy level appearing to emanate from a profound spirituality rather than from any store of physical strength. The epaulets that denote her rank as* subcomandante *(major general) seemed to dwarf her shoulders. The absolute serenity of her hands folded in her lap contrasts with the vivid expressiveness of her large brown eyes and the pixie quality of her smile.*

"I wondered if you'd be able to make time for our interview," I said, once introductions were complete. We had been ushered into a large conference room, one wall of which exhibited a series of phrases on little tan cards. I noticed that the author of one of the phrases was the Argentine/Cuban revolutionary Ernesto "Che" Guevara; another was the founding mother superior of the Catholic order of La Asunción.

Aminta helped us find an outlet for the tape recorder. "I would have called to cancel," she said, and then added: "This might be the only country in Latin America where we can order our police not to fight back against a mob of armed protestors, and they won't!"

Still I wondered, in these conflictive times, how long we would be able to talk. I wanted as much of this woman's story as she was willing to give. When we were fully set up and I could see that she was ready, I asked her to begin by telling me about her childhood, her family, her earliest memories:

Well I was born into a very wealthy family, in the city of León. I had one of those absolutely privileged childhoods—especially in a country like ours—with all the luxuries and delights a little girl could dream of. My grandfather was probably my most important influence during those early years. He was a philosopher, a historian, and he loved nature. He was the one who gave me my respect for freedom and for other people, and my lifelong identification with all living, growing things.

I remember we used to go to the seashore and to the countryside. There my grandfather would give me little exercises in silence. He'd say, "Let's see if we

1. *Gente* [People] is a news magazine published by *Barricada* every Saturday. Sofía Montenegro is the editor.

can be silent for five minutes." Then he'd ask me to tell him everything I'd heard during those five minutes. At first I heard very little. He could describe the cricket's chirp, though, and the crackling of a small branch broken by a squirrel, each bird's song. That's how he taught me to appreciate nature and to seek a deep sense of harmony within myself, with others, and with the world. At the time, I wasn't conscious of how special this was, but looking back I realize that the experience gave me a greater sense of fullness than any I've known.

I'm the oldest of five brothers and sisters. We all lived with my grandparents for a while, and then my parents and my siblings moved to another house. But I continued to live with my grandparents because I didn't want to leave my grandfather's side. And his house was quite special, unreal in many ways. I don't think I ever heard a raised voice or an argument of any kind there. A spinster aunt played the piano. My grandfather read his literature, his philosophy. And all the poets of León would come over in the evenings to read their poems. Musicians came, too. As I say, it was a very special house.

I was born in 1952. So when I talk about my childhood I'm talking about the early sixties. The country was in turmoil; misery and exploitation were rampant. But I was oblivious to it all—until I was eleven or so and El Cerro Negro [Black Hill] erupted for the first time I can remember. That terrible volcanic dust fell as violently and heavily as it did during last year's catastrophe.[2] A few days after the eruption, my family decided we were going to move away; it was bad for our respiratory system, they said.

And I remember asking if everyone in León was going to leave, if the whole city was going to be abandoned. Of course, they explained, not everyone was leaving, not everyone had somewhere else to go. And that's the first time in my life I stood up to my family: "I'm not going unless everyone can go," I said. They argued that I was only eleven, that I couldn't stay by myself. Nevertheless, I did stay. My family moved to Casa Colorado, in Diriamba, and I remained in León with a group of friends from school, from La Asunción.

So you're another Nicaraguan revolutionary woman who studied at La Asunción! There certainly are a number of you. From your generation and several generations just a bit younger than yours, I've interviewed at least a dozen women over the years who studied at that school . . .

Yes, La Asunción is of particular importance here in Nicaragua, and in my own formation. And when that first eruption of El Cerro Negro took place, a group of students from my school and from La Salle got together to organize the evacuation of the population, aid brigades and the like. That was my first real contact with how people live here, outside the confines of my family. A

2. El Cerro Negro is a large hill of smooth, black sandlike volcanic ash outside the city of León. It has erupted periodically over the years, and each time a heavy rain of black ash descends upon the city and environs, doing damage to that year's crops. The most recent explosion was in 1991.

group of us began working in a neighborhood called Río Chiquito, where La Asunción now has a large school and where a great deal of public work is going on. But back then we were helping the people patch up their houses and just generally get out from under all that volcanic ash.

My boyfriend, who was older than I and already studying medicine at the university, helped set up a makeshift clinic. Our first site was under a tree. We got basic medicines and attended to the people as well as we could. And there were campaigns; for example, one day everyone at the school would bring one brick to class. Sheltered as I'd been, this whole experience was tremendously important for me.

That's when a strong social consciousness began to awaken in me, and my commitment to God pushed me to a commitment with the poor. I knew it wasn't right for some of us to have so much while others had nothing. And I also understood that we had to do something about the situation of injustice in the country. The sisters at that time tried to get us to do a year of social service, once we were graduated from high school. They called it AMAS, Auxiliares Misioneras de La Asunción [Missionary Auxiliary of La Asunción]. They had a number of mission houses throughout Central America, and they urged us to spend a year or two working at one of them.

But my family wouldn't let me go. They wouldn't give me permission. Instead they insisted I go to Washington, D.C., to begin my university career. After college, they said, if I still wanted to do that kind of social service, I could. I wanted to study philosophy—I wanted to be like my grandfather—so I went to Washington and began my studies at Georgetown University. But the urgent need I felt to do something for others continued to grow; in fact, it was there in Washington that I made the decision to become a nun.

It's important to say that in Washington I lived with my aunt and uncle. My uncle was the Nicaraguan ambassador to the United States, Guillermo Sevilla Sacasa; my aunt was Somoza's sister. The tensions and contradictions became more and more extreme in my life. I began to feel the painful conflict between my family's interests and the interests of the masses of Nicaraguan poor as I never had before. And I identified with the Sisters of La Asunción. I saw them as fully realized women, living lives of service to others.

This was 1969, '70, '71. My boyfriend and I had broken up when I finished high school and tried to go off on that year of mission work. And, as I say, I ended up going to Washington instead. Nevertheless, one summer vacation we started going together again and we'd practically set the wedding date. But the idea of marriage only pushed me further in my knowledge that my life seemed set upon a course I didn't really want. I knew that if I married Henry—that was his name, he lives in the States now—I'd be condemned to the kind of life the other women in my family have. And in spite of the fact that I believed I was in love with this man, I knew that wasn't what I wanted.

So one day I called Guatemala, the provincial center of La Asunción. I talked to Mother Fermina, and I told her I wanted to enter the convent. The sisters didn't believe I was serious: they'd seen me with Henry, they knew me as a happy-go-lucky young girl who loved music, who loved to dance—well, I guess they just couldn't picture me in the convent. But I insisted and finally they said, "All right. If you continue to believe that this is what you want, you must first do a year of missionary work in Ecuador. And you must leave on such and such a date." It was January.

I immediately sold my car, packed my guitar, my accordion, and three pair of Levi's and took off for Ecuador. I wrote a letter to my father, another to my grandfather, and one to my boyfriend. I asked them to respect this decision of mine, to believe me when I said that this was what I had to do.

That year as a missionary in Ecuador was beautiful. It was a time of tremendous solitude, because as a missionary you're not one of the sisters and you don't really belong to the religious community. You live among them but you're not one of the family. They have their routine, their hours for prayer and so forth, a whole series of things in which you're not permitted to participate. And for me it was also the first time I'd lived completely away from the protection of my family.

I'd completed two years of philosophy by then. And I went to work in a child-care center, alongside the indigenous people of Gapal. Like the other women, I washed my clothes in the river. My hands were raw, all sorts of things happened to me . . . because, of course, I wasn't used to that kind of a life. Still, it was a wonderful year. I was able to take a great deal of pleasure in nature. And I learned that solitude is a prerequisite to being able to really communicate profoundly with people.

Solitude never made me sad. The sisters had their life in which I couldn't take part, so I'd walk through the mountains or go down to the river. I remember one Sunday afternoon: I must have spent four hours just sitting and looking at the river. The Yanuncay is beautiful as it flows past the city of Cuenca. There were these very smooth stones in the water that fascinated me. A local priest came by on horseback and asked me what I was looking at, and I told him I was just enjoying looking at those stones.

He asked me if I'd ever seen what the stones looked like higher up where the river was born. And I told him no. "Let's go," he said; and he took me on horseback, higher and higher. At the top, of course, the rocks were sharp and cracked, very different from the way they looked down below. And this priest—Father Blas was his name—told me that's how people are: all crude and sharp to begin with. But he said that contact with others, our contact with life itself, polishes us and makes us more beautiful. He said it was a matter of learning about life and being willing to make a commitment to it. And he quoted that line about it "not being the hammer that makes a perfect form, but water with its dance and song."

This experience sums up that year. I was a young woman who'd come from such luxury, such power, such waste. I even thought of Georgetown as a wasteful place, because the university offered so much in the way of possibilities, everything you ever wanted to study. And I came away from all that to a region of absolute poverty, an indigenous community where people literally had nothing. Where the women gave birth squatting on the earth, where I helped them deliver their babies and they themselves told me where to cut the cord. They'd give birth like that and then they'd get up, wrap their newborns in whatever they had, and go on down to the river to wash. There couldn't have been a greater contrast between my life in Washington and my life in Ecuador.

At the same time, I was living a very intense internal process, coming to the understanding that life was worth living only if you could live it in service to others. And at that particular moment I was convinced that the best way to live a life of service was as a religious sister. That became my challenge and my goal.

How did your father, your grandfather, and your boyfriend respond to the letters you wrote them? How did your family react to your leaving like that?

They tell me it was terrible, a terrible shock. My mother was very nervous; she cried a lot and became ill. Everyone suffered a great deal. Nevertheless, one day much later my mother confided in me that it wasn't until I left that she began to mature. Of course my decision affected my family. It affected my siblings because I was the oldest sister. I think the older sister in a family always has that sense of herself as a kind of second mother; she tends to want to protect the younger kids. We were a very united family. I think my sister cried the whole five years I was in the convent. It was also very hard on my youngest brother—he lives in the United States now, in Ohio. It was hard on them all.

Still, I think it's like the stones in that river near Cuenca. As Father Blas told me then, we help one another grow. Just as my family had once given me a sense of togetherness, a love of liberty, and my delight in nature, I think my choices and my attitude toward life have influenced and changed them. My boyfriend, too. My boyfriend told me I wouldn't last a month in the convent. He said I wouldn't be able to live without him, that I'd be back before I knew it.

Another break occurred after the year I spent in Ecuador. I returned briefly to be with my family, but I knew I had undergone a fundamental change. I knew what my own path was by then, and it wasn't the one they'd always imagined I would take. I tried to make them understand that in spite of my decision I still loved them as much as ever. But it was hard. And I went off to the novitiate in Guatemala.

For five years I was a member of the congregation of La Asunción—five very happy years. I no longer belong to the order, but I carry it with me always, like some indelible mark upon my heart. It wasn't only my years as a young girl in school, where the sisters taught us to pray, to know God, to relate to others, to serve; where they opened our eyes to the situation of poverty and injustice in the world. That sentence over there on the wall, it's by the founder of the congregation, Sister María Eugenia: "La voluntad de Dios es una sociedad donde ningún hombre tenga que sufrir por la opresión de otro" [God's will is a society where no man must suffer from the oppression of another]. That gives you an idea of the concept of God the congregation has, which they try to convey to those who work with them.

Those five years I spent as a sister of La Asunción were also unforgettable—
an extraordinary experience. If I were to do it all over again, I would make
exactly the same choices. My time in the order allowed me to study theology,
to continue to study philosophy, and to work with the Indians of Guatemala. I
was in Caulicán, in Alta Verapaz, in Tlaxtil in the state of Cobán, and in a
series of small villages way back in the mountains near the Mexican border,
where the sisters didn't even have an established mission yet. We novices went
out to open up that frontier, to attend to the needs of the Indian peoples there.

That's where I had my first contact with the Ejército Guerrillero de los
Pobres [Guerrilla Army of the Poor].[3] We began to work alongside the Jesuits
who were there, fighting for the liberation of Central America—that is, no
longer simply from a spiritual or social point of view, but with a political
commitment as well. And in my particular case that eventually brought me to a
military commitment, when I joined the FSLN.

I wish you'd explain that whole process, how it played itself out in you.
Because it's a pretty big leap . . .

It's not a process that's mine alone, or that belongs to the members of that
religious congregation. It's really a common one in our society, in all these
societies of ours that are so rife with institutionalized violence, so structurally
wrong. Unfortunately, we've had to learn that only through exercising another
type of violence can the system's violence be stopped and something new built
in its place.

But I'll tell you about my personal experience. I believe I went from a purely
spiritual experience to a social commitment primarily because I realized it
wasn't a matter of doing something for others but of doing something with and
[getting something] from the others. It was my relationship with God that led

3. The Guerrilla Army of the Poor, or EGP, is a Guatemalan guerrilla organization founded in
1972. In a country where the impoverished Indian and mestizo populations have been brutally
exploited by a tiny local oligarchy for generations, where whole villages and towns have been
napalmed, where death squads and torture are routine, and where some forty thousand human
beings have been "disappeared," the EGP joined a number of other armed-struggle organizations
in the fight against a succession of brutal military regimes. In 1980, the EGP formed an allegiance with the Revolutionary Organization of the People in Arms, or ORPA, the Revolutionary
Armed Forces, or FAR, and the leadership of the Guatemalan Workers' Party (Communist). In
1982, the Guatemalan National Revolutionary Unity (URNG), a more solid alliance of the
above-mentioned organizations, was established. The URNG has long opted for a political solution to the violence in Guatemala. Thus, in 1989, all of its member organizations met in Oslo,
Norway, with a National Reconciliation Commission and signed an accord aimed at a three-step
dialogue. In 1990, in El Escorial, Spain, the URNG met with nine mainstream Guatemalan
political parties, again to discuss a political solution. Although these talks have been a forward
step in the history of relations between the oppressed and their oppressors, as yet they have not
resulted in an end to Guatemala's daily terror, which only gets worse. In the mid-1970s, when
Aminta made contact with the EGP, it was a fairly young movement.

me to want to do this work—not from a position of privilege, of power, in which all my problems were taken care of, but by trying to walk alongside the people themselves, at their pace.

I guess I should say that from the age of fifteen, more or less, it's been a rare day that I haven't prayed. It's something I need, like I need to be with my children or my husband. More than I need to eat, because I'm someone who rarely feels hunger; I can't say I know what it's like to be hungry. But I do need a lot of sleep, so maybe I should compare my need for prayer with my need for sleep. This intimate personal contact with God is something I need in order to replenish my strength.

And what I've found is that this habit of examining myself before a Jesus who loves justice, and who asks only for love from those who follow him, has expressed itself differently at each stage of my life. Way back when I was a child and El Cerro Negro erupted, that self-examination found its expression through working with the people in Río Chiquito. Maybe later my relationship with Jesus expressed itself by my going off to Ecuador. But I also began to understand that even though we could do wonderful things, even though we could accompany people from the standpoint of their needs and desires, structural situations still exist that simply cannot be changed by that kind of work alone.

I came to understand that other methods are necessary. Unfortunately, real change requires a strategy that includes armed struggle; because nothing short of that has been capable of eliminating the old exploitative structures and replacing them with a society that is more humane, more just. And for me this just society, this world that is more humane, is God's will. Well, not only for me, but for the Sisters of *La Asunción* as well, for the founder of La Asunción.

So you learn that politics is necessary. I used to reject anything that smacked of politics because my family was political. The Sacasas were always part of Somoza's political world, and I grew up in that world. It was dirty, it was disgusting, and I rejected it completely. But then one day you wake up and realize that your country's liberation requires a political commitment, and you're not going to sit back and say, "No, I can't take part in that, it's dirty." You figure out how to participate in defense of the vast majority of the people.

And, of course, you figure out how to practice a different kind of politics—a different way, with a different focus, different objectives, different methods. In our case, that meant thinking about Nicaragua from the viewpoint of the poor, not from that of the bourgeoisie. It meant building a new Nicaragua in the interests of the poor, in the interests of the great majority of the population. This consciousness was what helped me make my political commitment.

At the same time, some of my cousins were already in the FSLN. They came to visit me and we talked. They shared some of what was going on in their lives. And it just happened that their visit coincided with my transfer to the school La Asunción had in San Salvador. I'd been working for five years with the indigenous people of Guatemala, deep in the mountains . . . a great closeness with people's suffering. But my health wasn't good and the congregation decided to move me. I had an acute case of anemia—corn was practically the only thing we ate there—and I also got typhoid fever and typhus. I was hospitalized for several months. The doctor who treated me told my mother superior that if I returned to the life I'd been leading in the mountains, I wasn't going to survive. So they sent me to this school in San Salvador; and it was quite a rigid structure, with sisters who were much older. The students were from the wealthiest families. You can imagine what a shock it was for me to come directly from the mountains of Guatemala to that school for rich girls in the city. And I realized that this wasn't the place for me; it wasn't the best place for me to continue my commitment to the people, and to God.

So on June 23, 1976, I decided to return to Nicaragua. I decided to leave the congregation. It really wasn't a difficult decision. I got along wonderfully with the sisters, including those at the school in San Salvador, but now I understood that my path was something different. I came back, entered the university, and began a career that was much more practical than my earlier university experience. My previous studies had been in philosophy, theology, the more ethereal disciplines. Now I said, "I need to come back down to earth." I began to study sociology. And in September of 1976 I joined the FSLN.

I began working with groups of revolutionary Christians. I was in Ciudad Sandino, in San Judas, involved with the organization's urban structure. The FSLN had divided into tendencies by then, and I joined the "Proletarian tendency." We organized workers in the cities, in preparation for the final insurrection; it was important to prepare all the people to participate.

I was full-time with the FSLN, but I never lost contact with La Asunción because, as I've said, the more tension I experienced, the harder the tasks, the greater the activity, the more I needed to validate those moments of communion with God, the more I needed to keep examining my actions in the light of the Scriptures. The Scriptures have been a constant guide in my life.

Because people always say, "You've lived so many lives! Your life before going into the convent, which was a life of luxury; then your years in the convent; then your life as a guerrilla fighter; and now your life as a military officer in the national police." But I tell them it's only the form that's changed. It doesn't matter what kind of uniform you wear. What's important is the attitude you carry in your heart.

For me, from the very first moment, the revolution was basically a system of ethics, of values. And from [the movement of] our victory in 1979, I knew that it would be as important to safeguard and consolidate our own ethical system as it would be to defend the revolution against all the counterrevolutionary plans and projects financed outside the country. Because it's the ethical character of the revolution that's always defined it, that continues to define it for me, even more than its political character.

Aminta, I'm wondering how difficult it was for you as a woman, as a woman who had lived for five years in a convent, to leave the congregation and join the FSLN. Was it difficult to do that, as a woman?

Joining the FSLN wasn't difficult. We were very united back then. What was difficult was what came later, after the victory. Those first few years of the revolution . . . I went to work at the Ministry of the Interior [MINT], and that was hard. The Party hadn't yet developed very mature concepts about certain things. And here I was, this young woman from the bourgeoisie, a Christian, who had been a nun; and I went to work at the place that had the most rigid political-military structure of all, which was the MINT. Of course it was hard.

Did you encounter a lot of prejudice on the part of your colleagues?

Yes, at first I did. Because of the kind of work that went on there, the MINT was a very strict workplace. It had to be. The selection process was a tough one, and once inside there were all sorts of rules and prohibitions. Many of the things considered appropriate for an ordinary member of the FSLN weren't tolerated in the ministry. The revolution's security apparatus was based there, along with the whole system of information: top secret information, that sort of thing. And that was precisely my area of work.

During the ten years of Sandinista administration, I was the MINT's chief of information and analysis. The department went by different names: first it was called Information and Analysis, then High Command, and later General Secretariat of the Ministry. But it was always the department that handled planning, control, information and analysis, statistics, the computer system. When the new government took over, of course, we had to relinquish all that to them, and that's when I transferred here to the police.

During the ten years of Sandinista administration, I'm interested in examples you may have, moments in which you suffered discrimination as a woman, either from your superiors or from your fellow workers . . .

I can't remember being discriminated against as a woman in the ministry. As I said, at the beginning, the first two years, I felt discriminated against as a Christian and because of my social class. But there were many women in positions of power in the MINT. Let's see . . . I was chief of information and analysis. Another woman headed the ministry's secretariat, another was head of immigration, another was head of the rear guard, and there was a woman who headed public relations. When the ministry's leadership council had its meetings, a good number of us were women. I don't remember being discriminated against because of my gender.

And outside the ministry?

You know, there was always so much tension here, right from the beginning; and during those ten years of revolution we lived under constant threat of aggression from outside. Defense was primary. I don't think we ever really stopped to think about our rights as women. We were too busy trying to keep the revolutionary project alive.

At the ministry we women carried the same work load as the men, we had the same responsibilities; they mobilized us for combat, and we pulled the same guard shifts. And then you'd go home at night and there was the house, your kids . . . I married in 1980. Fortunately my husband isn't the traditional macho. We've been together thirteen years now, and he's given me great freedom in terms of my own personal development. And we have three wonderful children: two daughters, who are eight and a half and six and a half, and a son who's going to be four.

My husband helps me with the housework, helps me with the children. But the basic responsibility is mine. If one of the kids is sick, if there's a parents' meeting at school . . . When they'd send me out on military maneuvers, I'd bundle up my kids and take them over to my mother's, or to my family in León. My husband is an economist; he works for the Ministry of Agriculture and Cattle Growing.

Tell me how you were affected by the FSLN's electoral defeat . . .

An information group like ours had its own polls, of course. And all our figures showed the Front winning just about the number of votes it ended up getting. Nevertheless, there was a large number of undecided votes, and that's where we made our mistake. I thought we were going to win. I really did.

The day of the election someone from NBC came to interview me at my office, and I remember he asked me a difficult question. He asked whether we were going to give up power if the FSLN lost the elections. I told him it depended on how he defined power. If he meant the government, the ministries and so forth, then the answer was yes. But, I said, if he meant power as I define it—the real power in the revolutionary consciousness of each and every member of the armed forces and the Ministry of the Interior—then no, that power wasn't something you could give up. Because that kind of power isn't up for grabs in an election; that kind of power we'd never give up.

When that reporter left my office I asked myself for the first time, "What if we lose the election?" It wasn't until February 25th that I actually asked myself that question. And I began to have my doubts, a tiny voice deep inside. I spent that night at the ministry's command post, and the reports from all the different polling places were coming in. By 10:00 P.M. I knew we had lost: the statistical trend was too difficult to turn around by that time.

It was terribly painful. I think I cried three months straight. I just couldn't get to feeling better about it. I don't think I would have felt as bad if we'd suffered an invasion with thousands of dead, if the revolution had been defeated by a foreign aggressor. What hurt so much was that the people themselves voted against the revolutionary project, voted us out of office. The same people for whom and with whom you've risked everything, your life, your energies: that's what was so painful. Especially during those first few months, because we didn't yet have a sense of what the defeat really meant.

I remember I felt so bad that I didn't even want to see my children. I didn't know what to say to them. It took me three days to gather the courage to face my kids. And I have a very close friend, a nun, who was in El Salvador at the time; she called, and I didn't even want to pick up the phone. I didn't want to speak with her either. I just didn't have the courage. It was a terrible blow.

At the same time I told myself, "You have to get a grip." I knew I had to find a way to define what had happened, to figure out what I as a revolutionary should be doing. We had to take this lesson that the people had given us and, humbly, as Christians and revolutionaries, respond appropriately. Little by little, very little by little, I began to assimilate what had happened, assimilate the defeat, and I began to assume a more positive attitude. It was especially important not to let hope die. Because if hope dies, what is there?

Aminta, in retrospect how do you interpret what happened? I'm not talking about the pressure put on Nicaragua by the United States, which we all know was considerable. How do you analyze the people's failure to trust the FSLN?

Look, I think it was a combination of things. Obligatory military service, the draft, was important here. It just became too hard for mothers to keep on losing their sons, to lose one and then have to watch a second go off. There were many many mothers who had lost two, even three sons. That was worse than the hunger. The war really battered the mothers. And it wasn't just the mothers. It was the sister who saw her brother in his coffin; it was the girl-friend, the wife. Fifty thousand dead this war cost us. And the weight was too great. This society just didn't have the strength to keep on sustaining that.

People believed that a change of government would mean an end to the war, an end to the draft, an end to this daily encounter with Death which was just getting to be too much for people here. So I think the war was the biggest thing. And then the economic situation. UNO's whole electoral campaign re-volved around those promises: "UNO can do it, UNO can bring about change, foreign aid will be forthcoming, inflation will end, the economy will improve." People really thought that they'd see an end to the most serious problems.

On the other hand, I also think that we in the FSLN were losing that vital contact we'd had with the people. We'd become alienated to such an extent that losing the election came as a big surprise. If we'd remained as close, as united with the population as we had once been, we'd have seen more clearly what was happening around us. Losing the election wouldn't have caught us off guard like it did.

Power is a dangerous thing. I remember my grandfather used to tell me how power corrupts. It creates a distance, because at times we assume a patronizing attitude or one of arrogance. And that distance between leadership and the people gets wider, deeper, and then it's hard to get back to where you were before. We begin to believe we can impose our ideas. So we need to rebuild the Party with better communication, more participation, a greater grass-roots par-ticipation. If we can do this, then perhaps the defeat will have been worth-while.

Of course, I can't speak officially as a member of the FSLN anymore. In the position of military leadership I hold, it's understood that I can no longer present myself as a Sandinista. But in the context of what I've been saying, Sandinism is more of an attitude about life than about membership in a political party. Sandinism, for me, is a philosophy, an attitude, a system of ethics as I said before.

Tell me something about the work you're doing here in the police . . .

Here in the police I'm doing the same thing I did in the ministry. I'm head of the Police Department's general secretariat. I'm directly responsible for the whole apparatus of information and analysis—statistics, planning, control, computer systems, special investigations—that permits us to see how our own work is going. And, because of my position, I also belong to the national police's high command.

Are there many women in that command?

There are two women and seventeen men.

Here in the police have you had any problems with discrimination because you're a woman?

In the ordinary everyday work I haven't. But something interesting has begun to happen. I mentioned before that throughout the ten years of revolution we women really didn't have the opportunity of thinking about ourselves as women, about the contradictions, the discrimination we suffered, or anything like that. But since the election, a movement has started among women in the military structure, and we've begun to acquire a consciousness that as women we can and must do things for other women.

I'll give you an example. Here in the police I noticed that we weren't looking at crime by gender. That is to say, our statistics showed victims and perpetrators of crimes, but we didn't bother to compute what percentage of the victims in this country are women. I decided to do some research, and I found that 70 percent of the victims of violent crime in this country are women and only 1 percent of the perpetrators are women. In other words, violence here is gendered.

We began to do some analysis. There hadn't been any sort of analysis based on gender before. So we thought, "We'll do this. We'll see what we can offer by way of information to the growing women's movement." And we began to ask, "What about rape?" And we found that while crime in general had increased by 7 percent and 8 percent in the past two years, incidents of rape had increased by 23 percent and 25 percent. We women in the police took this further than a mere statistical study; we went out into the rural areas and found that the statistics we were getting didn't even reflect what was really going on. Many more rapes occur than are reported, for example, because women are afraid of the police.

And we'd been making women feel responsible for the crimes committed against them! The very questions we were asking: "What did you do to provoke this? How were you dressed? What were you doing?" Women weren't being treated like victims but as if they were in some way responsible for the violence perpetrated against them, and we women inside the Police Department said, "This has got to stop."

We'd never before participated as policewomen in any of the women's movements, in forums or meetings, workshops, anything like that. I don't know if we were never invited or if we didn't think we had the time . . . In any case, now we began to meet with other women, with the National Assembly's Commission on Women, Children, and Young People. And we began to ask what kinds of things we might be able to do, together, to make things better for women—all this since the electoral defeat.

The letup in the war has given us some space. Which is not to say that the tensions we face today, as police, aren't in many ways more difficult, more serious, than those we faced before. But we're able to think as women, to feel as women, to act and struggle as women and for women.

Has this new way of seeing and thinking about yourself made a difference in your personal life as well?

A tremendous difference! I've begun to think of myself as a woman, perhaps for the first time—and to understand that as a woman I must situate myself in the world, as a woman I must assume the challenges. As I've told you, life has always seemed like a series of stages to me. And now I not only think of myself as a Christian, a revolutionary, a mother, a wife, but as a woman as well. In my personal life this new consciousness has been very gratifying, because it's allowed another dimension of my being to surface and grow—a dimension that had been suppressed. Now I'm a woman not just because I speak like a woman or because I'm a mother to my daughters: I'm a woman on the job and in the struggle itself.

Are you seeing much domestic violence here, Aminta? Do the police deal with that?

Of course. We're looking at what we, in the police, can do, although we're not the only institution involved. We're aware of the fact that with domestic violence, as with other sexual violence, we've got to approach the problem holistically. Right now we're working on a project with the National Assembly. The National Assembly has to define the legal aspects; our job is to confront the problem on a daily basis. Police work alone isn't enough; that is to say, the legislators can make their laws and we in the police departments can enforce them, but this still doesn't solve the problem. Because it's a social problem. It's a question of how we relate to one another, and we've got to become involved at that level as well. I think it's important that we do more than define the crime, arrest the criminal, and mete out the punishment. That's where the other entities come into play, and the women's movement itself.

Something I'm very excited about is a pilot project we hope to have up and running by the end of this year [1992]. It's a "women's precinct": a whole separate police station staffed completely by women officers and specialists, where women can go to file sexual assault claims. We've been studying what they're doing in Brazil and in Argentina, where women's self-help groups exist all over, where women who are victims of violent crime get together to talk with each other and with psychologists, therapists, social workers, and so forth; where there are groups for male perpetrators as well, so they can receive help.

We're looking at our women's precinct from two angles. We're trying to get a piece of land or a building, completely away from the ordinary station house, and we want to fix it up so it doesn't look like a police station. We'll have lots of pictures on the walls, and plants. And we hope women will feel invited to come, knowing they won't be treated as objects or in some way made to feel responsible for the crimes committed against them. We want the forensic specialists to be women as well. We want to start treating this whole problem with respect and tenderness, as women must.

Then there's the training we want to give to the women who will staff this precinct. We won't just be schooling them in investigative methods, in the "police aspect" of the work; we'll be giving them gender studies as well. Since we don't have enough money to open one of these special precincts in every city in the country, we're planning on starting with the pilot project here in Managua. In the other major cities we'll begin with a women's complaint office, within the existing station house.

I wanted to mention this project particularly because you asked before if I'd ever felt discriminated against as a woman. I mean, here on the police force. On the police force in general I don't think I've ever felt discriminated against as a woman. My superiors have always considered me efficient, capable, a good policewoman.

But the minute I got involved in this women's project, the guys started right in: "So you've become a feminist, huh?" My own comrades! "Watch out or you'll turn into one of those crazy women running around out there! You who have always been so centered." The word "centered" should be in quotes, because it's only now that I've acquired some awareness of myself as a woman that I'm truly beginning to feel centered.

We've got a long way to go. Because everything's been a struggle: getting the building; raising the money; convincing the national police chief to give us the people we need; convincing people that this is an important project, a project that deserves support. I've been told, "Sure, go ahead. It sounds like a good idea. But don't you get involved. We need you on more important jobs." As if this type of project is less important than the others, as if a women's project can't be that important!

And we have to fight our own preconceived notions and prejudices, too, so as not to give in. Sometimes it feels easier just to say, "Okay, this is creating too much of a problem for me. I'm going to have to let it go." So there's that internal struggle as well.

What percentage of the police force is female?

Thirty percent.

That's interesting, because it's the same percentage more or less as in the Sandinista forces that fought against Somoza. Aminta, would you call yourself a feminist?

I don't think I know enough about the term, I mean theoretically. As I've said, my life experience has led me to define myself first as a Christian, then as a revolutionary Christian, and more recently as a woman. As a woman I assume certain attitudes, relate to people in a particular way, and bring a woman's consciousness to my job. I believe that as a woman I have something special to say, and something to do for other women. Is that a feminist?

"It's True: We Can't Live on Consciousness Alone, but We Can't Live without It"

Doris Tijerino

Doris María Tijerino Haslam was born in Matagalpa in 1943, one of eleven sisters and brothers. Not yet fifty, she may well be the woman alive with the longest continuous participation in Nicaragua's struggle for liberation.

Her father was an electrical engineer who worked for Somoza's National Guard until he resigned in protest during his daughter's first imprisonment and torture. Her mother, who cherished from her own childhood a copy of Maxim Gorky's The Mother *and passed it on with love to this particular daughter, was enormously influential in Doris's formation. Doris's mother would cover for the adolescent Doris not when she attended parties or dated, but so she could participate in her earliest political meetings.*

She also encouraged her daughter in what Doris remembers as her first act of conspiracy. The girl was twelve or thirteen at the time. A rifle had to be delivered to Ramón Raudales's guerrilla camp, and the mother, believing a child would be a less likely target of suspicion, asked the daughter if she was willing to risk the trip.[1] Doris said yes.

1. General Ramón Raudales was one of a few remaining guerrillas from Sandino's "crazy little army" active between 1927 and 1934. Sandino, before his assassination on February 21, 1934,

The little girl traveled by bus, and when the driver asked what was in the odd-shaped bundle she told him "Communion candles." Fortunately, he must have been a sympathizer. He instructed her to put the candles beneath her seat and pretend she was asleep. She followed his advice, "slept" through a series of police checks, and made it with her cargo to its destination. It would be the first of a lifetime of such endeavors—many infinitely more dangerous and some, tragically, not nearly so successful.

Doris's youth in the north-central coffee-growing city of Matagalpa was typical for a child of the middle class. She spent time on her grandparents' farm, meeting and playing with peasant children but conditioned by the philosophy that God made some people rich and others poor. Her primary education came from Catholic sisters who schooled her in the practice of conventional charity. At age ten she wanted to be a nun. When she remembers her childhood and growing up, her statement of earliest consciousness may be: "I wasn't tall or blond, and I didn't have blue eyes. I knew I was Nicaraguan."

The United Nations would proclaim 1975 to be the International Year of the Woman. I lived in Havana, Cuba, at the time, closer to the liberation struggles being waged throughout much of Latin America than my friends in the United States. Most of them would have found it difficult to identify Nicaragua on a map, much less imagine that its forty-year-old dictatorship was only a few years away from being toppled by an army of youngsters called the FSLN. A surprising number of those youngsters were women, and it occurred to me that one of these women's stories might make the war in Nicaragua more real to people everywhere.

I wanted to tell that story, and so I approached the FSLN's Cuban representation. Carlos Fonseca and other Sandinistas in Havana at the time were enthusiastic and helpful. Within days I was introduced to Doris Tijerino. Much later I would learn that she had come to Cuba the month before for military training but had been unable to begin the course when it was discovered she was pregnant. Ordered to remain on the island until her child was born, she had plenty of time for a project like the one I had in mind. We worked together for almost a year and eventually produced a book about her life entitled Doris Tijerino: Inside the Nicaraguan Revolution.[2]

My introduction to the Spanish-language edition of that book presents a woman's experience interwoven with the statistical summary of a very poor, very troubled Central American nation. Nicaragua was of geopolitical as well as economic interest to the United States; before Panama was chosen as the

---

had ordered the young combatant to keep watch at the Wiwilí camp. Twenty-five years later, by then an old man with a long white beard, Randales was killed at Yaule. That was the beginning of another upsurge in Nicaragua's long history of resistance. A number of men had stayed on in the mountains, among them Raudales and Santos López, and they eventually became the link between the movement of the thirties and the Sandinist National Liberation Front which was founded in 1961.

2. The Spanish-language version was *"Somos millones . . ."* (*La vida de Doris María, combatiente nicaragüense*) (Mexico City: Editorial Extemporáneos, 1977).

ideal site, there was talk of an interoceanic canal across its lake-filled land-mass. And so the U.S. Marines had invaded the country repeatedly since the mid-1800s, occupying it and even briefly installing a North American president, William Walker. Likewise, since 1934, the brutal Somoza dynasty had received full U.S. backing. Franklin Roosevelt's comment in justification for this support has been widely quoted: "Somoza may be a son of a bitch, but he's our son of a bitch."

But by the time our book appeared in English, one year after its publication in Spanish, a new introduction became necessary. Doris had since returned to Nicaragua, and I was forced to write that "on Thursday, April 13, 1978, eight kilometers from the Honduran border in a village called Los Encinos . . . a battle took place between Sandinista forces and the Nicaraguan National Guard. According to information released . . . one Sandinista combatant, Mauricio Cajina Pérez, was killed, another managed to escape, and Doris María Tijerino Haslam was taken prisoner."

It was not the first time Doris had been arrested. In July 1969 she and veteran urban guerrilla Julio Buitrago had been discovered and surrounded in a Managua safehouse. He had gone down fighting; she had been captured, severely tortured, and imprisoned. It was then, faced with the evidence of his daughter's physical scars, that her father resigned from the National Guard. Doris remained incarcerated until an FSLN commando made its famous surprise appearance at a society Christmas party, obtaining the release of all the country's political prisoners in 1974. Now it was 1978 and she had been re-captured by the same authorities who had battered her almost a decade before. A group of us, by this time deeply involved in the Nicaraguan struggle, hurried to get Doris's story translated into English. We believed publication in that language might lead to international solidarity on her behalf; perhaps it would even prevent her death. A Canadian edition appeared within three months, making Doris's story available to an ever-wider circle of readers. But the FSLN had a more effective plan through which they would obtain her release— and that of dozens of others. In August they attacked the National Palace, taking some thirty five hundred hostages. It was the most spectacular and successful operation in the organization's history. Less than a year later these "youngsters" would defeat Somoza.

Doris Tijerino is a modest-looking woman of medium build. An almost electric tension underscores her gaze and conversation. Several lifetimes ago her olive complexion waged its own teenage battles with acne. Her dark-brown hair is naturally wavy; sometimes she pulls it back, at others it hangs just above her shoulders. Doris's brown eyes reflect more experience, anguish, and loss than most of us will ever know; and so they are steady, disciplined, sometimes engaged on a plane whose images we can only imagine. She has a quiet reserve mistaken by some for severity, even coldness.

When the FSLN took power, she was Comandante *Doris María Tijerino: the only woman to have achieved the rank of full commander in the Sandinista army. By that time she had lost two relationships to the horrors of war and at least one in the more typical circumstances where lovers simply drift apart.*

Early Sandinista leader Ricardo Morales, with whom she'd had the daughter born in Cuba, was captured and tortured to death just before we began work on that book about her life. I won't forget the day she came by for our daily taping session after having listened to the awaited details of his cruel death.

I reconnected with Doris after the 1979 victory, when I came to Nicaragua to gather material for Sandino's Daughters. *It was then that she told me how she'd learned that her most recent partner, José Benito Escobar, was dead. She spoke of her 1978 imprisonment: "We were a number of women in that particular prison," she said, "and although we weren't permitted much contact, we managed to shout from cell to cell to one another. I'd been there for about three months when José Benito was gunned down in Estelí. Unknown to the guards, some of us managed to keep small radios; and we'd listen to the evening news. We generally tuned out before the summary, so the batteries wouldn't wear out so fast.*

"One night a strange intuition prodded me to keep my radio on. And that's when I heard the flash: José Benito was dead. There was nothing I could do but call out to another of the women, a comrade named Rosa Argentina Ortíz. I knew she had a radio, too, and I asked if she was awake. 'Yes, sister,' she shouted, 'I'm awake.' And then Margine Gutiérrez, from her cell farther along the gallery, shouted even louder and clearer: '¡Todas estamos despiertas. We're all awake!' It was the greatest show of solidarity I could have received; my sisters knew what I was going through."[3]

Not only has Doris suffered from the deaths of innumerable comrades, among them men with whom she shared important years of her life, but the daughter fathered by Morales died in a plane crash at age twelve. Loss has been too common and too jarring an experience for this heroic woman, and stoicism is her trademark; at least it is the face she shows the world.

The ten years of Sandinista government brought Doris a variety of tasks, including several years as national chief of police—certainly she is the only woman in modern history to hold such a position. Tijerino has been elected to the Nicaraguan legislative body for every term since its inception, and she continues to be an FSLN senator even after her party's presidential defeat.

"I'm not a woman revolutionary," Doris once told me, "but a revolutionary who happens to be a woman." She will probably continue to argue that view of gender all her life. She does not consider herself a feminist in any radical definition of the term, yet she has defended women consistently and headed AMNLAE from 1989 to 1990. (The organization was about to cap an energetic process of democratization by electing its own national leadership when the all-male directorate intervened and named her to the office. Unwisely she accepted her party's designation. It was to be a stormy, and ultimately unworkable, arrangement.)

3. This account comes from the Spanish-language version of *Sandino's Daughters*, entitled *Todas estamos despiertas* (Mexico City: Siglo XXI, 1980). The book's Spanish title comes from this anecdote, but because of the non-gender-specific nature of the English language, it couldn't be translated.

To Doris's credit, she never wanted to preside over the FSLN's women's organization. She was happy as police chief and hated being removed from that position. Many in AMNLAE, on the other hand, profoundly disappointed at being manipulated once again, saw her as the policewoman sent to keep them in line. But Doris had been a Party loyalist all her life: an order was an order.

In retrospect, Tijerino has important criticisms of the FSLN's handling of the women's movement, and since its 1990 electoral defeat she has also been willing to voice her own anger over gender discrimination at the hands of her superiors. An edge of bitterness surfaces when she recounts some of the more blatant incidents, borne at the time with dignity but remembered with anger by this woman who had learned respect for the chain of political command so well.

Doris wasn't easy to locate when I looked her up in July 1992 for the interview that follows. I finally found her living with her grown son, a grandchild, and several adopted children in a small house on the outskirts of the capital. She was standing in the doorway when we drove up, wearing a loose-fitting T-shirt and a pair of shorts. Our immediate embrace made up for almost twenty years. "I was just about to take a shower," she said with a smile. "It'll only take me a few minutes. Why don't you wait for me here on the porch and I'll have them bring you some coffee. Do you still drink it black?"

We settled ourselves in the traditional rockers and sipped the good Nicaraguan coffee. I could hear water in a nearby bathroom beating briefly against the tiles. The house looked comfortable but strangely unlived-in. Later, Doris would tell me that she's never really been able to accustom herself to having a home. "I seem to keep a few necessities nearby," she confided. "I guess I'm always expecting to have to leave in a hurry."

As promised, in a matter of minutes Doris was changed and settled into a rattan love seat, its back against the porch's dark-tile wall. I started by reminding her that it had been nearly twenty years since we began this conversation. "Although I'm sure you thought I was interviewing you," I added, "I've always believed that we interviewed one another. I guess what I really want to know today is: What have these years meant for you, as a person, as a combatant, and as a woman? What's happened in your life since 1975?"

That's a pretty big question. Since we did that first interview, there's the period leading up to 1979: my entire life at that time was dedicated to the FSLN's efforts to take power. And there wasn't much variation. From 1975 to 1979, those comrades inside the country experienced terrible losses but also increasingly frequent victories. For someone like myself, who had been involved in the struggle continuously since 1965, that was a time I should have been able to spend here, on the inside. But it wasn't to be. The leadership wanted me outside the country, working in the area of international solidarity, so that's where I remained. And it was tremendously frustrating for me. In fact, I wasn't even here on July 19th.

Sometimes, reminiscing, I've said that I never really saw our victory. I was in Mexico at the time. Somoza's escape caught up with me on a plane between Venezuela and Mexico; and when our troops marched into Managua, well, I just wasn't here to see it. I wasn't able to savor the sweet taste of triumph like so many others did. And you know, often since then—as we began to see the project that so many had died for take shape, as we realized it was going to turn out this way rather than that, as we saw what was possible instead of what we had dreamed would be possible—often I've found myself telling people: "The thing is, I haven't even seen the victory yet."

It's our particularly Nicaraguan way of making light of our own frustrations, our own pain. Because, needless to say, the revolution we were able to make wasn't the revolution I pictured in that first interview of ours. All those ideas we had, they had to be put to the test. Could we really do this, or that, as we'd always dreamed? And what happened? We were working toward socialism but it never became socialism. Many of my ideas, as part of the leadership cadre, crumbled along the way.

At the time, I remember, I had this great big shoulder bag I used to carry around. And people would tease me. They'd say that's where I kept all the plans, all the broken plans; they were broken, but I still hauled them around with me wherever I went. I've always maintained that those weren't just broken plans, they continue to be viable dreams. Just because we weren't able to bring them to fruition doesn't mean they're not valid.

On the other hand, there's a great deal we were able to accomplish, a great number of projects we did get off the ground, that took shape during the ten years we had power. The quality of the average Nicaraguan's life got better, the suffering of our peasant population was greatly mitigated, agrarian reform was successful to a large extent, and there was the literacy crusade. I mean, we managed to do so many beautiful things that the fact we couldn't pull off a socialist revolution became secondary somehow.

Through it all I began to understand that the theory of socialism is something you read in books, but when it's real life, well, books are a help but it's your everyday experience that shows you what needs to be done. So, for me, these years have been personally enriching; they've offered important lessons in the relationship between theory and practice. Marxism isn't a dogma. The revolution can't be constructed according to recipes or prescriptions. It's really the creativity of the people themselves that shows you how to proceed at a given time and in a given place.

Take the experience with the Christian community, for example. In our book I remember talking about the participation of Christians, the incorporation of Christians; but here in Nicaragua the Christian experience was very profound, and very rich. It wasn't a matter of one group participating in a project being launched by another. All you have to do is look at the document the FSLN put out, outlining the Party's position on religion. Sometimes I think our revolution wasn't understood so well, even by some of the Sandinistas themselves.

Now that we no longer control the government, now that the political and moral authority of the national directorate has been demystified to a certain extent, now that people are speaking out and saying what's on their minds—

pretty directly, even crudely at times—I can see that many who call themselves Sandinistas didn't really understand the revolution. Because I don't agree with all the criticisms that have been leveled, not at all. It's the same throughout history: there's always a tendency to judge what's happened by what we know at the moment of judgment, not in the context of what was going on at the time.

For example, there are those who still criticize the revolution's relationship with the Church. And we know that an important sector of the Church never supported the revolution, never. So I think that's an unjust criticism. If we go back and look at the Party platform, and at the concrete actions on the part of the FSLN, it's clear that the revolution never tried to curtail people's legitimate religious expression—never. Religion grew during the revolutionary period. Some denominations, in fact, like the Evangelicals, quadrupled during those ten years. The revolution did practice democracy with regard to the Church; it just wasn't willing to subordinate itself to Church control.

The Catholic hierarchy here conspired against the revolution. It seems to me that some Sandinistas want us to get down on our knees and kiss our enemies' feet. I bring this up because it's one of the most important areas of discussion right now. And it's about ideology. We've got people in leadership running around criticizing the Party for its alleged [unfair] treatment of the Church, and I don't think that's fair.

I don't think it's fair because I don't believe there was religious persecution here. And if certain members of the clergy were targeted, well, what right does the cloth give a person to conspire against his country, to take part in international campaigns against the revolution? I don't think anyone should have that right, and the revolution must retain the right to defend itself.

The counterrevolution here meant the assassination of peasants, the destruction of schools, of health clinics—why, it got to the point where we couldn't even carry out a census in the rural areas because they'd murder anyone who went door to door to gather the information. We'd try to build a road, and they'd ambush the highway workers. And I ask you: Does religious faith or ministry justify that?

The thing is, those who talk about democracy have a very narrow concept when they apply it to the other person; it's much broader when they apply it to themselves. So, to get back to your question, the ten years of revolutionary government were rich ones for me, filled with important experiences and important lessons. Maybe I didn't take as much advantage of them as I might have. Because, you know, my natural tendency is to isolate myself, to stay apart, and that also increased during this period. I think it was a consequence of the difficulties, the problems . . .

What you say about the Church is important, especially concerning the criticisms being leveled now against the Party's attitude toward religion or its relationship with the Catholic hierarchy during the ten years of FSLN government. I wonder if you could give me your analysis with regard to women. What kind of relationship did the Party and/or government establish with women during that same period? It's clear that the revolution made a great many concrete changes, positive changes, in women's lives. Yet women voted overwhelmingly against the revolutionary project in the 1992 elections. Why?

It's true: people say women voted against the revolution, against the FSLN. But I don't know. I don't know if that's not a bit too simplistic. Maybe just because women are in the majority here . . . But votes don't have gender. I mean, there's no way to know for sure if a particular vote is male or female. You can go by the polls, but I'm not convinced. Women may have voted against the FSLN, but I don't really think they voted against the revolutionary project. It just wouldn't make sense.

What I believe is that among the many things the revolution wasn't able to finish was the profound and necessary change in human consciousness. We weren't really able to get people to understand what the literacy crusade meant, what the improvement in public health meant, what our educational programs meant. Ideologically, the revolution wasn't what it should have been. Tomás Borge once said, "The war isn't going to be won by those who fire the most rounds, but by those who raise the most consciousness." And I think that has a lot to do with what happened in the elections.

After the United States invaded Grenada, and even more so after Panama, we literally saw an "invasion psychosis" here. People were terrified that the U.S. was going to invade Nicaragua. And it wasn't as if this was farfetched: there were enough signs; the message was quite intentional. And people opted for the simplest route: elect a government the United States wants. As simple as that.

Because people's lives had improved; there's no question about it. The Sandinista government initiated an agrarian reform program; people were given ownership of the land they worked. If you couldn't pay your electric bill, we never cut off the power like Somoza did. You just went and explained your problem: there was a new level of understanding of people's needs. And we extended electrical power to remote mountain areas where people had never seen a light bulb before. We opened child-care centers where they'd never existed; before the revolution we didn't even have those in the *cities*!

But in spite of all these improvements, the United States kept on funding and supporting the counterrevolution. It was clear all along that they were going to keep on doing everything possible to undermine the revolutionary process, to defeat Sandinism. We were in the midst of a terrible economic crisis here, and it wasn't only a result of the U.S. blockade; it was a part of the global recession. Plus there were extensive areas of the country where you couldn't even travel because of the war. So this was the situation; I don't blame people for voting for a government favored by the United States, although their naiveté may be painful. The UNO vote was a vote for peace. How else can you explain the fact that people continue to demand the very same things the revolution had begun to provide?

It reminds me of the situation among a fair percentage of Cuban exiles, in Miami and elsewhere, people who fled to the United States, who detest the

Cuban Revolution. Yet they are astonished that there's no health care available to them, that drugs and crime are such problems, that there's such a high unemployment rate . . . The social services they'd come to expect from the revolution are suddenly not available in the country of their dreams. They've been victims of some very convincing propaganda . . .

But I know you want me to talk about women, specifically. Women did benefit under our revolutionary program. Peasant women, for example, got titles to the land along with peasant men—although it's true there were problems with the application of agrarian reform; it never really worked as it was supposed to, as it was conceived. I remember we frequently had to protest the fact that women weren't benefiting as they should have from the land reform.

Nevertheless, don't think sexism alone is to blame, on the part of the institutions, the policies, or the men themselves. The problem is, the women who complained or protested were always a small minority: leadership women, or some small group of women who saw things more clearly, who were more ideologically advanced than the majority of the female population. A minority of women were organized here. And this is where I believe our greatest political failure lies. We never did the ideological work we should have done.

An example: up in Matagalpa, over near Sébaco, you'll find communities—somewhat off the beaten path, it's true, but accessible to anyone who wants to go there—where the situation of women is truly dramatic. The role assigned to them during the decade of revolution, and which they themselves assumed, was an absolutely subordinate one. And I'm not blaming the women. It was up to our leadership to have made sure they understood that there were other possibilities. We had the organization and we didn't use it. And in barely two years of UNO government, without an organic structure anywhere near what the FSLN has, it's incredible to see how those women have retreated, without so much as a protest, back into the most traditional roles . . .

Doris, you were the national head of AMNLAE just before and just after the elections. That's a period which has elicited a great deal of discussion, particularly among women. How do you see what happened?

I have a great many complaints about the Party from that period . . .

That's precisely the question I'm getting at. Because it's not only an issue that's relevant here in Nicaragua; it's something that's being debated in many parts of the world. Should a mass women's organization or movement be subject to a political party—almost always controlled by men—or must it be autonomous to really function?

I know the consensus today is that an autonomous movement is necessary. But I think there's an initial period in which the Party has to keep control of the different mass organizations. The problem here was that we let that initial period go on too long. During the Somoza years there were no serious organizations of any kind: just a bunch of bourgeois parties that played the dictator's

game. And then there was the Sandinista National Liberation Front. Two opposing forces, that was it. Everyone and everything that moved in Nicaragua
moved under the influence of one or the other of those forces.

Then, too, the revolutionary project here had a single name: FSLN. It wasn't
like El Salvador where the FMLN is a coalition of several different organizations, each with its own structure, its own history.[4] In this country, the FSLN
was unique; it *was* the revolution, and all the different sectors of the population
were mobilized by broad-based, democratic organizations, launched by the
FSLN. Women here were organized by the FSLN.

You know the history. Women's organizing didn't happen here because
women themselves felt the need to unite. The FSLN felt it was important to
organize the sector, and the Party would make that a priority from time to time;
then, when there were other priorities, the idea of a women's organization
would lie dormant. I'm thinking of the Alianza de Mujeres Patrióticas [Patrio-
tic Women's Alliance]; the FSLN promoted that in 1969 with its own program
and relative autonomy. But it didn't work. For years people here saw their
main task as that of getting rid of the dictator, and they knew they weren't
going to be able to do that except through the FSLN.

So it's been a natural subordination, not really forced from above. It's like
when a child is born: there's a period in which that child is dependent upon its
mother, its father, the family in general. But then there comes a time when the
child has learned to stand on its own two feet. Then it's up to the parents to let
him go. I think we prolonged the period of dependence too long.

We can justify this subordination to a certain extent because of the war and
the fact that the overall defense of the larger revolutionary project was our
priority, especially during those last difficult years. But the problem remains:
how do you defend the overall project? Now the errors are more obvious. We
can see that it was a mistake to maintain the subordination, for example, in the
case of AMNLAE.

During the year before the elections, I remember that the women themselves
began to talk about autonomy. And on March 8, 1989, there was an official
demand for autonomy on the part of AMNLAE. The Party began to discuss
this, to cede its position and loosen its hold. That was the beginning of the
public discussion, as far as I know. I think the consensus was finally that
subordination to the Party would be maintained through the membership of
individual women in the movement, no longer conceived of structurally as it
had been up to that point. Let me explain: if a woman with a leadership posi-

---

4. In May 1980 the Farabundo Martí National Liberation Front (FMLN) was founded in El
Salvador to coordinate the various guerrilla organizations. At the same time, the Democratic
Revolutionary Front (FDR) was set up to coordinate all leftist political opposition; it became the
FMLN's civilian arm. Farabundo Martí was a revolutionary leader of El Salvador's frustrated
uprising of 1932, when more than thirty thousand workers and peasants were murdered in a
matter of months by the dictator Maximiliano Hernández Martínez. See Thomas P. Anderson's
Matanza: El Salvador's Communist Revolt of 1932 (Lincoln: University of Nebraska Press,
1981). Interestingly, Martí had previously fought as an internationalist with Sandino in Nicaragua.

tion in AMNLAE was a Party member, she would naturally continue to operate out of Party discipline, like any other member . . .

That's not real autonomy . . .

I know it may be difficult to understand. But you have to consider this within the political context. I think women have to find a way of wearing both hats. Because we can't allow ourselves to be swept away by separatist positions, to say that women shouldn't belong to political parties. Only the bourgeois project, the counterrevolutionary project, would benefit from that. It would be like removing the underpinnings of the revolution to limit women to dealing with gender issues, not allowing them to tackle the more general problems. So I think we were on the right track. We just didn't have the time to work it all out.

I don't think we're talking about the same kind of autonomy. I think history has shown us that until we women control our own organizations we aren't going to be able to address our gender-specific problems—which doesn't mean that we can't also participate in mixed organizations, with other goals. Clearly the very real pressures of war wrote a different history here, at least up to now. But these issues are being discussed, and I believe we'll come to see that only groups of people conscious of their real interests will truly defend those interests.
But Doris, I'd like you to go back some, if you will, and talk about your personal experience as a woman in an extremely high-level position. It wasn't the position alone; you were also one of the women with the most years in the FSLN and in the Nicaraguan struggle generally. When the revolution took power, you were promoted to a series of particularly demanding jobs. Could you talk about what it was like to be a woman doing the type of work you did?

I'm very critical of the FSLN in this respect, supercritical. I don't believe there's any use in making judgments if we're going to deceive ourselves. So before I say anything about my personal experience, I need to say that yes, it's true women participated here to an inordinate degree, but the higher up you go the fewer women you're going to find. Some people blame the women themselves. They say we run from responsibility. But others, and I count myself among them, understand that women often shy away from public responsibility precisely because they are so overburdened by responsibilities of other kinds: in the home, with their children, keeping the family together.

And let's face it: the FSLN hasn't really had a policy of promoting women to leadership positions. Women who have reached those levels here have done so at enormous personal sacrifice. We've knocked ourselves out and sacrificed all sorts of things along the way.

Believe me, I'm critical. Another woman told me once: "By the time they recognize your qualifications, you feel permanently offended." This was in the context of a speech made the day I was named national police chief. One of our leaders spoke, and I'll never forget what he said. The event took place on the police grounds near the Oriental Market, and there were a lot of people there.

He talked about my long history in the Party, my great organizing skills, my great ability to work with cadre, with the rank and file. He went on and on listing my many talents. And then he said they'd brought me into the police and discovered that I was an excellent chief!

I'll never forget how I felt that day. I asked that man, right there in front of all those people, if after twenty years of revolutionary militancy they'd just discovered that I can think. It made people extremely uncomfortable. They said that I was "difficult," that it was hard to work with me because I came out and said things like that. But, I can tell you, I felt continually attacked and offended. I had to make a huge effort, always, not to let bitterness get the best of me. My Party history won me authority and respect at the Ministry of the Interior, but I had problems the whole time, serious problems with the male leadership. All the women comrades did.

Could you be more specific?

For example, I often had to go to absurd lengths when I wanted something done. If I had an idea about how a particular problem might be solved, I learned never to make the "mistake" of suggesting the solution as if it came from me. I had to find other ways of suggesting things, such as saying that one of my subordinates had come up with the idea—a man, naturally—and that I agreed that it just might be workable. Or I'd say that I noticed this was being done somewhere else in the country, or in another unit . . . something like that. It was ridiculous. And the interesting thing is that I had the complicity of a whole series of subordinates in this; they knew what was going on and they went along with it. Because they understood as well as I did that it was the only way we were going to get anything done.

Did you ever bring this up inside the Party? Were you ever able to raise this sort of issue, or did anyone else raise it?

I brought it up continually. I'm still bringing it up, and I'm still being told it's inadmissible. On occasion I've been so angry that I've asked people to go and ask my superiors if what I'm saying isn't true. But of course they won't, and the superiors aren't going to admit it in any case. It's difficult to imagine that these guys could recognize their errors, especially the ideological ones. The sad thing is, they probably aren't even aware that I had to go to those lengths, or that their attitudes made it necessary.

They probably weren't aware. And for me it was denigrating, horrible. But I did it in order to keep a position that allowed me to get certain things done, exert a certain influence, or show that women can do these things. That's how I managed to continue for five years as a woman chief of police, nationally: something that was unimaginable for people in this country, in this society, or in the world for that matter. But the cost was enormous, believe me.

What years were you national police chief?

From 1985, or rather from the end of 1984 through the end of 1989. And, you know, the very fact that they nominated me as a candidate to the Senate, that felt like another attack. I thought I'd freed myself from that sort of obligation in 1984. In the 1984 elections I discovered they'd put my name on the list, and I had to go to unimaginable lengths, make use of my personal relations with the highest levels of Party leadership, and almost beg them not to make me run. Because I knew it would mean having to leave the Ministry of the Interior, being reduced once again to political or Party tasks.

It worked in 1984, but not in 1990. In 1990 I had to be a candidate. And, you know, I have the feeling I've lost this battle. They've won. Because it got to the point where I would talk to members of the directorate and they'd say, "All right. But we can't pull your name now. The campaign is in full swing. After the elections you can resign and go back to your post as chief of police if you want."

I said, "But that's not the point. It's not about my post as chief of police. What you don't understand is that you continually remove me from jobs where I feel that as a woman I can give something special in order to place me where, sure, I can do the work but, because of my personal characteristics, I know I'm not going to be able to accomplish as much."

Doris, this may be an old question by now, but I'm interested in your response in the light of what you've just said about your own experience. How do you analyze Dora María Téllez's not having made the national directorate? Outside of Nicaragua—and I know we often see things from a different angle— but outside of Nicaragua it was very difficult for many of us to accept the fact that a woman like her, or a woman like yourself for that matter, women with such extraordinary histories of struggle and such obvious qualifications, wouldn't at this stage of the game very naturally have been elevated to the highest leadership levels. Especially since the campaign was waged, and it failed . . .

The campaign was waged, and it failed because it wasn't handled correctly. Well, I think we always fail when we don't do things right. There was a position—and I should say that what I'm telling you now I didn't realize at the time—there was a position on the table that we didn't really understand. The problem was one of keeping the original directorate through this transitional period, in order to ensure a degree of continuity in terms of reform, the reforms and transformations necessary at this particular time. That was what voting the entire slate was all about, instead of voting for individuals, and I still believe it was the correct position.

Whoever was added to the directorate had to be able to fit in with this idea of continuity. And they said Sergio was an obvious choice, apart from his personal and professional qualifications, because of the role he'd played in the Sandinista government.[5] At the time, it seemed reasonable to me. But today I

5. Sergio Ramírez was vice-president under President Daniel Ortega, 1984–1990.

ask myself, "What about Dora María? She had been minister of state, she had her own history in government structures and within the Party." I think the mistake we made was focusing on sexism, when we could have argued Dora María's case in the same terms they used to argue for Sergio.

I've said this to people, and sometimes I get the feeling they think I have something against Sergio. That's not true. But I ask, "Why not Dora María? Or why not someone else?" I think we made a mistake when we made a woman the issue. Because, you know, back when AMNLAE proposed introducing a quota system for women in leadership positions, into the Party statutes, we never could get support for it—not from the men and not from the women either. And that was a while back. In spite of the fact that I'm not even sure quotas are such a good idea, because they might be limiting: what if you set a quota at 30 percent and then found you have women capable of filling up to 50 percent or 70 percent or even 100 percent of the positions? On the other hand, it's a beginning: if you've got a quota, you're committed to minimal representation. But we couldn't even get that proposal through.

Doris, you headed AMNLAE during the 1990 elections, and then you stepped down and Gladys Báez took over. Where did you go after that?

I kept my seat in the National Assembly, and I also went to work with AMNLAE in the Sixth Region: Matagalpa and Jinotega. I've still got both jobs.

How do you see women's organizing here now? How do you feel about AMNLAE, and about all the other groups that have sprung up? Do you see any possibilities for coalition?

I find it contradictory that in Nicaragua there are so many different women's groups among revolutionary women outside AMNLAE—in spite of the efforts being made to coordinate the work, to bring women together. Sometimes I look at the different programs and I can't even find the differences. At a certain point I thought my leaving AMNLAE's national office might make for a more cohesive movement . . . And that's another thing: I don't even know what to call what's happened. Are they movements? Groups? Organizations?

It seems to me that what we have is a whole lot of energy centers: women working in one or another of the popular organizations, in the trades or professional organizations, in the different sectors. There doesn't seem to be one organization that unites them all. And if you go down the various lists of demands, you're not going to find differences that justify so much dispersion. At least not the way I see it.

They said autonomy was the big problem, autonomy from the FSLN. But I thought it was more a problem of personalities. You had political secretaries— women as well as men—who respected AMNLAE's autonomy: people who just naturally respect the rights of others, who aren't jealous, who don't have to be in control all the time, who free people to do their own work. And then you have others who can't stand not being in control.

Doris, were you at the big gathering of women in January?

No, I wasn't. I've decided not to go to much of anything where the traditional leadership is. I've preferred to remain among the rank and file, working with women at the base. Because I find fewer problems there, fewer intrigues. But the way I look at what came out of that January meeting, women aren't interested in divisions, or in so much theorizing. None of that's going to solve the real problems. It seems to me that women talk about a "women's movement" no matter what it's called. And I think that's an expression of the fact that there's unity at the base.

When I retired from AMNLAE's national leadership in March 1990, what I thought was: "Okay, if they see me as someone too connected with the national directorate, too disciplined in the Party sense, too subordinated, it's better that I step down." I remember that one of the women from the movement called The 52 Percent [Majority] told me I was "too organic in terms of the FSLN." And I understood. I laughed to myself, but I understood it was a kind of punishment after the electoral defeat. They didn't want to have anything to do with anyone as historically involved with the Party as I am.

So I said, "Fine, I'll step down. In any case, it's not the position I have that's going to determine my participation or how I think. It's better if I turn the job over to someone capable of bringing the women together again." But it didn't happen. The divisions are deeper than ever.

On the other hand, the women on the other side haven't done much to mend the rift either. And they're split in all sorts of different directions. I understand that sectors of the FNT [National Workers' Front] also pulled out; they decided just to keep on working with women in the unions. When the women who attended the January meeting consulted among themselves about forming another organization, apart from AMNLAE, they didn't seem to feel that was justified. They tell me there's been criticism of the women who organized the January event—that their goal was the establishment of an independent women's organization, having nothing to do with AMNLAE. There are some very strange ideas floating around: vague, confused, about what autonomy really means, or democracy, or participation. I'm going to be very frank, Margaret, and maybe I'm wrong about this, but I really think these independent women have fallen into the NGO trap, the trap of the nongovernmental organizations.

The first thing people want to know here, when you ask for funding for whatever, is whether you're connected to a political party. They think you're hiding something—like suddenly it's a sin or a crime to belong to the FSLN. And I ask myself, "Wasn't it the FSLN that made the revolution? Why should AMNLAE, or any other organization, be ashamed of its links to the FSLN?" I agree we have to break with the subordination, in a practical sense, but why ideologically? Why do we have to stop being Sandinistas in order to legitimize ourselves?

To me it's just another form of imposition, another form of authoritarianism, under the guise of something called "feminism." Maybe I don't understand it like I should. But I think I've a right to some recognition. I deserve to be let in.

Why should I be discriminated against simply because I've achieved a certain level of leadership within the Party? There's a lot of talk about all of this, but I don't understand the problem.

I'd like to hear about your current work, with women at the grass roots. What are women demanding today? What are their problems? And what solutions are being suggested?

Well, I'm still the regional coordinator of AMNLAE, because those structures continue to function. They're not really structures so much as individuals who supervise AMNLAE's work in what used to be a particular region. Some say the model isn't valid anymore, but I think it is because it would be too awkward, too difficult, to direct programs or projects like those nationwide. There are approximately forty-two "women's houses" throughout the country, because sometimes one closes its doors or another opens them.[6] It would be hard for any one person to be in charge of them all. We're working toward decentralization. So the highest levels of leadership will eventually be determined by the way the country is divided: how many regions and so forth. Which is another discussion, because it implies forcing the women's movement to structure itself according to the administration of the country.

But we're also working with other women, women who haven't been organized before. In the Sixth Region we've got a group of thirty-nine women who are working at five child-care centers in the communities. I've been working with them on training, helping them with resources, but mainly training— because of how important that is for the children themselves, and for their parents. The child-care centers are a very concrete example of something the revolution was able to bring about that is still working. The women work voluntarily to keep the centers open, and the communities have assumed responsibility for them as well. And I'm proud of this project because Matagalpa is the only place the women's movement has taken it on.

The first thing Doña Violeta's government did when it came to power was to close the community service centers: health, child care, welfare, all that sort of thing. We're going to begin to open them again now, with the help of the women. First we wanted to concentrate on women's health clinics. But it's hard when you're right there in the community and a woman brings her child in, or the husband needs medical help. You can't say: "No, this is for women only." So we were going to start with gynecology and obstetrics, but then a pediatrician asked if he could volunteer his time. We've got the clinic going in Matagalpa now, and we're looking to extend this type of thing nationwide, as a project of the women's movement.

In Matiguas there's a group of women in AMNLAE who are also members

---

6. The "women's houses" are centers, begun by AMNLAE, where women can come for popular education and training, legal aid, and various activities. Some of these centers have separated from AMNLAE.

of UNAG;[7] they want to form a collective to work with leather, curing the skins. This is something that's happened spontaneously in Matiguas because it's a cattle-growing zone, and the only association of women cattle growers in the country is there. We're going to promote the curing operation and then hook those women up with a group of women in Jinotega who work the skins; they make shoes and bags and belts and so forth.

This kind of project serves a double purpose. It gives the women a skill, and it helps solve their economic problem. But the most important thing is that it brings them together, gives them a sense of solidarity with each other. And then we can begin to talk about other issues, issues that have to do with gender, political issues, do some solid ideological work with the women. Because I'm deeply troubled, not only by the tendency to move away from the Party that we're seeing in the women's movement, but by the general depoliticization that's going on.

This depoliticization is easily achieved through conditioning the resources. And we have to be aware of this to struggle consciously against it. Because it's all part of the plan to destroy the revolutionary project and replace it with the neoliberal one.

When the UNO government came to power, they found a perfectly viable economy, functioning in spite of the war. So they resolved the problem of the war—and that's relative because we don't really have a very solid peace here; what we have is an armistice. It's absurd to think we could have peace simply by proclaiming it: "Let's reconcile with our enemies," just like that. Simply because you see someone on one side embracing someone on the other, that doesn't mean there's real peace. It would be romantic, utopian really, to imagine such a thing.

The damage has been very profound here, very deep. We've got mothers who lost five children to the war, whole families that have disappeared. You can be as Christian as you like, you can understand the need for peace on an intellectual level, but emotionally it's not that easy. The most you can expect is that people will say, "Okay, we'll stop the killing." Beyond that, it takes time. We need time to resolve the deeper problems. And any day of the week you've got someone coming up to Doña Violeta and telling her right to her face, "I'm going to the mountains with four hundred men, because I'm fighting for my land." Or because she won't remove Humberto Ortega . . . or whatever the reason. So we're talking about a very relative peace here.

Doris, this reminds me of another question I wanted to ask. This may be more difficult to address, but I wonder if you could talk about how you've managed to live these years as a woman. I know that you've suffered irreparable losses, multiple losses that must be very difficult to bear. How have you managed it?

7. UNAG, or Unión Nacional de Agricultores y Ganaderos, is the National Union of Farmers and Cattle Growers.

I know I said this before, maybe in another interview. When I returned to Nicaragua in July of 1979, one of the things I did as a way of testing myself was to look for the people who had tortured me, the people who were in prison because they'd murdered someone close to me, people who had hurt me personally. I wanted to know how I'd feel face to face with those assassins, and I was surprised to find that I was absolutely indifferent. I thought I would feel rage. I thought I would want to attack them, now that I had the power to do so. But I felt indifference. I thought, "Perhaps indifference is my way of expressing repulsion." But I didn't feel hate.

That's interesting—and extraordinary—but that wasn't my question. In those cases it seems to me that your indifference was a way of coming out whole, a kind of victory. Because torturers don't deserve our hate. It's like giving them too much of our energy. Of course, different people react in different ways. But I was thinking more about loss in the sense that you, as a woman, have lost so many people close to you: lovers, even your daughter. This type of loss is something that's been shared by the great majority of people here in Nicaragua. My question is, As a woman do you believe you've had to accustom yourself to a particular type of solitude?

Yes, of course I have. I've talked about how hard it's been as a woman. How in order to gain certain leadership levels one has to work twice as hard as the men, show even more ability, put up with all sorts of things like those I've already mentioned. But the personal side is also a part of it all: the loneliness.

As a woman, it's been difficult and complicated keeping personal relationships going when you occupy leadership positions. For example, if you're a woman in a top-level job, people expect you to establish an intimate relationship with a man at the same level or higher. It used to be social status; with the revolution it became political hierarchy. In many ways it amounts to the same thing.

But I didn't see things this way. At a certain point, I established an intimate relationship with an ordinary enlisted man, someone without any rank at all. And I was a commander. The other officers were horrified, and I imagine the recruits were scared to death; I don't know what they thought. Needless to say, the relationship didn't prosper.

Why didn't it prosper?

There were a great many reasons. But I believe the difference in rank had a lot to do with it. Because relationships always engender personal problems of one kind or another. But in our case the difference in military rank complicated the situation, made it worse than it would have been. Unthinkable as it may be, the military hierarchy became a kind of social hierarchy here. But then, what did they expect a woman like myself to do? Above me there were only the nine Commanders of the Revolution. To begin with, they all had their relationships; and, secondly, I wasn't attracted to any of them.

So I married this man. But right away the problems began: the complexes, that male need to prove that just because you hold a higher military rank than he does, he's still "the man of the house." Dozens of problems. It just didn't work out. You know, it's unlikely that a woman who's reached a particular rank here will even be asked out to dinner, to the theater, even just for a walk. You have to do the inviting. You have to be the one to ask, "Would you like to go here or there?" It's hard. And this is what I mean when I say that a woman can make her way to the top, but the cost is enormous.

Society makes women with any degree of power pay. Powerful men have an easier time finding women who want to spend time with them; the more power they have, the easier it is. But I don't know if this is what you meant when you asked about solitude, about loneliness. Because, for me, there's another level of loneliness, more difficult to talk about. Even if I were to have a good relationship, even if I were surrounded by friends, people I love and who love me, I—Doris Tijerino—am a person who's long been accustomed to being alone, even isolated if you like.

This kind of aloneness is something I've lived with since my days in the underground. I told you when we first sat down to talk this morning: I don't live in a house; I live in a room. I don't have a wardrobe; I wear two or three outfits. I've been this way for years: I use the same clothing until people say I resemble a photograph. But enough of this. I want to get back to what I'm involved in now, and why.

This neoliberal project: you know, it's interesting. Internationally, they talk about this government having dealt with the economic crisis the Sandinistas are supposed to have created. Just look around you: there's something like a 60 percent unemployment rate. People are hungry. Once again we're seeing cases of night blindness, mongolism, epilepsy, inadequate nutrition—in numbers much greater than the norm. Maybe it's the accumulation of all these years of hardship. I'm not saying we were able to do away with these problems entirely—of course not—but at least we had health centers where people could go for free vitamins, for some kind of help.

Still, internationally, when it comes to the country's economic credibility, balance of payments, that sort of thing, we're supposed to be better off now than we were before. But there's one thing that hasn't changed, they haven't been able to change it, and that's the attitude people have. And this is where the great contradiction lies. People here agreed with the changes the revolution was making. Even UNO admits that. And people got used to demanding what they need, rejecting what isn't right.

That's why the change has been so complex. It's been hard for the new government to impose this neoliberal model. They've made some headway, but it's been slow. For example, since the revolution people here believe they have a right to health care. UNO has tried to make them feel ashamed that they believe they have that right. And the new solution to every problem is "Pay up." You have to pay for everything, everything has been privatized, everything has to be marketable, to make a profit. They've tried to make the Sandinistas feel ashamed of giving things away, and there have been a number of Sandinistas who have fallen into the trap.

But I ask you: What revolution doesn't have its quota of paternalism—if that's what you want to call it? I don't believe in giving everything away. I think people need to work for what they need. But I also believe the state has an obligation to take care of its citizenry, and that once people fight for and win the basic necessities, no one has a right to take those necessities away. Those are elemental human rights: health, education, work, shelter . . .

This government shut down the community service centers. It closed the child-care centers. It took away schools. And these are all gains that were won with blood. Ensuring the population's health isn't paternalism; it's giving people what's rightfully theirs. We subsidized basic foodstuffs, health care, education? Sure we did! Because ours was a revolutionary project, a humanist project. People accused the revolution of being irrational, socialist, communist—and all the while private property continued to exist here. Maybe we were romantics. But if a revolution doesn't have its dose of romanticism, it's not a revolution!

So what I'm most interested in doing right now is working with women at the grass-roots level so we can revive some of those projects that are so important, that we had and now we've lost: child-care centers, community service centers, neighborhood health clinics, and job training programs. It's amazing how ready and willing women are to build these projects all over again. Did you know that illiteracy has risen in the past two years? No sooner were the elections over than women were demanding another literacy crusade. People are asking for things as basic as that.

This is why I'm more interested in working with the rank and file. These women's groups with their feminist theories: they have jobs, they are well educated, and they sometimes lose sight of how ordinary women live. There's room for everyone, but I don't think we can discriminate against the woman who wants us to teach her how to read and write.

Doris, you hold a seat on the National Assembly. Can you tell me something about Article 204? How did it get passed? In your opinion, what is that struggle really about?

It was something terrible. Article 204 was already on the books, it's not something new. But it was less horrible, if you will, because [the old version] didn't include the provision about propaganda, promotion, what they call "introducing people to homosexual ideas." And that can mean anything: a film, a debate, a book—everything seems to be covered. Furthermore, in the new writing they left in the absolutely subjective phrase "practicing in a scandalous way." Who gets to measure scandal? What scandalizes you might not scandalize me and vice versa. The Sandinistas in the Assembly questioned that; we asked what they meant by "scandal." And one of the UNO representatives said something like "throwing a party with loud music." But, of course, heterosexuals throw those kinds of parties, and there's a misdemeanor code which addresses that. Yet, we couldn't get anywhere with our arguments.

Still, I believe it was a victory of sorts that we managed forty-one votes against Article 204: the vote was forty-three to forty-one. There are only thirty-nine Sandinistas in the Assembly. There was one UNO delegate who abstained; if we could have secured his vote, it would have been forty-three to forty-two. Another UNO delegate said he agreed with me and was going to vote accordingly—this was before we voted—but he ended up on the other side. Later he said he'd been confused. I don't know if he was really confused or if he just said that to get himself off the hook. If he had voted with us, we would have been able to defeat Article 204, forty-three to forty-two.

But really, what this is all about is prejudice. One of the senators from UNO—in a debate I was supposed to have gone to but didn't because I was ill—argued that it was evidence of our underdevelopment that we were fighting about whether or not to penalize homosexual activity here, when in Europe, he said, people are trying to get back to traditional family values. It's this old idea that so many people here have, that if something is happening in Europe it's progress; if it's happening in Latin America, it must be a reflection of our backwardness.

It seems to me like the campaign against sexual diversity here has been well orchestrated, among other reasons in order to divide the Left. Because the feminist movement has gotten so strong, and there are lesbian groups now doing extraordinary work in favor of nonsexist sex education, people working in AIDS outreach and education; there's so much going on. The line being taken by the extreme Right—and I have no doubt that Cardinal Obando y Bravo is behind this[8]—reminds me a lot of what was going on in Germany during the mid- and late-thirties, when homosexuals were also being discriminated against.

Margaret, you know I'm always being accused of paranoia when it comes to the United States. But it's interesting: I'm just now finishing up my university studies, and my classmates, who are much younger than I, tell me I blame everything on U.S. imperialism. But it seems to me that it's so much easier now than it was before for the United States to promote its line in a language Nicaraguans understand. Look at the debates around gay issues and the offensive against abortion taking place in the U.S. right now: we get the echo of all that.

It's a part of the neoliberal project. And it's worldwide. The U.S. has achieved such hegemony, such supremacy; that doesn't hurt the positions either. There's this backlash against gay rights and against choice in the United

8. Miguel Obando y Bravo was a Catholic archbishop during the Somoza regime and for the first few years of Sandinista government. He has always been a conservative, although circumstances forced him to take a stand against the dictatorship when it became clear that the FSLN was gaining power. He mediated some of the Sandinistas' important standoffs with Somoza, including the takeover of the Chema Castillo house in December 1975 and the occupation of the National Palace in August 1978. In May 1983, Obando y Bravo brought the pope to Nicaragua, where the latter publicly chastised Fr. Ernesto Cardenal and refused to hear the pleas of mothers whose sons had been assassinated by the Contras. Shortly thereafter, Obando y Bravo was promoted to cardinal. During the last years of the Contra war he, more and more obviously, represented the interests of the counterrevolution within Nicaragua.

States, and suddenly we're passing laws like this in Nicaragua. Since when have these issues been on our agenda here? Why we couldn't even get abortion legalized in cases of rape!

And, you know, our struggle is made more difficult by the fact that there is such dispersion, so many different groups, each going off in its own direction; so many power struggles. We've engaged in some heavy-duty criticism of this kind of leadership struggle within the political parties, but look what's happening among the women: the same sorts of jealousies, who's going to take charge . . . It doesn't matter whether they're lesbians or heterosexuals, or whether they're working in this area or that.

Doris, you mentioned that you'd gone back to school. What are you studying?

The university made me go back and start all over again; they wouldn't recognize my credits from before 1973. And, of course, I had to stop my studies when I became involved in the revolution full-time. So I had to start from the beginning. But it's been a great experience. I'm studying sociology— not so much for the degree, but to be doing something with people with whom I can have a different type of relationship. I wanted to do something totally different from working with women or in the police force. Sociology at UNAN includes political science and sociology; it prepares you for postgraduate work in either field.

Are you thinking of going for a graduate degree?

I'd like to continue studying, maybe not for a postgraduate degree in the formal sense; but I do want to finish my undergraduate work so I can take some courses that interest me, particularly in the area of criminology. I'm not interested in law as such, but I'm fascinated by anything that has to do with the penal system. I like investigation. Maybe I'll take some courses in investigative technique. But the most important thing, I think, is that I remain connected in some way with the student population.

My classmates don't treat me as a comandante or a senator or someone up there among the leadership. They treat me as one of them, a good or bad student, whatever . . . and that's refreshing. Of course, they're all much younger than I. And sometimes they joke about that. The other day we had a seminar on World War II. I raised my hand to talk about something, and one of the kids said, "Well, you certainly knew the answer to that!" I said, "Of course I did; I remember reading about it in the paper!" They teased me about having the advantage. I feel good in that class.

So this is my last year of undergraduate work. I think it will turn out to have some practical applications. And I'm not doing it just because I feel good being with the other students. After I finish this Senate term they imposed on me, I think I'd like to teach at the university. A number of Sandinistas are teaching now, and I think it's good for the university and good for the new generations. During the ten years of revolution so many young people stopped going to school; there was so much that needed to be done. Now people are going back to pick up where they left off . . .

What would you like to teach, Doris?

History. I'd like to teach history. You know, traditionally the university was a place where intellectuals and people of vision gathered, and taught. States-people, government ministers, and others were formed at the university. We need to continue producing people who can deal with the problems we have here.

Doris had to get over to the Ministry of the Interior, where she had a meeting about a project with delinquent children, a particular interest of hers. As I packed away my recording equipment, we continued to talk—about old times and about these new, much more confusing ones. It is painful when one remembers the hardships and uncertainty of guerrilla struggle as more joyous, or at least more energizing, than this fabricated peace. Yet this memory and its current counterpoint often dance drunkenly across our consciousness.

Before I took leave Doris had one more thing she wanted to say. She turned, looked at me for a moment, and then proclaimed—as if to anyone willing to listen—"You know, it's true: we can't live on consciousness alone; but we can't live without it."

"Nicaragua Is a Surprising Country"

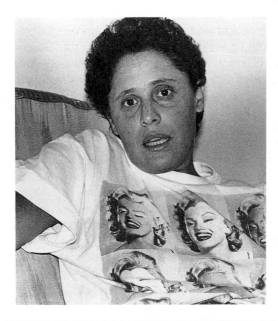

Dora María Téllez

In the last years of the war against Somoza a young woman became legend, first in Nicaragua and then beyond its borders. Her name is Dora María Téllez. She was twenty three when she made headlines as Commander Two in the 1978 takeover of Managua's National Palace.[1] A third-year medical student when she went underground with the FSLN, she quickly proved to be not only fearless in battle but intelligent and innovative when it came to negotiating with the enemy. She was the commando's spokesperson in Panama City when journalists from every major news service clamored for the story of how the young revolutionaries had brought the dictator to his knees.

Months passed, and this energetic woman with intense blue eyes, full lips, short-cropped curly hair and lithe body intentionally dropped from international sight. When she reappeared, it was only weeks before the war's end: June 1979. She and her high command of four women and two men occupied

1. In order to conceal their names, the Sandinista combatants identified themselves by number when they took part in operations that were sure to be reported on the news. The occupation of the National Palace, where Somoza's legislature was in session, was one such operation in August 1978. The FSLN took some thirty-five hundred hostages which enabled them to negotiate the release of all political prisoners captive at that time. Edén Pastora was Commander Zero in the surprise attack; Hugo Torres, Commander One; and Dora María Téllez, Commander Two.

*León, Nicaragua's second-largest city. They proclaimed it liberated territory
and proceeded to install the provisional Government of National Reconstruction. Less than a month later the dictator fled, the FSLN occupied Managua,
and those painful years of fighting had come to an end. Another, much more
difficult struggle was about to begin.*

*Dora María was to prove herself adept at rebuilding people's lives. From
the earliest days, peace was a complex process. A new, more humane society
had to be constructed, with all that implies in changing consciousness as well
as institutions, and it had to be done facing off against increased pressure from
the United States. Dora María left the military early in 1980 and brought her
unique mix of organization and creativity to bear upon a number of key posts.
Early on, she headed the FSLN party structure in Managua. Then she was
named minister of public health in a country where curable diseases were
epidemic, where resources were almost nonexistent, and where there were
forty thousand severely war-wounded alone. Téllez would hold this position for
almost a decade, until the electoral defeat of 1990. And in spite of extraordinary obstacles, preventative medicine and public health were among the
achievements of which the Sandinista revolution can be most justly proud.
Even the conservative who received the ministry from her hands attested to its
impeccable order.*

*During the Sandinista administration, overwhelming as it must often have
seemed, public health wasn't Dora María's only responsibility. She continued
to hold key posts in the Party, was a member of the Sandinista Assembly and—in
many people's eyes—was a sort of unofficial addition to the all-male, nine-
member national directorate. When the Council of State (Nicaragua's legislative body) was formed toward the end of 1979, she became its vice-president, a
position she would also hold, through numerous changes in the governing
coalition, throughout the decade. Today, although her party is no longer in
power, she retains her senatorial seat in Nicaragua's revamped National Assembly.*

*Just after the FSLN's 1979 victory, I arrived in Nicaragua to interview
women who had participated in the war. Everyone talked about Dora María,
and I naturally wanted to meet her. During those first euphoric months she was
always on the move; I'd hear I might find her in one place or another, then
arrive to discover she'd left hours or minutes before. In addition to the many
stories and news reports that wove the legend, my image of the woman was
also rooted in Daisy Zamora's poem, written as she watched the commando
that would occupy the National Palace leave from its safehouse—which was
also her country home:*[2]

> *Dora María Téllez*
> *twenty years old,*
> *slight and pale*
> *in her boots, her black beret,*

2. "Commander Two," in Daisy Zamora, *Clean Slate: New and Selected Poems*, trans. Margaret Randall and Elinor Randall (Willimantic, Conn.: Curbstone Press, 1993).

her enemy uniform
a size too large.

Through the banister rails
I watched as she talked to the boys
the nape of her neck
*   white beneath the beret*
and her freshly-cut hair.

(Before they left, we embraced.)

Dora María
young warrior woman
who caused the tyrant's heart
to tremble in rage.

Unexpectedly one night I caught up with the legend, and the woman. I was in the north-central city of Matagalpa talking with market women whose heroism included having hidden messages and munitions beneath vegetables in the baskets they carried on their heads. A young woman named Mary came by and said she knew I'd been looking for the comandante. "She's resting at a house near here," she said, "she's very tired. But she might be able to give you half an hour . . ." I remember almost telling Mary that half an hour wouldn't do. But I stopped myself. Half an hour was better than nothing. And, who knew? If we got to talking . . .

We did get to talking. Another one of the women comandantes was also there: Leticia Herrera. She was so tired she hardly said a word. Dora María looked exhausted, a pale figure in her dark uniform settled back in one of those old rocking chairs in the shadows of a dark room. But the warning of "no more than half an hour" faded out of memory as she spoke—about her life, the war, about women and their participation in the struggle just concluded.

I remember that a single yellow bulb hanging from the high ceiling didn't cast enough light for me to be able to focus my camera, and I didn't have a flash. But I wanted to record this woman's gestures as well as her words: the tilt of her head against the wooden slats of the rocker's frame, her pale forearm and hand as it gripped one cigarette after another. So I blindly shot several rolls of film and, later, in a dream, figured out how many minutes I would have to add to my developing time in order to obtain usable pictures.

That first interview, interspersed with pieces of a conversation I later had with María Dora—Dora María's mother—appeared in Sandino's Daughters. *The images, too, which had a magic about them. I was interested in talking to mothers and daughters in this country where so many young women had risked political commitment and then influenced their mothers to participate as well. In this most desperate of arenas, it was as if the traditional parent/child role had been reversed.*

María Dora showed me a story her daughter had left along with the note telling her parents she had gone underground in 1976. It was a very short story, sparse, almost raw, about her first delivery several years before. The woman giving birth was poor, the child had little to look forward to. Dora María was a medical student, and this was her first birth. After a simple description, including a reference to her own fear, she wonders about the baby: "Will his body survive? And what about his hopes? Have I completed my mission by aiding in his birth?" And then she responds: "I must say no. Our work will be done only when we can give these young ones a new and different world."

Over the years, from time to time we would talk again. I was privileged to be invited to a session in which the military command that occupied León came together formally for the first time after the war. Their task: to re-create the history of those heroic hours. It was a moving experience listening to seasoned warriors who'd never really talked about these events, at least not all together. One asked, startled: "You mean it was you on the other side of that wall? I had no idea . . ." Those of us there that night understood we were witnessing the recording of real people's history, not filtered through the prism of some elite historian but told by the protagonists themselves.

In May 1982, I and thousands of others would hear this extraordinary political leader in what must have been a particularly difficult assignment. Eight hundred mothers of young people murdered by Contra *forces had organized and marched into Managua, demanding the death penalty for those who had taken their sons' and daughters' lives. They were angry. Many carried photographs, framed portraits or tiny snapshots, often all that remained by which they could remember the child who was gone. I wouldn't want to have been the one designated to convince those outraged mothers that further death would not mitigate their loss. Dora María wasn't in uniform that day. She wore a* cotona, *the simple cotton overblouse traditional in Nicaragua's peasant countryside. And she spoke to the hearts of those women, from her own heart and mind.*

The night before I left Nicaragua, heading home to New Mexico in early 1984, a small group of women gathered to share their memories. Dora María was among them. The conversation centered on the pintas, *those words and phrases scrawled or stenciled on city and village walls through every stage of the struggle. They reflect popular demands, instructions, battles, losses, victories. Somewhere I still have the transcription of that tape: women talking about what it felt like to go out in the night and risk their lives, or to send others out. "It was dangerous," Dora María recalled, "because if you were caught that was it. But there's so much creativity in the* pintas; *you'll see whole poems on the walls. During the dictatorship, that was our freedom of expression here."*

When I returned to Managua in October 1991, I called Dora María and we met to talk again. The electoral defeat was already a year and a half behind us. The war had finally ended, and thousands of ex-Contras were reentering the country. No one, not even the opposition, had expected the FSLN to lose. Handing over the government had been as smooth as the revolutionaries had promised it would be, but the transition was more than just a change in administration. It wasn't like Republicans ceding the White House to the Democrats.

People were still in a state of shock. Dora María told me the goal was to defend those social and political gains which a decade of Sandinism had made possible.

"This is a different country," she told me, "than the one we inherited from Somoza. People here know who they are, and what they have a right to now. It's not going to be so easy to take away what's been won." It was while talking to Dora María that I got the idea of returning to do another book. I thought it would be interesting to search out the women I'd interviewed twelve years before, to learn how a decade of revolution and two years of conservative government had affected their lives. Dora María thought it was a great idea.

Once in the field and more in touch with current realities, my idea matured and changed. Surely I would go back to some of my original interviewees; but rather than mechanically trying to find all the women with whom I'd spoken in 1979 and 1980, it gradually became clear that the most interesting and useful book would be about Nicaraguan feminism. Whatever direction my project took, another interview with Dora María was essential; I knew that. So when I returned in July 1992, I again made plans to see her—and her mother. This time her father was also available, and I could see how much of her determination and dignity she gets from Don Ramón.

Although the interviews with Dora María and with her parents took place in different places and at different times, I have inserted bits and pieces from the latter at points where I believe María Dora's and Ramón's observations provide an interesting parental perspective. These proud people have had to struggle with their own feelings about a daughter who has risked so much. They have also been willing to share stories she is much too modest to reveal.

Dora María is a decade older now. Her entire adult life has been involved with the struggle for justice in her country, and there's no indication she will abandon that struggle. While other important FSLN cadre have gone into business or back to school since the electoral defeat, she remains a round-the-clock revolutionary. No one who knows her can imagine her doing anything else, and there is the unanimous belief—rare in Nicaragua—that this is someone whose history is absolutely clean. While several among the Sandinista leadership have been accused of straying from a commitment to the needs of ordinary people, and a few have slipped into varying degrees of corruption, Dora María has never been mentioned in connection with any of that. She is a model, even to her enemies.

This general and very solid popularity led to her being urged to run for a seat on the FSLN's national directorate, which would necessarily be renewed at the First Party Congress in July 1991. One of its members, Carlos Núñez, had died; another, Humberto Ortega, could no longer participate because of a conflict of interest with his position as commander-in-chief of the army. Both their places had to be filled. Days before the Congress, however, at a meeting of the Sandinista Assembly, the decision was made to approve an entire slate rather than voting for individuals. Dora María withdrew her candidacy when it became clear that the old guard had manipulated things to retain control of the governing body. Unity seemed to be the overriding consideration.

Answers to the questions "Why wasn't Dora María Téllez elevated to the FSLN's national directorate?" or "Why wasn't a woman made a member of the directorate?" elicit a number of responses, as we've seen. There are those who argue it wasn't the moment for such radical change. Many point to Dora María's strength of character, her independence and uncompromising honesty, her strong feminism. Some say she is a lesbian and that an organization as male-dominated and sexist as the FSLN couldn't overcome its prejudice, even as regards someone so obviously admired and beloved. Milú Vargas said she wasn't sure women should be seeking a place on the directorate: "We should be questioning the model itself," she insisted, "rather than trying to become a part of it."

What personal life Dora María enjoys is not something she is willing to discuss. For someone like myself, whose knowledge of this woman depends for the most part upon her public image, "warrior" is the word that most readily comes to mind. She exudes a unique mix of clarity and mystery, but "warrior"—in its ancient, more comprehensive definition—defines well her disciplined temperament and quick, ready intelligence.

All this and much else was on my mind the morning I went to interview Dora María for this book. The offices of the Sandinista congressional delegation, according to the Nicaraguan way of issuing street addresses, is "in Las Palmas neighborhood, across from the Mormon church." We knocked on a few doors and asked directions several times before we were able to find the house. Once there, beyond its simple façade a profusion of paintings and sculpture in the foyer and front halls came as a surprise.

A receptionist said that Dora María was still busy with the morning's telephone calls but that she'd be with me shortly. I'd barely finished the cup of coffee I'd been offered, and was still looking at the wonderful art, when the woman reappeared and ushered me into a utilitarian office: a desk in one corner, a file cabinet, a couple of pictures on the walls—and a small couch and two armchairs where she motioned me to make myself comfortable.

Dora María wore the neatly pressed Levi's, loafers, and T-shirt that have become her trademark. The shirt presented an interesting contrast with her uniform of other times: against a white background, Andy Warhol's Marilyn Monroe was pastel and frothy, repeated in six slightly different images across her chest.

The hardships, sorrows, and complexities of these years have left their mark: Dora María's features show a greater exhaustion, the skin beneath her amazing eyes is darkened and drawn. The cigarette remains a constant. She still responds to all questions with her particular combination of thoughtfulness and discipline. She still rocks as she speaks, or taps her foot. Her gestures are still angular, intense. And her grasp of how the world works, of how Nicaragua works in the world, and of how she has chosen to place herself within that overall dynamic is, I believe, of exceptional interest.

"We've done this before," she laughed, as she went to her desk for a clean notepad and mechanical pencil, then returned to settle herself in the chair across from mine. I knew she would scribble as she listened and responded to

questions, or she would doodle, or both. "Where should we start?" she asked.
"At the beginning," I said. "It's never the same story twice" . . .

Well, I began working with the FSLN when I got to the university. No, that's not true. It was before, in high school, during the student movement of 1970. Student movements here have traditionally included demands beyond the purely academic. That one had three goals: to raise teachers' salaries, to better the situation of nurses and health workers in general, and to gain the release of the country's political prisoners. We wanted the dictatorship to show us they were alive, and to release them. José Benito [Escobar] was in prison then.[3]

So even though I was still in high school at the time, our movement was very dynamic. And in Matagalpa we were able to establish ties with some members of the FSLN—not openly but clandestinely, you might say. That was the beginning of my real political involvement, although I had taken part in campaigns and demonstrations, that sort of thing, as far back as '68, '69.

I lived in Matagalpa then. My brother and I were born there, into a middle-class family with a fair amount of social status. I always say our social status was greater than our economic means. And we went to school there; I studied with the Josephine Sisters, which was the convent school where most of the families with money sent their daughters. After high school I went on to the university in León. That was just after the 1972 earthquake; I started college in 1973. I took the year of basic studies in order to go into medicine.

By the time I was in medical school my ties to the FSLN were more formal. I never really joined the FER [Revolutionary Student Front], but I was a student activist. And I became a member of the Sandinista National Liberation Front in 1974. My joining the organization coincided with an important number of cadre going underground.

During those first years of political activism in León, I mostly worked with the student movement and in some of the poor neighborhoods. We were also responsible for buying a certain amount of goods and supplies that were needed by the guerrillas in the mountains. And I typed and helped produce some of the documents the Front was circulating at the time. One interesting note: for a while I belonged to a security cell, a cell of militants who were designated to provide security wherever it was needed. We were all women except for the person in charge, a worker from León who happened to be the oldest member of the organization there. He was a good comrade. They killed him in November of 1978.

This guy didn't just take care of security; he was in charge of propaganda and supplies, too. We bought boots, clothing, medicines, and saw that they got to the mountains. We also secured safehouses, mostly there in León but sometimes in Managua, too. That's more or less the kind of work I was doing back then, besides the student movement.

---

3. José Benito Escobar, a longtime member of the FSLN, was killed at Estelí in 1978. The headquarters of the Sandinista Trade Union Central is named after him.

Dora María, looking back from the perspective you have now, can you talk about how men and women related to one another in the organization then? How were the women treated?

That was a period with very special characteristics. We were all very compartmentalized. No one knew anyone else except for the other members of his or her cell. So I can't really speak for the Front as a whole. And, of course, I thought the organization was huge, enormous! We all did, until we realized how few we really were! I don't know, there might have been four or five cells in León besides ours. And as I've said, the one I belonged to was almost all women. Three women, and the comrade in charge who was a man.

But there were lots of women in the student movement at that time—and a great many female leaders. Of course, there were more men than women in positions of power. But, for example, I was recruited into the FSLN by a woman: Ana Isabel Morales. She's second in command now in Immigration. Back then she was a student leader, she held an office in the FER, and she belonged to the FSLN.

When that group of cadre went underground in 1974 the percentage of women in the student movement rose. Most of the militants who went underground were men, although there were a few women as well. I remember some of the women from that time: Mónica Baltodano, Marta Cranshaw, Ana Isabel, Luz Marina Acosta, Mercedita Espinoza . . .

What was the political division of labor between men and women at that time?

I don't know. In my cell the kind of work we did was pretty ordinary: buying supplies, typing. If you look at it from today's point of view, it was typical women's work. The FSLN wasn't launching those big military-political operations yet. It was the period characterized by a silent, steady accumulation of power. But certainly there was a lot of sexism in the organization. In León, at least, the regional leadership was sexist in the extreme.

The comrade responsible for our cell was a worker, like I said, and we were three middle-class women. Our relationship with him was difficult at first. He gave us a hard time, he was very strict; but then that was the norm in the FSLN. Responsibility and discipline were essential. All the cells functioned that way. I can't really say if he was tougher on us because we were women or because we were middle-class women. But he had his quiet side, too. He could be very sweet. To tell you the truth, I never thought of him as sexist; although others among the leadership certainly were. When he was killed, there were just the three of us.

Who took charge of the cell then?

For a while we had to cool off. The [National] Guard found some notes with our pseudonyms, so we had to be careful. Later, one of the clandestine comrades was detailed to coordinate our work: Jorge Sinforoso Bravo. Our liaison with him was a guy who worked at the university, in the biology lab. He was the contact between the members of the cell and the clandestine comrade. But then one of the women began coordinating our activities; she was a biology student. Of the three women, one studied biology, one law, and then there was me in medicine. We continued to do the same sort of work: security, information gathering, buying and sending supplies to the mountains. Until 1975. I went underground in January of 1976, so I don't know what happened to the cell after that.

It's interesting today when I think about the three of us. The biology student became a professional in her field. I remember her husband was underground; he was arrested and was in prison for a while. But I think she continued in the organization until 1976 or '77. I see the law student every once in a while. She was the one you might have thought would have backed out before the rest of us: because of her fragility, she had one of those delicate personalities; her class background, too. But I see her around, in political activities, even today. In recent times I've run into her quite often.

Dora María's parents remember when their daughter went underground:

MARÍA DORA: It was so hard. We didn't know where she was, or how she was. I knew that some of the kids managed to send little notes to their parents. I'd get up early every morning and go to the door. I was looking for a note, some word from her, anything . . . We had some news just before her twentieth birthday. By that time she'd been gone for two and a half years . . .

RAMÓN: I couldn't understand it at first. My son and daughter and I had made a pact, that they would never make a serious decision without talking it over with me first. After the victory I asked Dora María, "Why didn't you come and tell me? Why did you go off like that, after the pact we made?" She said: "It's simple. If I'd come to you first, I wouldn't have gone."

MARÍA DORA: When the war ended, I thought she was going to come back home, come back to us and study medicine again. I thought, "Okay, they kicked Somoza out. That was the important thing." I always thought she'd come back home . . .

RAMÓN: The revolution was just beginning then! How could you have thought she'd be coming home, if the hardest part was just beginning?

MARÍA DORA: I know . . . and she always said, "I do what the Party requires of me. If they send me to be a night watchman somewhere, that's where you'll find me."

Dora María, when did the organization begin to plan the takeover of the National Palace? How was that organized?

That was an old idea. In 1977, sometime around the middle of '77, we began talking about it. And in 1978 we began more serious preparations . . .

So between January of 1966, when you went underground, and the end of 1977, when preparations for the attack on the palace got under way, what kind of work were you doing?

We left the country. A group of four comrades, three men and I, we left the country and went to Mexico. The idea was that we would go to Cuba. We were all medical students, and we went to get some special training in guerrilla medicine. I think it was the first time the FSLN actually invested in something like that. People usually went directly to the mountains. But this time they wanted us to have some basic training first, learn how to treat certain types of wounds, that sort of thing. So this group of four left Nicaragua in January of 1976 and headed for Cuba.

But there was a problem. We ended up staying four months in Mexico because the divisions within the Front were at their most critical point just then. Around the end of 1975 the first tendency had split off from the rest, but the situation still wasn't all that clear. So there was this group of us in Mexico, and there were problems with the trip to Cuba and problems within the organization.

Look, it's complicated; because the thing was, depending on where you happened to be, the situation looked different. Inside the country the political structures hadn't yet divided. And in Cuba there wasn't one clearly defined tendency either. But some of the leadership was in Mexico—Eduardo Contreras, Joaquín Cuadra—and Humberto and Daniel [Ortega] had been through, trying to mediate between the different lines. It was a mediation between one leadership group and another; one saw things one way, the other saw things differently. And things kind of ground to a halt, waiting for this mediation process to run its course. You'll remember that Carlos Fonseca reentered the country at the end of 1975, in November.

But the mediation wasn't successful. It was a long, complex process, and in the end it was the mediators themselves who formed the third tendency, the Insurrectionists. So there I was: first in Mexico and then in Cuba. And in Cuba no one talked about division; nothing at all was said. José Benito was in charge of us there, and he never breathed a word about any kind of division— as if it didn't exist. When I finally realized what was going on I was in Mexico, on my way back to Nicaragua; that was June 1977. And I found out purely by accident.

José Benito and I were traveling together. From the Mexico City airport we went to an apartment, and I remember he went into another room to talk with some members of the organization who were there. I stayed in the living room with a guy I didn't know. Later it turned out he was Saúl Lewites. And he asked me a question: what did I think of the Insurrectionist tendency? I didn't have the slightest idea. He mentioned the Proletarians and the GPP [Prolonged People's War], and I didn't know what he was talking about. I didn't answer him. I just turned it around and asked him a question, or remained silent; I don't remember. Later what I did was try to find out what was happening. I asked José Benito to tell me what he knew.

So the trip to Cuba was confusing, but the return to Nicaragua was worse. It was total confusion. I still had the picture I'd had when I left Nicaragua: that there were some tactical disagreements but nothing more. And besides, I had one version of what was going on; but then I found out there was another. When I talked to Eduardo Contreras in Cuernavaca, [Mexico,] he talked about unity, the typical mediator's line. The important thing was to bring the organization together. My sense was that inside the country everything was fine, that all the problems had been resolved. So it was a shock when I returned.

I had traveled from Cuba with José Benito more than anything because he needed a cover. As a woman I could cover for him; we traveled as a couple. If it hadn't have been for that, I don't know when I would have gotten out of Cuba. After the mediation José Benito was supposed to do in Mexico, he had to go on to Panama. So we went to Panama. He was supposed to make some contacts there, too, but it wasn't possible. So we went on to Honduras, where he was to meet up with members of the GPP. That didn't work out either. In Honduras he found some of the Insurrectionists: Daniel, Danto, Víctor. And whatever they talked about, I only heard about it much later. Then José Benito had to return to Mexico. He had a mission—I didn't know anything about that either—that had something to do with the Group of Twelve.

I stayed in Honduras at a safehouse that belonged to the Insurrectionists. José Benito had been there, too, before he had to return to Mexico. Lenín Cerna and I ended up staying there by ourselves. The Cubans didn't want any of us who had gone to study guerrilla medicine to end up in any of the tendencies; they didn't want to be seen as taking sides. But when José Benito left again, the organization sent me off to a school run by the Insurrectionists so I wouldn't have to hang around without anything to do. The Insurrectionists were preparing for the October 1977 offensive, and they wanted me to give some first aid classes to the comrades who were going off to fight.

I was glad when they sent me to that school. Because I'd been going crazy with Lenín in that safehouse all day, just talking and cooking! I was delighted. And it was at that school that I really began to understand the different viewpoints, what the differences were. But the school also served me in other ways. The comrades there had a fantastically high morale, the kind of morale you have when you're about to go into combat. I call it "carrying victory in your eyes"; that's the way I perceived it. It had to do with understanding that this was the moment for a military offensive against the dictatorship.

But José Benito was supposed to travel again. He was supposed to go to Cuba, to explain the situation to the comrades there, explain the offensive that was going to be launched. On the way he was scheduled to go to Mexico, to make contact with the Group of Twelve. I was to go with him again, to make good on our commitment to the Cubans that none of us who had studied guerrilla medicine were taking sides in the tendency dispute. And that's when José Benito and I had our big discussion. I said I didn't want to go. It seemed to me that if comrades were going off to fight, and I had all this training in combat medicine, well, the logical place for me to be was with them.

And, of course, I wanted to stay with the combatants. It felt good to be going back into the country. So we had this discussion. And I managed to convince José Benito. He decided to risk letting me off the hook. I stayed, and he left for Mexico and then Cuba. He was convinced that this was the moment for the offensive. He said, "We either launch our attack against the dictatorship now, or the FSLN dies." Those were his words. "This is our opportunity," he said. I know that he began to see things differently; maybe the comrades in Cuba changed his mind, or maybe it was in Mexico. I'll never know. Because he was killed in Estelí on July 15, 1978. I never saw him again.

A group of us reentered Nicaragua on September 22, 1977. We joined the northern front, the first deployment in the mountains of Dipilto. Our mission was to attack Ocotal, but that didn't turn out the way we planned. From September 22 to October 5, I was at a guerrilla camp there in the mountains. On the 5th we moved down to a camp near the highway—something we'd never done before—in order to prepare the attack.

On the 11th they sent me and Facundo Picado out to assess the enemy's position. We put on civilian clothes and went to the city, where we stayed the night of the 11th or—I don't remember—maybe it was the 10th or the 9th. In any case, by the 12th we were back at camp, preparing to surround the city. Everything went well at first. We had roadblocks on the highway, and we were stopping all incoming vehicles . . . until one of the roadblocks messed up and a vehicle managed to get through. They notified the [National] Guard, who thought we were bandits. And the guard came out. We were forced to start fighting some seven or eight kilometers outside the city. That was the 13th of October. The plan had been to attack Ocotal, but we couldn't pull it off.

I remained on the northern front until May 1978. Sometimes I'd travel to Tegucigalpa [in Honduras] to take part in planning sessions, but in May of that year a large group of us returned to concentrate our energies in the cities; we were preparing for the urban uprisings. The attack on the National Palace was in August of that year—and, of course, I had to leave the country again, with the commando and the hostages; we all flew to Panama. The month before, on July 15th, they'd killed José Benito. And I was back in Nicaragua for good by early 1979: the end of February, early March . . .

In Panama you were the spokesperson for the FSLN . . .

Something like that. And I had contact with [Gen. Omar] Torrijos, the solidarity committees, material aid, and [did] some political maneuvering: what remained of August, and September.

Ramón had this to say, about his daughter's experience in Panama:

I'll tell you about it, because it's history now. After the attack on the palace, the kids went to Panama, where they stayed for several months.

> Dora María was the treasurer of the group; she was the one in charge of the money that General Torrijos gave our revolutionary movement. And I want to tell you, Torrijos treated my daughter as if she were his own. I know that they opened a bank account with two signatories: Dora María and Manuel Antonio Noriega. That account started out with 12 million dollars in it, but one day Dora María realized that a million dollars was missing. She suspected Noriega. She didn't say anything to him, but she told Torrijos: "I want you to do me a favor. I want my name alone to remain on the account." He did as she said. But that Noriega stole a million dollars that belonged to the FSLN, just by writing one check! Much later, when Dora María went to Torrijos's funeral, his widow told her, "Be careful. There are people here who don't wish you well."

I'm trying to give you an idea of where I was, what I was doing up to the time I came back into the country for good. In December I was part of a unified delegation to the socialist countries, a delegation made up of one member from each of the tendencies; we wanted to explain what was going on in Nicaragua. I remember we went to the Soviet Union, Bulgaria, the German Democratic Republic, Czechoslovakia, Yugoslavia, and Poland. We didn't get to Romania. And then we went on to Algiers and to Libya. We were explaining the position of the FSLN, and asking for their support.

And, you know, no one believed us! Very few people anywhere believed what we had to say. Nobody really thought we could defeat the dictatorship. The most the Soviets were able to do was to begin—to begin—to form a new understanding of Nicaragua, to develop a new concept of Central America. The Soviet party had its ties with the Socialist Party here, Luis Sánchez and those folks, and their idea of what was going on was completely off base. Completely wrong. Of the socialist countries, the only ones who took us seriously were the Germans. Everyone else just listened, some more politely than others. The Germans were the only ones who really believed we were going to defeat Somoza.

Why do you think that was?

I don't know. We had a great deal of support from the German Democratic Republic. The rest considered us crazy Latin Americans. But it wasn't only the socialist bloc. We made contact with some of the leftist organizations in Western Europe, and they didn't believe us either. People just didn't think it was possible. They were sure the gringos would intervene, that we'd never be able to overthrow the dictatorship without the United States stepping in. I guess we just didn't manage to convince people what the real correlation of forces was.

Anyway we returned; it must have been February by then, February 1979. I entered by way of Panama. And we began to prepare the final offensive. I was in Granada for a while, in Managua, Chinandega, Chichigalpa, Masaya, Carazo, almost all the regions where the FSLN had a concentration of cadre. And then at the end I was in León . . .

Dora María, your occupation of León is history; you've spoken about it, and people have written about it extensively. I want to ask you: How do you explain the fact that your high command in León was so overwhelmingly female?

Pure coincidence. Look, the high command of the Insurrectionist tendency, there in León, was made up of Ana Isabel, Aracely Pérez, Carlos Manuel Jarquín, Roger Deshón, Edgard Lang, Leticia Herrera, Fanor Urroz . . . what a terrible thing memory is: I can remember his pseudonym but not his name! Oh, and Idania Fernández. The GPP had Mauricio Valenzuela and China Jirón. Marta Cranshaw was there for the Proletarians, although she spent most of her time in Chinandega. At least I ran into her in Chinandega; maybe she'd gone to Honduras by then. Anyway, as you know, they surrounded and killed a group of comrades in León: Carlos Manuel, Edgard, Roger, Idania, and Aracely.[4] So, who was left?

Ana Isabel was there that day, at the meeting where the others died. But she managed to get away. She passed herself off as a domestic; the other servants protected her, and she got out alive. Leticia Herrera was late, she didn't get there on time. So, what happened? After those comrades were killed, who did they have left? China Jirón and Mauricio Valenzuela for the GPP; the Proletarians didn't have anyone of stature in León at the time; and we were Ana Isabel, Leticia, and Fanor Urroz for the Insurrectionists. Lenín Fonseca and Carlos Brenes could have been there, too, but they were in Chinandega.

So when they named the joint command it was Mauricio, China, Leticia, Ana Isabel, Fanor, Polo Rivas, and me. It just happened that we were mostly women. Four women and three men. Then Fanor Urroz was killed on July 17th, or on the morning of the 18th. So we became even more of a female majority. But it was coincidence, that's all. What wasn't a coincidence was my designation as head of the command.

This brings us to the end of the war against Somoza. I feel like we've just finished another version of the interview we did twelve years ago. Now I'd like you to talk about your life since July 19th, 1979, after the war ended . . .

4. Although Dora María mentions only five names, six important members of the FSLN's leadership structure were assassinated in what would later come to be known as the Massacre at Veracruz (a neighborhood in León). It was April 16, 1979. The comrades were meeting in a house that had inadequate alternative exits. A man called "El Chino," who had participated in the Sandinista militia, was now a police informer. He accompanied the National Guard on the raid and identified Roger Deshón ("El Chele"), Edgard Lang Sacasa ("Aurelio"), Oscar Pérez Cassar ("El Gordo"), and Carlos Manuel Jarquín López ("Jacinto" or "Chinto") as important cadre. Consequently, the guard decided to liquidate them on the spot. They ordered the four men to turn their faces to the wall, but they insisted on dying face to face with the enemy. The two women, Idania Fernández Ramírez ("Angelita") and Aracely Pérez Darías ("Tere," "Argentina," "Pilar," or "Marta") were not known to El Chino. They were arrested but, once at the station house, were identified, tortured, and murdered. Leticia Herrera, another important member of the FSLN leadership at the time, was supposed to be at the fatal meeting. Something kept her from attending, though, so her life was spared.

Well, I remained in the army for a while. In León and Chinandega, which was the Second Military Region. In January of 1980 I was transferred to Managua, but by that time I had been demobilized from the army. I became political secretary of the FSLN's departmental committee in Managua, which was just then being formed.

What was that transition like, from military to civilian life? Was it hard after so many years of military discipline?

It wasn't easy. The peacetime army was just getting organized then, too, but there's always more discipline and more order in military life. By the time I left, it was pretty well organized. By comparison, the civilian apparatus was a mess. It was a hard transition for me. I'd been accustomed to a kind of rigid discipline, a military discipline, for years by that time. Because I'd been underground—which has its own disciplinary requirements—and then in the army. In civilian life we had to do some heavy duty political work; we had to move around a lot, get things going. I found it strange at first.

What was your experience as a woman in that arena? What were the power relations between men and women in the leadership of the political structures at that time? Were you treated differently in any way because you were a woman?

Not that I can remember. Of course, there may be things I wouldn't have noticed at the time that I might feel differently about today. As we gain in consciousness we see things with new eyes. But I don't remember anything in particular. And then, most of us in that early leadership of the Managua committee were women. In fact, Agustín Lara was the only man; the rest of us were women. And most of the women had been members of the Proletarian tendency. That was another thing: the differences between the tendencies. Our ways of seeing things were sometimes in conflict, and that caused problems.

But what was I doing during this period? Mostly I spent my time in the factories, among the workers—and in the neighborhoods. Talking to people, day after day. There were so many problems to be solved, everywhere you went. There were workers running factories on their own because the owners were Somoza people and they'd left the country. Labor relations were changing so fast you could hardly keep up with them. Workers were beginning to organize en masse: some into neighborhood block committees, others in the unions. I spent most of my time back then out in the streets, in the factories, in the workplaces, in the countryside—talking and talking to people. Four or five years of that.

There were days when I'd be at one factory in the morning, eat lunch with the workers at another, go somewhere else in the afternoon, and end up at a neighborhood meeting that night. It was an extraordinary experience. When you're out among the people you have a good sense of what's going on. And that was a very special time, because everyone was organizing, mobilizing; they were willing to listen to what you had to say, and they'd speak their own minds, too.

I remember they'd invite me to give political talks, to explain our political project. And people would ask thousands of questions. Life is like a sponge. For the first time, people were experiencing a political process in which they could be protagonists. In Nicaragua, neither Somoza nor the Conservatives had ever offered a political project that integrated anyone: they never even dialogued with people; they never explained who they were or what they wanted.

But ours was an integrated project that included everyone who wanted to take part. It made people subjects—instead of objects—of their own history. It was like a huge wave, something new; and people got enthusiastic, excited. It was also a contradictory project. For example, the relationship between bosses and workers was very difficult just then. It was as if the bosses hadn't been able to move beyond July 18th, and the workers gave birth to themselves on July 19th. And there were other contradictions, with state administrators and with technicians. Workers began to understand the production process, learn the statistics, the details of what they were doing. You have to remember: our tradition here was that workers be kept in total ignorance.

So everything was new. And those years were among the richest of my life. The first popular-defense mobilizations also began to take place at that time. The ex-guards, the Contras, began infiltrating our borders in 1982. It got worse through 1983, 1984. And the biggest mobilizations were from Managua, reserve battalions from the capital, mostly workers and young people. I worked with all that mobilization until the 1st of July, 1985, when I was named minister of public health.

That must have been a difficult transition, too. I mean, you were so involved with the work you've just described. Did you ask to be sent to Public Health? Were you surprised by the appointment?

You know, Margaret, I don't even know how to answer that question. My generation of revolutionaries was formed in the tradition of doing whatever had to be done. I wouldn't have stopped to ask myself what *I* wanted to do, not back then. Well, I had a sense that I would have preferred to stay in the army. Military life appealed to me because of how things functioned: the logic, the organization. Things worked more smoothly. Civilian life means you talk a lot more. You're talking and talking all the time. In the military you don't talk that much. You give an order and it's obeyed. Period.

So I guess the answer would be no. I never thought about whether or not I wanted to be minister of public health. I loved what I was doing. But I do know one thing: as much as I loved my job, I was ready to leave it. Why? Because I have this theory that five years is enough in any position. After that, you begin to slip. A change is good for you, and it's good for the organization where you've been working. Whoever takes your place is going to be fresher, more critical, have better ideas—if only because they're different ideas. So I'd been saying I wanted a change. I didn't know where I wanted to go. And it wasn't because I wasn't happy where I was; I loved what I was doing.

My appointment to the Ministry of Public Health gave me the opportunity of learning how things worked in the state apparatus. That was new for me. Because I'd traveled for the FSLN, I'd had experience outside the country, with the solidarity committees. I'd been involved in the military as well as in the political aspects of our work. I'd been in guerrilla operations, urban and rural. And I'd worked at the grass roots, with the people. The one experience I didn't have was with the state. That was the piece I was missing.

So it came at a good time. Of course, it wasn't easy. I'd studied medicine; but medicine is one thing and public health is another. The ministry was enormous. It was a large structure, complicated, with a big budget; and people made huge demands upon it. It was a also very difficult moment, with the war heating up. But I had a great deal of support, people were very supportive. I'd say I had a pretty successful tenure at Public Health.

I remember the speech the new minister, Salmerón, gave when you handed the ministry over to him. I think he may have been the only cabinet minister in the UNO government to publicly praise his predecessor. He was obligated to recognize the excellent job you'd done.

Yes, things were in pretty good shape. It was a complex situation at Public Health. There were always so many fewer resources than we needed. But it was good work.

RAMÓN: For me, Dora María's most important contribution to the Sandinista government was her position as minister of public health. She received the ministry in disorder, and she made a list of priorities. One by one she did what she had to do, until that place was in tip-top shape. They say that when she handed it over everything was computerized; you could predict an epidemic anywhere in the country. In spite of the war, she had a budget of 60 million dollars for medicines alone. The UNO government's not spending a sixth of that.

MARÍA DORA: When she handed over her job to the incoming minister, they tried to get him to say there were problems. But he said, "I'm a Catholic, I believe in God, and I'm not going to lie about anyone. I've received this ministry in perfect order." You know, she even had a car, from Germany I think it was. She handed everything over, even that car.

The one thing I didn't like about my job as minister was that you were stuck in the same slot all day long. I missed the larger political vision. The work I'd been doing before gave me a more complete sense of what was going on in the country. I'd talk to people in the factories, in the countryside, in the area of public health, teachers, people in the neighborhoods.

The ministry absorbed me completely, every hour of every day. But it did give me a perspective I hadn't had before. I saw things from a government point of view: the overall economy, what resources we had at our disposal, how we needed to organize things differently, all those problems, the transformations we were going through at the time. I came to the ministry just when the crisis began to deepen. Nineteen eighty-five marked the beginning of real crisis here. Then came the economic reform of 1988. And I was also a member of the Council of State and the National Assembly during that period. I was minister of public health until 1990. Come to think of it, I haven't held a whole lot of jobs in these twelve years.

Dora María, I'd like to hear your opinion about the period leading up to the 1990 elections, the electoral campaign, how you feel that was handled. How do you see the nature of the campaign itself, and how people responded to it?

Well, it's not easy to talk about how I saw it back then, not easy to make a critical judgment. Because what I thought at the time is one thing; another is the way I may see it now, from this perspective. I might not be the best person to talk about this. It might not even be fair. I will say this, and we were aware of it at the time: we were at a very difficult juncture. Among the Sandinistas, there was a general awareness that it was an extremely difficult moment. And the campaign itself was unusually long. It practically started with the Esquipulas II Accords.[5] That is, from the moment those accords were signed, we were forced onto the campaign trail. The campaign didn't last four months like people say, but more like a year and a half.

So this is the first thing I want to make clear: we're talking about something eternally long, terrible. It wore us all down. We knew we were in a crisis situation. When the campaign as such got off the ground, we'd just completed the economic reforms of 1988—unpopular reforms that restricted government subsidies. We'd had to liquidate almost all aid, we'd devaluated the córdoba, we were trying to control inflation. We'd been forced to let government employees go. We were beginning to see increased unemployment.

We couldn't put an end to the draft because we had no guarantee that the war was going to end. The United States was always very careful not to say they wouldn't keep on attacking Nicaragua, no matter who won the elections. And the U.S. conditioned the results of the elections in Nicaragua. If UNO won, they would stop arming the Contras. If the FSLN won, who could say? That was Bush's line, [James], Baker's line, consistently. And what was Gorbachev's line? "Until we see who wins the elections, we're not giving further military aid to Nicaragua." [Foreign Minister] Shevardnadze said that right here in Managua: "And furthermore, whoever wins, the Soviet Union will continue to help Nicaragua."

5. In August 1987 the presidents of Costa Rica, El Salvador, Guatemala, Honduras, and Nicaragua signed the Esquipulas II Peace Accords, promising reductions in the countries' armed forces, free elections, the formation of national reconciliation commissions, and freedom of the press, among much else. That same August Nicaragua became the first signatory to establish a national reconciliation commission.

But the United States, no. What the United States said was, "If Doña Violeta wins, we'll lift the blockade and demobilize the Contras. And we'll give economic aid to Nicaragua. If the Sandinistas win, who knows? We probably won't." The message couldn't have been clearer. So, it was a critical moment. No one could guarantee that if the Sandinistas won—as we believed we would—the United States would disarm the Contras. We couldn't run the risk of eliminating the draft.

Looking back, I ask myself, "Could we have done away with the draft?" I don't know. I really don't know if we could have done that, if it would have been the right decision. We knew it was one of our biggest problems. We knew that. Maybe we didn't know *how* big a problem it was, big enough to lose us the election. But I'm not even sure we could have won if we'd announced we were doing away with the draft. Why? Because there'd been an erosion of confidence by then. People might have said, "These guys are saying they'll do away with the draft, and then when they win they'll reinstate it." I don't know if I'm being clear. Honestly, some days I think it was exactly what we should have done; other days I think we couldn't have done it, no matter what. It's like we just didn't have a crystal ball.

So ours couldn't be a campaign against the draft. Our campaign was uphill all the way. We couldn't make a lot of demagogic promises about the economic situation getting better—because we weren't the ones controlling the blockade. All we could say was that a Sandinista victory would guarantee peace. But peace with what? Peace with dignity, peace with sovereignty. Like I say, uphill all the way.

UNO definitely had the advantage. They could wage a campaign against the difficult situation we were going through, and a campaign *against* is always a good campaign. To a certain extent, they had the truth on their side: they could tell people, "Hey, we'll do away with the draft law, and things will get better because the gringos will give us money." And that's a terrific campaign. You don't even need a whole lot of publicity. But we needed publicity, and we went overboard with our publicity.

On the one hand, I think we waged an overconfident campaign. And on the other, I don't think we always offered the most appropriate message. But here we have another point of discussion: in an electoral campaign, what is the most appropriate message? I mean, if you ask me what an appropriate electoral campaign message would be in the United States, I can tell you. But what would the most appropriate message for Nicaragua have been? As a political force you're not always going to find that the message that'll win you votes is the one you think you should be offering. When you're honestly trying to change society it's much more complicated.

I know we were overconfident. The messages we designed for this sector or that, they didn't really work. But then again, how could they have worked? You know, the votes the FSLN obtained in the 1990 election were nothing short of extraordinary! And I think it shows that people here had, and have, a considerable level of consciousness. During the campaign I spoke in literally hundreds of places: neighborhoods, factories, municipalities, all over. And what did I tell people? "The FSLN is your only guarantee of real peace. We can't promise that the economic crisis is going to be resolved tomorrow. It's going to take years. We're going to have to work like hell. It's our country, but we're going to have to work hard. If the FSLN wins the elections, we may be assured of better conditions in our search for peace. The draft is necessary because the gringos haven't demobilized the Contras."

That was my messsage wherever I went. It was an honest message, but a hard one. What could we tell people? I wasn't going to go out and repeat our motto: "Everything's Going to Get Better!" Nothing was going to get better. I knew it, and they knew it. All they had to do was watch television. Bush's message was on TV every day, and Gorbachev's and Shevardnadze's. So I don't think it's all that difficult to figure out why people voted as they did.

Like I say, our campaign was uphill all the way. You'll tell me the song about the cock was sexist.[6] Sure it was, sexist in the extreme. But do I think that sexism is what kept housewives from voting for the FSLN? No. I don't even think it kept feminists from voting for us, Margaret. Why? Because the housewives' vote is a conservative vote. Women who have to deal with putting food on the table every day are the first to suffer from an economic crisis. Three times a day, or whenever they have to go to the grocery store, they're confronted with the rising cost of staples. Housewives here went through most of the war on a ration card; and then they had to deal with the middlemen, the speculators, the whole nine yards. So, no, I don't think it was that damned song about the cock that did us in, but rather the everyday situation, what people here had to endure.

And then there was the obligatory military service. Almost every mother was up in arms about that, her sons forced to go to war, and so many of them not coming back. Just the daily struggle to transform society, that was something, too. People worked all day and then went out at night: if it was a working person, to his or her union meeting; if it was a young person, to a youth group meeting. On Sunday it was the militia. Christmas vacation you went to pick coffee. It took a lot of time, a lot of energy. People were exhausted. And I think women resented this a lot. I'd hear women saying, "My husband never comes home any more. Could he be seeing another woman? And whose fault is it that I never see him? The Sandinistas!"

Social transformation is hard enough when you don't have the U.S. breathing down your neck. It's hard work, radical work. You remember how it was: young people going off to pick coffee, going off to teach reading and writing in the countryside. And you remember how the Right was always saying, "Your daughters are going off like that, they're becoming prostitutes . . ." In a society like ours, rooted in conservatism, all that is very difficult. It's total dissension. And who feels it most? The father whose son has become independent much more quickly than he expected; the father and mother who have political

6. The FSLN's electoral campaign used the slogan *El Gallo Ennavajado* (The Cock with His Fighting Blade) to describe its presidential candidate, Daniel Ortega. It is an extremely sexist symbol, strongly objected to by feminists and indicative of propaganda that was shallow at best.

differences with their children, differences they never had before, who feel their family is being torn apart. And, you know, we never managed to do adequate ideological work, with the women especially. We just didn't.

Why was that, Dora María? Why do you think there was such a lack of ideological work?

In the first place, because of that damned philosophy, typical of the Latin American Left, which we were guilty of as well: you're guerrillas, you won the war, and people will follow you no matter what. In the second place, from 1982 on we were forced to confront the gringos. I'm not even putting these reasons in any order of importance. Maybe it was the other way round—or both things were true. AMNLAE, which was the organization that should have dealt with raising women's consciousness, put all its energies into defense, full-time: defense and production. We didn't have time for more. When you look at it, ten years aren't that many if we're talking about radically changing society. It's no time at all, and under extremely adverse conditions.

This is where we ask ourselves if a women's organization should be autonomous or not. The war was certainly an important factor, and the economic crisis. But many of us now feel that if AMNLAE had been more independent, it would have been able to deal more effectively with raising women's consciousness. I know it's complex . . .

It's very complex. Because, you know, during the past few years we realized there were things we were doing wrong. We analyzed them, we discussed them, we made some decisions about the Front's policies with the mass organizations, including AMNLAE. In 1988 we issued a proclamation specifically addressing women's problems, women's rights. But the truth is, most of us were 90 percent, 100 percent occupied with trying to deal with the war. And with the economic crisis. The priorities took our energy, our time, our efforts; they absorbed us almost completely. All the rest was secondary. When a society is simply trying to survive, even violence against women has to be considered secondary.

So what I'm saying is, it's easy to go back now and say this was done wrong or we made that mistake. Sure we did! The song about the cock was sexist; of course it was! But is that what lost us the female vote? I don't think so. We had profound structural problems here, much more serious than that song. People say that Doña Violeta waged the campaign of the Virgin Mary. She did. But I really don't think people voted for the Virgin Mary here . . .

They voted for the mother figure . . .

They voted for a woman who was apolitical, a woman with prestige, who used simple language. All that was very attractive to people in general. Violeta's message was a simple one: "I'm going to do away with the draft, because our sons can't go on dying like this. And I'm going to make things better economically, because all the countries of the world will help." That was it— no more, no less. UNO didn't need to organize all that much, they didn't need great publicity; all the conditions were there. People wanted to hear two things and two things only: that the war would end, and with it the draft; and that the economic blockade would be lifted.

Dora María, were you as surprised as everyone else when the FSLN lost?

Of course. We understood what was happening pretty early on the evening of the 25th. I got to the FSLN's headquarters by 7:00 that night, and the first telegrams from the Supreme Electoral Council were already beginning to come in. I remember the first three telegrams were from Region Five. Things were looking good for us, but something told me it wasn't good enough.

I was detailed to Managua's electoral command post, so I went on over there. We were monitoring 10 percent of the results, and we began to hear from the first polling places. The trend was pretty consistent: it began to look like we were losing. At 8:00 I was still telling people, "We have to wait and see what happens." But by 9:00 we had sixty ballot boxes counted and the rest were all backed up. We were having trouble with the communication system, but by that time we could pretty well see how it was coming down. It was more-or-less consistent throughout the country. We'd lost Managua, and we knew Managua was crucial. But maybe the provinces would save us. We called the provinces. It was the same all over the country. Then we knew we had lost the elections. And we called the national directorate and told them what had happened. Period.

We never hesitated about what we had to do. Our generation is prepared for blows like this. Every one of us has been forged in struggle, prepared to face the worst. What was the electoral command's reaction when we knew we'd lost? First we were concerned; then we were anguished; and then we just gathered up our strength, put our best face forward. By 9:00 that night we were asking, "Okay, now what do we do?" We called the directorate. We knew we'd lost, there was nothing to be done. It was a very difficult moment for every Sandinista. We talked to members of the directorate, and the first thing they told us was to split up so we could cover the city of Managua. Not a tear on anyone's face. Everyone imperturbable. Concerned, yes. Sad, yes. But imperturbable.

I got to Tipitapa around 2:00 in the morning, to talk to our comrades there. We had to tell people, "Okay, we lost the elections, we lost them in these particular circumstances, there's nothing to be done. No use waiting for the results of one more province, of one more region. We've lost, and that's that. Now let's all stand behind our party." The impact was enormous on everyone. There were thousands of questions. No one could have answered all the questions people had. "At 6:00 in the morning the new president is going to address the nation on the radio. We have to listen to what she has to say. Keep your radios tuned in, and be ready for what we'll be communicating as well. Keep busy, stay united. Talk to the other comrades." That's what we told people.

From Tipitapa I went home to shower and change. I called my parents because I knew they'd be worried. And I was worried about their reaction to our loss. I wanted to give them some encouragement. Later the next day I went by to see them, to try to put their minds at ease. But first, that morning, I went off to the press conference at the Olof Palme [Convention Center].

RAMÓN: I was surprised when Dora María called us at 5:00 that morning to say we'd lost the elections. Her voice was low, shattered. "Papá," she said, "we lost." And then she hung up. I have a bad heart. And she must have known I'd been up all night, waiting for news . . .

But, you know, sometimes I ask myself what would have happened if we'd won. It might have been worse. Because the duplicitous have fallen away, and the real Sandinistas have stood firm. I don't really think there's been that much desertion . . .

You never know how you'll be able to take the hardest blows. I think this is the worst blow we Sandinistas have ever had to endure. It was terrible. And, you know, it messes with your mind. Because in spite of the situation, I never thought we would lose the elections. I always had faith that somewhere, somehow, the people would vote on the side of justice.

You were elected to the Assembly . . .

Yes, those Sandinistas who were elected to senatorial seats immediately became members of Congress. And then there was that whole transition process. It was unbearably long. The elections were in February, and the new president didn't take office until April: too long a transition, for my taste in any case.

Tell me what the transition was like for you . . .

Handing over the ministry was the easy part. If you've got things in order, that's not a problem. And the people who worked with me were very supportive; they helped a lot. It was the political transition that was the most difficult. It's that same formation I mentioned before: the ability to do what has to be done and not let yourself feel it until later. We didn't get upset first and then do what had to be done; we did what had to be done and then allowed ourselves to feel what we were going through.

The emotional transition took place on April 25th. That was when it really got tough, emotionally speaking. For various reasons. In the first place, on April 25th we all woke up at home. All my adult life, practically since I'd gone underground, I'd always gotten up in the morning to face a tremendous amount of work. I'd get up at 5:30, maybe 6:00. And there were always a million things to do. Later, during the Sandinista administration, I was invariably at my office by 7:00. Or wherever I had to be that day, whether it was in the Party structure or at the Ministry of Public Health. And I wouldn't get home until 10:00, 11:00 at night. Dinner at 10:30, 11:00 was the usual for me. And I never knew what it might have been like to be able to get home for lunch.

So on April 26th, which was a workday, I got up. I showered, I dressed, and then I sat in a chair. I read the morning paper. And that's when the other part of it hit me. Here there were all these problems, but I no longer had the power to do anything about them. What resources there were, were in someone else's hands now. Even finding out what's going on by reading it in the paper: that wasn't something I was used to. So that was what it was like for me, a total and absolute change.

And I'm giving you a picture of what it was like for someone like myself: one of the lucky ones. Because I was still a senator. And that meant I had a job, a salary; at least my personal anguish wasn't economic. The Assembly would be going into session in a month. But then, maybe I'd have preferred economic anguish.

I found myself at home, someone who had never experienced that. I'd never been at home at 11:00 in the morning! I'd write a little, organize papers, look at my house, take stock—perhaps for the first time in my life—that I even had a house! Around 5:00 in the afternoon maybe I'd cross the street and drop in on my mother. The kind of life I'd never had. Besides, my address book, my telephone book: they weren't good anymore. We were used to calling each other at work. Now we had to begin to call our comrades at their homes. I'm talking about the biggest changes down to the smallest.

Did people's personal relationships suffer from such drastic change?

Of course they did. Most people were left without a job, the vast majority of Sandinistas at any rate. And no one offered us work. The new government began firing Sandinistas right away, and the private sector wasn't interested in hiring us. Literally thousands of comrades flooded the streets, trying to figure out how to survive. Maybe you could buy and sell rice, beans. Maybe you could sell fruit. Whatever you could think of.

Carlos Fernando gave me an office at *Barricada*.[7] So after a few days I'd leave my house in the morning and go over to my office, with my computer. It wasn't all that much different; I still didn't have enough to do. But I felt a lot better, because I was in an atmosphere where I could talk to the journalists, discuss what was going on, write a little. At first the subject of conversation was invariably survival; you'd hear ten, fifteen, twenty comrades a day talking about not having enough to make ends meet—"What can I do . . . ? Where can I find work?" And then, of course, we were trying to reorganize the Party.

Those first couple of months were complicated, very complicated. The last

7. Carlos Fernando Chamorro was editor-in-chief of *Barricada*.

time I could remember living for myself, so to speak, free from Party responsibilities or government responsibilities, was back in 1975; and, who knows, maybe it was 1974. Now all of a sudden we were on our own, people who were accustomed to our party telling us, "You do this . . . You go there . . ." We didn't know how to think about what we might want, as individuals. That whole internal process was very difficult.

I'm very interested in the process in which you began to realize it was possible to make certain choices. . .

Yes, make choices. And have your own life.

Can you talk about how this has been for you?

Like I say, it's been very complicated. For others, for people who haven't lived the kind of life we've lived, I imagine it's just the opposite: what's been normal for us must seem difficult, maybe even impossible for them. But for us it was the other way round. For example, I'm used to going and finding out what needs to be done, what I can do. So now I find myself doing what I think needs to be done, even when it's not necessarily what I want to be doing. And I tend not to do the things I'd enjoy but don't feel politically obligated to do. To a certain degree, I continue to function according to that logic.

But, of course, you become adapted, little by little. We're all becoming more integrated, I think. I see my parents much more than I used to. I go to the movies, just to give you an example. And that's great. I find I have time to read, to think, to go to an art exhibition, to talk to a friend for the sheer pleasure of the conversation. We were all under constant pressure here; and it was a philosophical pressure, something terrible. For those of us who were in government, it was a pressure that never let up.

Because it's not the same if you come to a government position with the mentality of the guy who's going to administer something he's not really committed to. We were truly committed to changing things here. If we knew someone needed medicine and didn't have any, we felt responsible to that person. If we knew someone was hungry, we felt responsible—if someone slipped and fell, if the traffic was all snarled up, whatever it happened to be. We approached everything that way.

And that's an excellent mindset when you really want to get things done, when you're committed to change. I'm convinced of it. But that's not the way most government officials function. You take a minister in today's government, or in other governments: if someone talks about being hungry, they're going to tell you that he or she should work harder! Sure, when things reach a crisis point, when things get really dramatic, then maybe they'll consider it a social or political problem. But if José doesn't have the wheelchair he needs, who really cares?

We cared. That's the problem. We cared about absolutely everything: where someone was going to be buried, the coffin, even the hole in the ground! The newborn baby, the baby who didn't get born—everything! When you're suddenly free of that degree of responsibility, it's totally disconcerting. And the thing is, you're never really free of it. It doesn't go away.

They took it from you . . .

They removed the weight of our believing we could deal with things because we were in power. But they'll never be able to remove the weight of what happened here. The thing is, we have to adjust to the situation we have now. We have to get used to being an opposition party or a revolutionary movement not in power, get used to doing what we can from the position we're in now. And people have to get used to our being unable to do what we could do before. People still come up to us and say, "Comandante, I've got a little piece of land . . ." This happened to me only yesterday. It was a woman in Boaco. She said, "Comandante, I've got this little piece of land, but I haven't been able to build my house. I need some building materials." It's been two years since we lost! And I had to explain, "Look, comrade, we're no longer in power. We just don't have the resources."

Sometimes, you know, you feel worse than before. It's as if you were a batting coach who used to be a player. You've got two men on base, and the other team's winning three to nothing. If the guy at bat hits a home run, it'll be a tie; and if he doesn't, it won't be. You were a batter once, and now you're a batting coach. You know this pitcher, you know how he's going to throw the ball, and you wish it were you up there at bat. You feel like if it were you, you'd have a good chance of hitting that ball.

If the Sandinista National Liberation Front were in office right now, we'd still have to face the economic crisis. But we'd have greater social support than this government has. We might even be forced to take some of the same measures this government's being forced to take. But we wouldn't be talking about making poor people pay five pesos to go to grade school; we wouldn't be doing that. The ordinary Nicaraguan feels abandoned now. It's not about great social programs or anything like that. It's about survival, with a certain amount of dignity. It's impossible to remove ourselves completely from what's going on.

Dora María, I wonder if you could talk about the FSLN's First Party Congress? Was it mostly concerned with reorganizing the Party, or was there also some analysis of the political moment?

That Congress was complicated, traumatic really, because we had to deal with a number of issues. There was the crisis of the electoral defeat, which also meant the crisis of the Party's political activism, made all too clear through the defeat itself. Then there were the different—sometimes contradictory—perceptions people had about the historical moment and what we should be doing. Along with these major issues, there was the whole process of democratization and electing leadership at the different levels.

All in all, I consider the Congress to have been a positive experience, positive because we weren't prepared for what happened. We had to figure things out as we went along. We weren't prepared for an open political debate, yet we managed to have an open debate—with all the problems, with all the prejudices. But it was a strong debate, a good first step. The whole democratization process, that was also difficult for the organization. Because there were those who wanted to go faster, those who wanted to go more slowly, and those who didn't want to move at all.

In the midst of all these differences, there was the problem of maintaining unity. If the FSLN had split, it wouldn't only have meant the death of Sandinism in this country; it would have been a disaster for everyone. Why? Because somehow or other Sandinism is this country's backbone, it's spinal cord; and our equilibrium, our sense of national stability runs through that spinal cord. I say this because the FSLN is the only political party we have that really has a social base, a social base with confidence in its party. There's no other organization here that can say that, and I'd wager it doesn't exist in many other countries either.

At the Congress, I think we managed to do right by the moment. Those of us who would like to have moved faster had to slow down some; those who wanted to move more slowly had to pick up their pace. We had to compromise, for the sake of unity, in order to preserve the Party's strength. And we're all still moving. The process wasn't conclusive, in that democratization must go deeper and we have to continue the political debate. We were able to resolve some things at the Congress; others could not be resolved there. People probably had more expectations of the Congress than the Congress was able to fulfill.

What was it like for you, Dora María, when you weren't elected to the national directorate?

By the time the Congress was held, I already knew I wasn't going to be on the national directorate. Because the Sandinista Assembly took place before the Congress, and my candidacy was something we'd presented to the Assembly to see if we could convince the delegates of its viability. Some were in favor, other's weren't. The Congress simply rubber-stamped what had been decided in the Assembly.

This brings us back to what I was talking about before: what was possible at that particular moment in time? What was possible was what we did, which turned out to be withdrawing my candidacy. I hadn't launched a campaign among the rank and file. My candidacy was discussed at the level of the Assembly; and when the Assembly voted that I shouldn't be a candidate, I accepted that. I didn't campaign at the Congress.

I know it was a disappointment to a great many comrades that you weren't elected to the directorate, that the traditional configuration prevailed . . .

It was a disappointment to me as well. I campaigned before the Assembly; but once that decision was made, I didn't campaign any longer. Clearly, this was a problem for me. But I think we have to consider what was possible. I believe I did what I had to do, and that was to withdraw my name. At that particular moment, in the Sandinista Assembly, that was what I had to do. The next day I might have been able to do something different; fifteen days later, there might have been another option. There might even have been other options at the Congress itself. But at the precise moment at which I withdrew, I'm convinced it was the only thing to do.

It was the only decision that wouldn't have had serious political risks. Up to a certain point we could agree, beyond that point we couldn't. This was as far as we were able to walk together. Absolutely. In a situation like this, if you pull too hard, something's going to break. You have to agree to disagree. It may mean you're not going to move as fast; I know that. But the problem is, can we think about moving faster if not everyone can come along? I don't think so. There comes a time when it's better for everyone to be moving at a pace that everyone can share. Because the alternative is that some are going to keep moving and others are going to be left behind, or that some are going to go in one direction and others in another.

What was my defeat about? All sorts of things: human considerations, subjective factors, political factors, the unity issue and, yes, personal issues too. When you're dealing with changing a leadership that's been around as long as ours has, with the personal histories of each of the individuals involved, when you're dealing with a directorate that still enjoys an enormous amount of prestige, it can be very complex. We're not talking about changing the directorate of the U.S. Democratic Party. Most people wouldn't even know who belongs to that; there wouldn't be much drama involved in making changes there. The national directorate of the FSLN goes beyond the leadership of a single party; it's played an important part in the life of the country as a whole.

Do you feel that all the members of the national directorate continue to enjoy the same level of prestige, what with the piñata and everything that's happened?

It's not a cut-and-dried matter, of course. But I believe the national directorate, as a body, retains the level of authority it's always had, at least among Sandinistas. If we're talking about members of the directorate individually, of course, there are differences of opinion. People feel differently about one or another. But if you see a document signed by the national directorate of the FSLN, you're going to take it very seriously. Each man alone is judged by his personality, his virtues and defects, his political capabilities, his public presence, his history, the job he was assigned, the role he had to play, everything. As a collective, though, the national directorate continues to carry enormous weight. And it should.

Dora María's parents have their own sorrow about their daughter not being elected to the directorate. María Dora talked about the sexist attitudes on the part of the Party leadership, but Ramón believes her honesty was what stood most squarely in her way. When we talked, he impulsively left the room and returned with a small postcard in his hand. One side was blank; the other contained a typed message and his signature. "I wrote this," he said, "but I never gave it to her. Maybe I didn't want her to know that I knew she was hurting." I asked Ramón if I could publish his message to his daughter. "Sure," he said. "I'll probably give it to her anyway one of these days. The card reads:

My little girl: When your spirit is sad or you feel hopeless, know there are many thousands of Sandinistas who look at you and see the face of the FSLN, turned to the future. You are a flag of hope for all of them. Be strong! Don't forsake them! Don't let them down! Keep on fighting like you always have: simple, tenacious, sweet and whole. My head and heart both tell me all will come in due time, although I may not be here to see it. Your father, Ramón.

Dora María, I want to ask you to talk about Sandinista women, those women—like yourself—who have held important political positions during the past administration. What's going on with you in the context of the revitalized women's movement we see here?

There's been a revitalization of the Sandinista women's movement. And it's gone beyond the question of organizational dispersion. Here the fact that there are a number of different revolutionary women's organizations, rather than only one, hasn't weakened the women's movement. On the contrary, in certain ways it's made it stronger. We really have an interesting situation in this respect. The organizational dispersion doesn't worry me, not in the women's movement. If it were the union movement, I'd be upset. Ditto for the farm workers. But in the women's movement, no.

Women are diverse to begin with. Unionism's problems are invariably linked to the problems of production, the economy, employment, salaries, workers' rights. But women conform to a broad spectrum. There are women whose area of struggle is mass media. Others come together around issues of education. There is the movement of women health workers, women fighting for their legal rights, others who are more interested in social issues or in the economy. It's a broad spectrum. And some women are much more politicized than others. Consequently we have some sectors of the women's movement with a sophisticated political consciousness, while others struggle with very basic issues.

I may be talking garbage now, but I'm not really worried about the fact that working within AMNLAE there are revolutionary women and others who feel they need to separate themselves from the organization and develop their struggles in other ways. I think there's an important consensus among all these women. There's consensus in the struggle against battery, against rape, for judicial reform, for women's right to health care, and a great deal more. There's consensus when we talk about violence against women. Women in the different professional and mass organizations share the consensus that they need to have greater participation in the political structures.

This is all very important. When it comes to these areas of struggle, there's no great distance between one group and another. The differences are more on a philosophical order. For example, one group may be against violence against women from the perspective of women controlling their own bodies: we're not second-class citizens, we're not going to allow ourselves to be used like that any longer, and so forth and so on. Another group may simply feel that violence against women violates a basic human right.

This was very clear in the protests against the passage of Article 204. Some of the more traditionalist political figures, who have frequently engaged in gay-baiting, still came out against the antisodomy law. I don't think they've changed their minds about homosexuality, but they've been able to join the more feminist groups in protesting the discrimination . . .

Exactly. That's why I say I'm not worried about the philosophical differences that exist, at least not in the women's movement. Those with a greater feminist consciousness and those with very little feminist consciousness are able to come together in political action. That's the important thing.

Why do you think the women's movement has grown and become so active at this particular time?

On the one hand, feminist movements everywhere are gaining in strength. In Nicaragua, the fact that there's been a depolarization, politically speaking, has also opened up a space for this sort of struggle. And I think there's something else, which may be the most interesting reason of all: this government and the political Right in general have pushed a very conservative line on women.

For example, when she was still running for office the president told a gathering in Chontales that women should stay at home. She said she was happy because she bears the "Chamorro brand," as if she were a head of cattle! That was the most offensive thing she could have said, Margaret, terribly offensive—and terribly conservative.

But internationally this goes against the grain. We've had our U.N. "Decade of the Woman." Every official proclamation, by every international organization, includes a feminist discourse now. In all its documents, UNESCO fights for nonsexist education. This organization, that organization: they're all riding the same train. Conservative as a government or political force may be, after they've come down on the Sandinistas for, as they put it, "perverting and subverting our women," they find out that our vision of women's role is more in line with the international consensus than theirs is. There have been tremendous advances in women's rights internationally, at least on paper.

So what do they do? Doña Violeta recently spoke out against battery and suggested Criminal Code reform. In a recent seminar on battery, you had Sandinistas, representatives of UNO, the minister of public health, women from

AMNLAE and from the Institute on Women (which is a government agency) all sitting down together. It's impossible for this government to continue to put out a conservative message on women. Of course, sometimes they slip up and do so anyway, but then they have to face the rest of the world. You can be sure that Amnesty International has its eyes on Article 204.

What do you think will happen with Article 204?

I don't know. Because even if Doña Violeta doesn't sign it, it will become law. The National Assembly passes it automatically; that's the way it works here. I haven't seen the latest *Gaceta*, so I don't know what's happened.[8] The conservatives have treated the whole thing with kid gloves.

Paradoxically, the feminist movement can take advantage of this moment. This is a good time for feminism here. Just like it's a good time for the Greens, the ecology people. For some movements it's a good time; for others, it's not so good.

I'm not concerned about the lack of unity in the feminist movement, because with all its differences it's essentially Sandinist in nature; its dynamic is Sandinist. And this is important. It doesn't matter that there are different philosophical tendencies if there's coordinated political action. This is an underdeveloped country; there are women who are more and less advanced. And women's issues can be very complex.

Take abortion. Within the Sandinist movement, there are those who are against abortion as a matter of principle. And there are others for whom the freedom to choose abortion is a matter of principle—inside the same movement. It's a difficult question, and we've discussed it again and again and again. It doesn't surprise me that there are some women who are philosophically more advanced than others.

What would bother me is if the feminist movement itself wasn't Sandinist. That would bother me. But that's not the case. All these women are Sandinistas, each with her own version of what feminism is, each with her own emphasis. It's the ground swell that's so important. It seems to me that AMNLAE has a role to play. The 52 Percent Majority has a role to play. There's room enough for everyone. The UNAG [National Union of Farmers and Cattle Growers] Women's Secretariat has a role to play. The women's secretariats in the various unions have their roles. It all adds up, and it's all positive.

One interesting thing is that right now the feminist movement is having more impact on the political ideology of the FSLN than it ever has. Before, during the Sandinista administration, the FSLN's line on women weighed heavily upon the Party's women's organization. Now it's the other way round. This is important.

Why do you think this is?

8. *La Gaceta* is the Nicaraguan congressional record.

Because the feminist movement is strong and very assertive. But we've also gotten freer in certain respects. We Sandinista women have more space for our feminism because there's no priority pushing it down. Defense is no longer a priority that relegates all else to second place. We no longer feel there's a contradiction between feminism and our political work. They're not mutually exclusive.

At the Congress this was very clear. The national directorate, Daniel [Ortega] in particular, was forced to respond to the specific question women asked. And the question was, "Shouldn't there be women at the highest leadership levels of the FSLN?" At the closing session, the national directorate itself was forced to respond to this question. So now we have committed ourselves to there being women at the highest levels of leadership by the time the next Congress comes along.

This couldn't have happened before. At the very most we might have heard something like, "We need more female cadre" . . . whatever. Now we women are demanding our place at the top. And the feminist movement has made its mark everywhere: in the trade unions, in all the other sectors. They're careful to elect women to top positions. Before, if a woman was elected, fine. If not, that was okay, too. But the feminist dynamic has influenced everyone now. The feminist movement is much more versatile than it was. And there can be no doubt that autonomy has helped; it's helped a great deal.

Dora María, is there anything else you'd like to say?

I'd like to say that I think Nicaragua is a surprising country. That's the way I see it, and I've lived here all my life. It's surprising because things aren't always what they seem. I'm not being chauvinist, or saying that we Nicaraguans are better than anyone else. Not at all. What I *am* saying is that the logic by which we function here isn't always easy to understand. Even we don't understand it at times. Take the feminist movement: why is it so strong right now, when everything else is in the doldrums? It might seem like a contradiction, but it's the kind of thing we've come to expect here.

The thing is, for the past thirteen years Nicaragua has attempted to make itself viable, to function as a nation. The cost has been enormous, and the conspiracy against our being able to achieve this viability has been all but overwhelming. And, you know, we're seeking a viability that doesn't exist anywhere in Latin America, a continent where nothing is really viable. Think about it for a moment: none of the political systems in Latin America works any longer. Why? Because neoliberalism has done them in.

Take Venezuela: neoliberalism has dealt the Venezuelan political project a severe blow. The same is true in Peru. And in Guatemala . . . Neoliberalism has hit at the whole complex web of Latin American political projects; our institutions, our parties, they've all suffered. The neoliberal project is like a steamroller: it's flattened everything in its path. And it's deepened the already profound contradictions within our Latin American reality.

If you need a dictatorship in order to impose the neoliberal program, well, what does that tell you? You're imposing a model in total contradiction with the current international discourse. You're forced to do away with political democracy, with the slightest hint of democracy, if you're going to impose the neoliberal program. What they're really saying is that economic salvation is possible only if you do away with democratic political institutions. So you have one government after another going into crisis—as well as all the political parties, every possible alternative.

This makes for a tremendous contradiction. Even the odd man out, the guy who wasn't a politician to begin with—like [Fernando] Collor de Mello in Brazil, or [Alberto] Fujimori in Peru—even those guys who didn't come out of the traditional political mold, end up like everyone else. Fujimori was forced to engineer a coup against himself, and Collor de Mello has a really complicated crisis on his hands.[9] Because in all these places, for a country to be able to resolve its economic problem it must impose some sort of control. And there's no social support. Who among them cares about social support, anyway? Everyone's life just gets worse and worse. People are angry, and why shouldn't they be: without work, living as they are in utter misery? It's a vicious circle, because when people are that angry there's crisis.

In Latin America each and every political alternative—of the traditional kind—has shown itself to be unworkable. Then the Collor de Mellos and the Fujimoris come along, the so-called independents, and they say they're not neoliberals, that neoliberalism is a barbarity, that all politicians are corrupt, that the old parties no longer work. And then they end up with their own neoliberal projects, accused of corruption and in crisis. What's left? Nothing.

What's left in Peru? APRA [the American Revolutionary Popular Alliance] isn't viable any longer. [Mario] Vargas Llosa doesn't have the answer. Fujimori either. So what's left? The Shining Path, total violence? Neoliberalism is supposed to revamp the economy in these countries so that the masses of people will have a better life. But since the cure kills the patient, the patient resists. What did we expect? Medicine's not going to do any good if the patient has no food, if the patient has nothing to eat.

All over Latin America you have political parties doing the opposite of what they say they're going to do. So no one believes in the parties anymore. All the judicial systems are corrupt. The parliaments don't work. The presidential plans don't work. No one can control the cabinets. None of the programs is viable. What we're left with is one gigantic crisis. Neoliberalism needs stability but creates instability. It needs political democracy but puts an end to democracy. And if someone comes along with a plan to alter the neoliberal program in some way, to make it more workable, well, then the World Bank and the International Monetary Fund won't give them the money they need, and you're right back where you started.

You had a real possibility for change in Haiti, so they overthrew [Fr. Jean-

9. Shortly after my interview with Dora María, in fact, Collor de Mello was forced out of office in Brazil.

Bertrand] Aristide. What else is new? Every time there's an honest attempt at solving the essential problems, you know they're going to bring you down. Nothing works, and nothing is allowed to work. No one has any answers. Nothing is viable.

Nicaragua is a country with the nerve to have attempted viability. For thirteen years, we tried to create a new system, to make it work in our own way, in line with our own history, our own possibilities. Our ideas might not have been good anywhere else; I don't know. In any case, we're not interested in selling formulas. We just wanted to make things work here. We tried to devise a revolutionary project that was right for us, and we effected real change.

The Nicaraguan people have more power, as a people, than all the rest of Latin America put together. The government here is forced to make concessions, to discuss, to negotiate. The political forces are held accountable. And even with the electoral loss, we can see the rise in people's consciousness. People's political movements are superdeveloped in Nicaragua. And the old model of the puffed-up demagogic political party is in total disarray; all we have to do is look at the parties that make up UNO.

Even with UNO in office, the model of a government totally dependent upon the United States is in crisis right now. Every time this government has to make a decision on its own, the United States suspends aid—and this is a government that's friends with the United States! We're not talking about the Sandinistas, a leftist government. We're talking about a bourgeois government, a government that's center-right, that wants a free-market economy, a neoliberal program, that's doing everything it's told to do! Whenever it tries for the slightest degree of independence, it gets its wrists slapped. The U.S. demands nothing less than absolute submission.

Still, there have been some fundamental changes over the past decade. In Nicaragua we no longer have an army capable of staging a coup. This is the only army in all of Latin America incapable of a military takeover. The only one. Unheard of on this continent! That's why I say this is a surprising place. You never know, we may become viable yet. Every other country on the continent is moving full steam ahead toward chaos. But things aren't quite that clear here.

The other thing is the United States itself. I don't know, but I think the United States is going to have to change, too. For a long long time the U.S. has policed the world, but recently there's been some serious resistance to that. Europe no longer wants the United States as a police force on its territory. The U.S. model in Latin America has worn itself out. Completely. So things are going to have to change. If the World Bank and the International Monetary Fund keep insisting that every country follow their recipe for change, independent of the conditions that exist, independent of what's going on in each of those countries, something's going to have to give.

Sooner or later these international institutions are going to have to realize that every twenty years or so they've tried to sell a different economic model to Latin America, and that none of them has worked. Thirty years ago "import substitution" was in vogue. We in Central America can tell you about that. And who was behind the import substitution model? The same people who are pushing neoliberalism today, and telling us that import substitution won't work. Who tried to impose protectionism? They did. Who imposed the "noncompetitive integration" model? They did.

Guatemala was supposed to produce toothpaste, and Nicaragua soap. The Guatemalan toothpaste factory was supposed to sell to all the other Central American countries, and Nicaragua was supposed to sell its soap. This was the model imposed by the international lending organizations thirty years ago, and now they tell us it's our fault it didn't work: that we were being protectionist, that we weren't competitive; free market this, free market that. Now it's a different song entirely.

I ask myself, "Thirty years from now what are they going to be saying? Are they going to be telling us that neoliberalism was a disaster, that it couldn't have worked, that the free-market philosophy destroyed our economies, that diversification of technology was impossible without great amounts of financing from the outside, and that great amounts of financing didn't exist?" That's what they're going to tell us thirty years from now. Meanwhile, Latin America moves further and further into the past.

But there's a point beyond which none of this can continue. And that point is the people. When the people say "Enough!" that's it. I don't remember who told me the other day . . ."The neoliberal program needs a little patience from people. It needs people to give it a chance, so the curtain can go up and the performance begin." I say, we've been waiting for five hundred years. How much longer can we wait? If you tell someone who's been waiting for five hundred years to wait just a little longer, that things really are going to get better, I wouldn't count on their believing you. And they'd be right not to believe you. It would be nothing less than absurd to think that one more of their inventions is going to make anything better.

"Coming Out as a Lesbian Is What Brought Me to Social Consciousness"

Rita Arauz

It turned out to be harder to pin down an interview with Rita Arauz than with any of the other Nicaraguan women whose stories I taped. I had looked for Rita the previous October, when I met with a group of lesbians active in the local movement. But in spite of having sent word to her via several intermediaries, she didn't show up on the designated evening. Neither was I able to reach her by phone back then. Later I would learn that she never received my messages, and that didn't seem to surprise her.

Now I was back in Managua. And I felt it more important than ever to locate this woman who had been so central to the founding of the gay and lesbian movement here. Milú Vargas is a close friend of Rita's; she provided me with her telephone numbers and agreed my book wouldn't be complete without talking to her. But although this time Rita turned out to be perfectly accessible by phone, as the days went by it became clear that she herself felt ambivalent about participating.

"I don't know what importance my story can have" was how she put it—in one way or another—each time we spoke. I'd explain the intention and scope

of my project, she'd seem half-convinced, and we'd set a time and place. When I appeared at the initial appointment, however, someone at the AIDS founda-tion she runs told me she'd phoned in sick that morning. "Call her, though," the woman added. "I know she'd like to meet you."

I, too, wanted to meet Rita. But I also wanted to interview her. Our on-again–off-again sparring contest continued up to a couple of days before I was to leave Managua. Just when I thought our conversation might not take place, something seemed to shift. Rita agreed, again, to be interviewed. I returned to the modest house-turned-office situated behind the Jesuit university just as she drove up in her weathered pickup. She was all smiles and nervous energy as she jumped from the cab, greeted me warmly, and ushered me back to her office.

We were the only ones in the building during the several hours the interview lasted. Bulletin boards dominated the entry, explaining the most common sexu-ally transmitted diseases as well as the basic tenets of AIDS education and prevention. Doors with little signs that warned KNOCK BEFORE ENTERING or PLEASE DO NOT SMOKE led from this entrance area to meeting rooms where workshops are held. Half-open boxes contained T-shirts on sale to benefit the foundation's multipronged work; like the large sign in front of the house, they bore catchy images of dancing condoms urging us to become informed and to practice safe sex. Everything signaled a ferocious activity carried out by a staff that is almost exclusively volunteer.

Later that night, continuing our conversation at Rita's home, I saw more boxes, mountains of them, stacked in one corner of the living room. "Books?" I asked, imagining the contents of most such stacks. "No," she laughed, "latex gloves. We'll distribute them all over the country . . ."

Rita Arauz is a small woman, with delicate features and closely cropped dark-brown hair. Her scrubbed complexion bears faint signs of teenage acne dealt with long ago. She's one of those people who says she almost always feels cold and, even in Managua's tropical July heat, wore a sweater over her Levi's and white shirt. Her manner is animated, her gestures forceful and quick. In spite of the difficulty I'd encountered confirming this interview, I immediately felt at ease with Rita, and I knew the story she was about to tell would fill in some serious gaps that still existed in my vision of Nicaragua's feminist movement.

Some books, a few posters, coffee mugs still containing the dregs from long nights of recent work, a fax machine that occasionally whirred and beeped as we talked, a bright bumper sticker that said STOP SIDA (SIDA is the Spanish acronym for AIDS): these were the visual elements that caught my eye as I set up my tape recorder and reassured Rita that her story is important. By this time I understood that she, like many leaders in incipient political movements, had once too often been the victim of movement jealousies, the target of antag-onisms. Perhaps she was tired of being a spokesperson; maybe she needed a break from the spotlight. But she was also the one most able to tell the whole story. She and I both knew that.

"Don't worry," she smiled, "you've convinced me. You've won. Where do we start?" As is my habit, I asked her to start at the beginning:

I was born in Matagalpa, into a petit-bourgeois family. And that's where I was raised and went to school. Later they sent me to Managua, to study at La Asunción; yes, here you have another graduate of La Asunción! It was while I was at that school, such an important part of the history of so many women of my generation, that my father was suddenly ordered to San Francisco. The family moved with him.

My father was in Somoza's diplomatic corps, and he was assigned to a post at the Nicaraguan consulate in San Francisco. It's interesting: most of the students at La Asunción would have given anything to have been able to go to the United States back then. I'm talking about 1967, 1968. But for some reason, in spite of the fact that I studied at that school for bourgeois girls, I wasn't that eager. I wanted anything but to move to the States. I'd never liked the English language. I'd never wanted to live north of the border. I tried to get my family to let me stay in Nicaragua, but they wouldn't. The move marked a pretty violent rupture in my life.

I'm the oldest daughter of five siblings. We all moved to San Francisco. I finished high school there and went on to college. Eventually my family returned to Nicaragua, but by that time I had been married, divorced, and had a little girl; I ended up as a single mother. When my husband and I separated, I started university at San Francisco City College. I was married for only two years. My divorce started a whole new process in my life: I began to acquire a consciousness of my socialization, and of my sexual identity. In retrospect, I can say that coming out as a lesbian was what brought me to social consciousness.

That's interesting, because for many women it's just the opposite. Although, of course, in the United States at that time, in the late sixties and early seventies, it wasn't that unusual . . .

I was a young woman from a social class that had a great deal of power, with a stable home environment, a family that was very religious and that enjoyed quite a bit of social status. I was also the oldest, "Daddy's little girl." You might say I had it made. But, of course, the moment I accepted the fact that I loved another woman, the moment I identified publicly as a lesbian, all that changed.

That abrupt change was my first experience with discrimination: how people are treated differently because of sexual, class, or racial differences. For the first time I knew what it was like to be marginalized. Through my lesbianism I came to understand that people are discriminated against: some because they're poor, others because of their color, others because we love someone of the same sex.

It was in this context that I began to participate in some of the struggles taking place in California at the time, and that's how I became involved in César Chávez's farm workers' movement, the grape pickers' strikes and all that. It would have been more difficult for me to have gone right into the Nicaraguan revolutionary movement because of the stigma associated with my being the daughter of a Somocista. Later I did a stint with the Puerto Rican

Socialist Party, working to free Lolita Lebrón and on all the campaigns against the forced sterilization of women going on in Puerto Rico at the time. Those were years of struggle for me, years in which I met many other women who would be important in the development of my growing political consciousness.

Finally the FSLN recruited me, there in San Francisco. And they recruited me as an open lesbian feminist. This was 1976, '77. The same year Casa Nicaragua was founded in San Francisco. San Francisco was the gay mecca of the world; it was amazing the number of different groups of gay men and women, of every social class and almost every race or ethnicity. And it was inside the homosexual community that I began to organize a movement of solidarity with the Sandinistas in the war against Somoza.

To raise funds for our struggle we held benefits among groups of gay Asians, gay indigenous peoples, gay Latinos, gay African-Americans. By that time I had joined a group that was called GALA, Gay Latino Alliance. We were the first group of gay Latinos in the United States. Rodrigo Reyes and I represented GALA at the first march on Washington, in October of 1979.[1]

By this time the FSLN had won the war in Nicaragua. And Aura Lila Beteta, the first Sandinista consul in San Francisco, issued us a strong letter in recognition of the work we'd done. It's a shame I haven't been able to retrieve that letter, because it's a part of the history of our work in San Francisco's gay community. We had the full and open support of the FSLN, and this shows the political dimension of the Front's ideological work back then.

We kept right on working. All the money we collected we sent to a bank account in Cuernavaca, [Mexico,] which was for the guerrilla effort. Once the war was over, things got even crazier, because we had one foot there and one foot here. We'd travel back and forth, doing whatever was needed, keeping up our ties with the support work in the Bay Area, keeping the solidarity going and also experiencing all the changes that were taking place here.

By that time, I had graduated in psychology and had been working for almost ten years for the Mission District Community Mental Health, in a residential halfway house in San Francisco. But I wanted to finish my studies before returning to Nicaragua permanently. In 1984, or the beginning of 1985, I came home for good. I'm sure you remember what the situation was like here in the mid-eighties, for women and for the lesbian and gay community.

I left Nicaragua in January of 1984. So I was leaving just about the time you were coming back. But I sense that women were still making enormous strides in terms of social participation throughout the early eighties. By the middle of the decade, with the intensification of the Contra war and the Party's failure to deal with a patriarchal ideology, things clearly began to go bad . . .

That's right. I've always been sorry I wasn't able to keep that letter written by the FSLN to Rodrigo and me, because it was an early declaration of sup-

---

1. Rodrigo Reyes was a Mexican choreographer and dancer who was a longtime activist in solidarity with Nicaragua. He died of AIDS in 1990.

port, concrete evidence that in those years, at least, the Party seemed to understand that the struggle for sexual liberation is part and parcel of the overall struggle. In other words, revolutionary change isn't complete if it doesn't include all the different struggles.

I came home without pretensions of any kind. I came with my daughter and a couple of suitcases, to go to work wherever I was needed. As it turned out, I kept on working in the area of solidarity, with the Nicaraguan Committee of Solidarity with the Peoples of the World, CNSP. We continued to provide channels of exchange: the construction brigades began coming down, and I helped with the logistical details, organizing them, that sort of thing.

The first brigade of women construction workers arrived. Its members received on-the-job training and worked in construction here in Nicaragua. What we'd do is facilitate the connections between the solidarity brigade and the local institution most appropriate to whatever [the brigade's] composition or interest might be. If it was women, it was AMNLAE; if farm workers came down, it was the ATC [Association of Farm Workers]; or if they were labor union members, it was the CST [Sandinista Workers' Central]. People came and built little houses, those famous little houses of the Sandino Project, for example. Or they built houses on the farming cooperatives, in San Juan del Río Coco, in San Carlos, or north of Estelí—all over.

But we began to have differences in regard to the way we visualized the work. Traditionally, in the Cuban Revolution and in Nicaragua's, too, most people saw this type of work as women coming to help the revolution, workers or peasants coming down to help the revolution. They didn't have a vision of the importance of women doing this *as women*, of what it could mean in terms of their own development. They couldn't see beyond the overall project to a macro concept of social change.

You came home as an open lesbian and began to do this work?

It was a very interesting experience. Because by then I hadn't only been a Sandinista for quite some time, but I was openly lesbian as well. And in those years, when the son or daughter of a well-known Somocista joined the FSLN, everyone sat up and took notice. In my case, my father was the head of Somoza's Diplomatic Ceremonial Corps, and as his daughter it turned out that I wasn't only a Sandinista but a feminist and a lesbian, too.

In fact it was Somoza himself who told my father that I was working with the FSLN. "Your daughter's in the Sandinista Front," he said, and my father took the next plane to San Francisco. For my family it wasn't just the stigma of one of their daughters having joined the FSLN, it was the fact that she was an open lesbian as well.

My father almost went crazy. He tried convincing me any way he could: with promises and with offers of all kinds. He was legitimately afraid, because I traveled on a diplomatic passport back then and I had access to high levels of power. He was afraid I'd take advantage of that, take part in some action or other, against the dictatorship . . . But I assured him that he didn't need to worry, that the level and type of my involvement wasn't going to jeopardize his position.

I told my father I would respect him if he would respect me, and that we'd just have to accept our differences—political, social, sexual, and religious too. Because my father was the type who went to Mass and took Communion every day. We managed to avoid talking about any of those subjects, so we were able to keep our family relations more or less intact.

As a revolutionary, were you alone among your siblings, or were others of your sisters and brothers also involved?

We're all progressive people. But I'm the only one of the five siblings who supported the FSLN. Today my brothers and my sister all live in the United States.

I didn't answer your question about being "out" when I came back to Nicaragua, though. I went from San Francisco, where I was completely public about my sexuality and my politics, to Managua where I entered a period of depersonalization. When I came home my old friends treated me as if I hadn't undergone a change of any kind, and those Sandinistas who didn't know my particular history tended to reject me as if I were one of those "July 19th revolutionaries."[2]

So on one level it was hard coming back, and complicated too. It was almost like having to come out of the closet all over again, going back through that process . . . and I'd forgotten what it felt like! On another level, it wasn't really that difficult because, this time around, I was much more aware; I had a different kind of respect for the process itself, and I'd learned something about the tactics and strategy to follow.

I knew how people in general here felt about homosexuality, how we've been conditioned to feel. But I also knew my comrades in the Front. I knew them as people who were very political, very capable, but who on this particular issue were dealing with something totally foreign to their experience: filled with erroneous concepts, myths, stereotypes, stigmas. In other words, they possessed all the necessary tools to understand sexual difference if it were presented to them intelligently, ideologically, with its political dimension, and by people they knew and trusted. Therefore, I didn't really mind having to come out of the closet again, if by doing so I could help achieve a political space for lesbian and gay rights.

I began to engage in a very personal type of campaign, very one-on-one, raising consciousness little by little. I'd work with people and make sure they knew who I was, my history—so they knew they could count on me politically—and then I'd tell them, "I'm a lesbian." And I'd begin to talk to them about what that means. Of course, this often led to a situation where people would say, "Well, I accept *you* because you're *different*. You're a political person, with both feet on the ground. But most homosexuals are . . . you know . . ."

2. "July 19th revolutionaries" was the term given those who identified as Sandinistas only after the victory.

So it was a process, like everything else. I felt it was important that this work be done from an ideological and political point of view.

Nicaragua is an ideal place to carry out this type of struggle. Because it's like the seed, the source if you will, of a much larger ideological battle. And my own experience has shown me that, although there's an extreme degree of sexism here, the revolution is also alive and well. It's possible to explain lesbian and gay rights within a vision of equal rights for all. I deeply believe that ours is a revolutionary struggle, a struggle that belongs to the overall revolutionary movement; and for that reason we must continue to struggle within the Left.

We were able to get the leadership of the FSLN to see that our demands belong with the people's demands. It wasn't easy, but we were able to achieve it at the leadership level, to get them to consider us as comrades, sisters and brothers in arms.

What level of leadership are you talking about, Rita?

All levels, right up to and including the national directorate. I can tell you that one of our greatest allies was Comandante Carlos Núñez. Through his wife, Milú Vargas, he had been able to understand the political-ideological dimensions of feminism; therefore, he was that much further ahead. And it wasn't hard for him to make the leap, to see the political-ideological dimensions of lesbian and gay rights. In fact, I'll tell you something: Carlos was able to understand all this before Milú was.

Was Carlos Núñez the only member of the national directorate able to understand this struggle?

I don't know. I didn't have access to them all. As I said, I came back to Nicaragua without any political pretensions, and you remember how inaccessible the highest echelons of leadership were. It just so happened that I got to know Carlos Núñez on a personal level. Tomás Borge? Tomás's attitude was probably more indicative: his line was that he supported us, that gay rights had to be part of the overall struggle; but he personally was just too sexist to really internalize it on a more personal level. In any case, I think it was an achievement to have been able to convince these guys, even at the ideological level. And I think it's been one of the Sandinista revolution's unique accomplishments.

Tell me how Nicaraguan lesbians and gay men first got together . . .

The lesbian and gay movement started organizing here around 1986. Prior to this there were small groups of lesbians and gay men, groups of friends. But in '86 we began to organize beyond the socializing that had been going on up to that point, and it was this early organizing that allowed people to perceive the political and ideological dimensions of gay rights. These were young people who were connected in one way or another with the FSLN; it was a natural leap from one type of political consciousness to another.

People would say, "Okay, in 1979 we liberated ourselves as a people. I'm free, and maybe I'm also successful at what I do, in my professional life, or as a revolutionary cadre. But what happens when people find out that I'm gay? All those credits go down the drain!" You can see what an organic process it was, a truly revolutionary process. People understood that if they didn't carry the process into their personal lives, the revolution would remain skin deep. Everything gained would fall away if we couldn't get people to continue to respect us knowing our sexual orientation.

We began to organize. But it wasn't easy, because the emergency measures were in place by then; all types of organization, outside the accepted political structures, were prohibited by law. We knew this, but we plunged ahead anyway. Sometimes there were more than sixty of us meeting at one time. About a year later we had a problem with state security coming down on us and destroying the organization we'd worked so hard to build.

In March 1987 we were summoned to Casa 50, the state security office. They mounted an operation where I was called in first—because, they said, I was the brains behind the whole thing. Naturally, I told them they were wrong, that I was a part of the movement, that maybe in a way people recognized my age and my history, but that many of us were involved. Still, they called me in first. And almost immediately after they called me, they summoned two others who were in the armed forces at the time. Finally they brought everyone in. They fingerprinted people and filmed the group session.

In my case, they actually arrested me. When I received the summons, I realized I wasn't going to be able to present myself on the day and at the time stipulated. I was going to be in San Carlos that day, with one of the brigades. So I went by the state security office and left them a note explaining why I wouldn't be able to make the appointment, but that I'd be glad to come in as soon as I got back from San Carlos. Their response was to issue an order for my arrest, and they simply picked me up.

I knew what was coming. I knew the only thing they could possibly be concerned about was this organizing of the lesbian and gay community. So I went to state security fully aware of what it was all about. They intended to imprison me. I spoke very firmly with the man who arrested and initially interrogated me. I told him he'd better hurry up and finish the interview, and that whoever else wanted to question me better hurry up and do it, because if they weren't through with me by 5:00 that afternoon, someone was going to show up and get me out of there.

I'd left word with my daughter that if she didn't hear from me by 5:00, she was to contact Milú and tell her where I was. The whole thing was an abuse of power on the part of those who carried out the operation. But we were able to defend ourselves, defend our political position. Not just me, but all the comrades who were pulled in. We defended ourselves with great dignity, from a political perspective, with pride and determination.

And, of course, that incident eventually led to a much more open struggle on our part, although at first it silenced us. When it happened, we agreed that we wouldn't make it public. We were revolutionaries, and we believed that if news of this repression got out, especially outside the country, it would be very harmful to the Sandinista cause. We knew we were at war, and we made a political decision to keep a lid on it for a while. Eventually one or two people did talk, but for several years most of us were able to keep the thing quiet.

The interrogation was pretty nasty though, downright morbid. The security officers assumed a voyeurlike attitude. They tried to get the information they wanted: names of all those who were in the movement, and names we knew of men and women in the revolutionary leadership who might be lesbian or gay. They got it all wrong from the very beginning: they thought we were going to name names, talk about individuals, but all we were interested in talking about was the ideological issue, political demands.

Another thing this guy kept asking me was, "Tell us who your lover is." I told him I didn't have a lover, and he'd come back at me: "You must have a lover, tell me who she is." I told him that I knew this was probably difficult for a macho like him to understand, because sexists think of lesbians as if they are men, and that he expected men to be machos, which intrinsically meant going to bed with as many women as possible; otherwise they weren't real men. But I said that isn't the case for feminist lesbians.

I also told him that it was hard for someone like myself to find a partner in a country like Nicaragua, that the repression is such that women aren't encouraged to explore their sexuality. I told him that just as I was sure he'd considered ideology and politics when choosing the woman with whom he wanted to share his life, I was looking for the same things in a woman.

State security's line at the time was that this was simply a "friendly warning." Those were the words they used. They claimed that the revolution couldn't have this sort of organizing going on, because the purpose of the revolution was to create "new men and women" and, well, faggots and dykes just didn't measure up; and they couldn't allow this type of organizing to go on in Nicaragua.

My position throughout the interview was that I believed my interrogator was confused. I spoke to him about my history with the FSLN. I told him I'd been recruited in 1976, '77, as an open lesbian. And I told him what I've just told you, that the revolution has to be for everyone, not just for heterosexuals. I said it was like teaching people to read: you don't teach them and then tell them they can read only certain books. If they know how to read, they must have access to all books. "We're liberating people," I said, "and we can't condition that liberation. We can't give people freedom and then curtail their options, especially when it comes to personal identity and choice." That was more or less the line I took that day. Nevertheless, the state security people held fast to their position. They told us we had to stop organizing, and that was that.

They let me go; they let everyone go. But they made it very clear that we were prohibited from organizing as lesbians and gays; the emergency measures were still in effect. And, of course, people got scared. A whole lot of people who'd been a part of this incipient movement, who'd attended the meetings and facilitated places in which to meet, just dropped out of sight. But some of us continued. We were absolutely aware that we needed to keep going with this work; and we did so, although our numbers were drastically reduced.

As I mentioned, all of us who had been called in to state security took the collective decision not to talk about it, not to reveal what had happened. We were a country at war, in a state of national emergency; and we were Sandinistas, the great majority of us supported the revolution. We felt that talking about this incident at that time could only hurt the FSLN. We knew it had been a mistake, and we were confident it would be righted at some point. Meanwhile, we didn't feel it was appropriate to share what they'd done to us with people who could easily use the information against the Sandinista revolution.

It was interesting: so many people were basically able to keep the secret. Some thirty of us had been summoned, and many more knew about it. Eventually a few did say something, but the rest of us kept on insisting it wasn't true, it hadn't happened. It was a case of their word against ours, which enabled us to keep a lid on it.

Later, there was the whole issue of AIDS. I had come from San Francisco, where I'd lived through the appearance of the virus and the tremendous impact it had on our community. But to come to Nicaragua and begin talking about AIDS: it just wasn't viable. I mean, I talked about the epidemic, and some of the others did too—but not as a campaign, not publicly.

About a year after that incident with state security, a group from San Francisco came to a health colloquium held in Managua, and they presented a paper on AIDS. This is when AIDS began to be a topic of discussion here. At that point the epidemic was still considered a "gay phenomenon." We knew that wasn't true; therefore, we had to make sure that when the virus hit Nicaragua it wouldn't be perceived that way. The popular myth was that there were no gays and lesbians here; and if people thought of AIDS as a gay disease, they weren't going to treat it seriously, which would only reinforce homophobia.

The top levels of the Sandinista Ministry of Health [MINSA] were very receptive and open to the idea of an educational campaign, and of carrying out preventive measures. The director of hygiene and epidemiology at the time was a progressive person and open to the question of lesbian and gay rights; his support turned out to be very important to our continuing struggle.

MINSA wanted to train people in the gay community to do AIDS prevention work. We wanted to become involved, and we felt the moment was right for us to work openly as lesbians and gay men doing AIDS education and prevention work. But to do so we had to resume our political organizing. How could we take part in this AIDS education work, as lesbians and gay men, if we weren't permitted to organize within the gay community?

At this point, a contingent of the incipient lesbian and gay movement met with the minister [of health] and her top-level aides to let them know about the incident with state security and the imposed prohibition on any future organizing.[3] These health officials were not aware of what had happened. Immediately

3. The minister of health at this time was Dora María Téllez.

the minister herself went to speak with the officer who had directed the operation against us back in 1987. By this time he recognized that the whole thing had been a terrible error; in a way, he was ashamed that he would go down in history as the bad guy.

In fact, it's not about a "bad guy" at all. It's a reflection of the extreme sexism in our society. These machos exercise so much power, yet at the same time they're so weak. They feel threatened by anything that might take away from their position, that might possibly alter the status quo—by the very idea that we might not need them for our survival, like they need us!

As I was telling you, we developed an AIDS education and prevention program within the Ministry of Health. We organized groups, a more complex process than the consciousness-raising we'd been doing around the issue of "coming out." These were therapy groups designed to help us deal with our own internalized oppression. And we provided courses in participatory methodology and in popular education, all within the context of our sexuality and around the problem of AIDS. We also studied epidemiology and prevention. This process gave rise to CEP-SIDA, the collective of popular educators in the fight against AIDS which still functions today.

The minister supported this program from the beginning. People at the ministry thought it was very solid. The therapy groups seemed a little short at first, but then they agreed that they were probably long enough. This was our opportunity, the open door we needed. CEP-SIDA was the only group in the country at that time doing AIDS education and prevention work, and we were officially recognized as a group of lesbians and gay men involved in this work. The ministry was 100 percent behind us.

For us, this also represented an opportunity to help develop a gay and lesbian political cadre, who could then go on to organize the gay community throughout the country. The work was very positive. We went everywhere, organizing and running these workshops; they sent us to schools, hospitals, and health centers. We really wanted to concentrate our efforts in the gay and lesbian community because we knew that we had a great deal to do there.

We needed to support our own people in ridding themselves of the internalized oppression they suffered, to provide them with liberating elements so they would be able to lead more integrated lives. Today there are a number of different lesbian and gay groups in Nicaragua; back then it was just us. We knew that educating about AIDS provided a space for talking about our sexuality. And as revolutionaries, we wanted to be able to speak about an integrated social and political participation. So we formed a collective of lesbians and gay men dedicated to working exclusively in the gay community.

We saw our struggle as part of the overall revolutionary movement. We wanted to create a gay and lesbian movement of the Left, something that hadn't existed before. We didn't want to be separatists. We recognized the need for certain spaces, but we didn't want to promote the visceral divisions that exist in the developed countries. We didn't want the kind of separatism that tends to exist between gay men and lesbians; we felt we'd be going backward if we allowed that to happen here.

What we really wanted was for our movement to be able to be a part of the FSLN, for the Party to get to the point where it would be able to include our demands in its platform.

Did you ever try to get AMNLAE involved in the lesbian issue? Did you ever believe there might be a way of getting AMNLAE, as the FSLN's women's organization, to take on the struggle for lesbian rights?

When brigades and other delegations began coming to Nicaragua and they'd meet with AMNLAE, women from the other countries would ask what was going on with women here, and eventually someone would bring up the question: "And what about lesbians?"

At first the AMNLAE women would respond, "There are no lesbians in Nicaragua." Gradually they had to admit that, well, we do exist. But they'd say, "There are very few; it's insignificant." Much later, when Lea Guido became secretary general of AMNLAE, I went to talk to her. But all I achieved was to become the "official lesbian." When PIE started up, I was their token lesbian, too.

I think what really got to them was that I'm a professional person. I identified as a lesbian feminist psychologist. That was just too much. Because they admitted that, yes, maybe lesbians do exist; but they're in the markets, or totally out of sight. At that time I was the only professional woman who was openly lesbian. Now there are more.

I'm sure you remember the struggle women were waging inside the Front at that time. There was this terrible symbiosis around "Papa FSLN"; and, in the final analysis, I believe that's what did AMNLAE in. The organization never could cut its umbilical cord with the Party. It was pretty amazing. A lot of these women were my friends: we socialized together, we went to the same parties, drank together and all the rest. But we couldn't succeed in convincing them of our position. Given their difficulty in accepting feminism as a valid instrument in the struggle for equality and as not antagonistic to revolutionary thought, AMNLAE was never able to accept us as part of the women's movement.

When you talk about going to parties, Rita, did you go with your partner? Could you have gone with your partner, danced with her, acted the same as if you'd been a heterosexual couple? Would you have felt comfortable doing that in this milieu?

I didn't happen to have a partner at the time, but if I had I certainly would have partied with her. As I say, I was openly lesbian, and assertive about the need for a lesbian movement. I'd ask those women, "How is it possible that lesbians and gay men all over the world are organizing, and you don't see the need for it here? The gay community can come together in a political front, from a position of gender, from a feminist perspective which is itself a political position. And it's not just a part of the feminist struggle; it's a part of the struggle for equality for all peoples, for real people's power.

"Here we are, all these different subgroups, all oppressed by patriarchal power: women, lesbians, gay men, children, everyone who is specifically oppressed and repressed by the patriarchy. Can't you see how important it could be for us to come together in a common front?" But, of course, the AMNLAE women were completely tied in to the patriarchal model, which was the FSLN. It was "National Directorate, tell us what to do!" right down the line. We tried, but there wasn't much we could do. And it wasn't just the lesbians who couldn't make any headway with AMNLAE; it was also the newly emerging independent feminists.

That was just the way it was. Since we continued to have our ties with feminist movements outside the country, and brigades were coming one after another, we'd always tell our foreign sisters, "Please keep asking about us. Ask about the lesbians. Ask for us by name—my name, the names of the others. Remind them that we exist, that we're here and we're not going away."

Little by little we were able to raise some consciousness about the issue, and I think in the long run we were successful. Because eventually we were able to make the revolutionary leadership understand that ours is a political struggle, an ideological struggle. It's been hard for them to see this, because it implies an internal revolution that they haven't really gone through as yet. At the intellectual level, at the political level, in their heads, they've come to accept our point of view. But in practice, at the gut level, they're still going to react with all their patriarchal instincts, all those typical reactionary responses.

I guess we shouldn't be surprised. Even in the more developed countries, where the lesbian and gay movements have such a long history, they continue to suffer from sectarianism; the gay world continues to be a ghetto, the groups are still compartmentalized, often completely alienated from one another. And the demands can be very limited. For example: that two women be allowed to marry. To my way of thinking, that's not all that relevant.

I feel strongly that our struggle needs to be about creating a healthy society. We need to struggle together for more humane and egalitarian conditions, and our demands must be linked to those of other marginalized groups, groups that are also repressed and discriminated against. What we need to do is build a movement that allows us to develop internally but also to reach out toward the outside world, toward the revolution as a whole.

Having a movement that's holistic in its approach to society is saying that lesbians and gay men need to be working together. We may need our own spaces for certain issues or events, but we also need the political and ideological clarity that allows us to maintain the unity necessary to building a movement capable of making a difference. And this is what we knew we needed here.

Of course, it was a bit utopian, considering there were so few of us. And we didn't have a well-developed culture. It was the first time anything like this had even been talked about in Nicaragua. We had no real models. While it's true we had a great deal of contact with the outside, our experience of the gay world was pretty limited. We did what we could, and I think we did pretty well, considering the context and its momentum.

I think our struggle to build a lesbian and gay movement in Nicaragua has been a success because we managed to raise our particular banner within the revolutionary context, and we managed to defend that banner in such a context. We believe our demands to be revolutionary in and of themselves, so it seemed only logical to us that we link them to that other, larger struggle. In many ways the Sandinista revolution provided the ideal framework for making these connections, and for showing how the gay movement can contribute to a consolidation of the larger revolutionary process.

I believe that to have been able to sit down with members of the national directorate of the FSLN, to discuss all this and have them say, "Politically and ideologically, we understand where you're coming from, but at the personal level I have a lot of trouble with this, my residual sexism makes it hard for me," I think that was an achievement, an important first step. We were able to engage them in honest discussion.

If we take a look at the gay movement in the United States—and it's a much older movement—we'll see that its demands are much more specific. The U.S. social system itself rejects homosexuality, or it's tolerated by virtue of the Constitution. In any case, the gay movement there doesn't much concern itself with broader social change. I'm not blaming this on the gay community itself. It's the fault of the system as a whole, how it's structured, the kind of society and the political system it spawns. Within the U.S. political system, they're forced to struggle in a vacuum. Although in many ways gays [in the United States] are no different from other people in the developed countries. And they all have this tendency of going off to the Third World and telling people what to do, how we should be living our lives, how we must structure our movements, often with a minimal knowledge of our history, our culture, our sociopolitical realities.

It's easy for people to come from somewhere else and tell us what to do. That's what cultural imperialism is all about. It's particularly ironic when it comes to the gay and lesbian community, because many of those who come from developed countries aren't even "out" to their own families back home. They come down here with their methodologies and their strategies, straight out of some gay mecca or other, but they haven't yet resolved their own basic problems.

To give you an example of what I consider inappropriate interference from outside: Initially there was a lack of AIDS education and information materials here. Some well-meaning comrades from abroad sent us some literature to be distributed in the gay community. The problem was, this literature described a series of practices prevalent in the gay communities of the industrially developed countries, practices like fisting and leather which are not a part of our culture. We said, "We'll write our own material."

Periodically, gay internationalists also tried to get us to talk about the incident with state security. But we wouldn't. We knew that if we talked, we weren't going to benefit as a movement. And the only thing we'd achieve in the context of the revolution would be accusations of human rights violations against the FSLN. The Party didn't need that then. None of us had been imprisoned; we were all living and working as we had before. We made the political decision to keep the story under wraps, and we feel it was the right decision at the time. But some of our gay sisters and brothers from other countries couldn't understand that.

This is what we wanted: a movement that would be eminently Nicaraguan, not dictated by outside forces, in which those involved would be able to deal with their own internal issues about being gay and at the same time could understand that our movement had to be part of the larger revolutionary project. It meant a great deal of work, and I don't think we really pulled it off on either count. There are many organized lesbians and gays in Nicaragua today who still haven't been able to process what it means to be gay. What I mean is, they think of themselves as gay because they go to bed with someone of the same sex, but they haven't taken it any further than that.

One thing we were able to achieve is that the lesbian and gay movement is now considered a part of the broader feminist movement. We even managed to convince a number of men of this. We have men here now who understand that lesbian and gay rights are a feminist issue. Our movement is unique. This is why I've been against celebrating Gay Pride in June. I have nothing against Stonewall;[4] it's an important event in international gay history. But we have our own history.

I support holding our yearly celebration the week of March 6 through 13, to commemorate our battle with state security in 1987, defending an openly lesbian and gay political and ideological position within the context of the Nicaraguan revolution. This is an important part of our history. I don't know how many people agree with me; there are so many groups around now. Maybe in the future. This past year CEP-SIDA was the only group to commemorate lesbian and gay pride in March.

I've had the sense that there've been some splits, that the movement here is divided . . .

Yes, unfortunately. Or, who knows, perhaps it's not so unfortunate, because there are many more groups now. Maybe it just had to happen this way. I've tried to stay away from the internal discussions. Because of my strong personality, my age—I'm in my forties—and because I'm a psychologist, the younger women and men have plenty of reasons to oppose me on certain issues.

Rita, tell me what you can about the electoral defeat. Did it surprise you? How do you think it affected the gay and lesbian community?

4. In 1969 the New York City Police attacked people coming out of a Puerto Rican gay bar on Stonewall Street in Greenwich Village. First a single lesbian and then large numbers of gay men and women fought back. The riot lasted through the night, marking the first public defiance of official harassment and abuse of lesbians and gay men. Stonewall is generally considered to mark the beginning of the current lesbian and gay movement in the United States, and is commemorated as well with Gay Pride marches and events in other parts of the world.

Yes, it was a totally unexpected blow. That day I was hosting a high-level delegation from the Socialist International—Mr. [Guillermo] Ungo from El Salvador and Ms. Monica Andersson from Sweden, among others. They'd come to observe the elections. These are highly experienced politicians, people with a great deal of objectivity. At a certain point some of them began to insinuate that maybe . . . But I insisted: "Comrade, there's no way we're going to lose!" When it happened, it was very hard to believe.

You've lived in Cuba, Margaret, and in Nicaragua. You know what it's been like. For a lot of people here, Sandinism replaced everything else in their lives. It became their identity in a very complex way. For many of those Sandinistas who were religious, Sandinism replaced their religious practice to an important degree. For those who lost their spouses, children, and families, Sandinism filled all their needs and empty places.

People threw themselves into the Sandinista project without a well-developed personal vision of the world. They weren't able to ask questions, they weren't able to conduct their own analysis, they couldn't engage in critical thinking. There was criticism and self-criticism, of course, but always within the prescribed mode. Many people used to say, "My life is the revolution," meaning and understanding revolution as a predefined, fabricated package that you adopt without asking any questions or offering any input; you simply become that idea of "revolution."

When you understand this, you can understand what the electoral defeat meant here. It was much more than a political defeat. It was much more than losing control of the government or, in an individual sense, losing our jobs, our livelihood. It's been a real loss of identity, one that hasn't been dealt with yet. People here weren't taught to think; we were always waiting for "the line." And we're still waiting for the line! At the same time, this triggers a lot of anger and resentment toward the FSLN and toward oneself, for going all the way with blinders on.

And there's something else. Carlos Núñez's death was also a terrible shock, in some ways more devastating than the electoral loss. When Carlos died so suddenly, I felt terribly alone. It caused me a great deal of sorrow and desperation. His death was a blow in particular to the lesbian and gay community, because he was our ally, someone we knew we could count on to defend our positions.

When I would go to international events, forums, or conferences, Carlos was never too busy to go over my speeches with me, make suggestions, help with our presentation of Nicaragua's gay community outside the country, and even inside the country. When we'd celebrate our movement's anniversary— every year we'd commemorate the time we stood up to state security, under the guise of celebrating the founding of CEP-SIDA—we could always count on Carlos's support.

I remember I was going to give an important presentation in San Francisco and another in Europe—representing Nicaragua's gay and lesbian movement. I wrote my speech and gave Carlos a copy, so he could give me ideas and suggestions; and I still have a copy of that speech, with his comments in the margin, written in his own hand. On that occasion he even added something at the end, something like: "We Nicaraguan lesbians and gay men . . . !" His identification with our cause was such that he even wrote a slogan as if he were one of us.

Carlos contributed enormously to our struggle, in more ways than I can tell you. I remember just before we celebrated the tenth anniversary of the revolution, I went to him and asked, "Carlos, don't you think it's about time the gay community participate as a movement? What would you say to our coming out this year, publicly, as a group?" "I think it's a great idea," he said. "And if they pick us up again?" I asked. "If security goes wild, will you defend us?" "Of course I will," was his answer, "but nothing like that is going to happen."

And we did come out that year, full force, for the tenth anniversary. A whole contingent of lesbian and gay Sandinistas, in our black T-shirts with the pink triangles—and, of course, our red and black neckerchiefs, our caps, the works. Lesbians and gay men openly marching in support of the revolution. The lesbian and gay international contingent marched right behind us. Because it was important for our group to be clearly Nicaraguan, rows of Nicaraguan faces. We couldn't afford to have people saying we were imports from another culture.

For the gay community, just as for the revolutionary community as a whole, the electoral defeat was traumatic. We had to pull ourselves together and try to figure out what we were going to do. We knew our struggle would be greatly altered; the balance of power was different from the moment the FSLN was voted out. That's when people began organizing all these different nongovernmental organizations. On the one hand, I think it's been a positive step; but on the other, I feel there's been a certain amount of distortion in the conceptions behind them.

Nimehuatzín is one of them. It's clear to me that we had to ensure spaces in which to continue our work, broad-based arenas where our movement could continue to grow. We didn't want to lock the AIDS work into that erroneous and fatal trilogy—homosexuality/lesbianism/AIDS[5]—which is why we needed a foundation dedicated exclusively to AIDS as it affects the population as a whole.

Tell me more about Nimehuatzín.

After the FSLN's electoral loss, I stopped working with CEP-SIDA. It was an amiable separation. I wanted to do AIDS prevention work aimed at the broader population. AIDS allows us to question the whole patriarchal power structure; and working with AIDS means tapping into the scientific community, the educational community, social work, other agencies. Class issues come up, the relationship between North and South, a whole world vision. Politically the epidemic facilitates taking on a wide range of issues with a broad spectrum of people.

---

5. In Nicaragua the term "homosexuality" is used to refer exclusively to gay men: there are "homosexuals" and "lesbians."

Founding Nimehuatzín, in March of 1990, made it possible for us to engage in this broadly based, inclusive work. And it also allowed us to fund other areas of AIDS work: research, for example, and overall sex education; as well as what CEP-SIDA does, which is education and preventive medicine. We work closely with them, and we've been able to complement one another.

The foundation's documents are drawn up from a particular political point of view. Because the traditional way of approaching the AIDS epidemic puts all the emphasis on the gay male community; the disease has been very much about men, very phallic. Women were virtually left out, or considered passive victims. That assumed passivity has put women at much greater risk. The campaigns have been pretty superficial, dealing with the tip of the iceberg so to speak.

One example of this superficiality is the campaign that expects women to "Demand a condom!" We live in a culture where women haven't been taught to demand anything, much less a condom, and even less from their men who are literally their owners. Traditionally, women here have been the givers, not the ones who make demands. So how can we all of a sudden expect women to demand that their men use condoms, without teaching them why it's important for them to change, to think of themselves, to be less sacrificial—and then teaching them how to make those demands? Conceived of broadly, AIDS work allows us to talk about all of this.

If proper ideological training is given, professionals in many different disciplines can help support a different way of looking at these issues. Doctors can address them from a medical point of view; psychologists, from their perspective; social workers . . . and so forth. Nimehuatzín works with all these different professionals. We've designed an integral program that puts out an integral vision: nonsexist, nonclassist, nonheterosexist.

In order to avoid duplicating our efforts, our main work with the homosexual community and with men who have sex with men is still done in coordination with CEP-SIDA. Currently we're in the process of consolidating the first collective of sexual workers in the struggle against AIDS.

We feel that in order to really want to prevent AIDS, or to keep ourselves healthy once we have the virus, we must first of all want to live—in the adverse conditions of poverty, misery, and depression that are so common in our country now. It doesn't do any good simply to tell people to use a condom if we haven't addressed the deeper issue of "Why live?"

Rita, what are the AIDS statistics here? Do you have statistics on the AIDS epidemic in Nicaragua?

Yes, we do have statistics, although AIDS is underregistered here as it is in most countries. The official statistics say we have 101 cumulative cases of people who are HIV-positive. Of these, 31 have been diagnosed as having AIDS; all but 1 have died. It's difficult to get exact figures, although the World Health Organization estimates that 1 statistical AIDS case represents as many as 100 or 125 people with HIV. So, if our statistics say we have 31 people with

AIDS, we can calculate that the number with HIV is closer to 3,000 persons.

I think there are closer to 5,000 people living with HIV in Nicaragua. Unofficially, experts at the Ministry of Public Health agree. We've got a tough job cut out for us. Basically, what we've been able to achieve so far is some educational work, but only at the level of the slogan. No significant portion of the population really takes the slogan to heart and incorporates it into his or her sexual practice. We believe that no more than 6 percent of Nicaraguans are currently using condoms. And women, particularly women who stay at home, without any social life to speak of except through their husbands, without even any contact with our campaigns: they're completely marginal to the whole issue. We have a great deal of work ahead of us, no question about that. And we need all the help we can get.

In spite of the electoral defeat, or maybe in some interesting ways because of that defeat, I have the sense that there's a very real opening for feminism in Nicaragua today . . .

I think you're right, Margaret. But as you know, where there's an opening for feminism there's an opening for everything else as well, and this represents a great danger. Because although it's true, feminism is stronger now and the lesbian movement has gained in strength, it's also true that we have the spread of fundamentalism and sectarianism, both of which have become stronger since the electoral defeat.

The Catholic and Protestant churches, as well as all the different sects in Nicaragua, are in the midst of a tremendous evangelization campaign, using every means at their disposal. This is particularly worrisome given people's psychological state owing to the destruction of our paradigms and the onset of the postwar period. We might say we are not exempt from suffering a generalized posttraumatic stress disorder, causing a collective existential crisis. And in the case of the Sandinistas this might well trigger a real identity crisis. All these elements place people in potentially vulnerable situations.

We must also acknowledge the long, drawn-out isolation left by the fact that the revolution failed to recognize the importance of the individual. Increasing numbers of Sandinistas, mostly women, have resumed a regular religious participation, many claiming they felt this aspect of their lives was repressed by the revolution.

The Sandinista revolution tried its best to be a unique model, not cast in the mold of previous revolutionary experiences. But it was run by human beings, fallible as humans are. Besides its resistance to feminism and to recognizing lesbian and gay rights, it's clear that it also had shortcomings with respect to people's spirituality. Now people feel a tremendous need to reconnect with their native roots. True revolution can't really be consolidated without this.

We must encourage our own particular spirituality—linked to our ancestors, free of sectarianism—which will strengthen and empower us to continue our struggle for balance, the midpoint of the pendulum's swing. As Rigoberta Menchú says, until we recognize the atrocities of colonization, we cannot speak of a *reencuentro* [reconnection], a meeting of two distinct cultures.[6] Until we recognize the imbalance of power that exists in the distribution of the world's resources, we cannot speak to one another from equal positions or begin to deal with egalitarian relations among peoples and countries. Nor will we be able to achieve the meeting of North and South, which is where the future of the planet is currently so tense.

The extreme Right and the religious sectors are doing an expert job of organizing. Take the issue of abortion, for example. They are very active in organizing against freedom of choice: they've published tracts, newspaper articles; they have their own magazines and hold public meetings and forums in conjunction with government institutions; and they're mobilizing women all over the country.

For our part, since we're still in crisis, we haven't really been able to get back completely on our feet. We haven't been able to articulate common goals. Thus, the feminist movement has grown, but it's grown in a number of different directions. The gay movement has grown, but there are several splits in it as well.

What do you see in the near future, Rita, in terms of how things will develop here? Where do you see the FSLN, and Sandinism in general, going now?

After the FSLN's electoral defeat, there has been an increasing number of people identifying as Sandinista but not as FSLN—some because they are angry at the Party; others just became disenchanted with the political game behind the ideology. Tendencies surface, but they'll make a public statement and die down, without anything getting consolidated; and the Party hasn't taken specific stands on these positions.

The idea or concept of "governing from below" has had a double-edged negative impact, mostly because the fine line between cogoverning and strong-voiced opposition has not been well understood, nor defined and therefore properly executed. This situation has created a vacuum in which extreme right-wingers have begun campaigning for president. This started almost as soon as UNO took power, and in these almost three years they've gained considerable popularity in the opinion polls.

It seems that the most disenfranchised—which in today's Nicaragua means the majority—would benefit more from the FSLN articulating a congruent platform within the framework of a strong and well-defined opposition party. But in spite of that, I think there may be some surprises on the horizon. We are

---

6. Rigoberta Menchú is a Quiché Indian woman from Guatemala. She began to be known beyond the borders of her country when the story of her life, *I, Rigoberta Menchú*, ed. and intro. Elisabeth Burgos-Debray (London: Verso, 1983) was published. The book was earlier published in Spanish as *Me llamo Rigoberta Menchú y así me nació la conciencia* (Havana: Casa de las Américas, 1982), and it has now been translated and published in many different languages. Menchú has traveled extensively, speaking about the conditions of poverty and repression in Guatemala. In 1992 she won the Nobel Peace Prize.

experiencing difficult times, no question about it; but we are also beginning to understand our historic role.

Conditions have been created here that don't exist in other places. Actually, it's only now that we're beginning to participate in a real political praxis at a deeper level. We've entered a tremendously rich period of political and ideological struggle; coalitions are being built. It's a great challenge. If we are able to achieve a minimum of political maturity, we'll have the opportunity of creating a state based on respect for human rights within a framework of economic, social, and cultural development.

"Who Was Going to Trust
a Montenegro?"

Sofía Montenegro

Sofía Montenegro wasn't in Sandino's Daughters. *When I arrived in Nicaragua, right after the revolutionary victory of 1979, hers was not one of the names I heard repeated as I went from place to place, from one woman to another, listening to the extraordinary stories of strength and participation, always asking who else might be willing to share their story. Yet Sofía had been as involved and active as many of those women I'd interviewed a dozen years before. Speaking with her now, hearing the particular contours of her personal history, it wasn't hard for me to understand why she hadn't been one of my original informants. Sofía was probably seen as a little too iconoclastic back then, perhaps too independent a thinker, not at all the kind of interview likely to have been suggested to a foreign journalist.*

The Sandinistas call July 17th the Day of National Joy. It's the day Somoza fled the country and just two days before the victorious rebel army marched into Managua, all more than a decade ago. Today everything has shifted. The joy is strained. Somehow, though, it seemed appropriate that our conversation be scheduled for this date. Somoza's long hold on Nicaragua had especially complex implications for Sofía's family. His defeat signaled an important beginning to the liberation of her dreams, even as it made definitive the tragic tearing apart of those closest to her.

Sofía used to manage the editorial page of Barricada, *one of Nicaragua's three major dailies. The paper was the FSLN's official publication throughout the Sandinista administration; since the electoral loss it has redefined itself as independently progressive. Along with this high level of ideological responsibility—still somewhat unusual for a woman within the Party ranks—Sofía is editor of* Gente [People], *a weekly supplement that is provocative and profound: the best sort of journalism.*

When we arrived for our interview, people at the paper told us Sofía had been home for several days. She'd injured her back. But she'd left word for us to come over to her small apartment, a two-story structure unusual among Managua's more typical courtyard-encircling homes. There we found her in pain, but willing and ready to talk. She quickly showered and changed from a short Japanese-style kimono into a patterned summer-print dress. On this hot July morning, her shoulder-length brown hair was held back by a paisley headband. Sofía's eyes are what most steadily rivet your attention; they are liquid brown, at times profoundly sad but containing an energy that pulls you into her sophisticated intelligence.

Sofía's is a feminist as well as a female intelligence. This is not a woman to whom you would pose the question "Do you consider yourself a feminist?" Her gender analysis is as widely known as her grasp of international affairs or her complex understanding of Nicaragua; it has represented her, in fact, beyond national borders—in essays, articles, and published interviews. Her life experience has been exceptionally rich.

With a cup of black coffee and a fresh pack of cigarettes, Sofía positioned herself on the floor, her lower back against a hot water bottle held in place by half a dozen pillows and cushions. One cigarette butt after another quickly filled to overflowing the ashtray at her side. And she began to talk . . .

You want me to start at the beginning. Well, I'm thirty-eight. My father was a major in Somoza's army: Alfonso Montenegro; he died in 1978. And my mother was your ordinary Nicaraguan housewife, although as I grow older I think I see more of my mother in myself. So, how to define my life? You might say I came to Sandinism through the back door. On the other hand, my feminism came earlier; I grasped it almost intuitively.

Back in the 1930s my father fought against Sandino—a hell of a legacy, huh? And my oldest brother was also a military man, my father and mother's firstborn. He, too, fought against the Sandinistas, for seven years. When they killed my brother, in 1979, he had risen to the rank of lieutenant colonel. I guess you could say that I come from an upper-middle-class family, petit bourgeois more or less. My mother's and my father's families both had a certain amount of land. They weren't rich, but ours was a comfortable life-style.

You didn't go to La Asunción, by any chance?

No, fortunately that's not part of my résumé. When I was younger I went to religious schools, of course. But with so many older brothers . . . well, I was what you'd call a tomboy. I was always fighting to be included in their group, to be allowed to play with them. And that's when you might say my infantile feminism got nurtured. In retrospect, at least, it seems to me that my earliest discovery of difference, my first rebellion, was in response to the difference between the ways that the boys and girls were treated in my family.

I was a skinny little runt, and a girl to boot. My other sisters were older, so I was this tiny little female person among a bunch of brothers. It was in that context that I began hearing the phrase that would mark my growing years. Although we had a maid, my mother always cooked and ironed. She'd send me with the maid to the market. And I had to wash my own clothes, which was something my brothers didn't have to do; or I had to help with the ironing, and this was back when everything was starched.

So I'd ask my mother, why do I have to do all this when my brothers don't? I was nine or ten, maybe younger. And when I'd ask my mother why I, who was younger and smaller and weaker than the men, had to do all the men's work, she'd invariably answer with the phrase "Because you're a woman." Sometimes she'd say it in anger, sometimes with a great sadness, sometimes it was an order. It's something that's stayed with me, all my life. Little by little I understood that having been born female meant having to eat shit, in industrial quantities.

I never took this lying down. I was always rebelling. And instead of one father I had eight, because I had seven brothers. All of them hit me, all of them ordered me around, all of them flew into jealous rages when it came to decisions about my life. And what was worse, when I was fourteen or so they took away my skates, forced me off my bike, and locked me up. I didn't understand why this was happening, why I wasn't allowed to play in the street anymore, why they took my shorts and tennis shoes away and began dressing me in ribbons and ruffles and little hats. I was furious.

Growing up, I only heard about Sandinism in hushed tones; my father and oldest brother or my other brothers would make me leave the room because it was "men's talk." My oldest brother was an idol in our family, and at home he was a very loving person—with his tragic history and all. I'd be privy to snatches of conversation. And in the pages of *Novedades* I'd see pictures of the corpses of those they referred to as "the bad ones," who'd been killed by my brother and his friends. That was my introduction to the Sandinistas.

And, you know, my father was someone who felt guilty about what he was doing. He was a liberal, not in the U.S. sense of the term, but as the French understand liberalism: a freethinker. He'd really made a mistake when he joined the National Guard. My father was ashamed of the monstrosity the guard became. In the beginning he believed all that stuff about violence being necessary to put an end to the war, the usual; but later he saw things more clearly.

So my father sort of disgraced himself, in the eyes of other family members—uncles of mine who were also military men—and within the guard itself. This was never really talked about in our family, but I think it was the year I was born, the April 1954 crisis: there was some kind of conspiracy, a coup planned against Somoza; they were going to kill him or something like that.

The thing is, they were never able to prove anything against my father; but they basically kicked him out of the Guard.

So those were important moments in my early years. Otherwise, it was the typical life of a very controlled female child, all the usual rebellions at home. And then came the first incident signaling some sort of change. For me it was a very important change. When the guard massacred a group of Sandinistas on January 22, 1968, my oldest brother was wounded, the same brother who would later lose his life. Right there by Government House, on that corner, he received a gunshot wound.

The massacre had already been perpetrated. A couple of my brothers, a little older than I, had gone off to watch the Conservative demonstration. I think I must have been thirteen, more or less. And I remember something that would have a tremendous impact on me. Later I read something similar in a [Gabriel] García Márquez novel. One of those brothers of mine, watching the massacre where another of our brothers was wounded, took refuge in a tall building. He had to spend the night there, because they declared a state of siege, martial law, it was that type of a situation.

Actually, he was forced to stay there for two nights, and he says that he personally witnessed four hundred bodies being loaded onto trucks and taken to mass graves. He counted the bodies. Well, he came home and repeated this story, and everyone told him to shut up. Because in the next day's paper, I remember it well, an AP cable established the number of dead at thirty. But my brother insisted that he had counted the bodies being loaded onto the trucks and that there were hundreds of them. We never knew for sure how many people had been killed; but I got goose flesh. Years later I read a similar scene about a train on a banana plantation in one of García Márquez's novels.

So, in 1968, a tremendous discussion began in my family. Little girl that I was, I wasn't really included. But I have a sister living in the U.S., and she began to put pressure on the rest of the family to send me out of the country, to get me away from that atmosphere of terror. Finally my father agreed. So I went to continue my schooling in West Palm Beach, Florida. The idea was for me to finish high school and, if possible, go on to college—and, if possible, get married and never come back. And that move turned out to be important for me, because that was when women's liberation began to explode, blacks were organizing, demonstrations against the Vietnam War were beginning. West Palm Beach wasn't exactly New York or Chicago, but I watched a lot of what was happening on TV.

In the United States I discovered my first feminist readings, writings by U.S. feminists . . . and I can't remember the author's name right now, but I'll never forget the book that changed my life. It was called *Born Female*. The same phrase I'd heard over and over from my mother, only this author gave me the explanations my mother had been unable to provide. With my half-baked English and the use of a dictionary I went crazy; I didn't understand half of what that book was about, but what I did understand was enough.

I remember that when I put the book down I cried. I cried for all the lies I'd been told for so many years, and also because I finally knew it wasn't me who was crazy; I was okay. I'd always been made to feel like the weird one, the crazy one. From then on, it was Marx, Engels . . . because I saw that every other page or so there was a quote by this guy named Marx, and this other guy named Engels. With my poor English, going through the bibliography at the end of that first book, I began to find out who these men were who talked about these things. That was my introduction to Marxism.

That's why, when people ask me how I became a feminist, I always say, "The opposite of most everyone else." It was because I was a feminist that I became a Sandinista. That's not the way it's generally happened here. With a very eclectic reading list, and in a language not my own, I began devouring everything I could find. You probably remember that in those days that kind of reading material was literally prohibited in Nicaragua. There was no way in the world you were going to get your hands on anything like that. The list of censored books was as thick as the Bible.

So I returned from West Palm Beach with my incipient understanding of feminism and with this new awareness that I wasn't the crazy one. That's terribly important. Because if I hadn't learned that, early on, I'm sure that at the rate I was going the search itself would have destroyed me. Now I understood and was able to articulate my own rebellion within the family, within the roles it's possible for a woman to play.

And then there was my experience of racism in the United States. While I was studying there, the first blacks were integrating into the public schools, at least in Florida, and that was hard for me. I'm not saying there's no racism in Nicaragua: of course there is; it's part of the social fabric. But in comparison with the U.S., it's minimal. The culture shock and the shock of such violent racism were difficult. I'll never forget, one day I was getting undressed for gym class and a group of girls made a circle around me. Some white girls on the edge of the circle were saying things like, "We want to know if yours is like ours 'cause you're from Nicaragua." I remember the only thing I could think of was to ask if they thought mine was horizontal . . .

My sister defended me, and I managed to get by. But then I'd see how these same white girls treated the black girls at the school. No one ever sat by them; they made fun of them, taunted them, called them names. It made me feel terrible; the taunting felt like it was meant for me. And I had my own white friends by that time, but I began sitting next to the black girls at lunch. And then the white girls got on my case; they said I had no need to sit with them, because I was brown. They said brown was different from black.

So I began getting in trouble at school, over the treatment of the black students. One day I had a fight with one of the white girls. She hit me, I hit her back; it got to be a big deal. The school suspended me, my sister had to come and get me, that sort of thing; and I started wanting to leave West Palm Beach, a small community back then. I began telling my family, "I'm coming home." Well, that wasn't in my father's plans, nor in my mother's, nor in my sister's. But I toughed it out, and they finally had to let me go back.

Sofía returns to Nicaragua. I was sixteen, seventeen years old by then, an adolescent, and much more mature because I'd learned to live away from my mother's overprotective and rather authoritarian presence. And that's when I can pinpoint a third experience that contributed to my formation. Even though I'd finished high school in the States, I had to do another two years here. Because Nicaragua didn't recognize my Stateside diploma; they considered it deficient. I had to go to school two more years at night in order to earn my Nicaraguan high school degree.

Beyond that, I was obsessed with the idea of getting a job. So I began looking for something part-time; and it was extremely rare in Nicaragua back then for a young girl like myself, from my social class, to work part-time. It was a struggle getting my parents to agree to let me work. But I finally managed it. And since I earned my own money, I paid for those last two years of education. Finally it was time to start college.

I had a brother I was very close to; he's an architect now, and he lives in Panama. But back then both of us wanted to be artists, painters. We talked about studying something related to that, and we decided to study architecture. I decided I wanted to be an architect. It wasn't that easy to pass the university entrance exams back then. Say a hundred students applied, maybe fifty would get in. My favorite brother and I said, "What the hell, we'll see what happens." And we both took the exam. Well, I passed and he failed.

That caused a family crisis. Obviously, since my brother hadn't passed, he'd have to choose another career or go abroad to study; but my brother insisted that he was going to study architecture or nothing. And you can imagine the number of university careers my parents were paying for by then; all my brothers were studying. Since he insisted on architecture and he couldn't get in here, he'd have to go to Mexico or to Panama. But there wasn't enough money for that kind of an investment with both of us in school. One of us had to be sacrificed.

The discussions were endless. I argued that I should be allowed to study, since I'd been the one to pass the exam. But to make a long story short, my parents and my other brothers got together and decided to put it to a vote. The outcome was that my brother would study abroad and I wouldn't study at all. I cried. I kicked. I asked my father, who loved me, how he could do this to me. And I'll never forget his response—that same old phrase, "Because you're a woman."

My father said he knew that I was right, that I'd been the one to pass the exam. "But you're a girl," he said. "You'll find some fool to take care of you. Your brother will have to support a family." The typical role stuff. In the end, I was denied the opportunity of going to college, while my beautiful brother was sent away to study; he's an architect today.

So that's how my education was taken away from me. And I began to look around for something to do. I decided I wanted to be a painter; if I couldn't be an architect, I'd be a painter. I went to art school, and it was there that I began meeting people—students and professors—who were involved in the political struggle. I began hearing about the FSLN, that it was engaged in this or that; and the time came when I felt that I, too, wanted to become involved. I was angry with everyone from God on down. I knew I'd been fucked over because I was a woman. And I could see that rebelling at home had gotten me nowhere. The whole system was at fault. I was eager to destroy the system, beginning with my own family.

I began to see the revolution as a way to dislodge the whole bloody mess. I was clear about individual rebellion being absurd; I knew we had to toss out the whole business. And so I set out to do just that, with the milk of Marxism barely wetting my lips and with my incipient notions of feminism. This brought on my first real crisis. I stopped painting. I said, "Fuck it, I don't want to paint the world. I want to change the world. Painting's not going to do it for me." I was looking for my weapon, an appropriate weapon for a weakling like myself. Maybe words could be my weapon. So I made a hundred and eighty degree turn and decided I wanted to go to the university, to study journalism.

As a woman, it seemed to me that the only real weapon I had was my mouth, my writing hand. I couldn't picture myself as the great guerrilla fighter. But it wasn't just my own sense of myself as a weakling . . . My surname also became a terrible barrier. Who was going to trust a Montenegro? Having the surname I had made everything that much more difficult. These were some of the reasons I couldn't visualize myself as a member of the FSLN, all organized and tidy like that. I saw myself more as a sniper, a sharpshooter, out there alone against the world.

That was my feeling about things when I started university. We're talking 1976, '77, and you'll remember the FSLN was in the middle of a period of great turmoil then: divisions, infighting, the whole mess. It was a philosophy professor, Carlos Cuadra, who first realized that I was serious about participating. That's when I started studying Marxism for real. And I was an A-student. On the one hand, I didn't understand the FSLN's tendencies that well; and on the other, the Sandinistas as a whole weren't that keen to have me around. People heard the name "Montenegro" and they backed off fast. Everyone knew who my father and brother were.

None of the different groups of Sandinistas wanted me, but Carlos was convinced I was serious. So he finally recruited me into MAP.[1] In the process I became a Maoist, a total ultraleftist, one of those deadly-serious rebels. By that time I had also met the man I would later marry, a German much older than myself. I kept on studying at the same time as I was participating full-time in the struggle.

Through my militancy in MAP, I got to know something about the political situation. I was educating myself, one way or another, and I understood the proposals of feminism a little better. I was reading. I had friends who would sneak me books. Because if there are comrades today who consider feminism suspect, back then it was infinitely worse. Every time I'd start talking about women, quoting Engels to back me up, I'd get it from all quarters: "Those are petit-bourgeois notions. The masses come first," the old line. [It was] my first

1. MAP is the Movimiento de Acción Popular (Popular Action Movement), a small ultra-Left group of Maoist orientation, made up mostly of university students.

experience with that whole miserable line the dogmatic, orthodox Left is so good at pushing.

The line was that we had to topple the system, the dictatorship and, once that was taken care of, there'd be time for all the rest. From my experience within my own family, I understood that everyone was obsessed with the problem of the dictatorship. If you talked about feminism, people looked at you as if you were from Mars. So I decided just to keep studying on my own. If I found someone who seemed receptive, I'd haul out my feminist ideas.

Although Carlos Cuadra was a member of MAP, his wife was a Sandinista. She was with the Proletarian tendency, the faction closest to MAP. I still don't understand how those two managed to live together, with their political differences—and they're still together! Nineteen seventy-eight came around, and they killed Pedro Joaquín [Chamorro]. We considered the Sandinistas adventurers, militarists; we wouldn't even speak to the Terceristas.

About then I began writing for a little newspaper published by MAP and the FO.[2] It was called *Nueva Opinión Cultural* [New Cultural Opinion]. I had the MAP line down pat. We believed that we had to organize the workers in the cities, that the mandate was to organize the urban proletariat. The Terceristas inspired the least confidence of all; we saw them as total militarists, completely crazy.

Before the 1978 insurrection, I remember some of us asking Cuadra and other older militants what we were going to do. The Sandinistas were calling everyone to arms. Were we going to join or not? And I'll never forget their answer: they said they'd given it a lot of thought and had come to the conclusion that this was total madness; it was going to be a massacre. But they also told us they couldn't prevent our going off to fight if we wanted to. And I remember saying, "You guys are as irresponsible as they come! You've never even trained us to fight. Besides, this isn't some kind of picnic: if you want to go, you're welcome and if you don't, well, that's all right too. We're not talking about a party here."

So it was a pretty confusing time. I was working as a translator for some foreign journalists by then, and I figured I could find out something about what was going on in the country through them. And that's how I ended up observing the 1978 insurrection, through the eyes of those journalists. I saw the massacres perpetrated by the National Guard, but I also saw the people's courage. That's when I said to myself, "The Sandinistas are right. There's nothing left to do here but to blow this government sky high."

That's when I decided I was wasting my time with such a timid, wishy-washy group as MAP. After the 1978 insurrection, I quit and a whole bunch of comrades quit with me: of course, they called us "petit-bourgeois deviants." Later we realized that in fact they *had* trained some of their people, but only those of pure proletarian stock. They were just using the rest of us, taking advantage of what we were able to offer, and that made me angry. Because, I

2. FO is the Frente Obrero (Workers' Front), a small ultra-Left organization.

said, "If I was willing to risk myself, why did I have to be a genuine, bona fide worker for them to give me military training?"

I crossed right over to the Sandinistas. Or, rather, the Proletarian tendency of the FSLN began a recruitment policy with those of us who had given up on MAP. One day, one of their emissaries visited me, Chico Meza. He asked if I was interested in collaborating and later joining the FSLN. I said yes right away, and that's when my history with the Front began.

But they never really trusted me completely. I remained a collaborator for a while. Even though I had proved myself in a dozen different ways, I guess there was always the feeling that I might be infiltrating the organization, because of my father and brother. I remained a collaborator. I had a safehouse; I was a driver for Luis Carrión and Carlos Núñez, for lots of them. I was a messenger, I moved people from one part of the country to another, or to Costa Rica, and they used me to leak information to the foreign press.

To make a long story short, that's the kind of work I was doing when 1979 came around. At the time, I had a job selling insurance for a company called American & British; they insured boats. My clientele was pretty exclusive, and since I spoke English I was earning a very good salary. It was really a terrific salary for those days; here they had this attractive young woman who spoke good English, and my clientele was made up of some fifty or so men who owned boats and planes here in Nicaragua, among them Somoza.

So that was a source of important information: what kind of planes and helicopters there were, who flew them, and so forth. And I'd report to the FSLN—until they asked me to leave my job. They needed me to work for the Party full-time, as well as serving as a legal cover. So I was never underground; I was legal to the end of the war. Owing to my last name I had considerable freedom of movement, I was able to come and go, get information, make contacts.

And the funny thing—tragicomic, when you think of it—was that we were all very compartmentalized. Everyone used a pseudonym, everyone belonged to his or her own little cell. But in 1979 I lost contact with my cell. And the problem was, no one but those five people knew that I was a member of the FSLN. Yes, I'd finally become a member by then, but only those five knew. So it was rough. When we won, people began looking at me again as so-and-so's daughter or so-and-so's sister.

On July 18th they captured my brother. Victory found me with my heart in pieces. And my brother's story is pretty horrible. His wife and two kids were here. I tried to convince my sister-in-law to leave the country, because it so happened that I'd heard Somoza's last conversation with my brother; I'd heard it by scanner, on the radio. Somoza fled on the 17th, on the 18th my brother was arrested, and the FSLN entered Managua on the 19th.

On the 17th I went looking for my sister-in-law, to tell her that Somoza had split. I'll never forget the scene, because when I got to their house I found them armed to the teeth: that woman with her eleven-year-old daughter and nine-year-old son, just waiting to be captured. And I asked them what they thought they were doing. "We're waiting to die," was what they said. "We're waiting for them to come and kill us." I'll always have that image: the girl with her rifle, the little boy with his pistol, and their mother.

I got down on my knees. I pleaded with them. I tried to convince them that at this point my brother either had left the country or was dead. But his wife wanted to go out looking for him. He'd been stationed on the southern front. After some pleading, I was finally able to convince my sister-in-law to at least take her children to the airport; she could always return later and look for her husband. It was a mess anyway, because what ended up happening was that in the confusion the boy was put on a plane that was headed for a refugee camp in El Salvador, and the girl boarded another that took her to Guatemala. And when their mother tried to leave the airport, an officer recognized her and said, "Where do you think you're going?" He forced her onto yet a third plane, and she ended up in Miami. They were completely separated.

By the 18th I was in León. That's where Dora María found me. She said, "We have your brother"; and that's when victory turned bitter for me. I asked myself, "Jesus, why didn't he escape? Or why didn't they just kill him?" The other major figure in this whole story is my mother, because my father had died the year before. And, as he lay dying, the last thing he had begged my brother to do was to leave the National Guard. He said Somoza was going to be defeated, and he begged him not to defend the regime, not to end up making the same mistake he had.

But my brother refused, which in Nicaragua was a pretty dramatic thing to do, to deny your father his dying wish. On top of that, my brother already knew that some of his siblings—myself and some of the others—had joined the Front, that we were on the other side. And we, too, had tried to get him to desert or to leave. In fact, we were actually talking politics as my father lay dying in the next room. But it was in that discussion that I lost all hope, because there's this one statement of my brother's I'll always remember. He said, "Look, kids, in this room we're brothers and sisters. But if we come upon each other in the street and you have a gun and so do I, you'd better shoot. Because you can be sure I will." That was it; I knew there was no hope. He was going to die as he had lived: a proud member of the National Guard.

So we'd tried to prepare my mother for the possibility of her children dying, on one side or the other. We'd tried to make her see that death was logical in the situation in which we lived; in the midst of all that fighting it would have been illogical to imagine we'd all escape without being hurt. But the problem with my brother's death is that he wasn't killed in battle: they shot him in October 1979. I don't know if you've read Christopher Dickey's book;[3] he tells the story of my brother's death. And it's something that's tormented me all these years. It continues to torment me.

In that last telephone conversation I overheard between Somoza and my brother, my brother was begging for reinforcements. He was saying, ". . . in order to take that hill." He was referring to a hill controlled by the Sandinistas;

3. Christopher Dickey, *With the Contras: A Reporter in the Wilds of Nicaragua* (New York: Simon & Schuster, 1985).

it had been taken by Edén Pastora. And he was asking for experienced troops, troops that knew how to fight because, he said, his men were nothing more than boys, without adequate training. My brother wanted the dictator to send him helicopters, munitions, and experienced combat troops. Somoza assured him that he would: "Just hang in there," he said. And the son of a bitch fled the country the very next day.

So my brother had no alternative but to retreat, with some three hundred guards, and he made his way back to San Juan del Sur. They prepared two boats. He stayed behind with thirty men, covering the retreat of the bulk of his force, which took off in one of the boats. The guys who managed to get away reached the Gulf of Fonseca; they made it to El Salvador, and they were the beginning of what was to become the Contra army. My brother and the thirty guards he had with him boarded the other boat, but they didn't have enough gasoline. And when they ran out of gas, the tide pushed them back onto the beach. There was a Sandinista column on shore, so their only option was to fight from that boat that was out of gas or to surrender. That's when they were captured and taken to León.

So that's where I found my brother. He was being held in a school there in León. And that's where the whole family drama began to unfold. The first meeting between my brother and me was terribly painful, and also very dignified. I was particularly impressed with his dignity in defeat. He said something like, "We lost. I'm a career officer and I know that we lost. You won a clean victory, and I'm ready to deal with that. All I ask is that I be judged by military law and that you respect my rank." He asked me to get him a good lawyer, and he didn't want my mother to see him in the state he was in. And, of course, he asked me to do what I could for his wife and kids.

But it was impossible for us to restrain my mother. And that was the beginning of a veritable calvary, a drama that ended only on the day they killed him: October 6, 1979. He never went to trial; they just shot him. A lot of people say they executed him. My very personal opinion is that he provoked his own death: a kind of suicide. My brother was extremely intelligent, and very proud. They moved him from prison to prison. He was one of those war machines, trained by the U.S.: an expert in counterinsurgency, black belt in karate, parachutist, mountain climber, a crack shot. He was thirty-eight when he died, and he and I looked alike: the same dark complexion, slender bodies; he had a body of steel.

He'd asked for a trial befitting an officer, but he was also worried about what it would do to my mother. He was probably trying to figure out how to escape; I know for sure he wasn't the type who would have accepted prison lying down. I went to see him on several occasions, but that was a tug-of-war, too, because my mother begged me—thousands of times, she'd get down on her knees and beg me—to intercede on his behalf. I had to tell her I couldn't. If I'd interceded for him I would have had to intercede for all the National Guard. I couldn't do that; it wasn't ethical.

By that time the evidence against him was mounting. People actually came to me and said, in so many words, "Your brother tortured me." And there was the matter of Estelí. We had newsreel film, taken by Somoza's own television cameramen, showing my brother mounted on a tank leading the attack on Estelí—where they blew up the houses with all the people inside. And my family is from Estelí. There was no way that city was going to forgive one of its own sons heaping that kind of destruction upon it! I didn't see how my brother was going to get off with less than thirty years.

But my mother, in her limbo, didn't read the papers; she didn't watch television except for the soaps. And I guess I tried to protect my mother. It was a Jekyll and Hyde situation. There was my wonderful brother, who loved his little sister, and whom I loved, deeply; and then there was my brother who had tortured people, who had fired on a defenseless city. For me it was pure agony, but for my mother it was worse. In a situation like that, what's a mother to do? I can understand why she tried to get me to intercede. But I couldn't. I told her that we'd each chosen our positions consciously. He fought and killed for what he believed, just like I did. I told her that he had no problem with the outcome, that he'd accepted it. She was the one with the problem.

But it really was a problem for me. Because I had to get a safe conduct pass every time I went to see him. People were up in arms, ready to take revenge on anyone who they thought shared some responsibility for all the terror and death. Who can blame them? The Sandinistas, when they found out my brother was in prison, well, they thought I might be an informer, infiltrated into their ranks. The Guard, or Somoza people, they saw me as a traitor to my family. Those first six months after the victory I slept somewhere different every night. I never knew who might be waiting to pull the trigger. A no-win situation. Both sides were tearing me apart. I was always afraid, and it was also very painful because, after all, this was my revolution. But lots of people weren't so clear about that.

When they killed my brother, I fell apart. By late July things with the Sandinistas were beginning to right themselves in my life. One of the comrades, Leonél Espinoza, remembered; because of my surname, he knew I was getting it from all sides. And he asked me, "Hey, you were a journalism student, weren't you? Do you still want to be a journalist?" I told him yes, it was what I most wanted to do, but that I'd be satisfied with literacy work, whatever. Then he said, "Come on. We're going to start a newspaper."

The craziness having to do with my brother being in prison was intensifying, but on July 25th I showed up at *Barricada*. And I went to work there: as a secretary, as a gofer, whatever they needed. *Barricada* had risen from the ashes of *Novedades*, the dictator's paper. I'd had two years of journalism by then, and I hoped at some point I'd be able to continue studying. Not everyone on the new paper trusted me, but Leonél's word and Carlos Fernando Chamorro's saved me. There was a group of Terceristas, but most of us were Proles. And then October came along.

My husband had gone off to Germany. I'd stayed behind, alone. My brother was in prison. My situation was still painfully ambiguous, with respect to people really trusting me. And then they went and killed him. The story goes more or less like this. They were transferring two prisoners in a truck, from

León to Managua: my brother and another well-known torturer named Chele
Aguilera. The prisoners were riding in the back. Their hands were tied, but not
their feet. Somewhere along the way, the story goes, my brother struggled to
his feet and kicked one of the soldiers who was guarding them. Then he and
Aguilera threw themselves from the vehicle and started running. The guys in
front jumped out and gunned them down; then they finished him off with a
bullet to the head.

I was at the paper when I got the news, and my first thought was for my
mother. I rushed down to identify the body; it was him all right. There were the
wounds from the spray of machine-gun fire, and the single shot at the base of
his skull. But one of my worst moments came as I was approaching El Chipote,
the military camp where they had the body. Coming along the street from the
direction of the Intercontinental Hotel was a group of women in black, a procession of some two hundred women, all in mourning. At first I couldn't make
out what they were shouting. It wasn't until they were almost upon me that I
realized these were the mothers of the two hundred young kids Chele Aguilera
had murdered there in León. They were screaming for Aguilera's body so they
could tie it to a team of horses and drag it through the streets of their city. At
any moment I imagined a similar group of mothers was going to appear, shouting for my brother's body so they could drag it through the streets of Estelí. I
was in a complete frenzy when I finally got hold of my brother, cleaned him,
washed him, combed his hair, wrapped him as best I could, and brought him
home to my mother.

The whole thing was horrific. Because, on top of all this, something else had
happened just days before. One of my superiors in the FSLN had been Chico
Meza, the comrade who'd recruited me, and he'd been killed a few days before
the war ended. They'd buried him on a street corner, right where he fell. The
Front decided that the comrades who'd last seen him alive should be the ones to
dig him up and give him a decent burial. In fact, he'd left my house when he
went off to die; so I was the one.

I'd never experienced anything like that before. There was a small group of
us. I remember Julio López, and I don't know who else. Well, we dug him up,
put what was left of him in a bag, and prepared the funeral. And it was a hero's
funeral. Thousands of people came; there were chants and songs, the works.
Chico Meza had been like a brother to me, a brother in arms. So I buried him,
and a week later it was my job to prepare this other funeral, for my blood
brother, the antihero.

My mother, who'd suffered the beginnings of a heart attack when she got the
news, wanted to wait until my siblings from the United States could get here,
until my brother's wife could come: the whole family. But everyone was
stunned. I was the only one of us able to function, really. My mother's doctor
recommended that we bury my brother as quickly as possible, in consideration
of my mother's precarious health. So I simply took the bull by the horns and
arranged the burial. Needless to say, almost no one came, a dozen at most.

What I remember most about that funeral procession is how people closed
the doors of their houses as we rode past with the casket. Door after door

slammed shut—and windows. Almost no one was out in the streets. It's an image I still carry with me. And when we got to the cemetery it began to rain, hard. A few feet from where we'd buried Chico Meza just days before, we buried my brother. It was like something out of a Dracula film.

When we got back to my mother's house, she drew herself up as only she can, and said, "Well, I just buried my son. Now I'm going to bury my daughter. Get out of my house, murderer!" I don't know if you can imagine how I felt. That was the beginning of a very long and very problematic history with my mother.

Have you been able to make peace?

Not until I tried to commit suicide in 1984. I broke down completely. I was anorexic, hallucinating . . .

Sofía seemed to want to think for a few moments about the nature of her breakdown, to respond with some analysis as well as an attempt to re-create the painful feelings of that time. For a while her voice became quieter, more introspective . . .

It was as if I had lost everything, as if I had risked too much as a woman who is conscious of her womanness and also of her revolutionary commitment. I had put my whole soul into that struggle. Quite simply, I fell apart. It happened during the electoral process of 1984.

I felt incredibly alone, and I don't think that sense of isolation is something I've ever lost. Not completely. Maybe I'll never lose it. I've always felt set apart from other people, painfully conscious of this double burden of being a woman and a Montenegro. Still, I think of myself as someone with a great deal of determination—stubborn, if you will, and persevering. Take the newspaper, for example: I started there as some kind of gofer, and in six months I was in charge of the international page. My French was better than it is now, I spoke English, and I worked hard. But I had so much to overcome.

In the beginning I remember going out with more seasoned reporters, to get my first stories. On two separate occasions when I'd flash my I.D., someone would ask, "Wait a minute, aren't you the torturer's sister?" Once someone even spit in my face. Carlos Fernando, with great tact, suggested that I simply wait it out; that I do menial jobs around the paper until people's emotions calmed down and they could be more rational about me, could learn to trust me for who I am. He understood how vulnerable I was. And he understood that I'd been through quite enough already, without having to expose myself to more.

I think I mentioned that by this time I'd separated from the German. And that was another painful process. At first we'd agreed that he should remain outside the country, in case they captured me or in case the Sandinistas didn't win; he could always do more on the outside. But he couldn't stop worrying that I would be killed. And it got to the point where one day he simply said, "Okay, you've played at revolution long enough. There's no reason why you have to stay in Nicaragua. You've got the double jeopardy of being a woman and a Montenegro. You've done enough for your country. You've helped defeat the dictatorship; now let others build the new society." And, of course, I refused to leave. It got to the point where he said, "The revolution or me." The choice was clear. I told him, "Well, I guess there are always other men. But other revolutions, who knows?" And that was the end of our relationship.

What I'm saying is that at a certain point I felt I'd lost everything: my home, my father, my mother, my brother, my sense of family, my husband, absolutely everything. All that was left was this somewhat abstract and violent something called "revolution." The emotional investment had been enormous. I was conscious of my disadvantage as a woman, utterly conscious of that; and I accepted the burden, but I also never stopped struggling at the newspaper to put my ideas out there, to try to change the relations of power. I think the power relations are different now, but it's been a long haul.

Along the way, there were always those who helped. At the very beginning there was an Argentine, a guy named Nacho González. He was the one who convinced me I could write; he gave me confidence in myself. And Carlos Fernando, as I've said. Two men. It's interesting, but I can't think of a woman on the job who influenced me as much as they did. Carlos Fernando's family situation was similar to my own, of course. There were differences, too. Because I was a nobody, a female nobody, with a torturer for a brother; and Carlos Fernando was the son of Doña Violeta and Pedro Joaquín Chamorro, the great Conservative politician and newspaperman. Yet we both came to the revolution with that family burden, no working-class credentials, nothing more than our own personal conviction that you do what you have to do, you do what's right, no matter who gets in your way—even if its you yourself who ends up getting in your way.

But I was telling you about 1984. There was that terrible massacre at Pantasma, and I'd gone to the affected area. I was like a little lead soldier up there, working round the clock—and with all the pain and pressures I've already mentioned. They brought me back from Pantasma like someone just out of Auschwitz, a human skeleton. I was seeing a psychotherapist, and I had a prescription for three or four months' rest. But then there was the matter of that first electoral process the FSLN had to face. So two weeks after my breakdown, I was once again working every day from 8:00 in the morning until midnight.

The Party decided that Carlos Fernando should head the newly reconstituted Department of Analysis and Propaganda [DAP], besides running the paper. DAP was charged with planning the electoral campaign. He had a group of comrades working with him, and he wanted me on board to take charge of public relations outside the country.

I was already having problems with the Party. I resisted its dogmatic, orthodox, parochial vision of things. And when I came down from the mountains, they suspended my membership. They said I'd been stuck up, arrogant, and that I asked too many questions. Get the picture? I mean, I wasn't being punished for being a coward, I wasn't being accused of running from combat or anything like that. No. They said I was "too liberal." And here I was, having a breakdown.

In fact, it was another woman who suggested that maybe I wasn't ready to reassume the responsibilities of being a Party member. But at the same time, Carlos Fernando had given me the job of designing the FSLN's propaganda outside the country. I had to work with a group of comrades, and of course they were all people who had joined the Front much later than me. I was furious at the injustice, and it was also difficult to maintain my authority with those working beneath me. I became very rigid, very hard on anyone who didn't do his or her job. And then it was two more women who wanted to subject me to a sort of trial, an internal Party process. I ended up rejecting the Party altogether. It was during this time that I tried to commit suicide.

But as I say, I was also seeing a psychologist. And she helped me a great deal, she helped me put my emotions in some kind of order, to organize and understand my drama: the mother who had rejected me, my father, my brother, the Party. Consistent rejection was my particular cross, and I never bore it very well. The psychologist helped me see that instead of turning my righteous anger against all those little people who were making my life miserable, I was turning it inward, committing a sort of hara-kiri.

Once again, I was doing my job impeccably, but I had what they called a "bad attitude." Eventually they fired me. I didn't have a job, I didn't have the Party. For a while I was abandoned once again, without anything to do. But then I ended up going back to *Barricada*. The idea was, they'd let me work but I was being "punished" at the same time. That is, I was supposed to do all the shit work that none of the other journalists wanted; and, of course, I was forbidden to hold a position of any importance. Bayardo Arce's idea was that I humbly work my way back up again, from the very bottom.

I should say that although Carlos Fernando formally accepted this situation, he did what he could to make things bearable for me. I started working again, doing the stories no one else wanted. And what happened? I got hold of one of those stories no one else wanted—the Miskitos and the autonomy proposal on the Coast—and I threw myself into it body and soul. The series I wrote won the Cuban journalism prize in essay that year!

My problems didn't end with that prize, though. A number of the newspaper's best people were having problems in '86 and '87. Several of us had questioned Daniel Ortega's abuses of power: Xavier, Marcio, Arqueles Morales, me with my prize in hand. At one point they threw us all out. And Carlos Fernando was trying to juggle both the paper and DAP. The paper went into the biggest crisis of its life.

Once again Carlos Fernando came to see me about returning to *Barricada*, to help him fix the mess. This time I said I wasn't coming back, and that's when Carlos offered me the editorial page. The directorate had its own candidate, of course, but Carlos negotiated his preference, promising to "control" me as well as limiting me to a kind of trial run, to "see what I could do." That was another war of internal politics, where one group of comrades urged me to take the post: "If you don't, they'll put a Stalinist in there for sure," they said. And, of course, there were many who were against my getting the page.

But I accepted. I rebuilt the page. Another storm had passed, and I remained at the head of *Barricada*'s editorial page until 1989. In 1989 we were all more-or-less clear that the FSLN needed a profound process of democratization, and that we had the obligation in the pages of its paper to open up a discussion capable of facilitating such a process.

I was also clear about something else. The Sandinistas always talked about political-ideological work, but I was coming to the conclusion that we were doing a great deal of political and almost no ideological work. There was no discussion at all about that which is considered "private": daily life, people's values, the home sphere (which, of course, is also "women's domain").

And so, I sold the idea to Carlos Fernando, which he in turn sold to the directorate, of starting a supplement aimed at young people and at women. That was how *Gente* was born. And we opened up this space which has gradually become so widely read and so influential throughout the country. But by this time we'd lost the 1990 elections.

In Nicaragua, for Sandinistas and opposition alike, the 1990 election marked a dramatic before-and-after. For the Sandinistas the electoral loss was unexpected, inconceivable, and for many it brought with it a profound self-questioning that might well be defined as a collective crisis of identity. Despite all its errors, the FSLN had nonetheless installed the country's first government ever to put people's needs before dynastic greed. I wanted Sofía to think for a moment about the time leading up to the election, the loss itself, and the ways in which those events effected her life:

I'll be honest. For me it was an absolute given that the Front would win. What I wasn't so sure about was that it would win by a very wide margin. In fact, I remember someone from the *New York Times* interviewing me just before the election. I told him, "I want the FSLN to win, but I want it to win fifty-one to forty-nine, something like that." Because I thought that if the Front won by a good number of votes, this revolution would go to the dogs; all the shit would just keep piling up. I wanted us to win, but by a very slim margin, so that a more critical vision might stand a chance.

I was surprised, of course, like everyone else. And I was terrified that civil war would break out, a general civil war. My personal plans were that once the FSLN had won, I'd leave *Barricada*. I'd been offered a scholarship to study for a year in England. And I thought: "A few more months and I will have trained a good group of people. I'll be able to leave the supplement in good shape, and then I can take off." In October 1990 I planned to be on my way. It was time for me to do other things. I wanted to devote myself full-time to the women's movement.

But, of course, defeat changed all that. When the Sandinistas woke up that morning—stunned, paralyzed, in an absolute stupor—the newspaper was almost the only entity capable of responding. Those were the hardest editions we've ever had to publish. We produced them with tears in our eyes. But it was important that we say something that made sense, that we get something out there that would help people understand what had happened. And I believe that need to respond politically helped delay my own emotional collapse.

In some sense your personal life has gotten a bit lost in this story so far. I mean, your feelings about the political-ideological process as it connects with your life is clear enough. But what was happening for you in terms of relationships, or the option to live alone? How did you address the need for personal sharing and companionship? After the German left, what happened?

After the German, there was your regular "Stalinist." I loved him, and I'm sure he loved me; but he ended up rejecting me like everyone else. I'll always remember that phrase of his: "Love is a political weakness." It was terrible. After that relationship, Carlos Fernando and I were together for quite a while, but it was a difficult relationship. He's in better shape today, but back then he was pretty ambivalent about his family, and ambivalent with me. And ambivalence was the last thing I needed. Carlos Fernando and I have remained good friends, and colleagues, because there's a bedrock of respect there.

After my suicide attempt in 1984, I lived with a North American. He's a good person, and it was a very healing relationship; I'll always be grateful to him. We were both journalists, and we had all sorts of plans, all sorts of things we wanted to do together. For two years it was wonderful; I almost married him. But it was interesting: he'd rescued me when I was in pieces, but once I was able to put the pieces back together—as I became Sofía Montenegro again—he did a complete about-face. As I regained control of my life, he became possessive, jealous, sexist, insecure. The more sure of myself I became, the more insecure he was!

And so I had to get out of that relationship. It got crazy, really terrible. And it's interesting, because I've always felt that men are basically emotional vampires; they can latch onto you and suck you dry, suck the life right out of you. After my experience with this man, I decided to do one of two things: either I'd find myself a woman lover—maybe I'd have better luck with women than with men—or I'd live alone, with maybe an occasional affair. I even got myself a little dog. I said to myself: "This puppy is capable of loving me without complications. No problems; just pure, uncomplicated love."

And that's when this guy appeared, the man I've been living with now . . . we've been together for the past four years. His name is Alejandro. He's Nicaraguan, a Sandinista, and to tell you the truth I'd given up hope that men like him existed here. We're the same age; he's divorced, and he's got his own scars, his own history. A sweet macho, the guy—and open to change. He likes it that I'm a feminist, and he likes my feminist friends. Alejandro says his wife was a very traditional woman and that it was horrible living with someone so divorced from herself, so alienated. He says that we feminists are more in touch with ourselves, with what we want out of life, with what we want to do. I feel that at last I can have a relationship with someone capable of giving me some space. It'll last as long as it's good.

Sofía, when you said that if the FSLN had won the 1990 elections your plans were to involve yourself full-time with the feminist movement, what place did you visualize for yourself in that movement? What did you plan to do? Were you thinking about writing?

I wanted to learn enough to be able to work with theory. Because, you know, I'm still a self-taught professional. Everything I've learned about feminism I've taught myself. From the age of fifteen, I've read anything and everything I've been able to get my hands on. And I feel that it's time to achieve some sort of synthesis. My life, my discoveries, have been interesting, but I want to be able to formulate something beyond pure testimony. I feel like I need some sort of methodology with which I can theorize about what I've experienced and move to a higher level of consciousness.

As an intellectual, I think my role is to try to achieve a synthesis with which we can renovate our practice. We need to find a way out of the dead end the Left has brought us to, the dead end of the revolution, even feminism's dead end. Here in Nicaragua we've come up against all these brick walls. But I believe that, precisely because I've lived this revolution as a woman, with my particular disadvantages—and I've stayed in the fray, I haven't turned my back on it and I'm not going to turn my back on it—precisely because of all this, I've got some ideas about how we might break through the dichotomies, how we might search for a more integral, a more holistic, vision. We need to find an alternative proposal for changing society.

So those were my plans. I wanted to be able to invest the necessary time in myself so that I could look for new ways, go back over all we've experienced and work with other women toward some kind of useful synthesis. It may not be the finished product; but it might be a first, important synthesis of what we've done here. I'm not ashamed of any of it.

As a matter of fact, we're in the process of getting a collective of women together. We're calling it La Malinche Feminist Collective. We conceive of it as a small think tank of women who are continuing to struggle, because we're not really interested in the women who have given up. We want to talk and struggle and work with women who are in this thing for the long haul; women who have something to give, who are willing and able to build an organized feminist force; women who want to articulate a proposal for a utopia that is viable, workable—a proposal led by women, but one that men can use as well.

I know how ambitious this is. But there's a group of us already involved: both of the Blandón women, Gioconda Belli, Olguita [Espinoza], myself. And there's a Mexican woman name Lilliam Levi; she makes six. We're talking to a woman in Australia. Well, we're still in the planning stages. Most of us have been struggling for a while, in the countryside, in the cities. No one can accuse us of not having been actively involved. We've been in the political parties, we've been activists, we've picketed, what have you. But I think that at this stage of struggle there are already plenty of women petitioning the government or fighting with the Party. There's got to be a small group of us women who can devote ourselves simply to analysis.

Here in Nicaragua, at least insofar as Sandinism is concerned, the thinking was always done by the men. There were nine male leaders who took it upon themselves to do the thinking for the rest of us. It's time we women learn how to think for ourselves. Of course, there are a number of agencies already, where women head important think tanks. But we need to create a space where we can discuss these particular issues, politically, seriously, where we can develop our own research, toss around our ideas.

I'm wondering whether, within the FSLN itself, there's been any real analysis of the fact that the model used was one that set nine men at the top of a pyramid?

Yes, there has been some discussion and analysis of that. But we're still waiting for the truly critical process; what's happened so far has been pretty superficial. I for one haven't been satisfied with the level of discussion inside the Party. The most interesting discussions have raged outside Party structures, among particular individuals, around specific issues. And you know, Margaret, it isn't a problem of Party members not being willing, even eager, to talk. A tremendous breakthrough is necessary in order to move past the old model. We need a whole shift in consciousness, and among the Sandinistas there are some who are more capable of that than others.

I think there have been three basic responses to the defeat. There are those I call the "dinosaurs," who say, "We've got to go back to that golden age when we were all just pure guerrilla fighters, 'the boys.'" That's not even possible. Then there's the other extreme: those who say, "The revolution is finished. There's nothing to be done. It was all for nothing, and I've been had." They're trying to salvage what they can of their lives, each man out for himself and the hell with everyone else. But the bulk of the population is somewhere in the middle. These are the ones who are really trying to figure out what went wrong, and what to do about it. And I think this group is the healthiest, because we're still looking to the future. We have a healthier vision, more realistic. One thing I'm absolutely sure about, though, is that the old leadership is exhausted, in every way.

Sofía, when you talk about democratization and feminism, do you see a relationship between the two?

Of course I do. The essence of feminism is its democratizing character; feminism promotes a general as well as a radical democratization. So if the spirit of feminism were to be assumed by as broad a revolutionary movement as Sandinism is, it would be totally extraordinary. That's why I won't isolate myself from the FSLN. I mean, in spite of the fact that I'm no longer a member in the formal sense, that was their choice, not mine. And as far as I'm concerned, the exact right time to put forth an alternative is now—during the present crisis. We need to be saying, "Look at this shit, the Left's model didn't work. The only ideology that remains standing in today's world is feminism."

Because, you know, feminists have been critical of socialism as we've known it, and of the Left, for thirty years or more. And the socialists and the Left never paid any attention to our criticisms. Now that so much has crumbled, it seems to me that the feminist proposition must be seen as much more coherent. It's also more coherent in and of itself than it's ever been. And it's got a greater potential, enormous possibilities for emerging because— among other reasons—there's nothing else.

Wherever I go I talk about this. And at the grass roots, among the rank-and-file Sandinista women and men, even at some of the intermediate levels, there's a lot more openness than there once was. People have been humbled by defeat. That's why we organized that big meeting of women in January, in order to show people that there are many more of us than they imagine; something's going on that many people don't even suspect.

I want to hear about that meeting. But first, tell me about PIE. [The acronym means "foot" in Spanish.] What's that about?

PIE really began as a joke. Sometimes even we women don't take what we say or do that seriously. By around 1987, we were acutely aware of the fact that we hardly counted—I mean, in the sense that women with real power were such a tiny minority inside the Party. We knew we could shut up or we could become involved in a tremendous confrontation: those were the two obvious options. But we developed a third, a way of putting some of these issues on the agenda without actually breaking with the revolution. We knew that we needed more of a lobbying strategy—a lobbying technique if you will—because if we opted for confrontation, we were sure to lose.

We began to talk among ourselves. Yvonne Siu was part of this group, along with Malena de Montis, Gioconda Belli, Ileana Rodríguez, Olguita Espinoza, María Lourdes Bolaños, Ana Criquillón, Vilma Castillo, Milú Vargas, Alba Palacios, and myself. It began with telephone calls whenever something would happen, and we began to coordinate some action from wherever each of us happened to be. We'd touch on a particular theme. I'd write an article for *Barricada*, maybe Gioconda would talk to Henry Ruíz, Milú might introduce an idea over at the National Assembly. It was all very loose.

That was the sort of thing we were doing when we heard about the feminist gathering in Taxco, Mexico. Forty-four of us attended from Nicaragua; all of the members of PIE went. AMNLAE had its delegation, Benigna Mendiola and others.[4] And then there was this group of "crazy women"—ourselves— who traveled separately, because we knew AMNLAE wasn't going to take us with them. And when we saw the faces of all those women, women from all

---

4. Benigna Mendiola is a longtime peasant leader whose husband was murdered in one of Somoza's terrorist strikes against rural-based revolutionaries. During the Sandinista administration she continued to organize in Nicaragua's countryside, and she has been particularly active within AMNLAE.

over Latin America, and women from Central America there in force, we virtually started to hallucinate!

That Mexican meeting was important. On the way home we talked a great deal among ourselves. I remember that the main divisions at the meeting were between the more intellectual feminists from Mexico, and from other countries where there's an older feminist tradition, and the political women like ourselves who were involved on the Left or who somehow were doubly militant: as feminists and in the political parties or popular movements.

In Mexico we political women put war on the meeting's agenda: women and war. That was our life back then. We needed to look at that. And we also demanded that feminism be approached as a mass movement. Our feeling was that as long as we remained a few isolated groups of intellectuals, we wouldn't be able to make a difference. We needed to insert ourselves into the mainstream of the struggle.

Our position was that there are countries whose characteristics provide a natural context for feminism to take root, and that a false division is made which tends to separate the intellectuals from the masses of women. At least that was my position. I think this separation is a terrible thing. As a people it costs us so much to produce our intellectuals! And then sometimes we intellectuals ourselves do the isolating; at other times the masses dismiss us as if we can't work on their behalf. Our position was that we have to rejoin head and hands, body and brain.

That was part of the debate. Another issue was the fact that, yes, we *do* want power. I don't know who spread the rumor that feminists don't want power! We produced a document that exploded ten myths about feminism, and one thing we emphasized there was that it's important for women to achieve a measure of power, that we have to fight for power, regardless of the arena. That experience in Mexico was like a catharsis for us. We came back to Nicaragua feeling much stronger.

Upon our return, some twenty of the forty-four of us who had gone decided to organize ourselves more formally. We were still semiclandestine, and we still functioned as a kind of lobby; but by then we'd become a much more articulate lobby. It was Gioconda who had the idea for the name, Party of the Erotic Left. It was from a line in a poem, I think by a Guatemalan poet, but I can't remember her name.

I'm wondering if any of you had read Audre Lorde's essay on the erotic as power?

It was just an idea we had. And someone was always asking us why we didn't define ourselves as a sensual party, why "erotic" rather than "sensuous"? We explained that it referred to Eros—akin to life, love. We wanted to eroticize society because it had become so violent. And we identified with the Left, because we propose a radical, revolutionary transformation of society.

I shouldn't forget to mention, though, that some very concrete work has emerged from this little movement of ours: a number of research centers, for starters, and a magazine. My own *Gente* was one of the by-products. Lourdes Bolaños founded Ixchen. Vilma Castillo and Ana Criquillón founded Puntos de Encuentro [Points of Encounter], which publishes the bulletin of the same name. Milú Vargas modeled her Center for Constitutional Rights after the center with the same name in New York City. Malena de Montis founded Cezontle, which is a center for research on women. These centers have sown the seeds for a great deal of study and debate; they've prodded people to think and talk and act. And in one way or another we can trace them all to PIE.

What about the January event?

That's got a dual history. In the first place, from 1987 through '89 we managed to get our independent women's movement in motion. One of us was able to raise some money here, another there, and the centers started functioning. At the same time, there was the struggle with AMNLAE. We were struggling on two fronts: within the Party and with the Sandinista women's organization.

During most of this period, Lea Guido headed AMNLAE at the national level. I'd say her tenure marked the organization's period of greatest inclusiveness. But then Lea became ill and vacated the post. Although there was also some ambivalence on her part, because while in private she declared herself a feminist, publicly it was often "*¡Dirección Nacional, ordene!*" [National Directorate, give me my orders!]. In any case, Lea understood the need to revamp AMNLAE, to develop a more democratic structure; if that didn't happen, the organization was going to fall apart.

By this time, the independent women's movement was becoming quite strong. AMNLAE was an organization that had been conceived of as subordinate to a political party in which men were in control. And it had a peculiar classist vision, centering its work on housewives, women industrial workers, women farm workers. For AMNLAE, professional women, intellectuals, and women of the middle class don't count, except insofar as we can be used—the same utilitarian vision typical of the Left as a whole. What can they get out of us? How can they use us to do the work, design the programs, help them organize? But when we demand political participation, they tell us, "No, you're a petit-bourgeois intellectual, not sufficiently representative of the masses." We political women were fed up with that line.

So instead of continuing to argue with the leadership of AMNLAE, we thought we'd do better by going to the women in the mixed organizations who represent the different social sectors: the unionists, field workers, cattle ranchers, professionals, artists, and so forth. Milú Vargas was active in CONAPRO, María Teresa Blandón, Alba Palacios, and Olguita Espinoza were active in the ATC. It was in this period that the different Sandinista organizations began building strong women's secretariats. And we had women working among schoolteachers and federal workers. This work has had many concrete results, including the opening of women's clinics, and today it's taken for granted that a union or other mixed organization will have a women's secretariat.

The Front could see what was happening. Clearly we were breaking through that whole pyramidal structure they'd constructed. We weren't satisfied with AMNLAE as it was conceived, although some of us continued to function within the organization; so we went directly to the women in the different areas. And since it was obvious that we wanted change—a structure with sectorial representation and a collective leadership that would be both horizontal and democratic—AMNLAE wasn't happy with the situation. They replaced Lea with Doris Tijerino, who came directly from the police.

Once again, the people's will was stifled. The FSLN could see that we were gaining power in the different sectors and in the women's commission within the National Assembly. And the big concern at that point was the electoral process: "We can't do anything to take people's attention away from the elections," they said. And, of course, the women had different levels of consciousness as well; in the unions and among the farm workers especially, some of the female leaders began to feel guilty. What if they really were dividing the movement? Doris absolutely refused to enter into a discussion about any of this until after the election took place, and that's where things stood when we lost in February 1990.

Following the electoral defeat, we women were the first to react. We said, "Okay, we've lost the election, but now we're going to discuss women's role." Doris had been elected as a deputy to the National Assembly, and she moved to convoke an election in AMNLAE so that she could turn the organization over to someone else. I don't think she ever really wanted the job in the first place. The FSLN thought that a democratic electoral process would help the institution. But the Managua membership opposed that; or, rather, we in PIE opposed it.

What they did was call a meeting. Doris Tijerino and Mónica Baltodano issued the invitations. They said there'd be an election and that now we could really talk about a change. But we said, "Wait a minute . . ." We knew what kind of autonomy they were talking about. At that point autonomy meant, "You women do what you want, but don't count on any support from us because the Party's broke now; there's no money." We said we wanted a democratic discussion, from the grass roots up. We'd done too much work on our own simply to accept the male model all over again. We didn't even know if an election, within the same old structure, was what we wanted. It seemed to us that other questions had to be answered first: What kind of movement do we need? What do we need it for? And who should be part of it? We wanted some criticism and some analysis first. And we were particularly alarmed because it was clear in the election that the women's vote had gone against the FSLN.

We were the only ones to bring a real proposal to that meeting called by AMNLAE. We'd cooked it up in a hurry at Milú's house, a couple of nights before. But we aired it there at that assembly and proposed that an ad hoc committee be named to analyze the women's movement and to figure out what kind of movement we women needed now, in this new situation, from an opposition point of view.

Everyone agreed with us. Almost everyone raised their hands to volunteer to be on that committee. We got the committee together. We made our analysis.

Our proposal was called "Project to Relaunch the Women's Movement in Nicaragua." We worked on this throughout all of 1990, and we came up with a series of proposals which included putting AMNLAE's electoral process on hold and convening women to address the basic questions we all had. We tried our proposals out in a group of fifty women, and that was where it became clear that a national discussion was needed.

We worked hard, and it was all volunteer work. We were everywhere. But the opinions we were getting from the masses of women scared the AMNLAE leadership. They could see that women wanted to do away with the whole pyramidal structure. We wanted real democracy, a movement that was truly autonomous. It scared them. So, after allowing this whole process to get under way—and for some of us this concluded a five-year struggle!—they simply stopped it cold. Gladys Báez was designated by the Party to take Doris's place. And she called us every name in the book: lesbians, prostitutes, feminists, CIA agents, counterrevolutionaries—you name it. She even revived that old accusation that we were trying to divide the FSLN.

We realized there was no way we could keep struggling within AMNLAE, so we refused to do so. We broke with the organization. We wrote articles, we went public with the whole mess, because we'd had enough of being used and taunted. I published the entire process in *Gente*. And the male leadership of the FSLN, in its wisdom or cowardice, washed its hands of the whole affair. When AMNLAE's leadership went to the national directorate and asked it to put us in our place, the leadership responded, "You wanted autonomy. Deal with it. We're not going to take sides."

So that's the story of the split. But we still knew what we wanted to do, and we knew that we weren't going to be able to count on AMNLAE to do it with us. So we decided to do it ourselves. We continued the process we'd started, of discussion at all levels and in all the different sectors. That group of ten women who had formed the ad hoc committee began to contact other women, and we just kept going. We took the rest of 1990 and all of 1991, and in January 1992 we finally had our national event.

The goal of that January meeting was for us to put forth our general message and our points of agreement, to decide upon an agenda capable of meeting the needs of Nicaraguan women at this point in time. We wanted to work on the most urgent priorities, so we organized the encounter by themes: the economy, violence, sexuality. Those were the three central concerns we'd come up with out of all the discussions with women at the base.

AMNLAE tried in every way possible to boycott the event. At first it tried to prevent its members from attending, but many did attend as individuals. And the important thing is that we were able to hold such a conference completely outside the Party, without government sponsorship, without direct support from the unions or other mixed organizations. It was extraordinary: more than eight hundred women attended! And when the AMNLAE women saw that this was going to take place, with or without them, they decided to send a delegation. It included some fifty women; Marta Cranshaw was more or less its spokeswoman.

We purposely did not start out with documents that had already been written up. We wanted to do this differently. We had a series of questions, and we hoped that through genuine discussion from the floor the answers we needed would come. In some ways, AMNLAE was successful in its boycott. Because the second question on the agenda was, "how should we organize ourselves?" and the AMNLAE women fought hard against a real discussion of that question. They also spread rumors saying that what we really wanted was just another organization with ourselves as leaders. Two organizations, they said, would divide the women's movement.

The movement was already divided! But we were committed to a democratic process. If the women didn't want to discuss that point, we weren't going to force them to discuss it. And we didn't. So the new kind of organizational structure that we'd hoped for didn't get off the ground. Instead, we formed networks to continue our work in different areas: the economy, violence against women, sexuality, education, women's health.

In March [1992] we hosted a Central American feminist meeting, at the seaside resort of Montelimar, and a hundred Nicaraguan feminists attended. A few years back we could count those Nicaraguan women who called themselves feminists on the fingers of one hand; there were maybe four of us. Now there are at least a hundred. So I'm optimistic. Feminism has grown in this country. And it's a feminism that ranges from the lightweight variety all the way up to those of us who understand that misery isn't going to go away here, poverty isn't going to go away, our struggle isn't going to go away, and there needs to be a group committed to thinking about these issues from a feminist perspective. If there are four of us today, then that's what we'll start with, and we'll see who joins us along the way.

About the Author

Feminist activist Margaret Randall has published more than fifty books, in addition to being a poet, journalist, teacher, and photographer. She was born and raised in the United States but has lived for long periods in Mexico, Cuba, and Nicaragua. Having relinquished her citizenship when she married a Mexican, she was denied residency and ordered to be deported from the United States when she returned in 1984. The grounds given were the political content of her writings. She finally regained her citizenship after a five-year immigration case in which she was joined by many prominent writers and others. She now lives in New Mexico where she continues to write, traveling frequently to read her poetry or lecture, and occasionally teaching at such colleges as Trinity in Hartford, Connecticut.